D1196849

Two Irelands beyond the Sea

Reappraisals in Irish History

Editors
Enda Delaney (University of Edinburgh)
Maria Luddy (University of Warwick)
Ciaran O'Neill (Trinity College Dublin)

Reappraisals in Irish History offers new insights into Irish history, society and culture from 1750. Recognising the many methodologies that make up historical research, the series presents innovative and interdisciplinary work that is conceptual and interpretative, and expands and challenges the common understandings of the Irish past. It showcases new and exciting scholarship on subjects such as the history of gender, power, class, the body, landscape, memory and social and cultural change. It also reflects the diversity of Irish historical writing, since it includes titles that are empirically sophisticated together with conceptually driven synoptic studies.

1. Jonathan Jeffrey Wright, *The 'Natural Leaders' and their World: Politics, Culture and Society in Belfast, c.1801–1832*

2. Gerardine Meaney, Mary O'Dowd and Bernadette Whelan, *Reading the Irish Woman: Studies in Cultural Encounters and Exchange, 1714–1960*

3. Emily Mark-FitzGerald, *Commemorating the Irish Famine: Memory and the Monument*

4. Virginia Crossman, *Poverty and the Poor Law in Ireland 1850–1914*

5. Paul Taylor, *Heroes or Traitors? Experiences of Southern Irish Soldiers Returning from the Great War 1919–39*

6. Paul Huddie, *The Crimean War and Irish Society*

7. Brian Hughes, *Defying the IRA?*

8. Laura Kelly, *Irish medical education and student culture, c.1850–1950*

9. Michael Dwyer, *Strangling Angel: Diphtheria and childhood immunization in Ireland*

10. Carole Holohan, *Reframing Irish Youth in the Sixties*

Two Irelands beyond the Sea

Ulster Unionism and America,
1880–1920

LINDSEY FLEWELLING

LIVERPOOL UNIVERSITY PRESS

First published 2018 by
Liverpool University Press
4 Cambridge Street
Liverpool
L69 7ZU

British Library Cataloguing-in-Publication data
A British Library CIP record is available

ISBN 978-1-78694-045-2

Typeset by Carnegie Book Production, Lancaster
Printed and bound by TJ International Ltd, Padstow, Cornwall, PL28 8RW

Contents

Acknowledgements

I could not have written this book without guidance and encouragement from many people. My thanks must first go to my thesis supervisor at the University of Edinburgh, Alvin Jackson, and to Owen Dudley Edwards. I am also grateful for support from colleagues and friends, including Megan Ledford, Eóin McLaughlin, Devon McHugh, David Ritchie, Rusty Roberson, members of the Scottish Irish History Group, and the University of Edinburgh postgraduate community. My thanks also to colleagues at Colorado College including Dennis Showalter and Carol Neel. I am grateful for conference feedback from various stages of this project, and I have also benefited from correspondence with several historians, particularly David Wilson, Andrew Holmes, my MPhil supervisor Eugenio Biagini, and Enda Delaney. My thanks to Richard English and Ewen Cameron for their critiques and support as viva voce examiners of the thesis on which this book is based, and to the anonymous reviewers of the book manuscript at Liverpool University Press and Palgrave Macmillan for their feedback and suggestions.

Through the years I have benefited from funding from the University of Edinburgh and Colorado College, for which I am grateful. This book would not have been possible without the aid of resources and help of staff at the University of Edinburgh Libraries, National Library of Scotland, Public Record Office of Northern Ireland, Historical Society of Pennsylvania, Irish Presbyterian Historical Society, Queen's University Belfast McClay Library, University of Colorado Norlin Library, British Library, and Library of Congress. Thank you to the deputy keeper of the records at the Public Record Office of Northern Ireland for granting permission to quote from materials deposited there. My thanks to Mykaila and Matt DeLesDernier for providing the absolute best place to stay while conducting research in Washington, DC, and to Maggie Garfield, my writers' group, and James Hart at the University of Oklahoma for their encouragement of a love of history.

Finally, special thanks to my dad and Renée Prud'Homme for reading thesis draft chapters and partaking in ramblings on Irish and American history. Thank you to Paula Dumas for having gone through all this before me and offering endless encouragement. To my parents and Jordan, and the rest of my family and friends, I am grateful for all of the help and support through the years.

Abbreviations

AIHS	American Irish Historical Society
BNL	*Belfast News-Letter*
DUP	Democratic Unionist Party
HSP	Historical Society of Pennsylvania
IHS	*Irish Historical Studies*
ILPU	Irish Loyal and Patriotic Union
IPP	Irish Parliamentary Party
IRA	Irish Republican Army
IUA	Irish Unionist Alliance
LOI	Loyal Orange Institution
LOL	Loyal Orange Lodge
Noraid	Irish Northern Aid Committee
NYT	*New York Times*
PD	Parliamentary Debates
PRONI	Public Record Office of Northern Ireland
PSIS	Pennsylvania Scotch-Irish Society
RBP	Royal Black Preceptory
SIF	Scotch-Irish Foundation
SISA	Scotch-Irish Society of America
UJC	Unionist Joint Committee
ULAU	Ulster Loyalist Anti-Repeal Union
UUC	Ulster Unionist Council
UUP	Ulster Unionist Party
UVF	Ulster Volunteer Force
UWUC	Ulster Women's Unionist Council

1

Introduction

A t Parliament's Government of Ireland Bill Committee meeting of 18 June 1912, Robert McMordie argued against the third Home Rule Bill. McMordie, Lord Mayor of Belfast and Unionist Member of Parliament for East Belfast, declared that Ulster's unionists would not accept Home Rule on any terms, implying they were seriously considering militant opposition if the bill passed. McMordie asserted Home Rule would sweep away available capital, thereby destroying the linen and shipbuilding industries in Ulster. He also predicted a large number of Ulster Protestants, faced with the conditions of Home Rule, would immigrate to the United States:

> They were driven there before, and they have made their mark there. It was the Ulstermen in the United States who started and carried on the War of Independence to a successful issue. You want to send some more there. If this Bill passes, you will have disaster in commerce and in manufactures, and you will drive people abroad who will carry with them a hatred of this country as happened before.[1]

McMordie's argument was that links forged with the United States over two and a half centuries of migration from Ulster would continue to play important roles in Ireland's future. McMordie emphasized threats of renewed American migration, which would drain Ireland of the Ulstermen whom he saw as the nation's most industrious, economically successful citizens. They would settle in the United States, a country which, with the help of Ulster emigrants, rivalled Britain as a world power in the years before the First World War. They would aid America in increasing its economic, techno-logical, and military might. Moreover, Ulster emigrants in America provided an important precedent for the actions of Ulster unionists: Ulster emigrants had successfully defied the British during the American Revolution, and

1 Parliamentary Debates (PD) Commons 5th Ser., Vol. 39, 1527.

Ulstermen in Ireland would defy the British and Irish nationalists who attempted to force Home Rule upon them.

McMordie's speech used the United States as a symbol to justify unionist actions and implicitly threaten the British. America was intertwined with his basic arguments against Home Rule such as the dangers presented by self-government to Ulster's economy. Moreover, McMordie's rhetorical use of America represented only a single aspect of the multifaceted Ulster unionist approaches and attitudes toward the United States. During the Home Rule period from 1880 to 1920, Ulster unionists employed a complex combination of political thought, rhetoric, and action involving the United States. Like McMordie, many drew upon links with America forged through shared ethnic and religious heritage, and utilized American historical and political examples to lend legitimacy to the unionist cause. Unionists eagerly sought support for their own movement in the United States. At the same time, they responded anxiously to the threat of Irish-American extremism and repudiated American government involvement on the Irish question.

Irish unionism is typically considered to be a very insular movement compared to Irish nationalism. Unionists are portrayed as a group primarily concerned with banding together against both Irish nationalists and the British government, with less interest in the wider world. Unionists themselves had diverse origins. They combined the forces of Toryism, the Church of Ireland, landlordism, Orangeism, and Presbyterianism. As Alvin Jackson describes, they developed at least in part as a reactionary body responding to the challenges of nationalists and the British government.[2] By 1885, faced with the threat of Home Rule, an Ulster party emerged in Parliament, representing uneasy alliances between northern and southern unionism, and between Liberals and Conservatives.

Over the next three decades, the Ulster party maintained a constant presence in the Westminster Parliament, returning at least 19 MPs for each election between 1885 and 1918. The party continued to evolve as it responded to two Home Rule crises in 1886 and 1893, the devolution crisis of 1904–1906, land reforms, and expansion of the electorate. By the time of the third Home Rule Bill, Ulster unionism was beginning to set itself apart from the rest of Ireland. The concept of a separate Ulster identity emerged at the same time as the revival of Scotch-Irish ethnicity was taking place in the United States. Both the Scotch-Irish and Ulstermen were celebrated for traditions of radical populism and pioneering spirit.[3] In the present study,

---

2   Alvin Jackson, *The Ulster Party: Irish Unionists in the House of Commons, 1884–1911* (Oxford: Clarendon Press, 1989), 21.

3   Graham Walker, 'Ulster Unionism and the Scottish Dimension', in *Ulster and Scotland, 1600–2000: History, Language, and Identity*, ed. William Kelly and John R. Young

the term 'Ulster Scots' is used to refer to those Presbyterians in Ireland who had their roots in Scotland, while 'Ulster unionists' is used to refer to those who supported unionism more generally.

The historiography of Irish unionism has significantly expanded since the end of the 1960s.[4] While historians have created a more complete view of the complex political, cultural, social, and religious elements of unionism during the Home Rule period, scholars have yet to fully explore the participation of unionists in the world beyond Ireland, the United Kingdom, and the Empire. There are only limited references to the reciprocal relationship between Ulster unionism and the United States. Discovery and examination of the details of this relationship are the driving forces behind the present study.

In recent years, the use of transnational approaches to examine historical interactions has gained prominence. Transnational history stresses the importance of movement, exchanges, and circulations of people, ideas, and products across national boundaries, recognizing the 'entangled condition' of the world throughout history.[5] Irish history has been a fruitfully developing area within transnational history, due to the size and visibility of the diaspora. The Irish have long called upon connections with the wider world, developing networks and engaging in reciprocal relationships with immigrant communities. The concept of a 'greater Ireland beyond the sea' harkens back to medieval sources, tied to an ideal of shared identities and nationhood that impacted both the homeland and immigrant host societies.[6] The present

(Dublin: Four Courts Press, 2004), 36. See Ian McBride, 'Ulster and the British Problem', in *Unionism in Modern Ireland: New Perspectives on Politics and Culture*, ed. Richard English and Graham Walker (Basingstoke: Macmillan, 1996), 7.

4 See, for example, Jackson, *Ulster Party*; Patrick Buckland, *Irish Unionism II: Ulster Unionism and the Origins of Northern Ireland, 1886–1922* (Dublin: Gill and Macmillan, 1973); David W. Miller, *Queen's Rebels: Ulster Loyalism in Historical Perspective* (Dublin: University College Dublin Press, 2007); Peter Gibbon, *The Origins of Ulster Unionism: The Formation of Popular Protestant Politics and Ideology in Nineteenth-Century Ireland* (Manchester: Manchester University Press, 1975); John Harbinson, *The Ulster Unionist Party, 1882–1973: Its Development and Organisation* (Belfast: Blackstaff, 1973); A.T.Q. Stewart, *Narrow Ground: Aspects of Ulster, 1609–1969* (Belfast: Blackstaff, 1997); James Loughlin, *Ulster Unionism and British National Identity since 1885* (London: Pinter, 1995). For a more detailed overview on unionist historiography, see Alvin Jackson, 'Irish Unionism', in *The Making of Modern Irish History: Revisionism and the Revisionist Controversy*, ed. D. George Boyce and Alan O'Day (London: Routledge, 1996).

5 C.A. Bayly, et al., 'On Transnational History', *American Historical Review* 111, no. 5 (Dec 2006); *The Palgrave Dictionary of Transnational History: From the Mid-19th Century to the Present Day*, ed. Akira Iriye and Pierre-Yves Saunier (Basingstoke: Palgrave, 2009).

6 Hilary M. Carey and Colin Barr, eds, Introduction to *Religion and Greater Ireland: Christianity and Irish Global Networks, 1750–1950* (Montreal: McGill-Queen's University

study uses a transnational approach to examine the circulation of popular politics, religion, ideas, and ethnic identity between Ulster unionists and America, discovering the ways in which unionists called upon what they viewed as a 'greater Ireland' of their own.

Across the Atlantic Ocean, Irish-American nationalist involvement in the movements for Irish Home Rule and independence has been well-documented. As Kevin Kenny notes, the history of the American Irish is closely linked to developments in both Ireland and the United States.[7] Nationalist leaders from Ireland frequently visited the United States to garner financial, political, and organizational reinforcement. They mobilized Irish-Americans in support of independence. Irish-American nationalism became so politically important that, as Alan Ward asserts, what was originally Britain's 'Irish problem' became an issue for successive American governments as well.[8]

In the United States, support for Irish nationalism was especially prominent compared to other Irish diaspora countries, in part because Irish Catholic immigrants retained close connections to their own ethnic community in the face of American anti-Catholic sentiment.[9] Tight-knit Irish-American Catholic communities remained closely tied to their Irish roots. They were drawn into Irish nationalist activities for several reasons: (1) they believed a free Ireland would raise the status of the Irish in the United

---

Press, 2015), 17–18. On Irish transnational history, see, for example, Enda Delaney, 'Our Island Story? Towards a Transnational History of Late Modern Ireland', *IHS* 37, no. 148 (2011); *Transnational Perspectives on Modern Irish History*, ed. Niall Whelehan (New York: Routledge, 2015); Kevin Kenny, 'Diaspora and Comparison: The Global Irish as a Case Study', *Journal of American History* 90, no. 1 (Jun 2002); *Ireland in the World: Comparative, Transnational, and Personal Perspectives*, ed. Angela McCarthy (New York: Routledge, 2015); Enda Delaney and Donald M. MacRaild, eds, Introduction to *Irish Migration, Networks and Ethnic Identities since 1750* (London: Routledge, 2007).

7 Kevin Kenny, *The American Irish: A History* (Harlow: Longman, 2000), 172.

8 Alan J. Ward, 'America and the Irish Problem, 1899–1921', *IHS* 16, no. 61 (Mar 1968), 64. David Brundage's *Irish Nationalists in America: The Politics of Exile, 1798–1998* (New York: Oxford University Press, 2016), highlights the extent to which Irish and Irish-American nationalism were intertwined for two centuries, impacting the history of both countries.

9 Lawrence J. McCaffrey, 'Diaspora Comparisons and Irish-American Uniqueness', in *New Perspectives on the Irish Diaspora*, ed. Charles Fanning (Carbondale: Southern Illinois University Press, 2000), 20. The extent of the impact of anti-Catholic sentiment on Irish immigrants is debatable – the need for greater comparative history in different Irish diaspora countries is addressed by Malcolm Campbell, 'The Other Immigrants: Comparing the Irish in Australia and the United States', *Journal of American Ethnic History* 14, no. 3 (Spring 1995). Donald M. MacRaild points out that Irish who settled in Britain took even longer to gain a foothold in their new society than American Irish: 'Crossing Migrant Frontiers: Comparative Reflections on Irish Migrants in Britain and the United States During the Nineteenth Century', *Immigrants and Minorities* 18, no. 2/3 (Jul/Nov 1999), 41.

States; (2) nationalist organizations also furthered other social, political, and economic goals within American society; and (3) they believed in the cause of self-determination for Ireland.

Organizations such as the Clan-na-Gael, Ancient Order of Hibernians, Friends of Irish Freedom, and United Irish League of America worked for decades to raise funds, rally Irish-Americans to the causes of Home Rule and independence, and lobby the United States government. Leaders of these organizations maintained close ties with nationalists in Ireland. At times the same people directed movements on both sides of the Atlantic. Kenny notes, 'The experience of these individuals in the United States, combined with the material and political support of Irish Americans, accounts for the significant phrase in the proclamation issued by the new provisional government of Ireland on Easter Monday 1916, which declared that Ireland had risen up in rebellion "supported by her exiled children in America"'.[10]

Scholarly accounts of the Irish in America during the Home Rule period detail the political, religious, economic, and social experiences of the Catholic nationalist immigrant community. Previous studies have not focused on Americans who supported the cause of Irish unionism, many of whom were of Ulster Protestant heritage. Approximately 360,000 Ulster Presbyterians migrated to America from 1680 to the start of the nineteenth century, along with substantial numbers of Protestants from other parts of Ireland.[11] The influx of Irish Protestants continued throughout the nineteenth and early twentieth centuries in a steady but decreasing flow. This immigration reached such numbers that Donald Akenson has concluded, 'The bulk of the Irish ethnic group in the United States is, and probably always has been, Protestant'.[12] In his study of *The American Irish*, William Shannon dismisses the Scotch-Irish as not actually Irish.[13] Thomas Brown, while not as explicit, focuses solely on Catholic Irish-Americans as he discusses how their American experiences contributed to their political and social views.[14]

---

10 Kenny, *American Irish*, 172, 195.
11 Kenny, *American Irish*, 14–23; R.F. Foster, *Modern Ireland, 1600–1972* (Harmondsworth: Penguin, 1988), 216; Patrick Griffin, *The People with No Name: Ireland's Ulster Scots, America's Scots Irish, and the Creation of a British Atlantic World, 1689–1764* (Princeton, NJ: Princeton University Press, 2001), 67, 97–101, 165.
12 Donald H. Akenson, 'The Historiography of the Irish in the United States of America', in *The Irish World Wide*, Vol. 2: *The Irish in the New Communities*, ed. Patrick O'Sullivan (Leicester: Leicester University Press, 1992), 99. See Rankin Sherling, *The Invisible Irish: Finding Protestants in the Nineteenth-Century Migrations to America* (Montreal and Kingston: McGill-Queen's University Press, 2016), 3–23.
13 William V. Shannon, *The American Irish* (New York: Macmillan, 1963), viii–ix.
14 Thomas N. Brown, *Irish-American Nationalism, 1870–1890* (Philadelphia: Lippincott, 1966) and 'Origins and Character of Irish-American Nationalism', *Review of Politics* 18, no. 3 (Jul 1956).

Kenny's *American Irish* sets out to tell a more inclusive story of both Irish Protestants and Catholics in the United States, but underlines the need for further research on Irish-American Protestants after the mid-nineteenth century.[15]

The literature dedicated to the study of Irish Protestants in America emphasizes their role in the eighteenth-century colonial and Revolutionary periods. However, the number of Protestants leaving Ireland continued to exceed the number of Catholics until the mid-1830s.[16] Kenneth Keller asserts, 'This seldom-studied, early nineteenth-century wave of emigration added a larger proportion of Ulster people to the overall American population than had the important colonial migrations'.[17] The migration of Irish Protestants to the United States continued steadily until the 1920s. Migrants from Ulster comprised almost one-fifth of all Irish immigrants to the United States from 1900 to 1909, and one-fourth of all Irish immigrants from 1910 to 1914, though by this time over half of Ulster migrants were Catholic.[18]

Some studies maintain Irish Protestants were fully assimilated into American society by the 1830s despite their continued migration.[19] The Anglo-Irish, of English origin and Episcopalian religion, are almost entirely neglected in historical study. The label 'Scotch-Irish', which originally applied largely to Presbyterians who migrated first from Scotland to Ulster and then from Ulster to North America, has been applied to all Protestants of Irish origin. Kerby Miller writes that the basis of this expansion of the 'Scotch-Irish' term is unclear, 'but surely it was associated with the dilution of Protestant denominational boundaries wrought by evangelicalism in both Ireland and America, and, in Ireland, the emergence of a pan-Protestant political bloc in opposition to Irish Catholic nationalism'.[20] Irish Protestants in America may have been similarly united through participation in

---

15 Kenny, *American Irish*, 3.
16 Malcolm Campbell, *Ireland's New Worlds: Immigrants, Politics, and Society in the United States and Australia, 1815–1922* (Madison: University of Wisconsin Press, 2007), 7.
17 Kenneth W. Keller, 'What is Distinctive about the Scotch-Irish?', in *Appalachian Frontiers: Settlement, Society & Development in the Pre-Industrial Era*, ed. Robert D. Mitchell (Lexington: University Press of Kentucky, 1991), 73.
18 Kenny, *American Irish*, 182; Donald H. Akenson, *The Irish Diaspora: A Primer* (Toronto: P.D. Meany, 1993), 222, 248–255.
19 Most prominent is James G. Leyburn's classic study, *The Scotch-Irish: A Social History* (Chapel Hill: University of North Carolina Press, 1962), but the historiography in general emphasizes the eighteenth century far more than any continuing Scotch-Irish identification in later years.
20 Kerby A. Miller, '"Scotch-Irish" Myths and "Irish" Identities in Eighteenth- and Nineteenth-Century America', in *New Perspectives on the Irish Diaspora*, ed. Charles Fanning (Carbondale: Southern Illinois University Press, 2000), 80.

anti-Catholic and nativist movements. Some also chose to participate in specifically Scotch-Irish associations such as the Scotch-Irish Society of America and Orange Order.

The Scotch-Irish are notoriously difficult to track after the American Revolution. They had diverse origins within Ulster and indeed all of Ireland. Once in America, the Scotch-Irish became a difficult ethnic group to define because they were English-speaking, highly mobile, and highly adaptable.[21] They carried an amalgam of traditions from Scotland and Ireland, and were influenced by encounters with other peoples in the two nations. Their culture also changed through adaptation to their new lives in America. Patrick Griffin concludes, 'Identity was always malleable and conditional, comprised at times of Old World traditions and at others from New World innovations, but ultimately responsive to circumstance'.[22]

The term 'Scotch-Irish' in itself has faced debate and criticism from historians. As Griffin emphasizes, the group's background makes it difficult to determine a fitting name, with divergence between what the group has been called by others versus what they have called themselves. The term 'Scotch-Irish' was embraced in the mid-nineteenth century, artificially homogenizing all Protestants from Ireland, and concealing complex historical realities. Contrastingly, the group never self-identified as 'Scots Irish'.[23] With no clearly appropriate terminology available, the present study refers to the group as they referred to themselves during this era, as 'Scotch-Irish'.

Despite difficulties in defining the Protestant Irish in America as an ethnic group, there are several indications of continued Scotch-Irish identity after the 1830s: continued emigration from Ulster; isolation of Scotch-Irish settlements in the southern backcountry; increasing popularity of the Orange Order and prominence of Scotch-Irish participation in American nativist organizations; recurring conflicts between Protestant and Catholic Irish in such cities as New York, Philadelphia, and Newark; and revival of the Scotch-Irish ethnicity in the 1880s.[24] These factors indicate the Scotch-Irish

21 H. Tyler Blethen and Curtis W. Wood, Jr., eds, Introduction to *Ulster and North America: Transatlantic Perspectives on the Scotch-Irish* (Tuscaloosa: University of Alabama Press, 1997), 2; Griffin, *People with No Name*, 172–173; Keller, 'What is Distinctive', 72.

22 Patrick Griffin, 'The People with No Name: Ulster's Migrants and Identity Formation in Eighteenth-Century Pennsylvania', *William and Mary Quarterly* 3rd Series, 58, no. 3 (Jul 2001), 589.

23 Griffin, *People with No Name*, 2, 175; Leyburn, *Scotch-Irish*, 327–334; David N. Doyle, 'Scots Irish or Scotch-Irish', in *Making the Irish American: History and Heritage of the Irish in the United States*, ed. J.J. Lee and Marion R. Casey (New York: New York University Press, 2006), 151–152; Miller, 'Scotch-Irish Myths', 76–82.

24 See T.G. Fraser, Foreword to *Ulster and North America: Transatlantic Perspectives on the Scotch-Irish*, ed. H. Tyler Blethen and Curtis W. Wood, Jr. (Tuscaloosa: University

were not simply and wholly absorbed into mainstream America after the Revolutionary period. Some recent studies of nineteenth- and twentieth-century Irish-America have integrated elements of the Protestant Irish experience with the more conventional narrative of Catholic Irish-America. Francis Carroll's studies of diplomacy, politics, and opinion in the United States and Ireland at times shed valuable light on the Scotch-Irish experience.[25] Kenny also sets out to incorporate the Protestant Irish into the overall story of Irish-America.[26] Miller and David N. Doyle investigate development of a unique Scotch-Irish identity while maintaining the context of Catholic Irish-America's expansion.[27] Rowland Berthoff also provides insight on the Scotch-Irish within the larger British migration to the United States.[28]

In contrast to the historiography of Catholic Irish-Americans, however, historical studies generally do not illustrate reciprocal links between Protestant Irish-America and Ireland. For the late nineteenth and twentieth centuries, there is little indication of continuing correspondence between Protestants in America and Ireland, interest of the ethnic group in Irish political movements, or comparison of experiences between Ireland and America. One exception is Maldwyn Jones's insightful article in the *Harvard Encyclopedia of American Ethnic Groups*, which provides the most comprehensive view of Scotch-Irish associational and political participation throughout the nineteenth and twentieth centuries.[29]

By the time of the first Home Rule Bill, the United States and Britain were experiencing profound changes in their relationship, which would eventually lead to the United States overtaking Britain as a world power. America was a rival to Britain as the world shifted in the late Victorian era.[30] Global

of Alabama Press, 1997), vii–viii; Maldwyn A. Jones, 'Scotch-Irish', in *Harvard Encyclopedia of American Ethnic Groups*, ed. Stephan Thernstrom (Cambridge, Mass.: Harvard University Press, 1980), 906–907.

25 Francis M. Carroll, *The American Presence in Ulster: A Diplomatic History, 1796–1996* (Washington, DC: Catholic University of America Press, 2005) and *American Opinion and the Irish Question, 1910–23: A Study in Opinion and Policy* (Dublin: Gill and Macmillan, 1978).

26 Kenny, *American Irish*.

27 Doyle, 'Scots Irish or Scotch-Irish'; Kerby A. Miller, 'Ulster Presbyterians and the "Two Traditions" in Ireland and America', in *Making the Irish American: History and Heritage of the Irish in the United States*, ed. J.J. Lee and Marion R. Casey (New York: New York University Press, 2006) and 'Scotch-Irish Myths'.

28 Rowland Tappan Berthoff, *British Immigrants in Industrial America, 1790–1950* (Cambridge, Mass.: Harvard University Press, 1953).

29 Jones, 'Scotch-Irish'.

30 Philip S. Bagwell and G.E. Mingay, *Britain and America, 1850–1939: A Study of Economic Change* (London: Routledge & Kegan Paul, 1970), 1–22; Duncan Bell, *The Idea of Greater Britain: Empire and the Future of World Order, 1860–1900* (Princeton, NJ: Princeton University Press, 2007), 238–239.

economic connections were increasing, illustrated by networks formed by the United States with Belfast's shipbuilding and linen industries. Technological improvements, particularly in transportation and communications, allowed people and goods to move throughout the world with greater ease, leading to increasingly integrated economies.[31] Political and religious figures could embark on transatlantic visits in numbers previously unseen, allowing for the development of transnational political, religious, and ethnic organizations. Links between the British and American governments also increased by the turn of the century, aided by Anglo-American rapprochement. Transnational linkages between Ireland and America grew increasingly important as Irish nationalists used American public opinion to pressure the British government over the issues of Home Rule and independence. American, British, and Irish economic competition, technological innovation, and government interactions formed important contexts for Ulster unionists in their views toward the United States.

The present study analyses the actions of Ulster unionists in the face of these developments and in light of historic connections to America. Even though the study will focus on unionist and Protestant elements within Irish society, it is not intended to perpetuate the divide between the 'two traditions' of Catholic/nationalist and Protestant/unionist in Irish and Irish-American history. Miller asserts this model 'ignores or de-emphasizes the similarities, common interests, and instances of co-operation between Protestants and Catholics. Also, it un-historically homogenizes both traditions, slighting the diversity, the complexity, and the socio-cultural and (among Protestants) denominational conflicts within each group'.[32] One of the problems inherent in transnational study is losing sight of the different divisions, identities, and groups within each movement, each of which had diverse origins and religious and political traditions.

While acknowledging the diversity within the movements, this study complements scholarship on Irish nationalists and unionists, and American

---

31 Graham Brownlow, 'The Political Economy of the Ulster Crisis: Historiography, Social Capability, and Globalisation', in *The Ulster Crisis, 1885–1921*, ed. D. George Boyce and Alan O'Day (Basingstoke: Palgrave Macmillan, 2006), 43; Bernadette Whelan, *American Government in Ireland, 1790–1913: A History of the US Consular Service* (Manchester: Manchester University Press, 2010), 98–102; Griffin, *People with No Name*, 88–89; Philip Ollerenshaw, 'Industry, 1820–1914', in *An Economic History of Ulster, 1820–1939*, ed. Líam Kennedy and Philip Ollerenshaw (Manchester: Manchester University Press, 1985), 74–79; Líam Kennedy, 'The Rural Economy, 1820–1914', *An Economic History of Ulster, 1820–1939*, 31.

32 Kerby A. Miller, *Ireland and Irish America: Culture, Class, and Transatlantic Migration* (Dublin: Field Day, 2008), 373; Patrick Griffin, 'The Two-Migrations Myth, the Scotch-Irish, and the Irish American Experience', in *Re-Imagining Ireland*, ed. Andrew Higgins Wyndham (Charlottesville: University of Virginia Press, 2006), 244–246.

Irish. The study explores Ulster unionist-American relationships to provide a more complete view of interactions between Ireland, Britain, and the United States during the Home Rule period. This study does not examine the lives and times of the Scotch-Irish in general. Their actions and rhetoric are reviewed only to the extent they were directly related to Ireland and the Irish political situation. Rather, the study focuses on Ulster unionists themselves, examining their paradoxical views toward the United States as they reacted to and attempted to harness support from America during the Home Rule period.

Given the gaps in the current literature, several themes remain to be examined, which this study will treat in turn. Each chapter examines an important element of Ulster unionists' American strategy during the Home Rule era. Chapters 2 and 3 provide an overview of the relationship between Ulster unionists and the United States from 1880 to 1920. During this time, unionists responded to Irish-American nationalism and involvement of the United States government on the Irish question, and attempted to garner support for their own movement. Chapter 4 turns toward the United States, investigating Scotch-Irish ethnic revival and associational culture at the end of the nineteenth century. Two organizations in particular, the Scotch-Irish Society of America and Loyal Orange Institution of the United States, are analysed in terms of their continuing links to Ireland and attitudes toward Home Rule. The chapter then looks at the ways in which Ulster unionists utilized Scotch-Irish identity and actions to aid in the formation of a separate 'Ulsterman' identity. Chapter 5 provides case studies of visits by unionists to the United States as they endeavoured to counter nationalist influence and build up a unionist following. Chapter 6 builds on the connections between Ulstermen and the Scotch-Irish by exploring the impact of religion on unionists' relationship with the United States. Religion was a significant theme in interactions with America, and religious institutions provided opportunities for transnational promotion of unionism. Chapter 7 examines intellectual impacts of American history and politics on Ulster unionism. Examples from the United States were regularly employed to justify unionist stances and oppose proposed Home Rule settlements. Finally, Chapter 8 concludes that the inability of Ulster unionists to deal effectively with the United States in the modern era has roots in the relationship between unionists and America during the Home Rule period.

In analysing the relationship between Ulster unionism and America, this study utilizes a wide variety of primary printed and manuscript sources. In determining which sources to use, a balance was sought between examining the views of the unionist leadership and Members of Parliament, and popular unionism. British and southern Irish unionist views are also included when they proved particularly illuminating on the relationship between unionism and America, as they help to provide the context in which Ulster unionists were working. Such views are also included where they were giving speeches in Ulster or promoted in Ulster, such as Irish Loyal and Patriotic Union pamphlets disseminating the views of Joseph Chamberlain, the Marquess of Hartington, and George Goschen. Archival sources are used from the Public Record Office of Northern Ireland, Historical Society of Pennsylvania, and Library of Congress, including previously underutilized materials on the American Orange Order. A wide variety of other sources are also employed in an attempt to gain a representative cross-section of views on the relationship between Ulster unionists and America. This includes government documents such as the Parliamentary Debates, organization minutes and reports, pamphlets and leaflets, journal articles and essays, and books such as novels, historical, ethnic, and political studies, and memoirs. Newspaper sources are used to document editorial opinions, public speeches, and organizational reports.

Examination of political and intellectual interactions between Ulster unionism and America allows a richer understanding of how Ulster unionists approached their own movement and responded to Irish nationalists. This book explores Ulster identity, the Scotch-Irish experience in the United States, and transnational links between Ulster and America. Ultimately, *Two Irelands beyond the Sea* aims to illuminate the complex ties between Ulster unionists and America during the Home Rule era, which sparked a theme of United States involvement in the affairs of Northern Ireland which endured to the end of the twentieth century and beyond.

2

Ulster Unionists and
Irish-American Nationalism
in the Late Nineteenth Century

During the present century there has not been a parallel for
the crimes perpetrated in the comparatively brief period to
which we refer. The Land League derived its strength from
the liberality of American and Irish-American contributors to
the fund; the conspiracies in this country were organized by
agents from America; and the most serious assaults upon life
and property were planned or perpetrated by men wearing
American masks.

Belfast News-Letter, 2 July 1883

Throughout the second half of the nineteenth century, Irish unionists
increasingly associated Irish-America with violence and extremism.
Inspired by such figures as Patrick Ford, John Devoy, and Jeremiah
O'Donovan Rossa, Irish-American nationalists were heavily involved in the
Fenian Brotherhood and Clan-na-Gael. They conducted attempted invasions
of Canada in the late 1860s and early 1870s, helped orchestrate the dynamite
campaign and land war of the early 1880s, and supported the movement for
Irish Home Rule, which culminated in two Home Rule crises in 1886 and
1893. The extremist image of Irish-America was so powerful that unionists
began to associate the whole of Irish nationalism with the violence and
separatism propounded by 'men wearing American masks'.

This chapter offers an assessment of unionist characterizations of the
United States and responses to Irish-America through the last two decades
of the nineteenth century. Unionist rhetoric and dialogue was strategic
discourse focusing on elements of violence, extremism, and militancy within

nationalism regardless of how representative these elements were in reality. The dynamite campaign, land war, and first two Home Rule crises provide the context for the unionist relationship with America during this period. Unionists denounced American funding of Irish nationalism, condemned Irish Parliamentary Party (IPP) connections to violence and crime, and feared the threat of separatism. Unionists also emphasized the international appeal of their own movement as they attempted to draw support from the United States in their campaigns against Home Rule. Ultimately, the unionists' approach to the United States was paradoxical and multifaceted, as they attempted to condemn Irish-American influence and extremism while at the same time seeking American aid for their own movement.

Irish-American Community, 1840–1880

As Irish Catholic immigration increased in the 1840s, the United States was a society in transition beset with economic turbulence and political tension. An estimated 1.5 million Irish immigrated to the United States between 1846 and 1855 as a result of the Great Famine. They were mainly poor, unskilled workers from rural areas.[1] Irish immigrants arriving in the United States were faced with ingrained Protestant hierarchies and socioeconomic structures, during a time of Protestant revivalism. Persistent nativism also pervaded, coming to a head with Know Nothingism in the 1850s. Irish-Americans turned inward to their own community for support, developing a unique communal identity based on the Catholic Church, Democratic Party, labour movements, and nationalist organizations.[2] The development of ethnic identity was central to national self-identification in the United States. Kevin Kenny asserts, 'In neither Britain nor Australia did ethnicity (Irish or otherwise) assume the historical importance it has had in the United States'.[3] Assuming an Irish-American ethnic identity was an important step in assimilating to American society. Even as increasingly close ties with the Catholic Church and Democratic Party led to conflict

---

1 Kenny, *American Irish*, 89–90; Kerby A. Miller, 'Class, Culture, and Immigrant Group Identity in the United States: The Case of Irish-American Ethnicity', in *Immigration Reconsidered: History, Sociology, and Politics*, ed. Virginia Yans-McLaughlin (New York: Oxford University Press, 1990), 108; William Forbes Adams, *Ireland and Irish Emigration to the New World from 1815 to the Famine* (New York: Russell & Russell, 1932), 221–222, 228–229.

2 Ward, 'America and the Irish Problem', 64; Miller, *Ireland and Irish America*, 8; McCaffrey, 'Diaspora Comparisons', 20; Arnold Schrier, *Ireland and the American Emigration, 1850–1900* (Minneapolis: University of Minnesota Press, 1958), 33.

3 Kenny, 'Diaspora and Comparison', para. 4.

with mainstream American society, these same organizations helped Irish-Americans gain a foothold in their local communities.[4] Participation in religious, political, and labour organizations was a means for eventual advancement in American society.

Throughout the country, Irish immigrants were closely associated with the Democratic Party. In New York City, they fell under the influence of Tammany Hall machine politics. From the 1840s, Tammany Hall lobbied for the support of prominent Irish constituencies in the city such as police, volunteer fire companies, and saloon keepers. William 'Boss' Tweed, though himself of Scotch-Irish descent, used a system of patronage to guarantee the support of New York City's Irish. A *New York Times* article in 1869 noted the Tweed Ring gave only 46 city jobs to Germans, while the Irish received 754.[5] Patronage from the Tweed Ring allowed Irish-Americans to gain key leadership roles and significant positions within New York City politics.

The deadly Orange Riots of 1870 and 1871, arising out of festering ethnic and class divisions, led New York elites to join with Irish-American representatives in a reform coalition which forced the Tweed Ring out of power. Having supported city elites in their reform efforts, 'Honest' John Kelly assumed Tammany Hall leadership in 1872. The Irish themselves now had direct control over New York City politics. New York City's first Irish-born Catholic mayor, William R. Grace, was elected in 1880.[6] Irish-Americans also gained prominence in other major cities as they grew in size, income, and social status. Boston's first Irish-born Catholic mayor, Hugh O'Brien, was elected in 1884.[7] The development of Irish-Americans as a more unified political group led the two main political parties to vie for Irish-American support on the national level.

The Irish were also closely associated with American labour movements. Irish-Americans were involved in the founding of such organizations as the American Federation of Labor and Knights of Labor. These organizations denounced the wage labour system and worked for educational programmes, land redistribution, and cooperative enterprise.[8] The Molly Maguires, a secret society of Irish mine workers in Pennsylvania, also protested against

---

4 Miller, 'Class, Culture, and Immigrant Group Identity', 113; Adams, *Ireland and Irish Emigration*, 374–375.
5 Hasia R. Diner, '"The Most Irish City in the Union": The Era of the Great Migration, 1844–1877', in *The New York Irish*, ed. Ronald H. Bayor and Timothy J. Meagher (Baltimore: Johns Hopkins University Press, 1996), 102.
6 Michael A. Gordon, *The Orange Riots: Irish Political Violence in New York City, 1870 and 1871* (Ithaca, NY: Cornell University Press, 1993), 2; Diner, 'Most Irish City', 102.
7 Thomas H. O'Connor, *The Boston Irish: A Political History* (Boston: Northeastern University Press, 1995), 141.
8 John R. McKivigan and Thomas J. Robertson, 'The Irish American Worker in Transition, 1877–1914: New York City as a Test Case', in *The New York Irish*, ed.

low wages, poor conditions, and military conscription in the 1860s. They became extremist and violent, linked with a string of killings from 1862 to 1875.[9] Based on the actions of the Molly Maguires, the attempted Fenian invasions of Canada, and Irish-American rioting, Irish unionists would later foster an image of Irish-America as inherently violent, corrupt, and immoral.

Nevertheless, the participation of Irish immigrants in political and labour movements contributed to a unique Irish-American identity. In many ways, involvement in these movements reflected a spirit of activism also present within the nationalist movement. At times, activism over American political and socioeconomic conditions went hand-in-hand with the cause of Irish nationalism, such as through Patrick Ford's prominent nationalist newspaper, the *Irish World and American Industrial Liberator*. Ford was an Irish-born journalist who immigrated with his family to Boston when he was four years old. After working under famed reformer William Lloyd Garrison, he founded the *Irish World* in 1870. Through its pages, Ford supported trade unions, strikes, and labour reform, at times backing the Greenback-Labor Party and even the Republican Party rather than the Democrats. Ford believed the labour struggle in the United States paralleled the struggle for land reform in Ireland, which grew in prominence throughout the 1870s.[10]

While participating in political and labour movements, Irish-Americans also built up a strong nationalist movement. The development of Irish-American nationalism was based on two major components. The first was genuine support within the immigrant community for Irish self-government, spurred by residual Anglophobia and perceptions that British actions had forced the Irish to emigrate.[11] The second, as Thomas Brown describes, was a response to the poverty and weakness of Irish Catholic immigrants within American society. Nationalists hoped that through the betterment of Ireland itself,

Ronald H. Bayor and Timothy J. Meagher (Baltimore: John Hopkins University Press, 1996), 304.

9   See Kevin Kenny, *Making Sense of the Molly Maguires* (New York: Oxford University Press, 1998); Brown, *Irish-American Nationalism*, 47.

10 David Brundage, '"In Time of Peace, Prepare for War": Key Themes in the Social Thought of New York's Irish Nationalists, 1890–1916', in *The New York Irish*, ed. Ronald H. Bayor and Timothy J. Meagher (Baltimore: John Hopkins University Press, 1996), 323; Eric Foner, 'Class, Ethnicity, and Radicalism in the Gilded Age: The Land League and Irish America', in *Politics and Ideology in the Age of the Civil War* (New York: Oxford University Press, 1980), 160–161; T.W. Moody, 'Irish-American Nationalists', *IHS* 15, no. 60 (Sep 1967), 440; Brown, 'Origins and Character', 350.

11 The idea that British actions had forced the Irish into exile is described in Kerby A. Miller, *Emigrants and Exiles: Ireland and the Irish Exodus to North America* (New York: Oxford University Press, 1985).

Irish-Americans could rise above nativist prejudices and gain acceptance, success, and prosperity in their new home.[12]

By the last quarter of the nineteenth century, the United States was transforming from a primarily rural, agricultural society to a more urbanized, industrial world power. As immigration levels soared, the country was home to immigrants not only from Western Europe, but all over the world.[13] Between 1870 and 1930, 2.5 million more Irish immigrants arrived in the United States, ensuring that as momentous changes were occurring in American and Irish society, Irish-Americans would play significant roles in both the United States and Ireland.

Coercion and Dynamite

Irish-American nationalist promotion of Irish Home Rule and independence was driven by a wide range of factors. Many Irish-Americans worked for their own advancement within American society through their quest for Irish self-government. Brown writes that immigrants supported collective action through which they 'would win Irish national freedom and thus the respect of Americans; and would also advance their material interests'.[14] Following the Civil War, Irish-Americans swelled the ranks of physical-force nationalist organizations such as the Fenian Brotherhood, organized in New York a few months after its Dublin counterpart in 1859. Fenians drew upon the ranks of Irish-American veterans of the Civil War to rise up unsuccessfully against the British in Ireland in 1867 and attempt to invade Canada in 1866 and 1870.[15] Many Irish-Americans joined the powerful Clan-na-Gael, formed in 1867 by Jerome Collins in reaction to Fenian factionalism. By the mid-1870s, Clan-na-Gael had 10,000 mainly working-class members, though it was under the control of middle-class leaders such as John Devoy and Dr. William Carroll.[16] Ford's *Irish World* was also an important force in both Irish-America and Ireland, becoming the most popular Irish-American

12 Miller, *Ireland and Irish America*, 14; Kenny, *American Irish*, 171–172; Timothy J. Meagher, Introduction to *From Paddy to Studs: Irish-American Communities in the Turn of the Century Era, 1880 to 1920*, ed. Timothy J. Meagher (New York: Greenwood Press, 1986), 11.

13 Meagher, Introduction, 3; Miller, *Ireland and Irish America*, 327–328.

14 Brown, 'Origins and Character', 352; Kenny, *American Irish*, 171.

15 Brundage, *Irish Nationalists in America*, 89–90, 99–106; Carroll, *American Opinion*, 6; Miller, 'Class, Culture, and Immigrant Group Identity', 113.

16 Brown, *Irish-American Nationalism*, 65–66; Brundage, *Irish Nationalists in America*, 107, 111–112; Terry Golway, 'John Devoy and the Easter Rising', in *Ireland's Allies: America and the 1916 Easter Rising*, ed. Miriam Nyhan Grey (Dublin: University College Dublin Press, 2016), 21–24.

newspaper of the late nineteenth century. His promotion of political and social movements on both sides of the Atlantic made Ford an ideal ally for Michael Davitt, the Irish land reform leader. Davitt visited the United States in 1878 and 1880 to promote the cause of Irish land reform, exchange ideas with Ford and other Irish-American leaders, and help lay foundations for the American branch of the Land League. Ford became the single most valuable source of support for the Land League Fund, raising $345,072 between 1880 and 1881.[17] In the minds of Irish unionists, Ford was the individual most associated with funding radical nationalist programmes, symbolizing American monetary control over Irish nationalism.

In his 1882 book, *The American Irish and their Influence on Irish Politics*, Philip H. Bagenal wrote that the root of American funding was the bitterness of second-generation Irish-Americans, who were often more 'Irish' in sentiment than their parents. Bagenal was an Irish civil servant and political writer who penned a number of books and pamphlets against Charles Stewart Parnell and the IPP. Bagenal described the 'vast Irish democracy' in the United States, living in tenements or factory towns, working as miners or domestic servants. He wrote, 'It is these who form the constituencies of anti-English demagogues, and who contribute their money to the various "funds" which have become, indeed, the root of all political evil in Ireland'.[18] Bagenal maintained, 'Without the American Irish aid and that material assistance which always forms the real sinews of business as well as of war, the efforts of Mr. Parnell and his party must have been comparatively feeble'.[19] According to Bagenal, Parnell recognized the potential of support from Irish-Americans who had been indoctrinated with anti-English attitudes and who were the driving force funding Irish nationalism and land agitation.

In the late 1870s, Irish-American nationalist leaders adopted a policy of close cooperation with Parnell and the IPP. During his 1878 American visit, Davitt worked with Devoy and Carroll to design the New Departure, calling for peasant land agitation to rouse the Irish populace to fight for separatism.[20] They hoped to pool resources between the revolutionary side

17 Miller, *Ireland and Irish-America*, 77; Brown, 'Origins and Character', 349–352; Moody, 'Irish-American Nationalists', 440; Carla King, *Michael Davitt* (Dundalk: Dundalgan, 1999), 16–19, 28–29; Shannon, *American Irish*, 133–134.
18 Philip H. Bagenal, *The American Irish and Their Influence on Irish Politics* (London: Kegan Paul, 1882), 33–36.
19 Bagenal, *American Irish*, 106–107.
20 Brown, *Irish-American Nationalism*, 89; Foner, 'Class, Ethnicity, and Radicalism', 154–155; Paul Bew, *Ireland: The Politics of Enmity 1789–2006* (Oxford: Oxford University Press, 2007), 309–310; T.W. Moody, 'The New Departure in Irish Politics, 1878–9', in *Essays in British and Irish History in Honour of James Eadie Todd*, ed. H.A. Cronne, T.W. Moody, and D.B. Quinn (London: Muller, 1949).

of the nationalist movement and the constitutional side, led by Parnell. In his 1884 pamphlet entitled, 'Two Irelands; or, Loyalty versus Treason', Edward Saunderson reflected on the New Departure as a turning point for Irish nationalism. Saunderson, a Cavan landlord and politician, would soon be elected MP for North Armagh and become leader of the parliamentary Ulster Unionist Party. He wrote, 'The happy family of Revolutionists in America quickly responded with money from the Fenian Treasury, while Mr. Parnell, the impoverished landlord of daring and unscrupulous temperament, having very little to lose and much to gain by the new move, threw himself heart and soul in with the others'.[21] In fact, Parnell never formally agreed to the terms of the New Departure, preferring to keep himself slightly detached from the proceedings while still profiting from American financial and political support.[22] The New Departure reoriented the focus of Irish nationalism toward land reform, while making the movement ever more dependent on the tacit support of Parnell.

According to Saunderson, leaders of the New Departure depended upon deception of American donors. When they donated money for the relief of Irish rural distress, the funds were instead used to support Parnellite MPs and violent Land Leaguers. Saunderson wrote that Catholic clergymen begged for funds to help their suffering flocks in distressed regions of Ireland, but received little aid. 'It was not for these purposes that the money was used, but in payment of the expenses of returning and keeping certain men in parliament, and in the providing of Captain Moonlight and others of that ilk with rewards for valour'.[23] Interestingly, Saunderson chose to show sympathy toward Catholic clergy rather than typical hostility of an Orangeman. This coincided with a strain of thought within unionism, which at times portrayed Irish and Irish-American nationalists as irreligious and anti-Catholic to underline the immoral and violent tendencies symbolized by the savagery of 'Captain Moonlight'. In Saunderson's interpretation, Irish and Irish-American nationalist leaders were betraying their American donors, the Catholic Church, and, above all, the interests of the Irish people.

The practices of the New Departure and Land League were officially legal and non-violent, though they were also linked with extremist rhetoric and a reliance on what R.F. Foster terms 'implicit violence'.[24] Parnell himself walked a fine line between promoting constitutional solutions to Ireland's problems and flirting with revolutionary nationalism. He arrived in the

---

21 Edward Saunderson, 'Two Irelands; or, Loyalty Versus Treason' (London: P.S. King & Son, 1884), 11.
22 Alvin Jackson, *Ireland, 1798–1998* (Oxford: Blackwell, 1999), 116–117; Moody, 'New Departure', 329–333.
23 Saunderson, 'Two Irelands', 17–18.
24 Foster, *Modern Ireland*, 405–410.

United States for a three-month tour starting in January 1880, speaking in 62 cities, addressing the House of Representatives, and raising $300,000 for the Land League.[25] Parnell's own turn toward radical rhetoric was symbolized by his speech in Cincinnati on 23 February, in which he reportedly declared that Irish nationalists would never 'be satisfied until we have destroyed the last link which keeps Ireland bound to England'.[26]

The *Belfast News-Letter* hoped Parnell's extremist language would turn the United States against him. An editorial on 6 February 1881 reported,

> There are unmistakable signs that the tide is completely turning against Mr. Parnell in America. 'The wretched agitator' ... is now being universally condemned by the Press of the United States for his attacks upon the Duchess of Marlborough and the Mansion House committees, and it is stated that the strong language in which he has indulged regarding them will probably complete the ruin of his mission.[27]

A Thomas Nast cartoon in *Harper's Weekly*, captioned 'Beware of Foreign Tramps', depicted Parnell begging hat-in-hand from an Irish-American domestic servant. She offered him 'food for Ireland' to relieve distress, but he demanded money.[28] Despite these depictions, Parnell grew increasingly popular with Irish-Americans. Through his use of extremist language, Parnell attempted to placate the revolutionary faction while steering Irish nationalist policy through a constitutional course. At the same time, he personally became very important to Irish-America as a leader and symbol of national unity.[29]

In Ireland, tensions increased over land disturbances. Land League demands for tenant rights and redistribution of land led to the eruption of a land war, which included boycotting and intimidation. Though the Land League remained officially non-violent, Conservative unionist writers

25 Brown, *Irish-American Nationalism*, 103–105; Kenny, *American Irish*, 176; F.S.L. Lyons, *Charles Stewart Parnell* (London: Collins, 1977), 98–115.
26 Lyons, *Parnell*, 111–113; Bew, *Ireland*, 316–317. Newspaper reports of the Cincinnati speech were inconsistent in their inclusion of the 'last link' phrase, and Parnell himself later denied ever using the words.
27 *BNL* 6 Feb 1881.
28 *Harper's Weekly* 24 Jan 1880, in Ely M. Janis, *A Greater Ireland: The Land League and Transatlantic Nationalism in Gilded Age America* (Madison: University of Wisconsin Press, 2015), 44–46. *Harper's Weekly* also printed several cartoons with negative depictions of dynamiters begging from Irish domestic servants. See Niall Whelehan, *The Dynamiters: Irish Nationalism and Political Violence in the Wider World, 1867–1900* (Cambridge: Cambridge University Press, 2012), 217–245.
29 Moody, 'Irish-American Nationalists', 438; Brown, *Irish-American Nationalism*, 97.

characterized it as extreme and terroristic. The root of Land League extremism, according to one unionist pamphleteer, lay in the United States: 'Subscriptions were pouring into its coffers from America, meetings were being held, violent speeches were being made, and the system of terrorism had been instituted'.[30] In another pamphlet, Bagenal presented rural distress in Ireland as manipulated by Irish-American separatists for their own purposes. He wrote, 'That agitation had its origin in the distress of the farmers of Connaught, which was skilfully used by American emissaries for the purpose of sowing the seeds of discontent and revolution'.[31] According to Bagenal, the Land League and Irish-American extremists were taking advantage of legitimate claims of rural distress to ignite rebellion and separatism.

However, the Land League and its goals for land reform were not solely the province of Irish Catholic nationalists in the late 1870s. Protestant farmers in the north of Ireland were also attracted to the Land League's principles and united with northern Catholics in the Ulster Liberal Party. Sectarian strife was at a low ebb as farmers and peasants joined together to combat landlordism. By 1879, Conservative party support in Ulster had weakened significantly. In less than a decade, this trend would be completely reversed as unionists formed a pan-Protestant bloc in the north in the face of the Home Rule threat. The 1885 general election saw the 'starkest possible polarization' of sectarian political parties, with 17 parliamentary seats in Ulster going to the Home Rule Party, 16 seats to the Conservatives, and none to the Liberals. As Brian Walker points out, from this point forward there would never again be such a close political alliance between Protestants and Catholics in Ulster.[32]

The mounting agrarian crisis led Prime Minister William E. Gladstone's Liberal government to introduce coercive measures through the 1881 Protection of Person and Property Act and 1882 Prevention of Crime Act. Goldwin Smith, an English Liberal intellectual and journalist who had settled in Canada, wrote that the government's coercive measures actually

---

30 Joseph T. Pim, 'Ireland in 1880, with Suggestions for the Reform of Her Land Laws' (London: W. Ridgway, 1880).

31 Philip H. Bagenal, 'Parnellism Unveiled; or, the Land-and-Labour Agitation of 1879–80' (Dublin: Hodges, Foster, and Figgis, 1880).

32 Frank Thompson, *The End of Liberal Ulster: Land Agitation and Land Reform, 1868–1886* (Belfast: Ulster Historical Foundation, 2001); Paul Bew and Frank Wright, 'The Agrarian Opposition in Ulster Politics, 1848–87', in *Irish Peasants: Violence and Political Unrest, 1780–1914*, ed. Samuel Clark and James S. Donnelly, Jr. (Madison: University of Wisconsin Press, 1983), 192–194, 218–225; Brian M. Walker, 'The Land Question and Elections in Ulster, 1868–86', in *Irish Peasants: Violence and Political Unrest, 1780–1914*, ed. Samuel Clark and James S. Donnelly, Jr. (Madison: University of Wisconsin Press, 1983), 230.

meant the removal of Land League coercion. He believed the land movement would have died out were it not for American financial support.

> It is from the United States, not from Ireland itself, that almost the whole of the money for rebellion is drawn. We cannot help admiring the love with which the heart of the Irish emigrant glows for his mother country; unselfish sentiment does honour to a race even though it may be misguided. But observation and inquiry have satisfied me that the Irish character in America, as well as at home, while strong in affection is weak in independence, and that many of these people subscribe to Fenianism under pressure, and, if they were left to themselves, would be glad to keep their hardly earned money in their pockets. They pay under the threat of Social Boycotting.[33]

To Smith, Irish-Americans rather than the Irish themselves were driving land agitation. Even the support of Irish-Americans was not genuine, however, as their actions were forced by intimidation from Fenian leaders. The blame for Irish disturbances was laid at the door of a few Irish-American leaders who were not representative of opinions in Ireland or America.

Along with coercion, Gladstone also attempted conciliation through the 1881 Land Law Act.[34] The *Belfast News-Letter* complained that conciliatory measures had little impact but to spur on violence and boycotting. 'What they have been taught hitherto', claimed an editorial, 'is that they have only to agitate and organize and be violent, and concessions will follow. The agitators, who find their countrymen in America contributing weekly their hundreds of pounds, are not likely to abandon so profitable a trade; and herein lies the source of many a future danger'.[35] In this view, concessions from the British government increased Irish-American donations which drove land agitation. Land agitation would not be abandoned as long as it remained lucrative for the perpetrators.

The United States was drawn into the situation when some land agitators who were arrested under coercion claimed protection as American citizens. James Russell Lowell, the American minister in London, was charged with protecting the rights of United States citizens in Britain and Ireland. While Lowell was sympathetic to Home Rule policies, he looked on Irish-American agitators as taking advantage of their American citizenship while their loyalties lay with a foreign country. He wrote in a State Department dispatch

---

33 Goldwin Smith, 'The Conduct of England to Ireland: An Address Delivered at Brighton, Jan. 30, 1882' (London: Macmillan, 1882), 31.
34 Jackson, *Ireland*, 119–121.
35 *BNL* 9 Jul 1881.

in 1882, 'Naturalized Irishmen seem entirely to misconceive the process through which they have passed in assuming American citizenship, looking upon themselves as Irishmen who have acquired American protection, rather than as Americans who have renounced a claim to Irish nationality'.[36] Though the American government did not want to hamper British prosecution of criminals, the State Department insisted on minimum guarantees of justice for American citizens, including prompt trials before a judge and jury. Chester A. Arthur's administration and the State Department worked to strike a balance between protecting rights of citizens abroad, maintaining Anglo-American relations, and addressing concerns of Irish-American pressure groups. Through the end of 1881 and beginning of 1882, Lowell continued talks with the British government. Ultimately, most of the prisoners were released after they agreed to return to the United States. This did not stop a mass meeting of New York Irishmen led by Mayor Grace and Democratic congressmen from condemning Lowell's 'sickening sycophancy to English influence'.[37]

A Tory writer in the *Quarterly Review* denounced Gladstone's inability to deal constructively with the land war and his agreement to return American prisoners, complaining, 'He has filled the gaols with "suspects", and his one idea appears to have been to keep them there, but the United States have already caused him to release some of the most dangerous of prisoners – the American Fenians'. The writer saw no end to land agitation so long as money came in from America: 'The funds with which the "social revolution" is carried on come almost entirely from the United States, and now it is advertised to the world that plots against the British Government may safely be carried on under its very eyes, provided that the plotters can show a certificate of American citizenship'.[38] The *Belfast News-Letter* also emphasized the profitability of extremism, meaning there could be no peace in Ireland as long as money came in from America. An editorial noted, 'The paymasters of the League are at the other side of the Atlantic, and they will button up their pockets if they do not get what they look upon as value for their money. An occasional landlord shot is an acceptable sacrifice to the dynamite Fenians. A recalcitrant tenant boycotted or carded is a tribute to their generosity'.[39]

36 Beckles Willson, *America's Ambassadors to England (1785–1928): A Narrative of Anglo-American Diplomatic Relations* (London: John Murray, 1928), 382.
37 Owen Dudley Edwards, 'American Diplomats and Irish Coercion, 1880–1883', *Journal of American Studies* 1, no. 2 (1967), 217, 227–232; David M. Pletcher, *The Awkward Years: American Foreign Relations under Garfield and Arthur* (Columbia: University of Missouri Press, 1961), 238–244.
38 'What Shall be Done with Ireland?', *Quarterly Review* 153, no. 306 (Apr 1882), 591–592.
39 *BNL* 26 Sep 1881.

The Land League's American funding was connected to more extreme elements within Irish-American nationalism, those who promoted dynamite attacks in major British cities starting in 1881. The dynamite campaign was the work of the Clan-na-Gael and Jeremiah O'Donovan Rossa, an Irish nationalist who permanently settled in the United States in 1871. They were supported by the Skirmishing Fund, set up in 1875 to finance guerrilla warfare against the British. The first dynamite attack came on 14 January 1881 on Salford Barracks. Further attempts were made in spring 1881 on the Mansion House, Liverpool Town Hall, and Liverpool's main police station. Even before these attacks, British diplomats were aware of the Skirmishing Fund, which was advertised in Irish-American newspapers including the *Irish World* and Rossa's *United Irishman*. As the threat of further dynamite attacks loomed in 1881, the British government began to investigate Irish-American newspapers and pressure the American government to suppress Skirmishing Fund subscription campaigns.[40] The *Belfast News-Letter* complained,

O'Donovan Rossa and others like him make their livelihood by advocating schemes of wholesale destruction and assassination; and it is impossible not to recognise the miserable fact that large numbers of Irish people in the United States are so utterly lost to all sense of rectitude and morality as to support and subscribe to assassination funds and journals which advocate the wholesale destruction of life and property.[41]

American newspapers were blamed for disseminating information about the funds, which led to the dynamite campaign itself.

H.O. Arnold-Forster, in his 1881 pamphlet, 'The Truth about the Land League', held similar bleak views on the role of the Irish-American press. He asserted, 'The *Irish World* is the advocate of – 1. Private murder, 2. Rebellion and treason, 3. Mutilation, 4. Plunder and robbery, 5. Assassination on a large scale by means of explosives'.[42] Furthermore, he believed the *Irish World* and Skirmishing Fund to be intimately connected with the Land League and Parnell. Arnold-Forster was an apologist of his foster father, then–chief secretary for Ireland W.E. Forster, who was associated with strict protection of law and order. Forster had Parnell arrested in 1881

---

40 Whelehan, *Dynamiters*, 70–86; Jonathan Gantt, *Irish Terrorism in the Atlantic Community, 1865–1922* (London: Palgrave Macmillan, 2010), 132–140; K.R.M. Short, *The Dynamite War: Irish-American Bombers in Victorian Britain* (Dublin: Gill and Macmillan, 1979), 38, 50–64; Pletcher, *Awkward Years*, 246.
41 *BNL* 28 Jul 1881.
42 H.O. Arnold-Forster, 'The Truth about the Land League, Its Leaders, and Its Teaching', 2nd edn (London: National Press Agency, 1882), 29–30.

and suppressed the Land League. Both Forster and Arnold-Forster broke with Gladstone when Parnell was released from jail on 2 May 1882 upon agreement of the Kilmainham Treaty.[43]

Just four days later, the new chief secretary for Ireland, Lord Frederick Cavendish, and undersecretary Thomas Burke, were murdered in Dublin's Phoenix Park. The murders were committed by a fringe nationalist group, the Irish Invincibles, which had only nominal connections with the United States. The *Belfast News-Letter* reported, 'In all its aspects the tragedy was terrible and revolting; but those who know how widely spread are the ramifications of Fenianism, and how broadcast the seeds of sedition have been sown, have long been prepared to hear of some such desperate attempt to destroy life or property, or both, in pursuance of the villainous designs advocated by the men of the O'Donovan Rossa school'.[44] The newspaper portrayed a growing atmosphere of violence in Ireland, fuelled by Irish-American extremism. The influence of America made an event such as the Phoenix Park murders tragically inevitable, even if Irish-Americans themselves were not directly responsible.

For the time being, the Phoenix Park murders cut off any possibility of a constructive relationship between the IPP and Gladstone's government. Irish agrarian violence temporarily abated, but the raising of money for the dynamite campaign continued. In response to this ongoing threat, the British government and consular officials in the United States hired Pinkerton Detectives and began early attempts at forming a secret service, gathering intelligence data and using undercover agents. Continued British objections to Irish-American newspapers had little impact, as the American government would not act without explicit evidence of connections to violent acts and was reluctant to risk alienating Irish-American voters.[45] The *Belfast News-Letter* believed it was hopeless to look for help from the American government because of this voter influence. The solidity of the Irish vote, the paper stated, 'depends on the line of policy adopted by such leaders as Ford of the *Irish World* and O'Donovan Rossa, of Skirmishing Fund swindle notoriety. For these reasons Republicans and Democrats are loath to offend the Irish party, whom they nevertheless cordially despise'.[46]

43 Margaret O'Callaghan, *British High Politics and a Nationalist Ireland: Criminality, Land and the Law under Forster and Balfour* (New York: St. Martin's, 1994), 56–79; Jackson, *Ireland*, 121–123.

44 *BNL* 11 May 1882.

45 Whelehan, *Dynamiters*, 99–103; Gantt, *Irish Terrorism*, 139; Short, *Dynamite War*, 75, 99; Murney Gerlach, *British Liberalism and the United States: Political and Social Thought in the Late Victorian Age* (Basingstoke: Palgrave, 2001), 85–86; Pletcher, *Awkward Years*, 246–247.

46 *BNL* 14 Apr 1884.

The violence and extremism of the dynamite campaign alienated potential American and British support for Irish nationalist causes. The American public was reluctant to sympathize with Irish-American revolutionaries, because their violent tactics degraded traditional associations with romantic nationalism. Both the American public and United States government increasingly supported Gladstone's efforts to find a moderate, constitutional solution to Ireland's problems.[47] In addition, disagreement over the use of the Skirmishing Fund led to factionalism within Irish-America. The Chicago convention in August 1881 broke up because of disagreements over dynamite, and Irish-American organizations suffered from internal divisions.[48] The violence of the dynamite campaign also reinforced unionist perceptions that the Irish could not be trusted to govern themselves.

Further dynamite attacks were made in Glasgow and London in 1883 and 1884. The new wave of attacks, orchestrated by Clan-na-Gael, had much greater potential to be deadly as they targeted railway stations and the London Underground. On 24 January 1885, coordinated dynamite bombs exploded at the Tower of London, Westminster Hall, and the House of Commons. Public opinion in America – as in Britain – was outraged, with newspapers denouncing the dynamiters, and congressmen condemning the events.[49] The *Saturday Review* commented,

> It must seem to every fair-minded Englishman slightly unreasonable to objurgate America for not restraining her Fords and her O'Donovan Rossas when we let agitators of every rank, from Mr. Parnell to the riff-raff of the Irish town councils, rave and insinuate as they please; which despite our knowledge that these men could break up the whole gang if they chose, we tolerate their toleration and wink at their connivance.[50]

Parnell was portrayed as having close control over all aspects of Irish nationalism, including American organizations and the dynamiters.

With Gladstone's conversion to Home Rule in late 1885, the dynamite campaign halted. The Clan-na-Gael faced further factionalism because of executives embezzling funds, which also impacted the dynamite campaign. When Parnell spoke in Parliament in support of the Home Rule Bill on 8 April 1886, he assured the House of Commons that the promise of such a bill would

---

47 M.J. Sewell, 'Rebels or Revolutionaries? Irish-American Nationalism and American Diplomacy, 1865–1885', *Historical Journal* 29, no. 3 (Sep 1986), 724, 729–730.
48 Brown, *Irish-American Nationalism*, 154–155.
49 Whelehan, *Dynamiters*, 94; Pletcher, *Awkward Years*, 253; Short, *Dynamite War*, 207.
50 Quoted in *Witness* 6 Feb 1885.

quell the extremism of Ford and the Clan-na-Gael, and that the dynamite campaign was not a reflection of the Irish in general.[51] Nevertheless, Irish unionists seized on extremist images of Irish-America and the dynamiters as part of their campaign to counter the Home Rule movement.

First Home Rule Crisis

Even before the first Home Rule crisis, unionists had developed an image of Irish-America which emphasized its violence and extremism. Unionists claimed that land agitation and dynamite outrages could never be stopped while Irish-America controlled the financing of the nationalist movement. Nationalists committed these outrages not for ideological reasons but because that was what Irish-American extremists demanded in return for their money. Irish nationalism was discredited by being funded and controlled by a foreign power, and unionists claimed nationalism had little genuine support in Ireland or indeed Irish-America. Dynamite and agitation were seen as lucrative trades controlled by an extremist minority, which duped average Irishmen and Irish-Americans who only wished to help relieve rural distress. This pattern of responses to Irish-American extremism would be utilized to an even greater extent throughout 1885–1886, as unionists formally organized for the first time in response to the Home Rule threat.

The November/December 1885 general election gave Irish nationalists the balance of power in the House of Commons. Lord Salisbury and the Conservatives managed to stay in government for only a month before the IPP combined with the Liberals to throw them out of office, initiating Gladstone's third ministry. With the imminent threat of Home Rule, unionists began to organize both in Ireland and the United Kingdom as a whole. Dublin's Irish Loyal and Patriotic Union (ILPU) formed in May 1885, leading the effort to spread information and propaganda for the unionist cause. In the south, unionists were generally Protestant landowners or merchants, with a small number of Catholic adherents.[52] In Ulster, local organization developed through the Ulster Loyalist Anti-Repeal Union (ULAU), a central association for agitation and propaganda founded in January 1886. Ulster Conservatives worked to forge an electoral alliance with local Liberals, who declared their support of Union in March 1886. In

---

51 Whelehan, *Dynamiters*, 295–303; Short, *Dynamite War*, 229–230; Pletcher, *Awkward Years*, 252–253; Brown, *Irish-American Nationalism*, 166. For Parnell's speech, see PD 3rd Ser., Vol. 304, 1124–1134.

52 Ian d'Alton, 'Southern Irish Unionism: A Study of Cork Unionists, 1884–1914', *Transactions of the Royal Historical Society* 23 (1974), 72.

Parliament, Conservatives and Liberals joined in an uneasy alliance to form the Ulster Unionist Party, led by Saunderson.[53]

Gladstone introduced the first Home Rule Bill on 8 April 1886. In debates from April to June, the United States played a prominent role. American historical and constitutional examples were frequently called upon, particularly by future Liberal Unionists such as Joseph Chamberlain, the Marquess of Hartington, and George Goschen.[54] Many unionists also attacked the claims of the Liberal chief secretary for Ireland, John Morley, that dynamiters and assassins would be delighted if Home Rule was rejected.[55] Goschen, the MP for East Edinburgh, condemned Morley's arguments, stating, 'The Chief Secretary continually recalls the Irish-Americans; and I trust the House will bear his warning constantly in mind, and then apply it to all of the analogies he used in favour of this bill. When the analogy of the Colonies is put to us, we may ask whether in that case, we have the same danger, or the same influences of the Irish-Americans?'[56] Unlike Morley, Goschen and other unionists were not worried about the reaction of Irish-America if Home Rule were defeated. Rather they were concerned about the impact of Irish-America on a Home Rule government which would surely retain the high levels of American influence including incitement to violence.

Unionists worried this influence would extend to a new Dublin parliament. Lord Randolph Churchill, Conservative MP for South Paddington, emphasized experiences of extremism, such as crime, outrage, assassination, and dynamite, which coloured views against Home Rule. He feared Ford and other Irish-American extremists would find places in the Home Rule government.[57] Goschen echoed this fear, asking,

---

53 Jackson, *Ulster Party*, 39–40, 44–50; D.C. Savage, 'The Origins of the Ulster Unionist Party, 1885–1886', *IHS* 12, no. 47 (Mar 1961), 193–195; Gibbon, *Origins of Ulster Unionism*, 129–130.

54 PD 3rd Ser., Vol. 304, 1205–1206, 1253–1254, 1481.

55 PD 3rd Ser., Vol. 306, 941.

56 PD 3rd Ser., Vol. 306, 1149–1150.

57 PD 3rd Ser., Vol. 304, 1339–1343. Lord Randolph Churchill himself played a substantial role in the attempt to form a Tory–Parnellite alliance in mid-1885. His remarks reflected his changing approach to Irish policy, revealing his pragmatism more than true horror at extremism and crime. According to Foster, his stances reflected strategic opportunism as well as the influences of Dublin Toryism and his own contacts within the unionist realm, causing him to evolve from being flexible on Irish policy to becoming one of Ulster's champions in less than a year. See R.F. Foster, *Lord Randolph Churchill: A Political Life* (Oxford: Clarendon Press, 1981), 224–260; Lyons, *Parnell*, 279–306; Nicholas Mansergh, *The Irish Question, 1840–1921: A Commentary on Anglo-Irish Relations and on Social and Political Forces in Ireland in the Age of Reform and Revolution* (Toronto: University of Toronto Press, 1975), 187–192.

Can we be sure that the new Irish Executive will not have a very difficult task to prevent the conspirators, dynamiters, and Nihilists from flocking into Ireland? ... I say it will be a difficult task for those whose movement has succeeded, if it does succeed, through the subscriptions which have come to it from Irish Americans, it will be a difficult task for the new Executive to close the doors in Dublin on their allies from the other side of the water.[58]

Irish-American financial influence was feared because it would lead extremists to control the Dublin parliament.

Francis Hughes-Hallett, Conservative MP for Rochester, feared separation would be the next demand of the Irish-Americans: 'Supposing the Parliament proposed by this Bill were established in Dublin, it seemed to him that the Representatives of the Nationalist Party now or in the future would be subject to wire-pulling by a Council sitting in Chicago or New York'.[59] The existence and influence of Irish-America meant separatism would always be a threat. Unionists argued that demands for further Irish autonomy would not stop if Home Rule was granted. Unionists maintained that preserving a full connection within the Union was safer than granting a half-measure like Home Rule which would allow Irish-American extremists to seize power.

Unionists also believed Parnell and other IPP members held separatist aims which were concealed in Parliament but revealed in America. William Johnston, Orangeman and MP for South Belfast, asserted that Parnell 'had never concealed [his aims] from sympathetic audiences in Ireland, and still more in America, whence he recruited his treasury. His aims were the disruption of the British Empire and the severance of the last link which bound Ireland to the British Crown'.[60] Saunderson also accused Parnell of revealing his true separatist intentions in America.[61] Unionists cited IPP speeches made in the United States, with George Trevelyan and Edward King-Harman both quoting Parnell's famous 'Last Link' speech, as well as T.M. Healy's 1881 'Begone Saxon' speech given in Boston.[62] Unionists drew upon these speeches to illustrate the extreme rhetoric in which nationalists indulged while in the United States. The Marquess of Hartington, Liberal Unionist MP for Rossendale and former chief secretary for Ireland, stated that even if Parnell did not personally advocate separatism, he was still guilty of failing to denounce American extremism. 'He seems to set up America as

58 PD 3rd Ser., Vol. 304, 1471.
59 PD 3rd Ser., Vol. 306, 537–538.
60 PD 3rd Ser., Vol. 304, 1227.
61 PD 3rd Ser., Vol. 304, 1392.
62 PD 3rd Ser., Vol. 306, 97–100, 1043–1047.

the true and only friend of Ireland; but in all his references to America he has never found time to utter one word of disapproval or misgiving about what is known as the assassination literature of that country'.[63]

Unionists alleged that Parnell's ambiguous stances were due to the influence of American money. Saunderson in particular focused on the American funding aspect in his speeches, stating,

> Let me suppose – which, of course, is very hard to suppose – that Russia succeeded, by corruptly subsidizing a certain number of Members of this House, in getting a Bill passed, and the Bill was passed by a majority of the men so bribed, should we not be justified in employing all the power we possess in contending against and in fighting against such a measure? Well, Sir, what is the case at present? There are 85 Members of this House paid by America.[64]

He was forced to withdraw the charges, but Saunderson's accusation of bribery revealed the extent to which the IPP was perceived to be controlled by a foreign power, Irish-America, rather than representing Irish interests. In fact, unionists argued, the cause of Home Rule did not appeal to most Irishmen at all. King-Harman, a unionist who had formerly been a Buttite Home Rule MP, stated,

> In Mr. [Isaac] Butt's time, the state of Ireland was very different from what it was now. Freedom of opinion was allowed, for there was no National League, no 'Boycotting', and no American agitators; and yet Mr. Butt could not with all his eloquence arouse the slightest degree of enthusiasm for the cause he espoused, and he (Colonel King-Harman) ventured to say there was little more enthusiasm now in the hearts of the people than there was in Mr. Butt's time.[65]

American agitation and funding had made Irish nationalist causes more prominent, King-Harman argued, but they did not have the support of the Irish people.

In addition, unionists maintained that Irish-American extremism and violence was not supported by Americans in general. Hartington declared, 'There is not an American that does not scorn it, and spurn it and loathe it, as you do'.[66] While Republicans and Democrats vied for the Irish–American

---

63 PD 3rd Ser., Vol. 305, 620.
64 PD 3rd Ser., Vol. 305, 1769.
65 PD 3rd Ser., Vol. 306, 1047.
66 PD 3rd Ser., Vol. 305, 620–621.

vote, Saunderson stated he very much doubted 'whether the language used at recent meetings in America is likely to gain either of these two Parties to the cause of Ireland'. He asserted that violent language would not attract the sympathy of the 'great American people'. In so doing, Saunderson implied that the support of the American public would be with the unionists.[67] Ulster was upheld as the one part of Ireland free from the degrading influence of Irish-America. Lord George Hamilton, Conservative MP for Ealing, contrasted the extremism in the south of Ireland with law-abiding Ulster. 'I have lived a great part of my life among the people of the North of Ireland', he said, 'and I assert that no more meritorious people are to be found on the whole face of the earth ... They have expelled crime and outrage, and, at the instigation of the Prime Minister himself, have shown themselves supporters of law and order'.[68] According to Hamilton, Ulster was at odds with the rest of Ireland, where nationalists were susceptible to resort to crime and outrage in return for American money.

Just as in Parliament, Irish-American extremism also formed a significant portion of unionist discourse in the public realm, as shown in their leaflets, pamphlets, journal and newspaper articles, and speeches. Many of these were facilitated by the ILPU, which in 1886 adopted an extensive programme of public meetings throughout Britain and Ireland, and established a press bureau. They published and circulated 11 million leaflets, 500,000 pamphlets, and over 20,000 posters and maps in that year alone.[69] Unionists made similar arguments both in and out of Parliament. Condemnation of American funding of Irish nationalism formed a major part of the anti–Home Rule campaign. Irish historian W.E.H. Lecky accused Irish nationalists of being under the control of a foreign power, working for policies demanded by Irish-Americans in exchange for financial support.[70] Reverend J.B. Crozier asserted that any attempt to appease the American-paid nationalists with Home Rule would be as craven as a father throwing his children to wolves. He cited Parnell's 1880 speech at Troy, New York, stating, 'Mr. Parnell had not scrupled to accept one hundred dollars from a person in America for the distressed Irish people on the stipulation that "thirty dollars were for bread and seventy dollars were for lead"'.[71] Unionists closely monitored and reported on speeches of Irish nationalists in America, and scrutinized Irish-American newspapers such as the *Irish World*. Parnell's 'Last Link'

67 PD 3rd Ser., Vol. 304, 1392–1393.
68 PD 3rd Ser., Vol. 305, 992–993.
69 Irish Loyal and Patriotic Union. Annual Report of the Executive Committee for the Year 1886, Public Record Office of Northern Ireland (PRONI) D989/A/7/1.
70 W.E.H. Lecky, 'A "Nationalist" Parliament', *Nineteenth Century* 19, no. 110 (Apr 1886), 638.
71 *BNL* 10 May 1886.

speech was frequently alluded to as proof of his true separatist intentions, which were closely guarded in Parliament but revealed in America.[72] Healy's 'Begone Saxon' speech was also repeatedly referenced, with an entire ILPU pamphlet devoted to publicizing his comparison of the British to Satan.[73]

Unionist pamphlet literature often recounted the history of Irish nationalist connections to Irish-America, through Devoy, Davitt, Ford, and Irish-American organizational treasurer Patrick Egan. Pamphleteers asserted that American paymasters dictated separatist policy in return for their financial support. If the British Parliament enacted Home Rule, it would be creating a perpetual source of weakness and eventually a hostile country on its neighbouring island.[74] Charles Lewis, MP for Londonderry City, stated that establishing a Home Rule parliament would mean submitting the loyal population of Ireland to the 'slavery of the Leaguers and dynamiters and Fenians of the United States of America'.[75] As in Parliament, unionists in the public realm worried over the influence which Irish-Americans would maintain over a potential Home Rule government.[76] Unionists in the public realm also argued that the Irish and Irish-American nationalists were not representative of the Irish people as a whole. They asserted that a 'foreign conspiracy' – in the form of Irish-American influence – was propping up a movement which otherwise would have long since died off.[77] Lecky wrote that much of the movement was of a superficial character driven by professional agitation, 'which American subsidies have made peculiarly lucrative'.[78] William Ellison-Macartney, MP for South Antrim, maintained that the Home Rule policy appealed to 'every other intelligence except that of the people whose interests were at stake'.[79] Unionists insisted that the quest for money was driving the Irish nationalist movement rather than the Irish people themselves.

---

72 See, for example, Lecky, 'Nationalist Parliament', 638; *BNL* 14 May 1887; 'Mr. Chamberlain and the Birmingham Association: Speech Delivered in the Town Hall, Birmingham, April 21, 1886' (London: Liberal Unionist Committee, 1886).

73 '"Begone Saxon!"': Mr. T.M. Healy at Boston', in *Irish Loyal and Patriotic Union: Publications Issued during the Year 1888* (Dublin: ILPU, 1888); Irish Liberal, 'Irish Issues: Letters Addressed to the Right Hon. John Morley, M.P.' (Dublin: E. Ponsonby, 1888).

74 Gilbert Mahaffy, 'The Attitude of Irish Churchmen in the Present Political Crisis' (Dublin: George Herbert, 1886); H. Brougham Leech, '1848 and 1887: The Continuity of the Irish Revolutionary Movement', in *Irish Loyal and Patriotic Union: Publications Issued during the Year 1888* (Dublin: ILPU, 1888).

75 *BNL* 24 Jan 1887.

76 Lecky, 'Nationalist Parliament', 637; *BNL* 8 May 1886.

77 *BNL* 9 Feb 1887; 'Ireland. No. XII. The Sources of the Parnellite Income', PRONI D989/C/3/5.

78 Lecky, 'Nationalist Parliament', 642–643.

79 *BNL* 24 Jan 1888.

The American example was utilized by unionists to emphasize that the Irish were not fit for self-government. Speaking in Belfast, Joseph Chamberlain described the power of the Irish vote in the major cities of America.

> The Government of New York – it was not called an Irish Parliament, it was known by the name of the Tammany Ring – that Government, according to all impartial American opinion, was the most corrupt, the most immoral, the most ineffective, with which a civilised people have ever been afflicted. Gentlemen, the experience is not encouraging to us, and for my part I cannot accept as desirable or possible the degradation of the great city of Belfast and the province of Ulster under a Tammany Ring in Dublin.[80]

Similarly, pamphleteer Henry Norton Palmer also argued that to judge by the example of New York, the Irish could never be peaceable, happy, or law abiding if granted self-government.[81] Tammany Hall was synonymous with government corruption and immorality, reflecting the inability of the Irish to govern themselves in any country.

Another theme in unionist rhetoric was the insistence that Americans would not support Home Rule measures if they were attempted in the United States. Goschen, in an interview with the *New York Herald*, stated,

> Mr. Gladstone's bill provided for neither such an authority as the United States Supreme Court to decide on the unity of legislation, nor such an authority as the Federal Executive. I do not believe that the American public would for one moment tolerate such a paralysis of the Central Executive in any American State as would have resulted in Ireland from Mr. Gladstone's plan.[82]

While analogies to American federal-state relations were part of an array of international examples used to support or condemn Home Rule, Goschen was here focusing on the United States in an effort to appeal to an American audience and attempting to relay the ill-planned and haphazard nature of Home Rule. He believed the state of conspiracy and rebellion in Ireland would never be tolerated by an American government. ILPU pamphlets also renounced land agitation, arguing that British land policies in Ireland

---

80 Charles W. Boyd, ed., *Mr. Chamberlain's Speeches*, Vol. 1 (London: Constable, 1914), 288–289.
81 Henry Norton Palmer, 'Ireland: Past and Present' (Exeter: Henry S. Eland, 1888).
82 *BNL* 27 Jul 1886.

were far more generous than anything allowed by the United States. They detailed how Irish land laws gave far greater rights than those in America, as the ILPU attempted to minimize Irish grievances.[83]

The American press closely followed the events surrounding the Home Rule Bill debates. The *New York Times* was critical of Parnell and his ties to Land League agitation and dynamite, viewing him as a 'demagogue' similar to the Irish-American bosses in United States cities. However, they discounted the right of unionists in Ireland to fight against Home Rule. 'The Protestants in Ulster are not entitled, by their numbers or by any other fact about them, to be treated as a separate people with national or quasi-national rights', an editorial opined, asserting that unionists should submit to majority rule. The editorial went on to say, 'When the Home Rule bill or its successor comes up again for discussion the Ulster Protestants are not likely to cut as conspicuous a figure in the debate as they have done thus far'. The *New York Times* did not see Irish unionism as a threat to the eventual adoption of Home Rule because, an editorial asserted, the visibility of Irish unionists was solely due to Tory party tactics in playing up sectarian divisions.[84] Like many American newspapers, the *New York Times* portrayed the battle for Home Rule as Gladstone and Irish nationalists versus English Conservatives. For many mainstream newspapers, admiration for Gladstone outweighed any dislike of Parnell, with widespread backing for a Home Rule settlement.[85]

Unionists attempted to appeal to America for support, closely monitoring attitudes in the United States. Both the *Belfast News-Letter* and the Presbyterian *Witness* reprinted articles on Home Rule from American newspapers, such as the pro-Union editorials of the *San Francisco Argonaut* and reports from the *New York Evening Post* and *New York Tribune*.[86] The *Belfast News-Letter* also printed letters of support from American Orangemen and monitored the pro-Union actions of United States Orange Lodges.[87] Unionists such as Lord Rossmore, an Orange leader, declared that the 'great Protestant nation' of America would hear unionist appeals just as well as those of Parnell.[88] James McCalmont, MP for East Antrim, emphasized the continued loyalty of Irish Protestants after emigration.

83 'An Irish Tenant's Privileges' and 'Irish and American Land Laws', both in *Irish Loyal and Patriotic Union: Publications Issued during the Year 1888* (Dublin: ILPU, 1888).
84 *NYT* 16 Nov 1880, 1 Aug 1883, 18 Aug 1883, 24 Jun 1881, 10 Jun 1886, 3 Jul 1886.
85 *Decatur Republican* 9 Apr 1886; *New York Sun* 8 Jun 1886; *Los Angeles Herald* 9 Jun 1886; *Sacramento Union* 8 Jun 1886; *Rocky Mountain News* 9 Jun 1886.
86 *BNL* 14 Jan, 16 Feb, 1 Mar 1886; *Witness* 24 Dec 1885, 16 Apr 1886.
87 *BNL* 13 Apr, 7 Jun 1886.
88 *BNL* 19 Feb 1885.

Mr. Parnell made a speech the other day in which he declared that all Irishmen as soon as they settle in the United States become disloyal. He (the speaker) absolutely denied that. His own family for the last two generations had been connected with the United States, but notwithstanding they would yield none in their loyalty to the Queen. (Applause.) That was only one instance, but he felt sure every Protestant from the North of Ireland would be the same, whether he went to America or anywhere else.[89]

Unionists drew upon connections forged over two centuries of Ulster Protestant emigration to the United States to promote the anti-Home Rule campaign. This in itself was a policy laden with pitfalls, as Irish-Americans were criticized for valuing Ireland more than the United States. The Scotch-Irish certainly would not want to be associated with doing the same thing. Organizations such as the American Orange Order had to walk a fine line to show that they were not monarchists and anti-American. Many Americans would have abominated the idea that the Scotch-Irish put Ulster or British interests before those of the United States, as McCalmont claimed.

Based in part on the historic connections between Ulster and America, however, there was still hope in the potential for American sympathy and support for the Union. Both the ILPU and ULAU adopted policies of appealing to the United States and dominions. The ILPU printed pro-Union pamphlets especially for the consumption of foreign and colonial audiences and distributed their weekly newsletter, *Notes from Ireland*, to newspaper editors throughout the world. The Executive Committee noted that America received special attention in their attempts to circulate pro-Union arguments. They even sent propaganda materials to the pro-Parnellite press in the United States.[90] Through the ULAU, Reverend Dr. Richard Rutledge Kane of Belfast's Christ Church, the grand master of Belfast's Orangemen, was authorized to correspond with loyalists in Canada and the United States, asking for their support during the Home Rule crisis. Reverend Dr. Hugh Hanna corresponded with those in Australia.[91] Kane was dispatched with George Hill Smith, a local barrister, to visit Canada and the United States on behalf of the ULAU to present the unionist cause to the people of North America.[92]

The Loyal Orange Institution provided one of the points of connection between Ulster and the United States. The Orange Order had grown in

89 *BNL* 21 Oct 1885.
90 Irish Loyal and Patriotic Union. Annual Report of the Executive Committee for the Year 1886, PRONI D989/A/7/1.
91 *BNL* 28 Jan 1886.
92 *BNL* 24 Jul 1886.

political importance in Ireland throughout the course of the first Home Rule crisis.[93] In a speech to Irish and Canadian Orangemen, Kane asserted that Protestant and Orange principles had found local habitation in every part of the globe, including the United States.

> When they think of how strong Orangeism was in the different parts of the British Empire and in America, they could afford to laugh at such figures of speech as were sometimes indulged in by men of the Michael Davitt type, who were very fond of talking about a certain ferocious animal which they called the wolf-dog, and who had his lair on the other side of the Atlantic wave, and who was ready, at the bidding of Fenian demagogues, to rush at the throat of Great Britain. He [Kane] was perfectly sure that when the said wolf-dog had done with the greater Britain that was on the other side of the Atlantic, there would be little breath left for him in the purpose of performing the gigantic task that they had been told of.[94]

According to Kane, when the Irish nationalist wolf-dog met with North American unionists, 'greater Britain' would be the victor. He felt sure Americans with Protestant and Orange sympathies would join the fight against Irish-American extremism. Kane and other prominent Orangemen such as Johnston frequently corresponded with Orange Lodges in the United States and Canada, receiving pledges of support for Ulster unionism.[95]

The Orange Order also helped provide the foundations of Ulster unionist preparations for armed resistance. In general, unionist militancy lacked central coordination and was used largely for rhetorical purposes.[96] However, some unionists believed if they were forced to take up arms against the implementation of Home Rule, the Protestants and Orangemen of the United States would rise up to aid them. T.G. Peel, at a demonstration in Richhill, asserted that arms were readily available in America.[97] Edward Jenkins, at a meeting of Belfast's Constitutional Club, declared that rather than giving way to priests and demagogues, the men of Ulster 'would appeal to their brethren in the colonies and America, and say to them – "We have resolved that whatever any British Government may do, whether it be Tory or Liberal, if it is going to sell our liberties to the Nationalists we will stand up to the last, shoulder our guns, and turning into the streets, fight to the

---

93 Gibbon, *Origins of Ulster Unionism*, 115–116.
94 *BNL* 11 Aug 1885.
95 *BNL* 22 Jun 1886.
96 Miller, *Queen's Rebels*, 91; Stewart, *Narrow Ground*, 167.
97 *BNL* 21 Jun 1886.

last man before we give way"'.[98] These unionists believed that, if it came to fighting, the 'great Protestant nation' of America would not allow them to be overrun by a despised Home Rule government.

Aftermath, 1886–1892

The Home Rule Bill was defeated on 7 June 1886, triggering a general election bringing Salisbury back into power. In the aftermath, unionists rioted in Belfast, leading to widespread condemnation from American newspapers. Editorials across the country declared their sympathy for Irish Catholics against the 'bigoted and barbarous behavior of the Protestants of Ulster'.[99] Land agitation was renewed as the National League initiated the Plan of Campaign. Parnell attempted to keep himself removed from the revolutionary side of the nationalist movement, though he and other Irish nationalists again turned to Irish-American organizations for financial support. As land disturbances and unrest intensified, *The Times* published a series of articles on 'Parnellism and Crime'. This series, published in March and April 1887, included a forged letter purported to have been written by Parnell condoning the Phoenix Park murders.[100]

In response to Irish land unrest, Conservatives instituted a new coercion act formulated by the chief secretary, Arthur Balfour.[101] William Henry Hurlbert, a prominent American journalist who corresponded with Balfour, visited Ireland in 1888 and wrote *Ireland under Coercion: The Diary of an American*. The 'coercion' he described was not referring to the policy of the government but coercion by nationalists to make governance impossible.[102] Hurlbert hoped to expose the true conditions of Ireland to his fellow countrymen because, he wrote, 'I know that America is largely responsible for the actual condition of Ireland, and because the future condition of Ireland, and of the British Empire, must gravely influence the future of my own country'.[103] Though he claimed to be supportive of Irish self-determi-

---

98 *BNL* 1 Sep 1885.
99 *NYT* 15 Aug 1886; *Bloomington Daily Leader* 11 Jun 1886; *Detroit Free Press* 19 Jun 1886; *Boston Globe* 11 Jun 1886.
100 F.S.L. Lyons, '"Parnellism and Crime", 1887–90', *Transactions of the Royal Historical Society* 5th Ser., no. 24 (1974), 124–125.
101 Bew, *Ireland*, 352–355; Conor Cruise O'Brien, *Parnell and His Party, 1880–90* (Oxford: Clarendon Press, 1957), 196–201; L.P. Curtis, Jr., *Coercion and Conciliation in Ireland, 1880–1892: A Study in Conservative Unionism* (Princeton, NJ: Princeton University Press, 1963), 146–147, 202–203.
102 William Henry Hurlbert, *Ireland under Coercion: The Diary of an American*, Vol. 2 (Edinburgh: David Douglas, 1888), 340–341.
103 Hurlbert, *Ireland under Coercion*, Vol. 1, xiii–xiv.

nation, his portrayal of Ulster and unionism was much more sympathetic than nationalism. His book was promoted by the ILPU.

Unionists in Parliament continued to denounce American funding of the nationalist movement. In what he described as the 'most desperate speech' he had ever attempted, Saunderson moved an amendment to the Address in Answer to the Queen's Speech which emphasized nationalist connections with American extremists.[104] Saunderson argued a divide remained between nationalists' parliamentary rhetoric, which emphasized constitutional methods, and the revolutionary policies propounded by their American paymasters.

> The Chicago and Westminster policies do not coincide. America was the El Dorado of Irish politicians, where they got those supplies which were necessary. He [Saunderson] understood that the advanced party found most of those funds, and amongst them there appeared to be a vision of action more dangerous, more perilous, and more heroic than moving the adjournment of the debate in the House.[105]

Saunderson contended that even as members of the IPP adopted constitutional methods by debating Irish policy in Parliament, the nationalist movement itself was driven by Irish-American extremists who controlled the flow of funds. Saunderson's amendment was never put to a division, but his emphasis on the importance of this speech revealed that he was passionately concerned about the impact of Irish-American funding and extremism on the Irish political situation.

Accusations of links between Parnell, the IPP, and American extremists came to a head with the Special Commission of 1888–1889. The Special Commission was held to investigate the claims made in *The Times'* 'Parnellism and Crime' series, which had attempted to link Parnell with rural violence and dynamiters. Henri Le Caron, the pseudonym for English spy Thomas Beach who had infiltrated the Clan-na-Gael, blew his cover to testify against Parnell. Le Caron was an associate of Devoy, Egan, Alexander Sullivan, and other Irish-American leaders, and had twice met with Parnell.[106] He reported to Robert Anderson, who worked as a Home Office advisor on Irish political crime. Anderson eventually used Le Caron's material to write the second series of 'Parnellism and Crime' articles.[107] Le

---

104 Saunderson to his wife, 2 Sep 1886, PRONI T2996/1/104; Reginald Lucas, *Colonel Saunderson, M.P.: A Memoir* (London: John Murray, 1908), 111–112.
105 PD 3rd Ser., Vol. 308, 1237.
106 J.A. Cole, *Prince of Spies: Henri Le Caron* (London: Faber and Faber, 1984), 154–169; Lyons, *Parnell*, 155–156.
107 See Robert Anderson, *Sidelights on the Home Rule Movement* (London: John Murray, 1906).

Caron's testimony at the Special Commission shocked nationalists and led to threats against his own life.[108] In his *Twenty-Five Years in the Secret Service*, Le Caron wrote,

> To me no more satisfactory result could attend my disclosures than the realisation by the poor deluded Irish in the States of the way in which they have been tricked and humbugged in the past years. For these poor weak people, animated by the purest, if the most mistaken of patriotic motives, who give their little all in the hope and trust that the day will come in their lives when Ireland will be a land flowing with milk and honey, I have the deepest and most sincere sympathy … But, for the blatant loud-voiced agitator, always bellowing forth his patriotic principles, while secretly filling his pockets with the bribe or the consequences of his theft, there can be no other feeling but that of undisguised loathing.[109]

Le Caron portrayed the IPP as loathsome swindlers and tricksters. However, while he illustrated the violent side of Irish and Irish-American nationalism, his evidence did not significantly advance the case against Parnell and the IPP.[110]

Sir Henry James, Liberal Unionist MP for Bury who addressed the Special Commission for twelve days, also attempted to link the role of Irish-American extremism closely to the IPP. He underscored that the New Departure had been initiated in America rather than Ireland, and that money for the Land League had come from Ford and the Skirmishing Fund. He stated, 'Everyone of the persons to whom he [Davitt] applied were members of the extreme or revolutionary party'.[111] The Clan-na-Gael, James believed, was closely connected with Parnell and the funding of the IPP. He accused the Clan-na-Gael of complicity in the dynamite campaign along with Rossa, only pausing their dynamite operation to see what opportunities the Home Rule policy of 1886 might bring them. James stated, 'I have instance after instance where the policy which controls the dynamiters in America is also controlling the men who in former times had no words to utter against outrage, but who are now, for policy's sake, saying, "stay your hand"'.[112] James portrayed Parnell and IPP members as having control over

108 Brown, *Irish-American Nationalism*, 174.
109 Henri Le Caron, *Twenty-Five Years in the Secret Service* (London: William Heinemann, 1892), 278.
110 Lyons, *Parnell*, 415–416.
111 Henry James, *The Work of the Irish Leagues: Replying in the Parnell Commission Inquiry* (London: Liberal Unionist Association, 1890), 111.
112 James, *Work of the Irish Leagues*, 850.

the revolutionary movement, but failing to halt the dynamite policies until it was politically expedient.

The Special Commission was in many ways a disappointment for unionists. Parnell was cleared of the charges made against him after Richard Pigott admitted to forging the letters that appeared in *The Times*. However, the Special Commission's report, published in 1890, did find close links between Parnellites and Irish-American extremists.[113] In light of the Pigott forgery revelation, the Commission findings were a double-edged sword for unionists. In the House of Commons debates over the Special Commission report, Lewis stated, 'No doubt hon. Members have been able to clear themselves of some charges brought against them, but the Commission has been the means of unmasking a gross conspiracy, and of showing how Ireland has been the victim of gross intrigues hatched in some cases across the Atlantic'.[114] Lewis felt unionists had been vindicated after years of accusations of Parnellite extremism. Another attack against Parnell's exoneration came from young unionist poet Rudyard Kipling, who wrote in his poem 'Cleared': 'They only took the Judas-gold from Fenians out of jail / They only fawned for dollars on the blood-dyed Clan-na-Gael'.[115] Kipling highlighted connections with Irish-American funding, accusing Parnell of inspiring murder and outrage. Despite the inherent difficulties with the Commission's findings, for years to come the Special Commission report was quoted in unionist speeches and pamphlet literature on the links between Parnell and Irish-American extremism. The revelations of the Special Commission, including the exposure of Le Caron's infiltration into the Clan-na-Gael, shocked Irish-America. With controversy also surrounding the murder of Dr. Patrick Henry Cronin in 1889, factionalism gripped Irish-American organizations. After the O'Shea divorce trial, the IPP split in 1890, and the death of Parnell in 1891, the Irish-American movement was further ravaged by internal divisions. The flow of money from America was severely diminished.[116] The weakness of the Irish nationalist movement on both sides of the Atlantic would persist for a decade, and in America would not wholly recover until after the Easter Rising of 1916.

---

113 Lyons, 'Parnellism and Crime', 137–139; Curtis, *Coercion and Conciliation*, 283–284, 292; O'Callaghan, *British High Politics*, 99–119.

114 PD 3rd Ser., Vol. 342, 48.

115 *Rudyard Kipling's Verse: Definitive Edition* (London: Hodder and Stoughton, 1966), 228; Owen Dudley Edwards, 'Kipling and the Irish', *London Review of Books* 10, no. 3 (4 Feb 1988), 22.

116 Brown, *Irish-American Nationalism*, 174; Moody, 'Irish-American Nationalists', 441; Curtis, *Coercion and Conciliation*, 308–318, 329; Brundage, *Irish Nationalists in America*, 128–131.

Second Home Rule Crisis

The 1892 general election returned Gladstone to government, with the balance of power once again held by Irish nationalists despite the split in the IPP. Gladstone was committed to initiating new Home Rule legislation for Ireland, introducing the bill on 13 February 1893. With factionalism decreasing the importance of Irish-American influence, parliamentary unionists were much less focused on countering Irish-American extremism than in 1886. David Plunket, MP for Dublin University, continued to emphasize that influence of Irish-American extremism would mean that separatism would be the end result if Ireland was granted Home Rule.[117] Edward Harland, MP for North Belfast, worried Britain's security would be threatened because Ireland would become a base for their Irish-American enemies to use against them.[118] While fears of Irish-American extremism decreased, use of American examples in support of the unionist stance – such as the Revolutionary and Civil Wars, federalism, and United States constitution – became increasingly prominent.

In the public realm, Irish-American extremism remained an important theme, especially in the run-up to the general election including the Great Unionist Convention of 17 June 1892. The Convention was held in Belfast's Botanic Garden, with speakers denouncing Home Rule and advocating passive resistance, though there were also allusions to militancy.[119] In their speeches and pamphlet literature at this time, unionists again utilized themes of Irish-American funding and extremism, Irish-American control over Irish nationalism and influence over a potential Dublin parliament, and lack for support for extremist policies across the United States as a whole.[120] The *Irish World* commented, 'It is not surprising, of course, that Orange Grand Masters hate Irish-Americans even more intensely than they hate Irishmen who live in Ireland. Through Irish-American love of Ireland and Irish-American money Protestant Ascendancy in Ireland has been brought to its doom'.[121]

Unionists continued to appeal to their historic connections with the United States, though this was to a lesser extent than in 1886. The *Belfast*

---

117 PD 4th Ser., Vol. 10, 1874–1875.
118 PD 4th Ser., Vol. 11, 941.
119 Miller, Queen's Rebels, 92; Curtis, *Coercion and Conciliation*, 394–395; Gibbon, *Origins of Ulster Unionism*, 131–132.
120 See speeches in *BNL* from May to August 1892; Imperium et Unitas, 'Irish Home Rule and British Industry. An Appeal to the British Voter' (Leicester: S. Barker, 1892); Robert Thynne, 'Plain Words from Ireland' (London: Swan Sonnenschein, 1892); W.E.H. Lecky, 'Some Aspects of Home Rule', *Contemporary Review* 63 (May 1893), 636.
121 *Irish World* 4 Nov 1893.

News-Letter published letters of support and sympathy from American Orangemen. The fraternal greetings of the United States Supreme Grand Lodge were read out at the Great Convention.[122] F.D. Ward, a Belfast businessman, believed unionists had the support of Americans as they held the Convention. He proclaimed, 'The eyes of the whole United Kingdom, as well as the eyes of their friends and sympathisers in America, were upon them at this time, and it, therefore, behoved them all to stand shoulder to shoulder, and act in such a way that the Convention would be thoroughly successful'.[123] Taking a more militant stance, Kane emphasized that if the unionists were forced to consider civil war to halt the implementation of Home Rule, they would be able to count on the support of friends in America. 'If there was any attempt to put over them mastery other than that to which they owed and were willing to give allegiance they would have something to say, and this million and a half would have the sympathy and be effectually aided by brethren in the United Kingdom, Canada, and America'.[124] Even as the influence of Irish-America over Irish nationalists was temporarily decreasing, it remained important for unionists to emphasize that they too had support coming in from the United States and dominions.

The *Irish World* repudiated the idea that 'Protestant Ulster' should determine the course of governance for Ireland, reasoning that 'Protestant Ulster' was itself a fictional construct. 'Ulster is not Protestant. It is not against Home Rule. The majority of its people are Nationalists and Home Rulers, and the majority of its constitutionally elected representatives are Home Rulers. They repudiate the claim of the Orangemen to speak for Ulster or for Ireland. All Ireland repudiates that claim'.[125] Furthermore, the newspaper dismissed the idea of unionists taking up arms to prevent the implementation of home rule as 'mere bluster'. 'The Orangemen won't fight', an editorial declared. 'Why? Because they are well aware they would be smashed if they tried it ... The Orangemen will swallow their brave threats as they have often done before, and submit like whipped curs to the inevitable that they have not the power to prevent or resist'.[126] The paper denounced the hypocrisy of unionists condemning nationalist 'extremism' while they were themselves threatening violence.

Other American newspaper editorials also played down Ulster unionists' militant threats. The Ulster 'scare' was again seen as the product of English Tories as they fought against Gladstone. The *New York Tribune*, recounting a

122 *BNL* 18 Jun 1892, 5 Sep 1892.
123 *BNL* 11 May 1892.
124 *BNL* 27 Jan 1892.
125 *Irish World* 16 Apr 1892.
126 *Irish World* 16 Apr 1892.

speech of Balfour in Belfast, praised Ulster unionists. An editorial drew upon the messages of the Scotch-Irish ethnic revival, stating, 'There is not a more industrious, courageous and public-spirited community on the face of the earth than Protestant Ulster. But when [Balfour] drops his compliments and deliberately justifies extreme measures for the defense of threatened rights he counsels nothing less than rebellion against constitutional government'. The *Tribune* insisted that majority rule and the right of Parliament to enact Home Rule should not be questioned. The *Washington Post* stated that it was difficult for Americans to understand or justify unionists standing against majority rule in Ireland. The *New York Times* wrote in praise of the Home Rule Bill, stating, 'Every objection made on the part of England, or on the part of the Protestant minority in Ireland, seems to be met by this project'. The *Boston Globe*, a strong supporter of nationalism, reported that as Ulster Protestants were educated about Home Rule they began to turn to it.[127]

The second Home Rule Bill was passed by the House of Commons but was quickly defeated in the House of Lords in September 1893. The Liberals remained in power until 1895, with warfare between Parnellites and anti-Parnellites continuing to divide the IPP. Under the subsequent Conservative administration, with Gerald Balfour as chief secretary, unionists attempted conciliation in Ireland on the issues of land and local government reform. The character of Irish unionist politics became increasingly popularized and localized as landed influence declined.[128] In power for over a decade, unionists would not again face serious demands for Irish Home Rule until 1911.

Conclusion

By the end of the nineteenth century, unionists had cultivated an image of Irish-America mired in violence and extremism. Spurred by the dynamite campaign and land war of the early 1880s, this image of Irish-America was propagated throughout the first Home Rule crisis and continued, though to a lesser extent, during the second Home Rule crisis. The extreme view of Irish-America was used to bring legitimacy to unionist opposition to Irish nationalism, providing a basis for which they could characterize the whole

127 *NYT* 31 May 1892, 4 Apr 1893, 29 Jun 1892; *Chicago Daily Inter-Ocean* 8 Apr 1893; *New York Tribune* 9 Sept 1893; *Washington Post* 26 Jun 1892; *Boston Globe* 31 Jan 1893.
128 Alvin Jackson, *Home Rule: An Irish History, 1800–2000* (Oxford: Oxford University Press, 2003), 97–104; Andrew Gailey, 'Unionist Rhetoric and Irish Local Government Reform, 1895–9', *IHS* 24, no. 93 (May 1984), 52–53; Jackson, *Ulster Party*, 229; Curtis, *Coercion and Conciliation*, 417.

of the Irish nationalist movement. Based on Irish-American extremism, they interpreted Irish nationalists as violent and unfit to govern Ireland.

Unionists characterized Irish nationalism as a foreign-run movement with little actual support in Ireland. America was the 'El Dorado' of Ireland, with Parnell and other nationalist leaders accused of pandering to Irish-American extremism to win monetary support. Condemnation of Irish-American extremism came from all sides of the unionist movement. Combining Ireland's northern Liberals and Conservatives with southern landowners, Presbyterians and Anglicans, British Conservatives and Liberal Unionists, and others, unionism in the mid-1880s was a diverse movement. Denunciation of extremism was used as a rallying cry to solidify the unionist cause. The emphasis on extremism also fostered an atmosphere which legitimized the unionists' own threats of militancy.

Unionist views of the United States during the last twenty years of the nineteenth century were paradoxical. On the one hand, they denounced American involvement in and funding of the nationalist movement. They condemned nationalists for being controlled by a foreign power. On the other hand, unionists themselves sought support for their own movement from the United States and emphasized the importance of international backing. They drew upon historic connections between Ulster and America to appeal to Americans, even at times going so far as to suggest that Americans would be willing to take up arms to fight against the implementation of Home Rule. The complexities of unionist attitudes to America ultimately limited the effectiveness of the unionist campaign in the United States. The paradoxical relationship of Ulster unionism and America would be further developed in the opening decades of the twentieth century, as the Irish political situation evolved through further Home Rule crises, the First World War, and the pressures of partition.

3

The Third Home Rule Crisis, the First World War, and Partition

And what about Irish feeling in America? We know that the Nationalist Party have to depend on America for their funds, and we know that in America the idea and the dream of every Irish Nationalist is, not these devolution proposals of the right hon. Gentleman, not even a separate Parliament with an Executive responsible to it, but an independent and separate nation.

James Campbell, 7 May 1907[1]

Throughout the first two decades of the twentieth century, Irish unionists feared the influence of Irish-America on the nationalist movement. Even as nationalism in both Ireland and America was recovering from divisions following the end of the Parnell era, Irish-America was seen as pushing the nationalist movement toward extremism and separatism through the power of finances. As expressed by James Campbell, MP for Dublin University, the influence of Irish-America was an important factor in the unionists' reluctance to accept even limited forms of devolution for Ireland. Unionists believed such measures would open the door for separatists and extremists to sweep in against the wishes of the majority of Irish people and force the establishment of an independent nation.

At the same time, the decline of landed power and greater democratic involvement meant Irish unionism was becoming increasingly focused on localities. Southern unionism weakened significantly due to changes in landlord-tenant relations, dismantling of economic positions, and decreased political power. As southern unionist identities diverged from those of Ulster, those in the south felt pressed to rely on Irish unionists sitting in English constituencies to represent their interests, rather than MPs from the north

1 PD 4th Ser., Vol. 174, 171–172.

of Ireland. Over time, unionists in Ulster focused on a distinctive Ulster unionist identity separate from the rest of Irish unionism. Landlords who had once led the unionist movement in both the north and south now gave way to an increasingly populist leadership.[2] Many unionists believed constructive policies at the turn of the century had addressed the grievances of the Irish people, thus forcing Irish nationalists to turn to Irish-America for support and funding. During the third Home Rule crisis, unionists portrayed Irish nationalists as unrepresentative of the Irish people because of the influence of their American paymasters. As the passage of Home Rule became more and more likely, Ulster unionists turned to open militancy. This was in part due to their fears of complete separation and the atmosphere of extremism. The moves toward militancy were partially justified by the image of Irish-America which the unionists themselves had cultivated.

The outbreak of the First World War made the United States government more influential on the Irish situation than it might otherwise have been. Ulster unionists were also more likely to respond to America than they otherwise would have been because of the need for United States support in the war. Unionists worried about nationalist propaganda in the United States, claiming if Americans only knew the truth about the Irish situation they would never support nationalism. They were sceptical about the importance of American attitudes toward the Irish problem, calling for Americans to cease their meddling in another country's affairs. The fact that unionists urged American non-involvement may have hurt their own movement as supporters for Irish-American nationalism remained vocal. The value accorded to American opinion by the British government helped add to the sense of betrayal felt by Ulster unionists. Ulster unionists felt they had proven their loyalty through sacrifice during the war years; this loyalty was rewarded by the British government placing more importance on American attitudes. Unionists propagated negative views of American government and public opinion, and condemned the influence of Irish-America. At the same time, unionists attempted to gain support from the United States for their own movement. They conducted letter-writing campaigns, published propaganda materials for an American audience, attempted to get pro-Union articles published in the American press, and conducted publicity tours of the United States.

This chapter explores the contradictory Ulster unionist attitudes toward America during the first twenty years of the twentieth century, particularly

2 Gailey, 'Unionist Rhetoric', 59; David Burnett, 'The Modernisation of Unionism, 1892–1914?', in *Unionism in Modern Ireland: New Perspectives on Politics and Culture*, ed. Richard English and Graham Walker (Basingstoke: Macmillan Press, 1996), 50–53; d'Alton, 'Southern Irish Unionism', 87; Ian d'Alton, '"A Vestigial Population"? Perspectives on Southern Irish Protestants in the Twentieth Century', *Éire-Ireland* 44: 3/4 (Fall/Winter 2009), 15–17.

focusing on the third Home Rule crisis, turn toward open militancy and threat of civil war, outbreak of the First World War, and the immediate aftermath of the war. The unionist movement evolved during this period to become increasingly militant, focused in Ulster, and gradually accepting of partition. Unionists sought both to discredit Irish-America and appeal to the American people to support their own movement.

Re-emergence of Irish Nationalist Politics

Irish local government reform in 1898 brought into stark relief Ireland's north–south divide as well as a nationalist–unionist divide within Ulster itself. The Local Government Act of 1898 was part of a wave of constructive unionist measures at the turn of the century under chief secretaries Gerald Balfour and George Wyndham. Constructive unionist policies were in many ways the natural result of the government responding to popular public demands. At times these measures were more generous than those proposed by the Liberals or Irish nationalists. The policies were also admitted attempts to 'kill Home Rule with kindness', aimed at resolving the root problems that were driving support for Home Rule.[3] Under the leadership of Henry Campbell-Bannerman, the Liberals had adopted a similar approach of gradual reform rather than focusing on demands to implement Home Rule.[4] The Liberals were unwilling to take a strong stance on Irish nationalism while split over the Boer War and faced with the disintegration of the IPP. The division of the IPP into Parnellite and anti-Parnellite camps in 1890 led to nationalist upheaval in both Ireland and Irish-America. The nationalist breach was healed through the reunification of the IPP in 1900, with John Redmond emerging as Parnell's successor.

Redmond visited the United States in 1901 on a fundraising mission for Home Rule. On the model of the recently launched United Irish League, he founded the United Irish League of America. The new organization established 200 branches in its first year and raised at least £10,000 for the IPP. Kevin Kenny writes, 'Like his predecessor Parnell, Redmond deliberately blurred the distinction between his own moderate constitutional position and full-fledged republicanism, thereby generating further support in America'.[5] Redmond and other IPP members were able to frame their statements with enough ambiguity that they appeared to endorse every position on Home Rule from moderate constitutionalism

---

3 Burnett, 'Modernisation', 49; Gailey, 'Unionist Rhetoric', 52–57.
4 Harbinson, *Ulster Unionist Party*, 22–23.
5 Kenny, *American Irish*, 193; Brundage, 'In Time of Peace', 325–326.

to radical separatism.[6] Unionist observers, however, believed any constitutional stance the IPP might take was ultimately to conceal their actual separatist intentions, which shone through in their American speeches. This was confirmed by one of William Johnston's Canadian correspondents, Hermann H. Pitts, who wrote him in 1901 to report, 'Redmond and his aides are having a Triumphal Tour through the United States, howling out treason and blasphemy and denouncing everything British'.[7] Pitts was the Orange Imperial Grand Secretary, and his Orangeism coloured his views of Redmond's visit. He feared Catholic influence on nationalists, and condemned the extremism and separatism espoused in the Irish leader's American speeches.

Meanwhile, as the Irish nationalists began to rebuild support within Ireland and America, Irish unionists were facing divisions of their own, in addition to the split between British Conservatives over tariff reform.[8] First, the influence of labour within Belfast politics led to the challenge of the Belfast Protestant Association and the Independent Orange Order.[9] Second, T.W. Russell, Liberal Unionist MP for South Tyrone, created a splinter group of 'Russellite' independent unionists, mainly on the basis of demands for compulsory land purchase.[10] Third, the devolution debacle in 1904–1905, entangling Wyndham, undersecretary Antony MacDonnell, and Lord Dunraven, led to increasing distrust of Ulster unionists for the British unionist elite and Dublin Castle.[11] The Ulster Unionist Council (UUC) emerged out of a conference held in 1904 to condemn Dunraven's devolution proposals. The new central unionist organization had 200 members representing local unionist associations, the Orange Order, MPs, peers, and other prominent Ulstermen. The creation of the UUC aided in the re-centring of the unionist movement from the south of Ireland to Ulster. However, both the UUC and its Dublin counterpart, the Irish Unionist Alliance (IUA), joined in the Unionist Joint Committee (UJC)

---

6 Ward, 'America and the Irish Problem', 66; Brundage, *Irish Nationalists in America*, 128–133; Francis M. Carroll, 'The Collapse of Home Rule and the United Irish League of America, 1910–18: The Centre Did Not Hold', in *Ireland's Allies: America and the 1916 Easter Rising*, ed. Miriam Nyhan Grey (Dublin: University College Dublin Press, 2016), 31–33.

7 Pitts to Johnston, 18 Nov 1901, PRONI D880/1/E.

8 Jackson, *Ulster Party*, 292.

9 J.W. Boyle, 'The Belfast Protestant Association and the Independent Orange Order, 1901–10', *IHS* 13, no. 50 (Sep 1962); Buckland, *Irish Unionism II*, 28–29.

10 Alvin Jackson, 'Irish Unionism and the Russellite Threat, 1894–1906', *IHS* 25, no. 100 (Nov 1987).

11 Jackson, *Ulster Party*, 160–168; F.S.L. Lyons, 'The Irish Unionist Party and the Devolution Crisis of 1904–5', *IHS* 6, no. 21 (Mar 1948); Blanche E.C. Dugdale, 'The Wyndham–MacDonnell Imbroglio, 1902–1906', *Quarterly Review* 511 (Jan 1932).

formed in 1907.[12] Unionist organizations closely monitored the treks of
nationalist leaders across the Atlantic. For example, the UUC scrutinized
Redmond and Joseph Devlin's September 1908 trip to America in its Year
Book. During the tour, Redmond seemed assured of the impending proposal
of a new Home Rule Bill in Parliament. He stated in Boston he believed
the majority of British people would support a Gladstone-style measure.[13]
At meetings of the UJC, secretary R.G. Carden reported he had taken steps
'to procure verbatim reports of Messrs. Devlin and Redmond's speeches in
America',[14] which were used in unionist pamphlets, leaflets, and speeches
to show the extremism of Irish nationalists.

As the House of Lords had blocked Home Rule in 1893 and would surely
block similar measures in the future, nationalists aimed to remove the veto
of the House of Lords over House of Commons legislation. At the IUA,
the General Council expressed 'the feeling of all Irish constitutionalists
when they state that the present movement by Irish and Irish-American
nationalists towards Home Rule by means of the removal of the Veto of
the House of Lords, is a direct assault upon the integrity of the United
Kingdom'.[15] Unionists saw the campaign for the removal of the House
of Lords veto as a direct attack on the Union itself. It would enable the
Liberal-controlled House of Commons to push through a Home Rule Bill
which would normally be halted by the more conservative Lords. This
attack on the House of Lords left some unionists searching for ways to
compromise without giving away Home Rule, leading to increasing appeals
for a federal solution.[16] In Ireland, unionists once again began to amplify
anti-Home Rule campaigning. They saw Irish-America as a significant
driving force behind Irish nationalism, and searched for ways in which
unionists could make a greater impact in the United States. The secretaries
of the UJC 'were authorized to see as to how far they could get articles
in the American and Australian Press, on the Irish Question'. They hoped
to promote unionist counterpoints to the escalating nationalist presence in
those countries.[17]

12 Harbinson, *Ulster Unionist Party*, 23; F.S.L. Lyons, 'The Watershed, 1903–7', in *A
    New History of Ireland: Ireland Under the Union II, 1871–1921*, ed. W.E. Vaughan
    (Oxford: Oxford University Press, 2010), 119. The IUA was formerly the Irish Loyal
    and Patriotic Union, which changed its name in 1891.
13 UUC Report 1909, PRONI D972/17.
14 *Unionist Associations of Ireland, Joint Committee Minutes* 12 Oct 1908, 14 Nov 1908,
    PRONI D1327/2/1B.
15 IUA General Council Minute Book 22 Apr 1910, PRONI D989/A/1/4.
16 Ronan Fanning, 'The Unionist Party and Ireland, 1906–1910', *IHS* 15, no. 58 (Sep
    1966), 147.
17 *Unionist Associations of Ireland, Joint Committee Minutes* 17 Mar 1911, PRONI
    D1327/2/1B.

In 1910, Walter Long resigned the chairmanship of the Irish Unionist Parliamentary Party. The position was taken over by Edward Carson, Dublin-born barrister and MP for Dublin University. As the nationalists predicted, the General Elections in January and December 1910 did not give the Liberals clear victories, forcing them to rely on the support of both the Labour Party and the IPP. The Parliament Act removing the House of Lords veto was passed in August 1911. This act, coupled with the desire to be identified as a popular movement, meant that unionists could no longer rely on Parliament as a primary venue to promote their cause. Militancy was increasingly advanced as a way to protect against the implementation of Home Rule. Because of this reliance on military strength, unionists in Ulster were even further divided from the isolated and dispersed southern unionists. In September 1911, plans were laid for the creation of an Ulster provisional government. Small numbers of arms were imported from German dealers. The plans were capped with a mass demonstration of Orangemen and Unionist Club members, held at Craigavon, home of prominent Unionist MP James Craig, on 25 September.[18]

British unionist leaders also came out strongly against Home Rule. At the Blenheim demonstration in July 1912, Andrew Bonar Law proclaimed that there was 'no length of resistance to which Ulster can go in which I should not be prepared to support them'.[19] Bonar Law characterized Home Rule as counter to the worldwide trend toward unity and centralization, as exemplified by the American Civil War. Moreover, he depicted Home Rule as the British government placing Ireland in the hands of extremists determined to destroy Irish liberty and prosperity.[20] Bonar Law and other British unionists believed a majority of voters throughout the United Kingdom had no stomach for the Irish nationalist cause. They attempted to leverage their support for Ulster unionism to force a general election specifically on the issue of Home Rule, but they were ultimately unsuccessful. Given the success of unionists in mobilizing support across Britain, it is likely a general election would have resulted in Unionist victory.[21]

---

18 Jackson, *Ulster Party*, 240, 285, 298, 313–318; Miller, *Queen's Rebels*, 94; Paul Bew, *Ideology and the Irish Question* (Oxford: Clarendon Press, 1994), 21.
19 Stewart, *Ulster Crisis*, 56–57; Patrick Buckland, *Irish Unionism, 1885–1922* (London: Historical Association, 1973), 24.
20 *The Times* 10 Apr 1912.
21 Jeremy Smith, 'Bluff, Bluster and Brinkmanship: Andrew Bonar Law and the Third Home Rule Bill', *Historical Journal* 36, no. 1 (1993); Richard Murphy, 'Faction in the Conservative Party and the Home Rule Crisis, 1912–14', *History* 71 (1986); Daniel M. Jackson, *Popular Opposition to Irish Home Rule in Edwardian Britain* (Liverpool: Liverpool University Press, 2009), 242.

Third Home Rule Crisis

The Third Home Rule Bill was unveiled in Parliament on 11 April 1912. When Redmond claimed the support of Irish-America and the British colonies, Craig emphatically countered that the true sympathy of Britain's dominions lay with the 'loyal men of Ulster'. He denied that a majority of Irish people supported Home Rule, because their demands had been satisfied through constructive unionist policies. Craig explained that the IPP relied

> not so much upon the justice of the case, as upon a false cry or sentiment, which hitherto has kept them in power by the collection of dollars from American-Irish who have gone abroad. If anyone doubts what I say let him read the hon. Member [Redmond]'s old speech. He said that support for Home Rule in Ireland from a monetary point of view was quite insufficient to keep it going, and that if it were not for the Americans it would be impossible to proceed with the campaign for Home Rule.[22]

Craig asserted that lack of support from Ireland forced the IPP to rely on American money to support their movement, as they had in the two previous Home Rule crises. Similar sentiments were expressed by Lord Claud Hamilton, MP for South Kensington. He suggested that if MPs went to Ireland and looked for the real feeling of the Irish people, they would find support for Home Rule steadily decreasing, which was why nationalists were reliant on America.[23] Peter Kerr-Smiley, MP for North Antrim, concurred with Hamilton's analysis in his 1911 book, *The Peril of Home Rule*.[24] Unionists portrayed constructive policies as successfully removing all legitimate grievances of the Irish people. They also continued to emphasize that constructive unionist policies and land laws were more favourable to agricultural tenants than any which would be allowed in the United States.[25] Unionists assumed that even those who would not normally support the Unionist Party, such as the labouring classes, were now satisfied to remain in the Union. In the unionists' view, this drastically reduced support for Home Rule, and forced Irish nationalists to turn to America for funding. They also portrayed Irish nationalists as working against the interests of the Irish

---

22　PD Commons 5th Ser., Vol. 36, 1476–1477.
23　PD Commons 5th Ser., Vol. 37, 1934.
24　Peter Kerr-Smiley, *The Peril of Home Rule* (London: Cassell & Company, 1911), 54.
25　W.E.H. Lecky, 'Ireland in the Light of History', in *Historical and Political Essays* (London: Longmans, Green, 1908), 86–87.

people, intentionally failing to address problems with land and poverty in order to force the Irish to back Home Rule.[26]

Unionists depicted Irish nationalism as unrepresentative of the Irish people. They insisted a new Irish parliament would be equally unrepresentative, dominated by Irish-Americans. Hamilton asserted that the moment Home Rule became law, the 'godless conspirators who are now on the other side of the Atlantic' would 'flock across to Ireland and in a very short time have complete control over Irish affairs'.[27] The menace of Irish-Americans returning to Ireland was all the more threatening because of their extremism. Andrew Long Horner, MP for South Tyrone, quoted resolutions from the national conference of the Ancient Order of Hibernians, held in Portland, Oregon, in which they pledged to bring about complete and absolute separation from England.[28] Unionists alleged that leaders of Irish nationalism catered to Irish-American extremism. Carson described Irish nationalists as resorting to 'perverted rhetoric' to gain the support of Irish-America.[29] C.C. Craig, MP for South Antrim, quoted Redmond's October 1910 speech in Buffalo, when he pledged to get Home Rule first and then demand more. Craig commented, 'I wonder how the hon. and learned Member gets over that. It seems to me that a man who uses that language is hardly likely to be content with what is contained in this Bill'.[30] Irish unionists in Parliament and in the public realm used examples of Redmond and other nationalist leaders in America to illustrate that they would never settle simply for Home Rule.[31] Craig questioned,

Can this Bill be said to comply with the description given to what they want? Obviously this Bill does not destroy the last link that binds them to England. Therefore, either they were humbugging the Americans or

26 Andrew Bonar Law, 'Home Rule: The Unionist Point of View. Speech in Bootle, on December 7th, 1911' (Westminster: National Conservative Union, 1912); Marquess of Londonderry, 'The Ulster Question', in *Against Home Rule: The Case for Union*, ed. S. Rosenbaum (London: Frederick Warne, 1912), 166–167.

27 PD Commons 5th Ser., Vol. 37, 1935–1936.

28 PD Commons 5th Ser., Vol. 38, 300.

29 Edward Carson, Preface to *The Truth about Home Rule*, by Pembroke Wicks (London: Sir Isaac Pitman & Sons, 1913), iv.

30 PD Commons 5th Ser., Vol. 37, 1764.

31 See, for example, 'The Home Rule "Nutshell" Examined by an Irish Unionist. (Being a Reply to "Home Rule in a Nutshell" by Mr. Jeremiah Macveagh, MP)' (Dublin: Unionist Associations of Ireland, 1912); Irish Imperialist, 'The Old Conspiracy: An Attempt to present in Popular Form the Leading Points in Connection with the Present Home Rule Agitation and to Demonstrate the Impossibility of a Final Settlement of the Irish Question by Means of the Proposed Legislation' (London: Simpkin, Marshall, Hamilton, Kent, 1911); PD Commons 5th Ser., Vol. 40, 837–839; Vol. 42, 1970–1971.

else – and this I think is a much more probable explanation – they are humbugging the British public when they say that they will accept this Bill as a final settlement of the question.[32]

Craig alluded to Parnell's 'Last Link' speech as indicative of the nationalists' ultimate goal – total separation. He urged any British Liberals who thought Home Rule would be the final, peaceful solution to the Irish problem to realize it would only open the door to even greater turmoil.

Imperial foreign policy and defence would also be impacted by Irish-America's influence on a potential Irish parliament. Carson wrote that Irish Home Rule would open Britain to additional threats in wartime, as Irish-Americans were avowed enemies of the Empire. He emphasized, 'We have only to imagine the element of weakness and disunion which would be introduced to our foreign policy'.[33] Many unionist speeches and pamphlets quoted American naval expert Admiral Alfred Thayer Mahan, who wrote, 'The ambition of the Irish separatists, realized, might be even more threatening to the national life of Great Britain than the Secession of the South was to that of the American Union ... The instrument for such action in the shape of an independent Parliament could not safely be trusted even to avowed friends'.[34] An Ireland ruled by American-influenced separatists was seen as a haven for the enemies of Great Britain. To some unionists, the American example proved the Irish were incapable of self-government. Lord Ernest Hamilton, former MP for North Tyrone, wrote,

Tammany, in America, stands for the most flourishing system of corruption and immorality on the face of the earth, and the reason that it intrudes upon the consideration of Ulster is because it is almost exclusively a Celtic Irish organization, and may, therefore, reasonably be taken as an indication of what might be expected were the Government of Ireland to be thrown unrestrainedly into the hands of the native element.[35]

32 PD Commons 5th Ser., Vol. 37, 1765.
33 Edward Carson, Introduction to *Against Home Rule: The Case for Union*, ed. S. Rosenbaum (London: Frederick Warne, 1912), 20–21.
34 Originally published in 'Motives to Imperial Federation', *National Review* (May 1902); reprinted in Alfred Thayer Mahan, *Retrospect & Prospect: Studies in International Relations, Naval and Political* (Boston: Little, Brown, 1902), 100. See, for example, George Cave, 'The Constitutional Question', 86; and Earl Percy, 'The Military Disadvantages of Home Rule', 202, both in *Against Home Rule*, ed. S. Rosenbaum (London: Frederick Warne, 1912); 'New Home Rule and the Old Objections' (Dublin: Unionist Associations of Ireland, 1909), 17; 'Home Rule and Imperial Defence: Admiral Lord Beresford's Views' (Belfast: Ulster Unionist Council, 1919).
35 Ernest W. Hamilton, *The Soul of Ulster* (London: Hurst and Blackett, 1917), 179.

For Hamilton, Tammany became shorthand for Irish machine politics in cities across the United States. In the face of Tammany influence, minorities were helpless.[36] F.F. Moore asserted that Tammany acted 'from generation to generation for the Ulstermen to point to as an example of the form of Home Rule which is the ideal of the Irishman'.[37] In the eyes of unionists, the Tammany example proved that corruption and immorality would be the ruling characteristics of an Irish parliament.

As Home Rule advanced in the House of Commons, Ulster leaders continued actively to prepare for the defence of their movement. The Carson Defence Fund was set up in early 1912 to carry out anti-Home Rule campaigning in English and Scottish constituencies. American Orange lodges were among those who donated.[38] Unionists built support through a series of mass meetings and the spread of political propaganda, their efforts culminating with Ulster Day on 23 September 1912. The signing of the Ulster Covenant on Ulster Day achieved mythical status with the defence of unionism and creation of an Ulster unionist tradition.[39] Almost half a million Ulstermen and women signed the Covenant, pledging to resist Home Rule by any means. While unionists concentrated in Ulster had the option of armed resistance against the implementation of Home Rule, in the south unionists were too scattered to consider the use of force. Unionists in the south were a dispersed minority and a fairly hetero-geneous group. They were mainly characterized as Protestant, anglicized, propertied, and aristocratic, but also included Catholic landowners, Trinity College intellectuals, and Protestant businessmen. Southern unionism was increasingly divided from its Ulster counterpart, which was becoming a more democratic, popularized force.[40] The Church of Ireland was also increasingly divided between south and north, with the southern portion willing to accept Home Rule while the north supported pan-Protestantism and exclusion for Ulster.[41] Ronald McNeill, Ulsterman and MP for St Augustine's, wrote,

36 Hamilton, *Soul of Ulster*, 181–182. Hamilton included an entire chapter on the dangers of the Tammany system, 'Tammany and its Offshoots', 179–188.
37 F. Frankfort Moore, *The Truth about Ulster* (London: Eveleigh Nash, 1914), 173.
38 Carson Defence Fund, PRONI D1327/2/10; see correspondence of Richard Dawson Bates, PRONI D1327/18/1A/12.
39 Alvin Jackson, 'Unionist Myths, 1912–1985', *Past & Present* 136 (Aug 1992), 164–165; Patrick Buckland, 'The Southern Unionists, the Irish Question, and British Politics, 1906–14', *IHS* 16, no. 59 (Mar 1967), 239–240; Miller, *Queen's Rebels*, 96–97.
40 Buckland, 'Southern Unionists', 234–240; Patrick Buckland, *Irish Unionism I: The Anglo-Irish and the New Ireland, 1885–1920* (Dublin: Gill and Macmillan, 1972), xiv–xx.
41 Andrew Scholes, *The Church of Ireland and the Third Home Rule Bill* (Dublin: Irish Academic Press, 2010), 150–151.

The events of the last three months, and especially the signing of the Covenant, had concentrated on Ulster the attention of the whole United Kingdom, not to speak of America and the British overseas Dominions. This was not of unmixed advantage to the cause for which Ulster was making so determined a stand. There was a tendency to more and more regard the opposition to Irish Home Rule as an Ulster question and nothing else.[42]

The position of southern unionists was played down in the eyes of Britain, the dominions, and the world as a whole. Ulster unionists portrayed themselves as separate from the rest of Ireland, particularly through the signing of the Ulster Covenant and emphasis on militancy.

Intensification of Militancy

The combined forces of militancy and focus on Ulster would only be amplified as the third Home Rule crisis wore on. In fact, militancy became so pronounced in Ulster that George A. Birmingham wrote a novel, *The Red Hand of Ulster*, based on the seeming absurdity of fighting against the British to stay in the Union. His novel drew on the mischievousness of American involvement in the Irish question.[43] Birmingham was the pseudonym of Belfast-born Church of Ireland clergyman James Owen Hannay, a prolific writer. In his novel, the narrator, Lord Kilmore of Errigal, becomes involved with Joseph Peterson Conroy, an American millionaire who had associations with the Clan-na-Gael. Conroy, who is bored, decides he wants to start a revolution, focusing on the Ulster unionists. The Ulstermen end up voting to fight against the British government to halt the implementation of Home Rule and form their own provisional government, but the British soldiers refuse to do battle. Ultimately, the provisional government appoints Kilmore as their ambassador to the Prime Minister. They tell Kilmore that their demands are to end all talk of Home Rule, and that the English must clear out of the country 'and leave us a free hand to clean up the mess they've been making for the last hundred years'.[44] Afterward, the Ulstermen insist that they will govern themselves, though maintain that they are thoroughly loyal and always have been. The British government, of course, agrees to

---

42 Ronald McNeill, *Ulster's Stand for Union* (London: John Murray, 1922), 128. On McNeill, see Jackson, 'Irish Unionism', 127–128.

43 George A. Birmingham, *The Red Hand of Ulster* (London: Smith, Elder, 1912). On Birmingham, see J.C. Beckett, *The Anglo-Irish Tradition* (London: Faber and Faber, 1976), 119.

44 Birmingham, *Red Hand*, 298.

all of their demands. Birmingham's novel highlighted real frustrations with Irish-American involvement and seeming contractions concerning Ulster militant policies.

In January 1913, the Ulster Volunteer Force (UVF) was established, bringing together units that had been drilling since 1911. They developed into a fairly sophisticated force of about 100,000 Volunteers.[45] Threats of civil war in unionist rhetoric ramped up the atmosphere of militancy. One unionist pamphlet warned, 'Civil war in Ireland would let loose these voracious vultures upon society ... Irish Americans of fighting breed would cross the Atlantic to the assistance of both sides. Irishmen in Great Britain would hasten to the aid of their respective parties'.[46] The same pamphlet described the threat of Irish-American nationalists crossing the Atlantic if Home Rule were granted.

> Fenianism – the Clan-na-Gael – the Land League, the plan of campaign of the United Irish League and the Ancient Order of Hibernians, proclaim the Irish in their native land to be the same born wire-pullers as their kith and kin in America, and to imagine that these secret societies will not continue to influence and in many cases wield autocratic sway over the Nationalist members of an Irish House of Commons is to imagine that the leopard will change his spots.[47]

In this view, fear of Irish-Americans' influence over a potential Irish parliament helped drive threats of civil war, with the expectation that the fight would draw Irish-American and British supporters to both the nationalist and unionist sides. In Parliament, Robert McMordie also insisted that unionists would have their own international backing in wartime. 'With regard to feeling in the Colonies, it is only right that hon. Members should know that the Unionists of Ireland have a special connection with most of our Colonies', he asserted.

> Right across Canada the sentiment is our sentiment. In Toronto there are already men enrolled to come over in case any trouble arises. If anything hurts Ulster you will not have a friend left from one side of Canada to the other. The same applies to Australia. We have our

---

45 Stewart, *Narrow Ground*, 168–169. On Ulster unionist culture and development of militancy in this era, see Jane G.V. McGaughey, *Ulster's Men: Protestant Unionist Masculinities and Militarization in the North of Ireland, 1912–1923* (Montreal: McGill-Queen's University Press, 2012).

46 Tom Bruce Jones, 'The Imperial Peril: One Hundred Reasons against Home Rule' (Edinburgh: Oliver & Boyd, 1914), 89.

47 Jones 'Imperial Peril', 75–76.

special connections there, and wherever our people have gone the link is not broken. We have a stronger connection still in New Zealand, and if you take the United States of America from east to west, so far as there is any sentiment relating to Ireland, it will go to us if there is the least trouble in regard to Home Rule.[48]

When another MP reminded him that American dollars tended to go to the nationalists, McMordie dismissively replied that the dollars came from servant girls and the real indication of sentiment was the lack of support for nationalists in both America and Ireland.

Many unionists, like MP for South Birmingham L.S. Amery, continued to fear Home Rule as only an 'instalment of the larger policy, a stepping stone to the "great goal of national independence"'.[49] In Parliament, James Campbell, MP for Dublin University, also maintained that the Home Rule Bill would not satisfy nationalist demands:

It was proclaimed for it that it would be a settlement, and that it would satisfy and conciliate Irish-American sentiment, but we know now that the Clan-na-Gael and Ancient Order of Hibernians in the United States have exploded and repudiated the idea, and we know as every week passes in Ireland itself Nationalist orators and newspapers reecho that denial. It was hailed as a message of peace to Ireland, and yet every line of it contains the seeds of certain harvest of future friction and trouble.[50]

Campbell emphasized the inadequacy of Home Rule proposals because of the extremist influence of Irish-America. Campbell insisted Home Rule, if implemented, would not bring peace to Ireland but only further trouble.

Fear of extremism and separatism in an Irish parliament helped steer the paramilitary activities of the UVF. The position of Ulster unionists was boosted through the Curragh incident of 20 March 1914, revealing the inability of the government to direct a military offensive against the unionists. Then, on 24–25 April, the Larne gun-running was orchestrated by F.H. Crawford, who went to Germany posing as an American to arrange for the delivery of guns to Ireland. Twenty-five thousand rifles and 3 million rounds of ammunition were successfully brought into Ulster. At the same time, the Irish Volunteers, formed in response to the UVF the

---

48   PD Commons 5th Ser., Vol. 46, 459.
49   L.S. Amery, 'The Case against Home Rule' (London: West Strand Publishing Company, 1912).
50   PD Commons 5th Ser., Vol. 55, 154.

previous November, were growing in significance. Their own gun-running at Howth in July brought in about 900 rifles.[51] Unionists were alarmed at the arming of the Irish Volunteers. R.J. Herbert Shaw at the IUA wrote to Pembroke Wicks, Carson's private secretary, 'It is practically impossible to know how many arms they have got, but we have every reason to believe that financial support has been promised by Irish Americans, and that they have promised a supply of arms and ammunition of the class that is being supplied to Mexico'.[52] In the months leading up to the First World War, Mexico was offered arms by the German government in exchange for an alliance.[53]

With increasingly open militancy in Ireland, partition began to be seriously considered as a constitutional solution, where previously it had primarily been used as a tactic to wreck the passage of Home Rule. Carson and other unionists recognized that partition might be their only option to avoid coming under the rule of a Dublin parliament.[54] Partition debates, mainly between Prime Minister H.H. Asquith, Bonar Law, Carson, and Redmond, developed from October 1913 to July 1914. By early 1914, the principle of special treatment for Ulster was solidifying. Proposals for four-, six-, or nine-county exclusion, Home Rule-within-Home Rule, and federalism were considered. Both the territorial scope and the duration of the policy were cause for disagreement.[55] Gradually, six-county exclusion came to the fore, with the emphasis on partition solidifying the divide between Ulster and southern unionism. Southern unionists, however, retained significant influence over the British Unionist Party as a whole, especially as several MPs with southern Irish roots sat for British constituencies.[56]

---

51 Jackson, *Home Rule*, 157; Stewart, *Ulster Crisis*, 106.
52 Shaw to Wicks 27 May 1914, PRONI D989/A/8/2/19.
53 See A.T.Q. Stewart, *The Ulster Crisis: Resistance to Home Rule, 1912–1914* (London: Faber, 1967), 116, 225–226 for connections between Germany, Ireland, and the situation in Mexico.
54 Jackson, *Home Rule*, 144–145.
55 Alan J. Ward, *The Irish Constitutional Tradition: Responsible Government and Modern Ireland, 1782–1992* (Washington, DC: Catholic University of America Press, 1994), 94–97. Ward notes that as late as September 1913 Carson still believed it might be possible to defeat Home Rule by insisting on the exclusion of all or part of Ulster. This was the reasoning behind support of the Agar-Robartes Amendment that promoted four-county exclusion, and Carson's own amendment to exclude nine counties. PD Commons 5th Ser., Vol. 46, 377; Jackson, *Home Rule*, 144–161; G.K. Peatling, *British Opinion and Irish Self-Government, 1865–1925: From Unionism to Liberal Commonwealth* (Dublin: Irish Academic Press, 2001), 76–81.
56 Buckland, *Irish Unionism II*, 92–96; Alvin Jackson, 'Irish Unionism, 1870–1922', in *Defenders of the Union: A Survey of British and Irish Unionism since 1801*, ed. D. George Boyce and Alan O'Day (London: Routledge, 2001), 125; Buckland, 'Southern Unionists', 243.

The Buckingham Palace Conference was held in July to resolve the issue of partition, but was ultimately unsuccessful. Prominent moderate Horace Plunkett wrote that any plans of devolution, federation, and exclusion would 'leave utterly unsatisfied the Home Rule sentiment in Ireland and, what is to my mind – I might almost say within my own knowledge – equally important, the sentiment of the great majority of the Irish people in the United States and throughout Europe'.[57] Plunkett's caution highlighted the importance of the worldwide Irish diaspora. Irish and Irish-American nationalists generally saw Ireland as an indivisible entity. They rejected any unionist suggestion that the island was composed of two nations, not one.[58]

The plight of Ulster unionists did attract sympathy, however, from supporters in Britain, the dominions, and the United States. Backing for the Ulstermen came from the British League for the Support of Ulster and the Union, which in March and April 1914 organized the signing of the British Covenant as a counterpart to the Ulster Covenant. Mass meetings were held in Canada, particularly among Orangemen; Australia; New Zealand; and South Africa. In the United States, Scotch-Irish and Orange gatherings expressed solidarity with Ulster.[59] Unionists also attempted to counter nationalist propaganda through direct appeals to the United States and dominions. One such appeal was made by Wicks, who wrote *The Truth about Home Rule* specifically for an American audience. He emphasized inconsistencies with nationalist policies on either side of the Atlantic, with a side-by-side comparison of speeches. Wicks also used American historical examples to justify the unionist position. He asserted that unionists were passionate in their defence of Union, while the rest of Ireland was apathetic to Home Rule.[60] The *New York Times* review of his book observed that Wicks 'produced the impression that what is now proposed can never work, and that what has been heralded as a settlement is likely to result in utter confusion'.[61]

American newspapers generally showed a changed understanding of Ulster unionism during the third Home Rule crisis compared to earlier years. The *New York Times*, which previously treated Ulster unionists as a tool of English Tories, now had a change of perspective. 'We had been led to believe that the Ulster movement was largely fostered by his Majesty's Opposition to delay the Home Rule Bill. Perhaps that was true at first, and

---

57 Horace Plunkett, 'A Better Way. An Appeal to Ulster Not to Desert Ireland' (Dublin: Hodges, Figgis, 1914), 21–22.
58 Buckland, *Irish Unionism II*, 94.
59 Stewart, *Ulster Crisis*, 138–140; Donal Lowry, 'Ulster Resistance and Loyalist Rebellion in the Empire', in *'An Irish Empire'? Aspects of Ireland and the British Empire*, ed. Keith Jeffery (Manchester: Manchester University Press, 1996), 192.
60 Wicks, *Truth about Home Rule*.
61 *NYT* 10 Aug 1913.

the movement has now runaway with its promoters', an editorial reasoned. 'In any case, the position so boldly assumed by Sir Edward Carson and some of his distinguished associates is surely full of peril'. The *New York Times* admitted that Carson and other unionists had displayed 'a remarkable and splendid manifestation of patriotism'.[62] The *Los Angeles Times* explained the difficulties for outsiders in understanding the Ulster crisis.

> Among the many things that make it difficult for unprejudiced, but interested, persons to understand the Ulster situation are the divergent presentations of the case by the home rule advocate and by the Ulster advocate. The former maintains that the situation would have a parallel in the United States if one or more of the States refused to abide by a Federal enactment. The latter insists that the case would be analogous if the Federal authorities of the United States were attempting to disunite California or some other State from the republic. Hundreds of thousands of people are feverishly sincere in one or the other belief, yet both contentions cannot be right.[63]

The editorial concluded, 'The situation in Ireland is both portentous and dramatic. The spectacle of two opposing citizen armies, each Irish and therefore enthusiastically determined, would be a menace to any government'. After the signing of the Ulster Covenant and the early stages of militancy, many newspapers viewed Ulster threats as a bluff. As the Ulster crisis continued into 1914, editorials expressed fears that civil war might come after all.[64] The *Chicago Tribune* hoped all sides would agree to temporary exclusion as a reasonable compromise. 'No one approaching the Ulster question without prejudice fails to have regard for the interests of both parties in the controversy. It is a question touching human nature in its most sensitive spots, a question of religion and nationality ... Indiscreet legislation might bring consequences abhorrent to Christianity'.[65]

In the United States, both nationalists and Orange lodges became increasingly active on the Home Rule question. Irish and Irish-American nationalists focused on leveraging political influence to disrupt the Anglo-American relationship, impact American foreign policy, and build international networks in support of nationalism.[66] Irish-Americans

---

62 *NYT* 11 Jul 1914, 1 May 1914, 26 Sep 1913, 12 Jul 1914.
63 *Los Angeles Times* 13 Jul 1914.
64 *Washington Post* 29 Sept 1912, 16 Mar 1914, 28 Jul 1914; *Boston Globe* 11 Feb 1914, 20 Mar 1914.
65 *Chicago Tribune* 10 Jul 1914.
66 Gerard Keown, *First of the Small Nations: The Beginnings of Irish Foreign Policy in the Interwar Years, 1919–1932* (Oxford: Oxford University Press, 2016), 17–18, 25–35.

continued to have a significant influence within the Democratic Party, leading some American politicians to excuse extreme nationalist tactics. However, the forces of Protestantism also influenced views – for example, Secretary of State William Jennings Bryan sympathizing with Ulster because of his strong Protestant convictions. Bryan appeared to favour a federal solution with a separate local government in Ulster.[67] The British Ambassador to the United States, Cecil Spring-Rice, wrote to Foreign Secretary Edward Grey that conflict in Ireland might cause unrest in America.[68] Carson himself echoed fears that the conflict might lead to Irish ethnic and religious strife in Britain, the dominions, and the United States.[69]

With the threat of war looming in Europe, the Home Rule Bill was passed but implementation was suspended for the length of the war. Asquith in part hoped this course of action would help Britain cultivate American goodwill.[70] In the House of Lords, George Curzon, representative peer for Ireland, condemned the government's decision. He accused the government of valuing the loyalty of the United States above its own citizens in Ulster. 'If you are considering the feelings of Ireland and the undesirability of disappointing any section of the Irish population in either this country or abroad, why not consider the feelings of Ulster? Why should Ulster be disappointed? In a word, why should the loyalty of Ulster be sacrificed to the loyalty of the Irish in the United States of America?'[71]

The First World War

In the opening years of the twentieth century, Americans generally pushed for a solution to the Irish question because they thought it would improve Anglo-American diplomatic relations and American domestic tensions. The outbreak of the First World War created temporary unity between Ireland and Great Britain, with Redmond pledging loyalty to the British Empire. For the majority of Americans, the importance of the Irish question significantly

---

67 Bernadette Whelan, *United States Foreign Policy and Ireland: From Empire to Independence, 1913–29* (Dublin: Four Courts, 2006), 51; Stephen Hartley, *The Irish Question as a Problem in British Foreign Policy, 1914–18* (Basingstoke: Macmillan, 1987), 12; H.C. Allen, *Great Britain and the United States: A History of Anglo-American Relations, 1783–1952* (Hamden, Conn.: Archon, 1969), 100.
68 Gantt, *Irish Terrorism*, 261.
69 J.A. Spender and Cyril Asquith, *Life of Herbert Henry Asquith, Lord Oxford and Asquith*, Vol. 2 (London: Hutchinson, 1932), 53, cited in Jackson, *Popular Opposition*, 234.
70 Hartley, *Irish Question*, 19.
71 PD Lords 5th Ser., Vol. 17, 715–716.

diminished in the face of war. One aspect of Irish-American nationalism was specifically impacted by the war's outbreak. Redmond's controversial loyalty to Great Britain devastated the United Irish League in America and the constitutional segment of Irish-American nationalism. For the moment, control of Irish-American nationalist organizations was assumed mainly by radical separatists. However, Spring-Rice reported that the majority of Irish-Americans were sympathetic to the Allied cause.[72] The British Foreign Office and War Propaganda Bureau at Wellington House agreed at the start of the war that propaganda was needed to ensure the United States did not enter the war on the side of the Central Powers. Britain recognized that the Irish situation in particular required intensive counter-propaganda in America.[73] As both unionists and constitutional nationalists rallied to the cause of Great Britain in the opening months of the war, revolutionary nationalists in Ireland and America were alienated from Home Rulers. Just as the German government worked with the revolutionary nationalists in Ireland, German-Americans were in close cooperation with Irish-Americans during the war.[74] For nationalists in Ireland, Redmond's position on the war split the Irish Volunteers, though by far the great majority remained with him as part of the National Volunteers.[75]

For unionists, the war was an opportunity to demonstrate commitment to British and imperial values. The separate 36th 'Ulster' Division gained the mass enlistment of the UVF. The new division was overwhelmingly Protestant and unionist, and was given permission to have the 'red hand' of Ulster on uniforms. The UUC passed resolutions pledging support for the war effort, but also vowed to maintain the UVF to resist the implementation of Home Rule if necessary.[76] At the outbreak of war, the UVF Headquarters Council offered the War Office a hospital to be set up in the Belfast Exhibition Hall. The UVF Hospital initially had 100 beds, but was eventually expanded through the Samaritan Hospital and an additional wing erected onto the Exhibition Hall. Several American individuals, as well as

72 Carroll, *American Opinion*, 19, 36; Ward, 'America and the Irish Problem', 73; Hartley, *Irish Question*, 22–23; Brundage, *Irish Nationalists in America*, 142–145.
73 M.L. Sanders and Philip M. Taylor, *British Propaganda During the First World War, 1914–18* (London: Macmillan, 1982), 152–153, 167–173.
74 Alan J. Ward, *Ireland and Anglo-American Relations, 1899–1921* (London: Weidenfeld & Nicholson, 1969), 115–116; Carroll, *American Opinion*, 55; Chris McNickle, 'When New York Was Irish, and After', in *The New York Irish*, ed. Ronald H. Bayor and Timothy J. Meagher (Baltimore: Johns Hopkins University Press, 1996), 350; Carroll, 'Collapse of Home Rule', 35–39.
75 Bew, *Ideology*, 122.
76 Gillian McIntosh, *The Force of Culture: Unionist Identities in Twentieth-Century Ireland* (Cork: Cork University Press, 1999), 11–12; Thomas C. Kennedy, 'War, Patriotism, and the Ulster Unionist Council, 1914–18', *Éire-Ireland* 40, no. 3/4 (Fall/Winter 2005), 201.

the Pennsylvania Scotch-Irish Society, donated money to the UVF Hospital during the war.[77]

Carson accepted office with the first British coalition government formed in May 1915. He served as Attorney General until resigning in October.[78] After Asquith's resignation in December 1916, Carson returned to office as First Lord of the Admiralty. He gave an interview with the *New York Sun* in March 1916 to appeal to American sympathy for the war effort. Carson urged all parties to observe a truce in Irish affairs.[79] Carson recognized that both he and Redmond were attempting to satisfy the demands of their segments of the Irish population while throwing all of their support behind the British war effort. Carson emphasized that if nothing else, the Irish ought to be able to put their differences aside when facing an even greater enemy in the war. He hoped internal Irish problems would not impact upon the fighting of the First World War. In just the following month, however, rebellion broke out in Dublin. Even before the Easter Rising, unionists linked extreme nationalists with 'rampant and unchecked pro-Germanism'. The IUA newspaper, *Notes from Ireland*, described a nationalist lecture from early 1916 at which the audience 'might have been composed of Irish-Americans their sentiments were so anti-British; at one point a voice cried out, "Gott strafe England"',[80] and the sentiment was loudly applauded. The *Freeman's Journal* reported that some Germans in America established a 'Defence of Ireland' fund. The article stated,

> Having exhausted apparently all other means of collecting money from their dupes the German agitators here (New York) have established a fund for the 'Defence of Ireland'. Neatly printed subscription cards soliciting donations to the fund have been despatched all over the country. The New York *Herald* has traced the origin of these cards to a German newspaper office. Apart from enriching German 'patriots' who have inaugurated the movement the purpose of the fund is not made clear.[81]

The creation of such a fund recognized the potential of Irish-American support for German causes, and underlined the links between the two groups.

77 UUC Reports 1914, 1916, PRONI D1327/20/2/1; UVF Hospital Report 1917, PRONI D1507/A/25/2.
78 Kennedy, 'War, Patriotism', 203; Hartley, *Irish Question*, 69.
79 Quoted in Bew, *Ideology*, 141–142.
80 'May God Punish England', a German army slogan during the First World War.
81 Notes from Ireland 1 Jul 1916, PRONI D1327/20/4/138.

Notes from Ireland reported a January 1916 lecture in Cork by Reverend Michael O'Flanagan, CC, of County Roscommon. The article noted that when the speaker related his experiences in America and remarked, "'I met a few Germans there", he was greeted with "loud cheers" from his audience'. The report went on, 'In his peroration the rev. gentleman continued to employ this easy method of fanning the fires of sedition amongst his Irish Volunteer audience. He spoke of the American Irish having effectively prevented an English alliance with the United States'.[82] O'Flanagan's Cork audience was not representative of the region as a whole, however, particularly in the months following the sinking of the *Lusitania*. On 10 May 1915, just three days after the disaster, the Cork County Coroner opened an inquest into the events, at which Captain William T. Turner testified. The jury, composed of twelve locals, returned a strongly anti-German verdict of 'wilful and wholesale murder' on the part of the submarine officers and the German Emperor and government.[83] The focus of *Notes from Ireland* on the O'Flanagan example illustrated the determination of Irish unionists to portray Irish and Irish-American nationalists as overwhelmingly extreme, pro-German, and anti-British despite evidence to the contrary, using divisive and militant rhetoric to obscure commonalities unionists shared with nationalists.

The outbreak of the Easter Rising in 1916 had several ties to Irish-America. Major American newspapers condemned the activities of the revolutionary nationalists. They viewed the Rising as foolish and futile in a time of war. With the news of the rebel leaders' swift executions, public opinion in both America and Ireland came out strongly against the British.[84] The United States consul used his influence to protect Americans involved in the Rising, including Éamon de Valera and Diarmuid Lynch. The Rising signalled the final death toll for the cause of constitutional nationalism amongst Irish-Americans. Huge numbers flocked to join or support the revolutionary side of the movement. Some 800,000 Irish-Americans joined nationalist organizations, raising over $10 million in support of Sinn Féin and the Irish Republican Army (IRA).[85] Following the Easter Rising, Irish-American nationalism gained a real vitality that had not been seen since the days of Parnell. By this time, much of Irish-America was American-born and economically well off. However, new immigrants still

82 Notes from Ireland 1 Jul 1916, PRONI D1327/20/4/138.
83 *The Times* 11 May 1915.
84 Kenny, *American Irish*, 195; Carroll, *American Opinion*, 56–57; Mansergh, *Irish Question*, 297–298; Richard English, *Irish Freedom: The History of Nationalism in Ireland* (London: Macmillan, 2006), 267.
85 Carroll, *American Opinion*, 63; Carroll, 'Collapse of Home Rule', 39–42; Miller, 'Class, Culture, and Immigrant Group Identity', 116.

arriving from Ireland helped to keep alive connections with Ireland and discontent with Britain which may have motivated their involvement. At the same time, Irish-American nationalist goals accorded with the rhetoric of President Woodrow Wilson. Wilson promoted ideas of democracy and self-determination for small nations. Wilson himself sympathized with the Home Rule cause, but he was not willing to jeopardize Anglo-American relations.[86] With the Home Rule Act already passed in 1914, though delayed from being enacted for the duration of the war, the period following the Easter Rising provided a chance for Irish nationalism to achieve significant headway on the goal of Irish independence.[87]

In the aftermath of the Easter Rising, British and American secret services began to keep routine surveillance on Irish-American activities, sharing intelligence and coordinating counterterrorism operations. British propaganda in the United States was renewed in an attempt to curb anti-British sentiment.[88] Unionists maintained that if only the British government had paid attention to the statements of nationalist leaders in America, they would not have been surprised by armed rebellion. *Notes from Ireland* of 1 July 1916 accused the British government of ignoring statements by Redmond while in New York, glorifying his efforts at importing weapons to Ireland.[89] In part, the IUA was playing down the UVF's own role in fomenting armed rebellion by placing blame back on the British government. Unionists also placed blame on Irish-American extremism, which helped to create an atmosphere of militancy and contributed to the arming of both unionists and nationalists in Ireland.

Major American newspapers condemned the British government for failing to reach a settlement on Irish Home Rule after the Easter Rising, and for the continuing conflict over the question of 'temporary' partition.[90] The *Washington Post* reasoned, 'What both sides should realize is that the Irish question should be brought out of the realm of theory and given the status of concrete action'. The editorial asserted temporary exclusion should be accepted by nationalists, who could win the Ulster counties to Home Rule through good governance.[91] The United States Senate passed a

86 Whelan, *United States Foreign Policy*, 57–58.
87 Miller, *Ireland and Irish America*, 345; Miller, 'Class, Culture, and Immigrant Group Identity', 117; Bayor and Meagher, Introduction to *The New York Irish*, 12.
88 Gantt, *Irish Terrorism*, 246–247; Whelan, *United States Foreign Policy*, 144, Sanders and Taylor, *British Propaganda*, 174–175.
89 Notes from Ireland 1 Jul 1916, PRONI D1327/20/4/138.
90 Carroll, *American Opinion*, 70; Robert Schmuhl, 'Bifocalism of US Press Coverage: The Easter Rising and Irish America', in *Ireland's Allies: America and the 1916 Easter Rising*, ed. Miriam Nyhan Grey (Dublin: University College Dublin Press, 2016), 269–281.
91 *Washington Post* 26 Jul 1916.

resolution in July, coinciding with the trial of Roger Casement, appealing to the British to exercise clemency in the treatment of Irish political prisoners. This did not prevent the execution of Casement, further inflaming opinion against the British. President Wilson, who was of Scotch-Irish ancestry, had his own troubles with the Irish-American community. He was seen as committed to pro-English stances and had attacked hyphenism among immigrants during the 1916 presidential campaign. Behind the scenes, however, Wilson was attempting to influence a solution to the Irish problem.[92]

David Lloyd George, then minister of munitions, was very aware of the impact of American support and supplies on the British war effort. He was deputed to find a compromise on the Irish situation. Lloyd George met with Carson and Nationalist MP William O'Brien at the Hotel Metropole on 30 May. He made clear his belief that the war would be lost if American support was not reined in.[93] O'Brien recorded Lloyd George saying, 'In six months the war will be lost', to which Carson replied, 'If the war is lost we are all lost'. Lloyd George explained, 'The Irish-American vote will go over to the German side. They will break our blockade and force an ignominious peace on us, unless something is done, even provisionally, to satisfy America'.[94] After further meetings with Lloyd George, Carson felt under pressure from the apparently unanimous support of the entire Cabinet for forcing through some measure of Home Rule. He agreed to go to the UUC and urge them to accept six-county partition. The UUC's official position since the signing of the Ulster Covenant was the protection of all nine counties.[95] Liberal unionist landowner and UUC member Hugh de Fellenberg Montgomery of County Tyrone was shocked at the turn of events. He wrote to his correspondents

92 Ward, 'America and the Irish Problem', 78; Carroll, *American Opinion*, 74; Nicholas Mansergh, *The Unresolved Question: The Anglo-Irish Settlement and Its Undoing, 1912–72* (New Haven, Conn.: Yale University Press, 1991), 90; Seán Cronin, *Washington's Irish Policy, 1916–1986: Independence, Partition, Neutrality* (Dublin: Anvil, 1987), 18–19; Dave Hannigan, *De Valera in America: The Rebel President's 1919 Campaign* (Dublin: O'Brien, 2008). On Woodrow Wilson and the Irish, see Michael Hopkinson, 'President Woodrow Wilson and the Irish Question', *Studia Hibernica* 27 (1993); William M. Leary, Jr., 'Woodrow Wilson, Irish Americans, and the Election of 1916', *Journal of American History* 54, no. 1 (Jun 1967); Robert Schmuhl, *Ireland's Exiled Children: America and the Easter Rising* (Oxford: Oxford University Press, 2016), 75–117; Bernadette Whelan, 'The Wilson Administration and the 1916 Rising', in *The Impact of the 1916 Rising Among the Nations*, ed. Ruán O'Donnell (Dublin: Irish Academic Press, 2008), 91–118.

93 H. Montgomery Hyde, *Carson: The Life of Sir Edward Carson, Lord Carson of Duncairn* (Melbourne: William Heinemann, 1953), 402.

94 William O'Brien, *The Irish Revolution and How It Came About* (London: George Allen & Unwin, 1923), 271–277.

95 Kennedy, 'War, Patriotism', 205; Hyde, *Carson*, 403–404; Jackson, *Home Rule*, 159.

that James Craig had been sent to him to explain the reasoning behind the push for a settlement:

> The most serious part of it was that the Cabinet were quite unanimous in considering it necessary to give Redmond Home Rule at once, in spite of all the obvious dangers which were implied. Sir Edward Grey insisted upon this as absolutely necessary to enable him to get over difficulties in his dealings with America and other neutrals.[96]

Montgomery believed the Cabinet was 'Asquixiated'. He asserted that 'all the ground they had gained in their anti Home Rule campaign before the war had slipped away under the influence of war'.[97]

Montgomery was stunned by the choice the UUC had to make, as he believed they were turning their backs on the Ulster Covenant and giving up hope of finding another solution. He wrote:

> The choice we had was really between all Ireland being placed under a Home Rule Parliament, or all Ireland minus six counties and I believe, odious as the position is, that we choose right. What is difficult to understand is (1) how the American pressure to which the Cabinet had unanimously yielded can be strong enough to justify their action, and (2) how it is possible that the sort of Home Rule it is proposed to give can satisfy the feeling that is at the back of this pressure.[98]

Ronald McNeill later reported that, while meeting with the UUC, Carson:

> outlined the representations that had been made to him by the Cabinet as to the injury to the Allied cause resulting from the unsettled Irish question – the disturbance of good relations with the United States, whence we were obtaining vast quantities of munitions; the bad effects of our local differences of opinion in Allied and neutral countries. He admitted that these evil effects were largely due to false and hostile propaganda to which the British Government weakly neglected to provide an antidote; he believed they were grossly exaggerated.[99]

Commitment to winning the war and staying in the good graces of the neutral United States forced the unionists to reconsider their official position

---

96 Montgomery to Charles Hubert Montgomery 9 Jun 1916, PRONI D627/429/27.
97 Montgomery to George F. Stewart 17 Jun 1916, PRONI D627/429/39.
98 Montgomery to Fane Vernon 13 Jun 1916, PRONI D627/429/32.
99 McNeill, *Ulster's Stand*, 247.

on Home Rule. With much regret, the UUC formally gave up claims on Cavan, Donegal, and Monaghan, committing itself to six-county exclusion.

Ultimately, the settlement was scuttled by a poorly defined period of partition. Carson believed partition would only end if the British Parliament formally decided against it after the war's end. Redmond was under the impression that partition was temporary. British Conservative backbenchers rose up in opposition to an immediate grant of Home Rule. British and southern unionist forces within the Cabinet shut down the possibility of settlement.[100] A statement issued by southern unionists read,

> It is common knowledge that they [the IPP] do not even now represent to the full extent the views and feelings of their constituents ... It might be suggested that it was worth the gamble if the so-called settlement would satisfy the Irish Nationalists at home or political Irish-American feelings: it will do neither one nor the other.

Southern unionists emphasized that Sinn Féiners and Irish-American extremists would not be satisfied with any deal that included partition. They explained that the settlement would 'in our view be regarded by Irish American opinion with even greater contempt than in Ireland, and will be tolerated only on the ground that it will give the forces of disloyalty free scope for further efforts'.[101] According to southern unionists, this measure of Home Rule and exclusion would only open the door to further trouble in Ireland. Sinn Féiners and Irish-American extremists hoped ultimately to achieve a far greater measure of self-governance.

Though it was unlikely Irish and Irish-American revolutionary nationalists would have been satisfied with the proposed settlement, this attempt at negotiating for Home Rule helped to mollify the opinion of the American public in general.[102] Wellington House and the Foreign Office also attempted to counter some of the extremist propaganda in the United States. Charles Hubert Montgomery, who worked at the Foreign Office and later travelled with the Marquess of Reading on his mission to the United States in 1918, wrote to his father,

> There is a lot of rubbish being talked in America about distress in Ireland which is said to need relieving. I believe collections are even being made for the ostensible purpose of relieving it and no doubt

100 Alvin Jackson, *Sir Edward Carson* (Dublin: Historical Association of Ireland, 1993), 53; Thomas Hennessey, *Dividing Ireland: World War I and Partition* (London: Routledge, 1998), 145–152; Jackson, *Home Rule*, 164–170.
101 Notes from Ireland 1 Aug 1916, PRONI D1327/20/4/138.
102 Hyde, *Carson*, 405.

those who collect the money will have no bother in finding a use for it. We are trying to arrange ways of disposing of these myths ... My impression is that the farmers are having the time of their lives and that there is no distress in any quarter.[103]

Montgomery believed Irish agricultural distress had been relieved, but the plight of the rural Irish was still being used to gain funding for entirely separate nationalist activities. While there were British attempts to appeal to American opinion and counter extreme nationalist propaganda, relations between Ulster and Britain were worsening. The high number of casualties faced by the Ulster regiments, particularly after the Battle of the Somme, was seen as part of their sacrifice for the empire. The casualties of war became martyrs for Ulster Protestant freedom. The Somme was paralleled with the Battle of the Boyne in Ulster unionist mythology, adding to the sense of separateness in Ulster. For Britain, as the war went on, frustration built with Ulster always standing in the way of settlement in Ireland which endlessly impacted on British domestic and foreign relations.[104]

After the United States declared war on Germany on 6 April 1917, Wilson for the first time instructed his London ambassador, Walter Hines Page, cautiously to urge the British government to implement self-government in Ireland. Though Page himself was sympathetic to the unionists, Irish-American opinion in favour of a settlement had gained substantial popular backing. Wilson attempted to appease them to win support for the American war effort.[105] Page received a memorandum from the White House instructing,

The President wishes that, when you next meet the Prime Minister, you would explain to him that only one circumstance now appears to stand in the way of perfect cooperation with Great Britain. All Americans who are not immediately connected with Germany by blood ties find their one difficulty in the failure of Great Britain so far to establish a satisfactory form of self-government in Ireland.[106]

Furthermore, Page was to impress upon Lloyd George that 'If the British Government should act successfully on this matter, our American citizens

103 Charles Hubert Montgomery to Montgomery 28 Sep 1916, PRONI D627/429/76.
104 Carroll, *American Presence*, 115–116; McIntosh, *Force of Culture*, 8–17.
105 Carroll, *American Opinion*, 89; Ward, *Ireland and Anglo-American Relations*, 120; Whelan, *United States Foreign Policy*, 123.
106 Burton J. Hendrick, ed. *The Life and Letters of Walter H. Page* (London: William Heinemann, 1922), Vol. 2, 255; *Papers Relating to the Foreign Relations of the United States, Lansing Papers, 1914–1920*, Vol. 2 (Washington, DC: Government Printing Office, 1940), 4–5; Cronin, *Washington's Irish Policy*, 19–20.

of Irish descent and to a great extent the German sympathizers who have made common cause with the Irish, would join hands in the great common cause' with the Allies in fighting the First World War.[107] The British government continued to make efforts to influence American opinion over Ireland. E.M. House, Wilson's foreign policy advisor, and Sir William Wiseman, a British intelligence officer who liaised between Britain and the United States, prepared a memorandum to be presented at the March 1917 Imperial Conference. The memorandum asserted that the Irish question was 'one of the greatest obstacles to a good understanding between Britain and the United States', but that 'the Unionist side of the question is little understood and never presented ... There are, however, many reasonable and intelligent Americans of Irish extraction who feel very strongly on the subject, and who might be persuaded to lend their assistance with all honesty to the settlement of this question at the end of the war'.[108] The British Foreign Office prepared propaganda materials for the United States, circulating pro-British views in the press. British-American organizations were prominent in the United States, particularly in New England and mid-Atlantic cities. Scotch-Irish organizations joined the ranks of other groups such as the Sons of St. George, the Order of Scottish Clans, and the Daughters of the British Empire. These organizations promoted Anglo-American cooperation and friendship, and were used as channels for British propaganda.[109] Additionally, the Loyal Coalition, English-Speaking Union, Ulster League of North America, British-American League, and others promoted pro-British agendas.

Notes from Ireland reported that Americans had been forced to change their stance on Ireland once they allied with Britain. A *New York Times* article was quoted, stating, 'As the friends of Germany and the enemies of England, Sinn Féin in Ireland and its abettors in the United States are necessarily enemies of the United States. They are doing all in their power to beat America, whose cause cannot be separated from any of her associates in the war'.[110] Arthur Balfour, then foreign secretary, went on a mission to the United States in 1917. Balfour spent four weeks in Washington as part of the British War Mission to liaise with the United States government and obtain further war loans.[111] He was instructed to telegraph back to Britain the attitudes in America regarding Ireland. Balfour met with secretary of state

---

107 Burton, *Life and Letters*, 255–256.
108 Carroll, *American Opinion*, 90.
109 Dennis J. McCarthy, 'The British', in *The Immigrants' Influence on Wilson's Peace Policies*, ed. Joseph P. O'Grady (Lexington: University of Kentucky Press, 1967), 89, 96.
110 Notes from Ireland 1 Feb 1918, PRONI D1327/20/4/140.
111 Sanders and Taylor, *British Propaganda*, 190.

Robert Lansing on 6 May, addressed Congress, and met with a delegation of leading Irish-Americans. In his report to the British Cabinet, Balfour minimized the importance of Ireland to the United States.[112]

Back in Ireland, Montgomery was also sceptical about the importance of American attitudes. He wrote to Sir James Stronge:

> My feeling is that, while it is on the whole wise for us to stick to the offer we made this time last year, it can do us no good in the public estimation to offer to make the setting up of a Parliament in any part of Ireland more easy than it is at this moment, that is to give a Parliament in which the majority, if not Sinn Féiners, will go in dread of Sinn Féiners power to assist the German submarine to command safe bases in all the Harbours and creeks of the West Coast. No doubt the attitude of a great part of the Press is most disquieting, but a great deal of the arguments with regard to the attitude of Americans is as baseless as the yarns we were told about America and munitions at Belfast this time last year.[113]

Montgomery recognized that the previously agreed UUC policy of six-county exclusion was probably the best course for the Ulster unionists. He revealed his frustrations with the continual way that the opinions of the American government and public were driving Irish policy. Montgomery believed that reports of the strength of American opinion were baseless, but were being used to support an agenda that went against the interests of Ulster unionists.

As talks progressed for organizing an Irish Convention, Ulster unionists recognized that in a time of war the United States was one of the driving factors influencing the British government. Unionist MP for South Tyrone, William Coote, wrote to Montgomery, 'I believe this whole Conference question is intended as window dressing for the Americans and a diplomatic move on the part of Lloyd George to ship the Responsibility from the House of Commons to Ireland. It is however fraught with great danger to Ulster and we will require to be very diplomatic'.[114] A unionist memorandum on

---

112 Carroll, *American Opinion*, 91–92; Sydney H. Zebel, *Balfour: A Political Biography* (Cambridge: Cambridge University Press, 1973), 234–236; Mansergh, *Irish Question*, 298–299. Balfour's place on the British War Mission was subsequently taken by Lord Northcliffe, followed by Lord Reading. See Sanders and Taylor, *British Propaganda*, 191, 197; J. Lee Thompson, '"To Tell the People of America the Truth": Lord Northcliffe in the USA, Unofficial British Propaganda, June–November 1917', *Journal of Contemporary History* 34, no. 2 (Apr 1999) and *Politicians, the Press & Propaganda: Lord Northcliffe & the Great War, 1914–1919* (Kent, OH: Kent State University Press, 1999), 148–169.
113 Montgomery to Stronge 5 May 1917, PRONI D627/430/4.
114 Coote to Montgomery 23 May 1917, PRONI D627/430/19.

the Irish Convention took the view that any coup to Home Rule would be dangerous to the war effort – a fact Americans would soon realize:

It is suggested that it is necessary to agree to some form of Home Rule in order to placate American opinion. It must be clear to intelligent Americans that the establishment of any effective form of Home Rule within Ireland would be equivalent to furnishing the Germans with a convenient Naval Base for attack upon the United States. If Irish unionists continue their resistance to any form of Home Rule till the American public generally understand better what Home Rule means, the desire to see Home Rule established in Ireland will disappear.[115]

Unionists aimed to counter the influence of Irish nationalist propaganda. They hoped if Americans were fully educated on the Home Rule question, there would no longer be demands from the United States for a solution to the Irish problem. However, though the United States was a significant rhetorical target throughout the period of the war, unionists in actuality never fully committed to executing wide-ranging propaganda in America. Instead they remained partially reliant on the efforts of the British government and Foreign Office.

Partition

Even though they deplored Home Rule, by mid-1917 Ulster unionists expressed openness to the idea of partition. The *Observer* credited Ulster unionists for doing their utmost to aid the war effort and accommodate the United States through their willingness to accept a partition settlement. An editorial on 6 May commented,

For the sake of the Allies' cause, and with honest regard for American opinion, [Ulster] has gone further, we believe, than would have been thinkable even a few weeks ago. Unionist Ulster has stretched out her hand. Is there a sane Irishman alive who does not realise what that means and what it might be made to mean by courageous and generous action, by responsive and reconciling statesmen, on the Nationalist side? Is the proffered hand of Unionist Ulster to be left ungrasped or flung back?[116]

---

115 Montgomery Papers PRONI D627/430/16.
116 Montgomery Papers PRONI D627/430/16.

The First World War had made American opinion on the Irish situation vitally important. At the same time, Ulster unionists were more responsive to America because of the ways in which the war effort, the Irish situation, and the United States were entangled.

The Irish Convention met from July 1917 to March 1918 under the chairmanship of Horace Plunkett. Plunkett was a former Unionist MP who had converted to Home Rule by 1911. As a correspondent of Woodrow Wilson, Plunkett was influential in Irish-American relations, and had experience in the United States through his efforts in cooperative agriculture.[117] The Convention has been depicted as a way to conciliate American opinion, but was also a genuine attempt to solve the Irish problem.[118] President Wilson refrained from commenting on the Irish situation while the representatives were in session. The Convention had separate representatives for Ulster and southern unionists, who were led by Lord Midleton and Protestant Archbishop of Dublin John Henry Bernard. Federalist proponents F.S. Oliver and Lord Selborne hoped to use the Irish Convention as an opportunity to launch the federal idea as a solution. They drew up a draft plan, which won over a few converts, but were unable to make much of an impact beyond the unionist elites.[119] With Sinn Féin unrepresented and difficulties finding common ground between Ulster, southern unionists, and nationalist representatives, hopes for the Convention soured by early 1918. The government linked the Convention's report with conscription, which was hugely unpopular in Ireland, thus destroying any remaining popularity of the pro-Home Rule, constitutional nationalists.[120]

The conscription crisis in April 1918 generated bitter anti-Irish sentiment in the United States. The British Foreign Office again felt this was a

117 Whelan, *United States Foreign Policy*, 43–44; Francis M. Carroll, *The American Commission on Irish Independence, 1919: The Diary, Correspondence and Report* (Dublin: Irish Manuscripts Commission, 1985), 6; Carla King, 'Defenders of the Union: Sir Horace Plunkett', in *Defenders of the Union: A Survey of British and Irish Unionism since 1801*, ed. D. George Boyce and Alan O'Day (London: Routledge, 2001), 138; R.B. McDowell, *The Irish Convention, 1917–18* (London: Routledge & Kegan Paul, 1970).

118 Alan O'Day, *Irish Home Rule, 1867–1921* (Manchester: Manchester University Press, 1998), 285–286; Christopher Harvie, *A Floating Commonwealth: Politics, Culture, and Technology on Britain's Atlantic Coast, 1860–1930* (Oxford: Oxford University Press, 2008), 244; Mansergh, *Unresolved Question*, 106.

119 D. George Boyce, 'Federalism and the Irish Question', in *The Federal Idea*, Vol. 1: *The History of Federalism from Enlightenment to 1945*, ed. Andrea Bosco (London: Lothian Foundation Press, 1991), 131; Jackson, *Home Rule*, 177–195; D. George Boyce and J.O. Stubbs, 'F.S. Oliver, Lord Selborne and Federalism', *Journal of Imperial and Commonwealth History* 5, no. 1 (Oct 1976); Whelan, *United States Foreign Policy*, 166–167.

120 Jackson, *Home Rule*, 185; Hennessey, *Dividing Ireland*, 221–226.

time in need of delicate propaganda efforts, which they directed toward American Catholics in particular.[121] Irish nationalists sent a letter to Wilson to justify their views of conscription. Ulster unionists responded by writing an admonishing letter of their own.[122] McNeill described,

> In the Nationalist letter to President Wilson reference was made more than once to the sympathy that prevailed in Ireland in the eighteenth century with the American colonists in the War of Independence. The use made of it was a good example of the way in which a half-truth may, for argumentative purposes, be more misleading than a complete falsehood … No mention was made of the fact that the members of the 'banished race' in Washington's army were Presbyterian emigrants from Ulster, who formed almost the entire population of great districts in the American Colonies at that time.[123]

McNeill went on to write that, conversely, it was the Ulster Presbyterians 'who best in Ireland can trace their kinship with the founders of the United States, and who are entitled – if any Irishmen are – to base on that kinship a claim to the sympathy and support of the American people'.[124] The unionists' own letter to Wilson was signed by Carson, the mayors of Belfast and Londonderry, and representatives of Ulster labour and commerce. The letter was transmitted to Washington with the help of Walter Hines Page, who embedded it into an official telegram from the embassy.[125] In the letter, unionists refuted the nationalist claim to American sympathy, stating:

> The Nationalist party have based their claim to American sympathy on the historic appeal addressed to Irishmen by the British colonists who fought for independence in America a hundred and fifty years ago. By no Irishmen was that appeal received with a more lively sympathy than by the Protestants of Ulster, the ancestors of those for whom we speak to-day – a fact that was not surprising in view of the circumstances that more than one-sixth part of the entire Colonial population in America at the time of the Declaration of Independence consisted of emigrants from Ulster. The Ulstermen of to-day, forming as they do the chief industrial community in Ireland are as devoted adherents to the cause of democratic freedom as were their forefathers

---

121 Carroll, *American Opinion*, 108; Sanders and Taylor, *British Propaganda*, 199.
122 Carroll, *American Opinion*, 131.
123 McNeill, *Ulster's Stand*, 273–274.
124 McNeill, *Ulster's Stand*, 273–274.
125 Whelan, *United States Foreign Policy*, 175.

in the eighteenth century. But the experience of a century of social and economic progress under the legislative Union with Great Britain has convinced them that under no other system of government could more complete liberty be enjoyed by the Irish people.[126]

The unionist appeal to the United States was based on shared history, and love of freedom and liberty. They emphasized their role in Ireland's industrial economy. Unionists believed that liberty and economic progress would best be achieved through continued participation in the Union. They therefore felt the maintenance of Union was consistent with the values they shared with America.

As well as the historical and ideological connections between Ulster and the United States, the unionists appealed to self-determination and wartime sacrifice. They also further attempted to discount the nationalists. They stated,

The claim of these men, in league with Germany on the one hand, and with the forces of clericalism on the other, to resist a law passed by Parliament as necessary for national defence is, moreover, inconsistent with any political status short of independent sovereignty – a status which could only be attained by an act of secession from the United Kingdom such as the American Union averted only by resort to civil war.[127]

Unionists' appeal against separatism would have been limited in its effectiveness for Americans, who would have been familiar with Irish-American calls for total independence over the four previous decades. Anti-clericalism was also a delicate subject in an American setting. While Americans repudiated clerical involvement in government, they also did not primarily view the Irish question in terms of religious conflict.

As president, Wilson was reluctant to take an open stance on the Irish question. He did not want to imperil Anglo-American relations. Other American politicians, however, were not under the same constraints. Many congressmen and senators strongly supported pro-nationalist measures, causing resentment among unionists in Ulster. As the war was coming to an end, Irish and Irish-American nationalists found in Wilson's calls for a new international order based on self-determination a possible route to

---

126 'Unionist Manifesto. Mansion House Claims Refuted' (Belfast: UUC, 1918), PRONI D1327/20/4/142.
127 'Unionist Manifesto'. The full nationalist and unionist letters can also be found in the appendix to McNeill, *Ulster's Stand*.

achieve their own goals.[128] McNeill commented, 'President Wilson's coinage of the unfortunate and ambiguous expression "self-determination" made it a catch-penny cry in relation to Ireland'.[129] The end of the war allowed Irish-American nationalists to resume vigorous work for Irish independence, without the insinuation that they were weakening the United States' war effort. They viewed the Paris Peace Conference as an ideal place for Irish causes finally to win international attention, as the Allies would be considering democracy and self-determination for small nations.[130] Dáil Éireann selected Éamon de Valera, Arthur Griffith, and Count Plunkett to represent Irish nationalists at the peace conference, to ask for international recognition of the Irish Republic. When they were not permitted to go to Paris, Irish-American nationalists selected three of their own leaders to promote the Irish cause. Frank P. Walsh, Edward F. Dunne, and Michael J. Ryan were chosen at the Irish Race Convention held in Philadelphia in February 1919. The three delegates formed the American Commission on Irish Independence.[131]

The commission members hoped to ask the British for safe-conduct passes for the Dáil Éireann representatives. When that failed, they sought to present Ireland's claims to the peace conference themselves. They travelled to Ireland to 'inspect conditions'. To the embarrassment of the Wilson administration, the delegates were vocally supportive of the republican government. In part because of their blunders, they were not allowed to present their cause to the peace conference. To Wilson's further embarrassment, the United States Senate resolved by an overwhelming margin that Dáil Éireann representatives should be permitted to supplicate the powers at Versailles.[132] The IUA passed a resolution admonishing the Senate resolution, stating, 'That this Committee of Irish Unionists, representative of both North and South, indignantly resent the intervention of the American Senate in pressing the Irish problem on the notice of the Peace Conference, as the questions of Irish Government and administration are, in the opinion of this Committee, purely domestic ones for the decision of the Imperial Parliament'.[133] Unionists also specifically addressed allegations about conditions in Ireland made by the American Commission on Irish Independence. One UUC pamphlet entitled 'The State of Ireland: American-Irish Allegations Refuted' corrected each point

128 Carroll, *American Opinion*, 120–121; McNickle, 'When New York Was Irish', 350.
129 McNeill, *Ulster's Stand*, 227.
130 Carroll, *American Opinion*, 122; Keown, *First of the Small Nations*, 36–46.
131 Carroll, *American Opinion*, 131; Ward, 'America and the Irish Problem', 83.
132 Carroll, *American Commission*, 13–16; Ward, 'America and the Irish Problem', 84; Whelan, *United States Foreign Policy*, 190.
133 Notes from Ireland 1 Aug 1919, PRONI D1327/20/4/141.

made in memorandums published by the Irish-Americans during their visit to Ireland.[134]

In a speech at Belfast's Wellington Hall on 2 September, Carson directly appealed to the United States. He stated,

> A word to Americans. Now, let us see what are the elements that the real statesman has to consider. He must first consider what it is we are asked to give up if we accept Home Rule, and this is very often forgotten. May I say to our American cousins they nearly always forget. We are depicted to them as having no constitutional government at all in this country. What have we got? ... Full and equal rights in the greatest Parliament that ever existed ... We are on equal terms, and we decline anything subordinate.

He went on to criticize Irish-Americans' calls for Irish self-determination, which went against the example of history in America itself: 'Self-determination is, in my opinion, one of the most misleading phrases that has ever been put forward, and it is being run, you know, for all they knew in America. Would they allow the South of America, the Southerners, self-determination for themselves? Why not?'[135] Unionists repeatedly asserted that if Americans only realized the true conditions of Ireland, that it was not oppressed by British rule, that the Irish were in fact over-represented in the British Parliament, then their interference would come to an end. *Notes from Ireland* remarked,

> The truth of the matter is that America is beginning to learn that the traditional Ireland, 'under the brutal heel of the oppressor', is the greatest bluff in history. A great nation cannot suddenly intervene in a great European struggle without learning something. American soldiers have visited Ireland and looked in vain for signs of oppression. Many of them have gone home and informed their friends that the bluff has been called, and that there is 'nothing doing'. The more America knows of the truth about Ireland, the less, we confidently prophesy, will she be inclined to interfere.[136]

Unionists hoped the United States' experience with Ireland during the war had created a more realistic picture of the Irish situation for the

---

134 UUC Pamphlets, PRONI D1327/20/4/142.
135 'Ulster and Home Rule. Unionist Council Meeting. Sir Edward Carson's Advice' (Belfast: UUC, 1919), PRONI D1327/20/4/142.
136 Notes from Ireland 1 Nov 1919, PRONI D1327/20/4/141.

American public. The conscription crisis and willingness of the unionists to compromise on partition were also war-driven events which the unionists hoped would impact on the views of the American public.

The unionists themselves made attempts to reach out directly to the American public. They tried to take advantage of the attitudes of those Americans who believed the United States had gone too far in its involvement in the Irish question. President Wilson received letters from both sides of the Atlantic urging him to ignore the demands of Sinn Féiners.[137] The Ulster Women's Unionist Council (UWUC) and the Women's Committee of the IUA were both involved in letter-writing campaigns to the United States.[138] The minutes of the UWUC Executive Committee recorded in 1920,

> Mrs. Allworthy [Chair of the UWUC Literature Committee] reported that four meetings of the Literature Committee had been held at which over 200 Newspapers had been sent to Women's Clubs in America ... That several members had responded to the appeal for papers, and she hoped that when the Committee met again in September, it would not be necessary to make a further appeal.[139]

Branches of the UWUC were linked with 53 American women's clubs who were sent leaflets and local newspapers.[140] Later that year, the UWUC Executive Committee weighed its options for continuing with propaganda work. Dehra Chichester commented that, 'It was almost too late now but a great deal might still be done if proper steps were taken. She read a letter from a friend in America testifying to the value of the Newspapers and literature sent out there combating the Sinn Féin Campaign'. The secretary, John M. Hamill, was instructed to write to the Loyal Coalition, a pro-unionist organization in Boston, to arrange for coordinated propaganda in the United States.[141] Orange lodges in the United States were also offered literature for circulation, 'setting forth true facts relative to conditions in Ireland' from the Propaganda Department of the UUC.[142] In the south, the

---

137 Carroll, *American Opinion*, 131–146.
138 On the UWUC, see Diane Urquhart, '"The Female of the Species is More Deadlier Than the Male"? The Ulster Women's Unionist Council, 1911–40', in *Coming into the Light: The Work, Politics, and Religion of Women in Ulster, 1840–1940*, ed. Janice Holmes and Diane Urquhart (Belfast: Institute of Irish Studies, 1994) and *Women in Ulster Politics, 1890–1940: A History Not Yet Told* (Dublin: Irish Academic Press, 2000).
139 Diane Urquhart, *Minutes of the Ulster Women's Unionist Council and Executive Committee, 1911–40* (Dublin: Irish Manuscripts Commission, 2001), 118.
140 Nancy Kinghan, *United We Stood: The Story of the Ulster Women's Unionist Council, 1911–1974* (Belfast: Appletree Press, 1975), 42.
141 Urquhart, *Minutes of the Ulster Women's Unionist Council*, 120–121.
142 *Orange and Purple Courier* I, no. 72 (May–Jun 1921).

IUA Women's Committee took on similar work. An IUA Annual Report stated, 'The Women's Committee undertook to carry on special propaganda work in America, and much useful work has been done by them by a regular supply of articles and letters. Many successful meetings were also arranged by the Women's Committee'.[143]

Edward Carson wrote to UUC Secretary Richard Dawson Bates about the establishment of an active propaganda department. He stated,

> I have had numerous letters from America pointing out how active our opponents are in that country in the Press and on the Platform in trying by the grossest misrepresentation to bring about an anti-English feeling in relation to Ireland. I am convinced that the time has come when we should establish an active propaganda department by which the true facts as regards Ireland and especially as regards Ulster should be made known.[144]

Bates confirmed that there was a branch of the London-based unionist operation at 25 Victoria Street which dealt with the American press.[145] He also wrote that a Mr. McClure had been employed by Carson to put Ulster's case before America.[146] This was probably Samuel S. McClure, Ulster immigrant, journalist, and former proprietor of *McClure's Magazine*. He would later appear in a Carnegie Hall debate against an Irish-American nationalist opponent, in opposition to Irish independence.[147]

Sinn Féin propaganda in America was a particular concern of Hugh Montgomery. He wrote to one of his correspondents, 'I have received a lot of literature from America which makes me feel rather uncomfortable at the apparently growing strength of the Sinn Fein view of matters there'.[148] He frequently corresponded with one of his former tenants, John E. Gunn. Gunn had immigrated to America and became the Catholic Bishop of Natchez. Montgomery wrote an impassioned letter to Gunn in early 1919, arguing:

> If Americans, who now appreciate the importance for the freedom and progress of the world, of the British Empire remaining united and powerful, can only persuade the Irish at home and abroad to devote

---

143 IUA Annual Report 1919–1920, PRONI D989/A/7/4.
144 Carson to Bates 21 Apr 1919, PRONI D1327/18/19.
145 Bates to Montgomery 5 May 1920, PRONI D627435/73.
146 Bates to Montgomery 14 Oct 1919, PRONI D627/435/5.
147 Jones, 'Scotch-Irish', 907. On McClure, see Peter Lyon, *Success Story: The Life and Times of S.S. McClure* (New York: Charles Scribner's Sons, 1963).
148 Montgomery to Ambrose Ricardo 23 Apr 1920, PRONI D627/435/51.

themselves to abandon their struggle for national independence which will be no benefit to Ireland, and undoubtedly cripple the British power, they would confer an immense benefit on this country and on mankind. Irish and English Unionists are really fighting for the same cause as President Lincoln fought for, and which I imagine all Americans, whichever side their fathers fought on in the sixties, are now practically agreed was the right course.[149]

In this letter, Montgomery revealed a hope that America might be the key to convincing Irish nationalists that independence would not benefit Ireland. He emphasized that the fight for national unity, embodied in American history, should have greater resonance for Americans in their views on the Irish situation. If Americans had learned anything from the experience of the Civil War and the First World War, they would realize that the Ulster unionists were fighting in the same spirit of national unity.

Montgomery also sent packages of unionist literature to Gunn. This included Richard Dawson's *Red Terror and Green*, which emphasized Bolshevik ties to Ireland, and Rodolphe Escouflaire's *Ireland: An Enemy of the Allies?*, which asserted that America had suffered from the 'ill-timed jests' of Irish nationalists during the war.[150] In turn, Montgomery read Gunn's recommendations on typical pro-Sinn Féin literature being circulated in the United States, including George Peel's 'Reign of Sir Edward Carson'.[151] Montgomery was alarmed by Judge Cohalan's pamphlet, 'The Freedom of the Seas', and the 'Congressional Record', which contained a large amount of material for Irish-American consumption. He worried that neither the IUA nor the unionists at 25 Victoria Street had 'taken effective measures to get themselves supplied from America with all these things'. Therefore, they might not be aware of the dire influence of Sinn Féin in the United States.[152] The materials recommended by Gunn were in parts incendiary and unrepresentative of Irish-Americans in general, the majority of whom were pro-Ally and reluctant heavily to criticize Britain during the war. Montgomery believed the British government's pursuit of Home Rule policies leading up to the new Government of Ireland Bill would only strengthen the anti-British propaganda released by Sinn Féin in America.[153]

---

149 Montgomery to Gunn, undated but apparently early 1919, PRONI D627/438/2.
150 Richard Dawson, *Red Terror and Green* (London: John Murray, 1920), 100–110, 121–122, 145–146, 260–261; R.C. Escouflaire, *Ireland: An Enemy of the Allies?* (London: John Murray, 1919), 217–220. See Keown, *First of the Small Nations*, 62, on context of Bolshevism and Irish nationalism.
151 See PRONI D627/438 for ongoing correspondence between Montgomery and Gunn.
152 Montgomery to H.M. Pollock 28 May 1920, PRONI D627/435/93.
153 Montgomery to Leo Maxse 7 May 1920, PRONI D627/438/16.

In the United States, Irish-Americans actively lobbied against the Versailles Treaty and the League of Nations at Senate hearings. Alan Ward writes, 'The Irish became the leading weapon of the anti-League forces'.[154] American supporters of Ulster unionism also attempted to influence the hearings. They submitted a brief of protest arguing against attempts by the Sinn Féin party to have the 'so-called Irish question thrust into the discussion in the Senate of the peace treaty and the league of nations'. Seven Scotch-Irishmen signed the brief, which was also published in pamphlet form and circulated by the UUC.[155] Nevertheless, the Treaty of Versailles was defeated on 19 November, with Irish-Americans having played a vital role.[156]

As a draft of the Government of Ireland Bill was prepared in the closing months of 1919, British statesmen considered American attitudes. The measure was designed to pave the way for a single united Irish parliament, with partition in place which would theoretically be temporary.[157] Unionists in the south protested against what they saw as the government acting with the excuse of placating Americans. *Notes from Ireland* exclaimed,

American Opinion! The apologists for the Statute [the Government of Ireland Bill] would have us to believe that some such Act was necessary to placate public opinion in the United States. We fail to see the necessity – or indeed the efficacy – of the means to promote the end. The anti-English party in the States is not going to welcome a half-way house to Irish independence; and our friends in the Republic are content to allow us to manage our own affairs.[158]

Notes from Ireland highlighted one of the major points of difficulty for unionists regarding the United States. Irish-American nationalist supporters were vocally in favour of measures far surpassing those offered in the Government of Ireland Bill. Those Americans more in sympathy with unionists merely urged the United States to refrain from involvement in the Irish question. Unionists in Ireland supported such a stance: they consistently expressed disapproval of the high levels of American influence. However, they may have been more successfully aided if they had gained greater outright support for their own movement from the American public.

154 Ward, 'America and the Irish Problem', 85.
155 Treaty of Peace with Germany: Hearings before the Committee on Foreign Relations, United States Senate, 66th Congress, 1st Session (Washington, DC, Government Printing Office, 1919), 903–904; McCarthy, 'British', 105; Whelan, *United States Foreign Policy*, 221–222.
156 Kenny, *American Irish*, 197.
157 Mansergh, *Unresolved Question*, 123, 129–130; Jackson, *Home Rule*, 195–199.
158 Notes from Ireland 1 Mar 1921, PRONI D1327/20/4/141.

Irish-American nationalism was wrought with factionalism, making the movement largely ineffectual by 1920.[159] As a result, when Éamon de Valera, president of the Dáil Éireann, secretly arrived in New York City in June 1919 to stay for eighteen months, he was able to take advantage of the power vacuum. He established the American Association for the Recognition of the Irish Republic in November 1920. This allowed him to control the Irish-American side of nationalism. De Valera also initiated a bond-certificate drive for Sinn Féin, which raised $5.5 million. He was unable to achieve his ultimate goal of securing official American recognition for the Irish republic.[160] As with previous nationalist visitors to the United States, Irish unionists closely monitored de Valera's activity. *Notes from Ireland* portrayed him as a comic figure, commenting,

What a figure of fun, according to all accounts, is de Valera cutting in the United States. One can picture this self-centred poseur, sitting in his 'State' apartments in a New York Hotel, talking in the King Cambyses vein about his new 'Republic', and the Irish loan to be raised by the issue of Republican bonds 'of small denomination to attract the small investor'. God help the poor dupes that lend money to the 'Irish Republic'![161]

De Valera was likened to Falstaff in *Henry IV, Part I*, when he speaks in the 'King Cambyses vein'. The unionists portrayed him as a fool playing the role of a majestic king. However, the unionists in actuality took de Valera very seriously. A delegation was sent from Ulster to America, led by William Coote, to represent the views of Irish unionists in the face of the de Valera propaganda.

Philip Whitwell Wilson, a special correspondent of the *London Daily News*, wrote a book for the consumption of the American public entitled *The Irish Case before the Court of Public Opinion*. He reiterated the Coote deputation's accusations that the American press was pro-nationalist, not giving fair hearings to unionist viewpoints. Wilson equated the citizens of the United States to a jury, 'sitting in solemn judgment on the great case of *Ireland versus England*'. He believed Ulster unionists needed unbiased consideration in the

---

159 Carroll, *American Opinion*, 166–168; Francis M. Carroll, 'The American Committee for Relief in Ireland, 1920–22', *IHS* 23, no. 89 (May 1982), 30.

160 Ward, 'America and the Irish Problem', 86–88. See also the account of de Valera's trip in Owen Dudley Edwards, *Éamon de Valera* (Cardiff: GPC, 1987), 81–94; Hannigan, *De Valera in America*; Cronin, *Washington's Irish Policy*, 25–26; Earl of Longford and Thomas P. O'Neill, *Eamon de Valera* (London: Hutchinson, 1970), 95–114; Brundage, *Irish Nationalism in America*, 149–162.

161 Notes from Ireland 1 Aug 1919, PRONI D1327/20/4/141.

United States.[162] Wilson recognized Ireland as an international question with the United States particularly interested in its solution. He also condemned Irish-American extremism. 'There is all the difference between study and incendiarism. For responsible American Citizens to aid and abet revolution in Ireland is improper. For them to aid and abet revolution in India in order to force England's hands, they think, in Ireland, is surely worse than a mere impropriety'.[163] Wilson portrayed American citizens as an irresponsible jury condoning extremism, failing to consider the situation without bias and treat all parties in Ireland justly.

The Government of Ireland Act was passed on 23 December 1920. The Act created separate devolved parliaments for six counties in Ulster and for the south, continued representation at Westminster, and formed an all-Ireland council.[164] The UUC had pressed for straightforward exclusion from Home Rule, but they accepted their new parliament as more secure than being under direct rule from Westminster especially given the increasing sense of betrayal they felt toward the British since the end of the war.[165] Initial elections in Northern Ireland produced huge Unionist majorities.[166] As the north attempted to cope with its newfound Home Rule status, the south degenerated into chaos with fighting between the British and the IRA. Anglo-Americans attempted to counter the increasing violence by emphasizing the extremism of Sinn Féin and the IRA. In the early 1920s, both the British and American press regularly described Irish guerrilla violence as 'terrorism'. The American consul in Dublin, Frederick Dumont, sympathized with the British. He enumerated for the State Department the outrages and attacks committed against British forces by Irish nationalists. The British and American governments began to work together to an extent to counter terroristic forces in both countries, though British reprisals in Ireland were also condemned.[167]

American newspapers applauded Ulster unionists' decision to compromise on the Government of Ireland Act while condemning the chaos in the south. 'Ulster has undertaken to try the experiment', a *New York Times* editorial praised. 'Instead of standing by its old idea of indissoluble union with England, it is ready to begin separation. Why should not the South

162 Philip Whitwell Wilson, *The Irish Case before the Court of Public Opinion* (New York: Fleming H. Revel Company, 1920), 4, 13.
163 Wilson, *Irish Case*, 107–108.
164 John D. Fair, 'The Anglo-Irish Treaty of 1921: Unionist Aspects of the Peace', *Journal of British Studies* 12, no. 1 (Nov 1972), 134; Jackson, *Home Rule*, 230–233.
165 Buckland, *Irish Unionism 1885–1922*, 30; Foster, *Modern Ireland*, 503.
166 Foster, *Modern Ireland*, 504.
167 Whelan, *United States Foreign Policy*, 252–253; Gantt, *Irish Terrorism*, 207–210, 220–221.

of Ireland act in the same spirit?' The *New York Times* editors hoped that good governance from Dublin could still win over Ulster and lead to a united Ireland, but they were sympathetic with the unionists' position. 'It is unpleasant to mention religious animosities of the old date, and perhaps much too much has been made of them. Ulster is a great industrial district. Rightly or wrongly, it feared that its economic strength would be injured under a Government dominated by the South and West'.[168] The *Los Angeles Times* went so far as to blame Sinn Féin for promoting violence which kept a peaceful settlement from being put into place. Their 'rabid attitude was responsible for the fears of Ulster and Ulster's long opposition to Home Rule. But even Ulster has long since made necessary concessions for a workable home-rule scheme … Ulster has now made her concessions, but Sinn Féin prefers to prolong the misery'.[169] Mainstream American newspapers, which consistently denounced chaos and violence, commended the actions of Ulster unionists and even exhibited understanding of unionist fears of militancy.

In the midst of the Anglo-Irish War at the end of 1920, Irish-Americans founded the American Committee for Relief in Ireland, chaired by Judge Michael J. O'Brien. An eight-member delegation, including several Quakers with previous relief work experience, was sent to Ireland to investigate conditions. They toured Ireland in 1921, determining that the country faced widespread destruction. When they returned to the United States, the committee initiated a national fundraising campaign for Irish relief, led by Captain John F. Lucey. The campaign attempted to make this a non-partisan exercise, expanding beyond their Irish-American base and gaining the endorsement of President Warren G. Harding.[170] The American Committee for Relief in Ireland raised $5,123,640. They dispersed the money in Ireland through the Irish White Cross. By the end of March 1921, Dumont sent reports to the State Department questioning the validity of the delegation's descriptions of destruction in Ireland. He feared they had been exploited by the Irish White Cross, an organization with close ties to Sinn Féin. In short, he thought American relief funds were going straight into Sinn Féin coffers. The British government was angered to find President Harding had endorsed an organization that was inadvertently funding Sinn Féin separatism. Anglo-American relations were already strained due to tensions over the Anglo-Japanese alliance and American naval building activities. It is possible at this time that the United States government threatened to recognize the Irish Republic to force Britain's hand in the other areas of diplomatic strife.

168 *NYT* 12 Mar 1920, 26 Oct 1920.
169 *Los Angeles Times* 13 Aug 1920.
170 Carroll, *American Opinion*, 166–168; Carroll, 'American Committee for Relief', 32–34.

This marked the first time the United States government was prepared to pursue an Irish policy that went against British interests.[171]

In June 1921, further controversy was generated when Rear Admiral William Sowden Sims, the Commander of United States Forces Operating in European Waters during the First World War, addressed a London meeting of the English-Speaking Union. In his speech, Sims accused Sinn Féin sympathizers in America of having 'the blood of English and American boys on their hands'. Sims stated that Irish-Americans who tried to interfere in Anglo-American relations 'are like zebras, either black horses with white stripes or white horses with black stripes, but we know they are not horses, they are asses. But each of these asses has a vote, and there are lots of them'.[172] These anti-Irish-American views accorded with his statements on Sinn Féiners in Ireland in Sims's Pulitzer Prize-winning book, *The Victory at Sea*. In the book, he described his experiences in Queenstown during the war. He stated that Sinn Féiners 'were not only openly disloyal; they were openly pro-German'.[173] Sims accused them of attacking American soldiers at Queenstown and taking attention away from the war effort, effectively prolonging the war. Sims was condemned for his 'jackass' speech by politicians and Irish-Americans. Secretary of the Navy Edwin Denby publicly reprimanded the Rear Admiral for overstepping diplomatic relations. Sims found strong support from Protestant churches and clergy, including Reverend Dr. Frederick Brown Harris, Reverend Harry Knight Miller, and Methodist Bishop Edwin Holt Hughes. The *New York Times*, *New York Herald*, and *Christian Science Monitor* defended Sims. He was also backed by such organizations as the Loyal Coalition, American Protestant Federation, Orange Order, and the Allied Loyalty League. Prominent individuals such as Harvard President Charles W. Eliot, eugenics theorist Madison Grant, Senator John Sharp Williams of Mississippi, former United States Attorney General George W. Wickersham, and others rallied to Sims's defence.[174]

Overall, the response of the American public revealed frustration with the Irish question after the First World War. According to Francis Carroll, the Sims incident illustrated to the British that they need not be swayed by American Congressional and Senate resolutions on Ireland. The American public was frustrated with the Irish–German relationship during the war and the prominence of the Irish situation in American politics. The climate

---

171 Carroll, 'American Committee for Relief', 37, 45–47.
172 Francis M. Carroll, 'Admiral Sims Incident: Irish Americans and Social Tensions in the 1920s' *Prologue* 25, no. 4 (Winter 1993), 338; Whelan, *United States Foreign Policy*, 336.
173 William Sowden Sims and Burton J. Hendrick, *The Victory at Sea* (Garden City, NY: Doubleday, 1921), 83–87.
174 Carroll, 'Admiral Sims Incident', 339–342.

of the United States following the First World War, with resurgent nativism, anti-Catholic and anti-immigrant ferment, and pseudo-scientific racism, helped to sway Americans in general against the cause of Irish independence. The same impulses which influenced views of the Irish situation also led to the substantial restrictions on immigration to the United States in 1921 and 1924.[175]

The signing of the Anglo-Irish Treaty in 1921 largely satisfied Irish-American demands.[176] An Irish Free State with dominion status was created. On the treaty's adoption, foreign secretary George Curzon stated that the Irish question had been a disrupting factor in British relations with the United States for the past fifty years. He hoped if they 'could wipe off from the slate here this Irish question, I know of no obstacle to impair the completeness of the understanding, and the closeness of the co-operation that should prevail in future between America and ourselves, and which is equally demanded by the traditions, the sentiments, and the need of these two great branches of the English-speaking race'.[177] Curzon argued that settling the Irish question was the key to good relations with the United States. Many Irish-American nationalists felt their goals had been achieved with the Anglo-Irish Treaty and Ireland was finally free, though a faction was stridently anti-treaty. The subsequent outbreak of civil war therefore came as a shock. The war received little support from an Irish-American nationalist movement that lacked motivation to fight another Irish battle.[178] As for Ulster unionists, even after the creation of the Irish Free State, concern remained for attitudes in America. The UUC continued its efforts to spread pro-unionist propaganda to the United States. The Year Book for 1923 noted that the press bureau was active in sending out 'articles and letters on the Irish situation' to counteract 'the false propaganda of our enemies'.[179]

Conclusion

Ulster unionists conducted a contradictory policy toward the United States in the opening decades of the twentieth century. They painted a picture of Irish-America as violent and separatist. Unionists emphasized the illegitimacy

175 Carroll, 'Admiral Sims Incident', 343–344; John Higham, *Strangers in the Land: Patterns of American Nativism, 1860–1925* (New Brunswick, NJ: Rutgers University Press, 1955), 265–293, 300–324.
176 See Fair, 'Anglo-Irish Treaty'.
177 PD Lords 5th Ser., Vol. 21, 30–31; Mansergh, *Irish Question*, 290.
178 Ward, 'America and the Irish Problem', 90; Keown, *First of the Small Nations*, 99–100, 110–111.
179 Ulster Unionist Council Year Book 1923, PRONI D1327/20/1/1.

of Irish nationalism because it was supported by Irish-Americans. At its worst, Irish-America was portrayed as a den for the cultivation of hatred against England, carrying everlasting bitterness from the Famine and a sense of exile from the homeland. It was these views from within the Irish-American community which unionists feared were influencing the actions of the American government. Ulster unionists' loyalty to the British Crown and Empire during the First World War meant they were forced to consider American opinion because of the circumstances of the war. In part because of this, they overturned their Ulster Covenant commitments to protect all nine counties of Ulster and reluctantly accepted the principle of six-county exclusion. However, they were resentful of American involvement in what they saw as a British domestic issue and this contributed to a sense of betrayal by the British for the valuation of American opinion over Ulster loyalty. At times unionists were divided over relying on British propaganda in the United States and attempting their own counter-propaganda to what they saw as deceitful nationalist misinformation. Ulster unionists also actively attempted to garner their own support base in America, producing written materials, conducting letter-writing campaigns, and forging connections with pro-British groups in the United States.

Unionist attitudes toward Irish-America were complex and it is difficult to tell exactly what the unionists thought they would gain by either discrediting or appealing to American views. At times, they were sceptical about the importance of American attitudes, wondering why another country should have any influence over British domestic policy. Unionists constantly urged the United States to cease its involvement in the Irish question. They hoped that the more Americans knew of the truth of the Irish situation, the less inclination there would be to interfere. There also appeared to be a vague and distant hope, emerging when it seemed that there may be no other way to hold the Union together, that America might be the key to convincing the Irish that national independence would not benefit Ireland.

The Irish unionist movement grew increasingly militant and focused in Ulster during the first twenty years of the twentieth century. While unionists remained interested in engaging with Americans, their sometimes-contradictory policies and uneven approach to the United States meant Ulster-American networks were not as fruitful as they might have been. This had the effect of making unionists appear increasingly isolated and entrenched in Ulster even as they sought international support.

4

Scotch-Irish Identity
and Attitudes to Home Rule

The term 'Scotch-Irish' represents the combination of three identities: the Scottish and Irish in an American setting.[1] In Ireland, Irish Protestants were members of different groups with varied backgrounds and traditions. The Ulster Scots were relatively recent settlers in Ireland, 'planted' in Ulster starting in the early seventeenth century. Their experiences with cultural adaptation were similar to what they would later encounter in the American colonies and republic. The difference of experience between those who settled in the southern backcountry in the early eighteenth century and those who joined the California gold rush in the mid-nineteenth century would have been drastic. In addition to their diverse origins and migration experiences, their language, mobility, and adaptability within American society made the Scotch-Irish a particularly difficult group to define. This was especially the case as the characterization of 'Scotch-Irish' widened to include all Irish Protestant immigrants and their descendants, regardless of denomination or region of origin.[2]

Historians of ethnicity emphasize the reciprocal interactions between immigrants and their host societies, as immigrants navigated the dynamic ground between ethnic resistance and assimilation.[3] In the United States, as Kevin Kenny describes, ethnicity assumed a historical importance as immigrants emphasized their ethnic identities to become more fully

---

1 Portions of this chapter have previously been published in the *Journal of Scotch-Irish Studies* 3, no. 4 (Fall 2013). My thanks to the Center for Scotch-Irish Studies for permission to include this material.
2 Matthew McKee, "'A Peculiar and Royal Race": Creating a Scotch-Irish Identity, 1889–1901', in *Atlantic Crossroads: Historical Connections between Scotland, Ulster, and North America*, ed. Patrick Fitzgerald and S.J.S. Ickringill (Newtownards: Colourpoint, 2001), 75; Keller, 'What is Distinctive', 72; Blethen and Wood, Introduction, 2.
3 Miller, 'Class, Culture, and Immigrant Group Identity', 97–98; Kenny, 'Diaspora and Comparison', para. 25.

'American'.[4] The role of ethnicity fluctuated depending on the challenges a particular ethnic group presented to assimilation and acculturation to American society. The Scotch-Irish, for example, would have been affected when the mood of the country was anti-Irish or Anglophobic.

As the volume of United States immigration increased throughout the latter half of the nineteenth century, both American and ethnic identities were expressed through civic and associational culture.[5] Associational culture became an increasingly important part of American civic life culminating in a 'golden age of fraternity' after the Civil War. Many Americans expressed their individuality through joining what Jason Kaufman describes as 'self-segregating' organizations based on gender, race, ethnicity, or religion.[6] At times these associations allowed 'friends' to join who did not claim membership of that ethnic group, such as Henri Le Caron's Clan-na-Gael participation.

In the mid-nineteenth century, expressions of ceremonial citizenship were changing. As Mary Ryan describes, during the first half of the century major American cities spawned hundreds of voluntary organizations, leading to the pluralization of civic society. By joining such groups, individuals were able to take part in parades and civic ceremonies which were an important part of city life. After the Civil War, societal elites withdrew from participation in these civic ceremonies. Increasingly crowded and chaotic conditions in cities led to clashes between different ethnic and religious groups. This was epitomized by the New York City Orange Riots of 1870 and 1871. The Orange Riots marked a turning point in American civic culture, as celebrations of public holidays became more private and less participatory. However, ethnic societies continued to flourish, emphasizing shared national identity, language, religion, rituals, and traditions amongst both older and newer immigrant groups.[7]

Irish-Americans had long celebrated their heritage through ethnic associations, as part of what Ryan terms 'a textbook case of ethnic sociability'.[8]

---

4 Kenny, 'Diaspora and Comparison', para. 24.
5 On immigration at the turn of the century, see Roger Daniels, *Not Like Us: Immigrants and Minorities in America, 1890–1924* (Chicago: Ivan R. Dee, 1997), 38–39.
6 Jason Kaufman, *For the Common Good? American Civic Life and the Golden Age of Fraternity* (Oxford: Oxford University Press, 2002), 8–9; Arthur M. Schlesinger, 'Biography of a Nation of Joiners', *American Historical Review* 50, no. 1 (Oct 1944).
7 Mary P. Ryan, *Civic Wars: Democracy and Public Life in the American City during the Nineteenth Century* (Berkeley: University of California Press, 1997), 74–75, 78–79, 224–234.
8 Ryan, *Civic Wars*, 79. See also Dale B. Light, Jr., 'The Role of Irish-American Organisations in Assimilation and Community Formation', in *The Irish in America: Emigration, Assimilation and Impact* (Irish Studies 4), ed. P.J. Drudy (Cambridge: Cambridge University Press, 1985).

They participated in church groups, temperance groups, mutual benefit societies, and nationalistic political organizations. They faced discriminatory attacks from nativist associations which were also prominent in the mid-nineteenth century. Along with nativist organizations, native-born white Americans joined associations dedicated to the celebration of Anglo-Saxon Protestant heritage. Such associations generally barred membership of people of other races, ethnicities, and religions.[9] The Scotch-Irish played prominent roles in and alongside nativist organizations and claimed places within Anglo-Saxon associations. However, many chose to separate ethnically from the 'native' Americans by forming their own ethnic societies, such as the Scotch-Irish Society of America (SISA) and Loyal Orange Institution (LOI). These organizations allowed the Scotch-Irish to celebrate combined Anglo-Saxon, Scottish, and Irish backgrounds, promote their historic contributions to American society, and preserve ties to Ireland.

This chapter will first focus on the immigration and identity formation of the Scotch-Irish in America during the nineteenth century. Next, the chapter explores two organizations prominent at the end of the nineteenth century which explicitly celebrated Ulster Scots origins and connections: the SISA and American Orange Order. While work remains to be done on many aspects of Scotch-Irish life within American society during this period, this chapter will look particularly at their ties to Ireland and their involvement in the Ulster unionist cause during the Home Rule era. Irish-American nationalists were prominent within the movement for Irish self-government, influencing the attitudes of Americans of non-Irish backgrounds and United States government policy. This chapter examines the ways in which the Scotch-Irish responded to these calls for Irish Home Rule and independence, attempted to support unionists, and remained connected to Ireland.

Along with reciprocal interactions between the Scotch-Irish and their American host society, connections with the society of origin remained important. The Scotch-Irish were influenced by and remained interested in conditions in Ireland. In addition, Ulster Scots themselves were affected by the actions and legacy of the Scotch-Irish in the United States. Their use of Scotch-Irish heritage to help form their own 'Ulsterman' identity will be addressed later in this chapter.

9   Kaufman, *For the Common Good*, 9.

Immigration and Identity

From the late seventeenth century onward, Protestants were over-represented in the numbers of emigrants from Ireland to America.[10] By the early nineteenth century, as Donald Akenson and Kevin Kenny emphasize, Irish-America was largely a Protestant place. There is no indication Irish Protestants would have felt socially threatened by minority Irish Catholics up to this time. Kerby Miller suggests the social and political issues that engaged Irish immigrants transcended religious divisions in the early American republic, leading to a broad Irish identity.[11] Large numbers of Protestant Irish had immigrated in response to the failed United Irish uprising in 1798, which in turn shaped perceptions of American and Irish politics moving forward. Early nineteenth-century Irish emigration was mainly motivated by economic distress. The emigrant group also included a number of professional men, political refugees, and others who were relatively well off compared to earlier phases of migration, which had included large numbers of indentured servants.[12] The flow of emigrants to America was temporarily halted by the War of 1812. Immediately after the war's end, an economic crisis in Ireland drove 35,000 to emigrate. These emigrants were mainly Irish Protestants of various denominations, the majority coming from Ulster. Many Ulster migrants went directly to British North America. Canada, along with other commonwealth countries such as Australia and New Zealand, had high levels of Irish Protestant immigration and maintained connections to Ireland through political unionism and the Orange Order.[13]

Through ancestral links, new United States immigrants were drawn to already established Scotch-Irish settlements in the southern backcountry. Significant numbers also settled in cities along the eastern seaboard, particularly Philadelphia and New York. The peak of Ulster emigration came

---

10 James White McAuley, 'Under an Orange Banner: Reflections on the Northern Protestant Experiences of Emigration', in *The Irish World Wide*, Vol. 5: *Religion and Identity*, ed. Patrick O'Sullivan (London: Leicester University Press, 1996), 46; Donald M. MacRaild and Malcolm Smith, 'Migration and Emigration, 1600–1945', in *Ulster since 1600: Politics, Economy, and Society*, ed. Líam Kennedy and Philip Ollerenshaw (Oxford: Oxford University Press, 2013), 141–146.

11 Akenson, 'Historiography of the Irish', 99; Kenny, *American Irish*, 44; Miller, 'Scotch-Irish Myths', 79–80, 83.

12 Maldwyn A. Jones, 'Ulster Emigration, 1783–1815', in *Essays in Scotch-Irish History*, ed. E.R.R. Green (Belfast: Ulster Historical Foundation, 1969), 49; Cormac Ó Gráda, 'Irish Emigration to the United States in the Nineteenth Century', in *America and Ireland, 1776–1976*, ed. David N. Doyle and Owen Dudley Edwards (Westport, Conn.: Greenwood Press, 1980), 98.

13 MacRaild and Smith, 'Migration and Emigration', 152–155.

between 1815 and 1847, with approximately 500,000 arriving in America. During this period, numbers of Catholics leaving Ireland first exceeded Protestant numbers. The region of departure shifted from Ulster to the south. For the first time, more people were setting out from Cork than Belfast.[14]

Identity formation processes in America were gradual and multidimensional. Miller argues that a particularly 'Scotch-Irish' identity developed between 1790 and 1820, before the Catholic Irish played any significant role in American society. Even during the American Revolution, the Protestant Irish ethnic group encompassed differences in their political leanings; while most joined with the American patriots, others were British loyalists or more concerned with local issues.[15] In the early republic, genteel and conservative Irish Protestants used 'Scotch-Irish' identity while attempting to undermine radical support for Jeffersonian Republicans, and to gain acceptance and influence in Anglo-American society. This mirrored similar struggles in Ulster following the failure of the United Irish rising.[16] They hoped to dissociate themselves from Scottish immigrants, who were viewed negatively as loyalists to the British. Anti-Scots sentiment in America lasted into the nineteenth century.[17] In addition, the term 'Scotch-Irish' was used to invoke shame with being associated with the Catholic Irish. The desire to be dissociated from the Catholic Irish would only increase as the nineteenth century brought huge numbers of new Irish Catholic immigrants. The 'Irish' identity in both Ireland and America was becoming more exclusively associated with Catholicism. These increased divisions between separate Irish communities were exemplified by New York City's first Orange–Green riots in 1824.[18]

As early as the 1820s Irish Protestants were prominent members of nativist and anti-Catholic organizations. Contrastingly, as late as the 1840s, some Scotch-Irish immigrants expressed anti-British and radical views. Irish Presbyterians were known as consistent supporters of Jeffersonian Republicans

14 Campbell, *Ireland's New Worlds*, 5, 7; Patrick J. Blessing, 'Irish Emigration to the United States, 1800–1920: An Overview', in *The Irish in America: Emigration, Assimilation, and Impact* (Irish Studies 4), ed. P.J. Drudy (Cambridge: Cambridge University Press, 1985), 19; Jones, 'Ulster Emigration', 63; Keller, 'What is Distinctive', 73. See Sherling, *Invisible Irish*, 205–243.

15 Leonard Dinnerstein, Roger L. Nichols, and David M. Reimers, *Natives and Strangers: A History of Ethnic Americans*, 5th edn (Oxford: Oxford University Press, 2010), 22–23.

16 Miller, 'Scotch-Irish Myths', 78; Miller, *Ireland and Irish America*, 135, 143.

17 Andrew Hook, *Scotland and America: A Study of Cultural Relations, 1750–1835* (Glasgow: Blackie, 1975), 47–70.

18 J.J. Lee, 'Introduction: Interpreting Irish-America', in *Making the Irish American: History and Heritage of the Irish in the United States*, ed. J.J. Lee and Marion R. Casey (New York: New York University Press, 2006), 17.

and Jacksonian Democrats, parties also supported by Irish Catholics.[19] Miller cites Ulster Presbyterian immigrant letters revealing liberal and radical sentiments. These letters suggest Irish-Americans inherited United Irish ideals, perhaps through the mass migration of Irish political radicals from Ulster to America. The transference of the United Irishmen's non-sectarian ideals across the Atlantic was illustrated by Irish Protestant aid to newly arrived, impoverished Irish Catholic immigrants, and by their membership in non-sectarian ethnic organizations.[20] Over time, this remained the case in southern cities such as Charleston and Savannah, where Irish networks often allowed for interconnections across religious, class, and generational lines.[21]

By the second quarter of the nineteenth century, Irish Protestants, especially in northern cities, were assuming increasingly defensive stances against large numbers of Catholics flooding into the country. As Thomas Brown describes, the term 'Scotch-Irish' became more prominent. Irish Protestant immigrants attempted 'to make it clear to all Americans that in religion, culture, and capacity for assimilation into American life they were very different' from the Catholic Irish.[22] Irish Protestants were also closely associated with the waves of nativism and anti-Catholicism engulfing America in the 1840s and 1850s. Nativism and anti-Catholicism were rooted in several different factors: (1) religious, economic, and social resentment felt toward immigrants, who were coming into the United States in dramatically increasing numbers; (2) fear of foreign radicals and attacks on foreign symbols; (3) the doctrinal concept of Anglo-Saxon superiority; and (4) uncertainties associated with times of change to traditional socioeconomic patterns.[23] For the Scotch-Irish, nativism and anti-Catholicism could also be

---

19 Kerby A. Miller, Bruce D. Boiling, and Líam Kennedy, 'Famine's Scars: William Murphy's Ulster and American Odyssey', in *New Directions in Irish History*, ed. Kevin Kenny (Madison: University of Wisconsin Press, 2003), 40; Miller, 'Scotch-Irish Myths', 79–80, 83; Lawrence J. McCaffrey, *Textures of Irish-America* (Syracuse, NY: Syracuse University Press, 1992), 94.

20 Miller, 'Ulster Presbyterians', 266; Miller, Boiling, and Kennedy, 'Famine's Scars', 40; McCaffrey, 'Diaspora Comparisons', 60; Brundage, *Irish Nationalists in America*, 33–47.

21 David T. Gleeson and Brendan J. Buttimer, '"We are Irish Everywhere": Irish Immigrant Networks in Charleston, South Carolina, and Savannah, Georgia', in *Irish Migration, Networks and Ethnic Identities since 1750*, ed. Enda Delaney and Donald M. MacRaild (London: Routledge, 2007), 42; David T. Gleeson, 'Smaller Differences: "Scotch Irish" and "Real Irish" in the Nineteenth-Century American South', *New Hibernia Review* 10, no. 2 (Summer 2002), 76–77; Brundage, *Irish Nationalists in Ireland*, 64.

22 Brown, *Irish-American Nationalism*, 35.

23 Colman J. Barry, 'Some Roots of American Nativism', *Catholic Historical Review* 44, no. 2 (Jul 1958), 139; Tyler Anbinder, *Nativism and Slavery: The Northern Know Nothings and the Politics of the 1850s* (New York: Oxford University Press, 1992), xv, 19.

used as a means of assimilation into American society. The very existence of prominent nativist organizations made the Scotch-Irish even more likely to seek to distance themselves from Irish Catholics, thus increasing sectarian fervour and divisions within the Irish community.[24]

The Know Nothing movement of the mid-nineteenth century was the second such wave of nativism in American history, following the time of the Alien and Sedition Acts of the 1790s. John Higham also identifies two other major periods of nativism: the late 1880s and during the First World War.[25] The deepening sectarian sentiment was symbolized by the burning of the Ursuline convent in Charlestown, Massachusetts in 1836 and the Philadelphia riots of 1844, when nativist attacks were made against the Catholic Church because of controversy surrounding the use of the Bible in public schools. In 1852, the Order of the Star-Spangled Banner was formed in New York City, and the 'Know Nothing' movement spread rapidly thereafter. Promoting an anti-immigrant, anti-Catholic, temperance, anti-slavery, and government reform platform, the Know Nothings attracted a wide range of support in both the northern and southern states. According to Tyler Anbinder, one of the reasons the Know Nothings attracted anti-slavery advocates was specifically due to anti-Irish sentiment, because 'native-born Americans were convinced that nearly all Irish immigrants supported slavery'.[26] The Know Nothings made significant political gains including electing numerous congressmen and state officials, contributing to the collapse of the Second Party System in the United States, but they never achieved their ultimate goals of tightening restrictions on immigration and naturalization. Divided by the slavery question embroiling the nation, the movement died out by the end of the 1850s.[27]

The Scotch-Irish were closely associated with the Know Nothings, as well as subsequent nativist organizations such as the American Protestant Association, Order of United American Mechanics, and American Protective Association. Higham writes that the significant participation of the Scotch-Irish in these nativist organizations was due to their overwhelming hatred of the Catholic Irish.[28] In the most extreme case, Ku Klux Klan propagandist Thomas Dixon identified his white supremacist ideals as Scotch-Irish in descent and inspiration.[29] Nativism ebbed following the outbreak of the Civil

---

24 Kenny, *American Irish*, 158; Campbell, *Ireland's New Worlds*, 25.
25 Higham, 'Another Look at Nativism', 181.
26 Anbinder, *Nativism and Slavery*, 9–15, 44–46, 103–126.
27 Anbinder, *Nativism and Slavery*, 99–101, 218–219; Daniels, *Not Like Us*, 42–43; Campbell, *Ireland's New Worlds*, 51.
28 John Higham, 'Another Look at Nativism', *Catholic Historical Review* 44, no. 2 (Jul 1958), 181; Blessing, 'Irish Emigration', 29–30.
29 G.K. Peatling, 'Thomas Dixon, Scotch-Irish Identity, and "the Southern People"', *Safundi* 9, no. 3 (Jul 2008), 247–254.

War, although anti-Irish sentiment was revived in the aftermath of the 1863 Draft Riots in New York City. Anti-Catholic protests erupted at times in the postbellum period, such as with perceived threats to public schools, but no nativist organization reached the heights of political influence of the Know Nothings.[30] Ultimately there is no way definitively to determine the levels of Scotch-Irish participation in nativist and Anglo-Saxonist organizations, or the degree to which 'Scotch-Irishness' influenced participation.

By the mid-nineteenth century, many Scotch-Irish families had been in America for a century and a half. James Leyburn argues that these families had assimilated into the overarching American culture by 1800, with the story of the Scotch-Irish people as a distinct group ending with the Revolutionary War.[31] Known as pioneering backwoodsmen, the Scotch-Irish had founded towns, colleges, and churches on the American frontier. The majority converted from Presbyterianism to denominations more easily transferable to frontier life, becoming Baptists or Methodists.[32] The election of Andrew Jackson as President of the United States in 1828 represented the pinnacle of Scotch-Irish achievement as they assimilated into the overarching American culture. To nineteenth-century Americans, Jackson symbolized the ultimate self-made and democratic frontiersman.[33] The election of Jackson, son of Ulster Presbyterian immigrants, illustrated the degree to which the Scotch-Irish had shed their ethnic distinctions and were identified simply as Americans. There is scholarly debate over the level of Scotch-Irish acculturation and assimilation into mainstream American culture from the 1830s onward.[34] How 'Scotch-Irish' did they remain? At what point can they be considered 'totally' assimilated?

Akenson argues that ethnic groups are a multi-generational phenomenon, and it is impossible to tell how long a sense of ethnicity will be passed through the generations.[35] For the Scotch-Irish, cultural continuities certainly existed in isolated backcountry settlements, where intra-marriage

---

30 Anbinder, *Nativism and Slavery*, 270–278.

31 Leyburn, *Scotch Irish*, xi, 317–325.

32 David N. Doyle, 'The Irish and Christian Churches in America', in *America and Ireland, 1776–1976: The American Identity and the Irish Connection*, ed. David N. Doyle and Owen Dudley Edwards (Westport, Conn.: Greenwood Press, 1980), 178; Akenson, *Irish Diaspora*, 272–273.

33 John William Ward, *Andrew Jackson: Symbol for an Age* (New York: Oxford University Press, 1955), 207–213.

34 See Leyburn, *Scotch-Irish*; Keller, 'What is Distinctive'; Doyle, 'Scots Irish or Scotch Irish'.

35 Akenson, 'Historiography of the Irish', 100. For more exploration of 'multigenerational ethnic groups', see Akenson's 'No Petty People: Pakena History and the Historiography of the Irish Diaspora', in *A Distant Shore: Irish Migration & New Zealand Settlement*, ed. Lyndon Fraser (Dunedin: University of Otago Press, 2000).

within the community was common.[36] Their sense of ethnicity was also renewed through continued emigration from Ulster. There was a significant number of newer arrivals, with a steady but declining stream of Ulster Protestant immigrants coming to the United States up to the 1920s. By the turn of the century, Ulster immigrants accounted for 19 per cent of all Irish immigrants to the United States.[37] Half of these were Catholic, meaning about 10 per cent of all Irish immigrants were Ulster Protestants – not an insignificant number.

Newcomers played important roles in filling the ranks of the American Orange Order.[38] Even in the SISA, which is generally associated with more distant Ulster ancestry, at least 20 per cent of members, and perhaps many more, had themselves emigrated from Ireland.[39] Undoubtedly, with waves of migration lasting over centuries, the levels of acculturation and assimilation into American society were extremely varied. Their perceptions and experiences of Ireland would encompass a wide range of views, as Irish Protestants themselves were a diverse group.[40] By the late nineteenth and early twentieth centuries, their views and experiences of the United States also differed dramatically. This is emphasized through Scotch-Irish support for Republicans, Democrats, and third parties at various elections throughout this era.[41] The Scotch-Irish were neither unified in their political views nor in their attitudes toward America and Ireland.

In his now-classic work on Irish-American nationalism, Brown posits that the great motivating factor behind enthusiastic interest in Irish nationalism lay in American political, social, and economic conditions.[42] Like their Catholic counterparts, the Scotch-Irish were motivated by American circumstances and their quest for advancement within American society. Even those who promoted celebration of Scotch-Irish ethnic heritage anxiously emphasized their allegiance to America first and foremost.[43]

---

36 Doyle, 'Scots Irish or Scotch Irish', 168–169.
37 Kenny, *American Irish*, 182; Jones, 'Scotch-Irish', 905–907.
38 See transfer certificates from Lily of the Valley Loyal Orange Lodge (LOL) No. 167, folders 2, 4–9, 12–18, Historical Society of Pennsylvania (HSP) MSS 103.
39 Calculated based on the biographies of members in the report of the Fifth Congress. I divided the number who declared an Irish birthplace by the total number of biographies; however, a significant number do not list a birthplace. *The Scotch-Irish in America: Proceedings and Addresses of the Fifth Congress, at Springfield, O., May 11–14, 1893* (Nashville: Barbee & Smith). Hereafter the meetings of the SISA will be denoted by the congress number. See bibliography for further publication information.
40 Miller, 'Ulster Presbyterians', 264–265.
41 For political views, see, for example, *Evening Star* 1 Nov 1888; *NYT* 25 Jul 1900; *Purple Bell* 25 Oct 1902; Higham, *Strangers in the Land*, 85–87.
42 Brown, *Irish-American Nationalism*.
43 McKee, 'Peculiar and Royal Race', 75.

As white Protestants whose families had originated in Great Britain, the Scotch-Irish could choose to join the legions of 'invisible immigrants' in the United States. The Anglo-Irish, who probably made up the overall majority of Irish Protestant immigrants, were likely subsumed as 'invisible immigrants', as there is little indication of their collective fate in the historiography.[44] For both the Anglo-Irish and Scotch-Irish, cultural differences were masked by common language and their ability to move more quickly into higher-paid jobs than most immigrants because of the industrial nature of British society.[45] They could emphasize Anglo-Saxon or Scottish ties, joining numerous popular organizations which celebrated Anglo-Saxonism and promoted closer British-American relations. The Loyal Coalition, English-Speaking Union, Ulster League of North America, British-American League, and others promoted pro-British, though not always anti-Irish nationalist, agendas.[46] Membership in Anglo-Saxonist and nativist organizations, in which many Protestant Irish joined with immigrants from Great Britain, could also encapsulate anti-Catholic and anti-Irish viewpoints.[47] Many Scotch-Irish joined such organizations as the American Protestant Association and the American Protective Association, which had close ties with the Orange Order.[48]

As emigrants from Ireland, the Scotch-Irish could continue the traditions of their United Irish forebears and forge ties with Irish-American nationalism in spite of its close association with the Catholic Church. Indeed, for years Irish Protestants had led such organizations as the Irish Society of Boston and the Society of Friendly Sons of St. Patrick, and during the Home Rule era Protestants continued as a source of support for Irish nationalism.[49] With their diverse backgrounds, coming out of Ireland throughout a wide period of time and representing a multitude of different political and social viewpoints, the Scotch-Irish were in a unique position among American ethnic groups. Those who joined such organizations as the SISA and the LOI were choosing to celebrate and promote a specifically Scotch-Irish ethnic heritage.

---

44 Akenson, *Irish Diaspora*, 252–253; Thomas J. Archdeacon, *Becoming American: An Ethnic History* (New York: Free Press, 1983), 52–53, 109–110.
45 Charlotte Erickson, *Invisible Immigrants: The Adaptation of English and Scottish Immigrants in Nineteenth-Century America* (London: Weidenfeld & Nicolson, 1972); Berthoff, *British Immigrants*; Blethen and Wood, Introduction, 2–4.
46 Carroll, *American Opinion*, 170–171, 278–279; Berthoff, *British Immigrants*, 200–205.
47 Dinnerstein et al., *Natives and Strangers*.
48 Kenny, *American Irish*, 158–159; Jones, 'Scotch-Irish', 906. On relationship between Anglo-Saxonism and Home Rule, see L.P. Curtis, Jr., *Anglo-Saxons and Celts: A Study of Anti-Irish Prejudice in Victorian England* (Bridgeport, Conn.: University of Bridgeport, 1968), 90–101.
49 Mary C. Kelly, 'The Hand of Friendship: Protestants, Irish Americans, and 1916-Era Nationalism', in *Ireland's Allies: America and the 1916 Easter Rising*, ed. Miriam Nyhan Grey (Dublin: University College Dublin Press, 2016), 229–237.

Scotch-Irish Society of America

Throughout the late nineteenth century, Americans celebrated their ethnic heritage though the formation of historical associations commemorating the achievements of their ancestors. Groups asserted older American roots against the newer tide of emigrants from eastern and southern Europe.[50] Seeing the ways in which such groups as the New England Puritans, Dutch-Americans, and German-Americans memorialized their historic contributions to America, several Scotch-Irish were driven to form their own ethnic society.

Colonel Thomas T. Wright, a Nashville businessman, was credited with the idea of an organization to 'record and make history of the achievements of the Scotch-Irish race'.[51] He contacted Governor of Tennessee Robert Love Taylor, and received an enthusiastic response to his proposition of forming a Scotch-Irish society.[52] Around the same time, other Scotch-Irish also discussed the formation of an ethnic society. In July 1884, preliminary meetings were held in Belfast, where several prominent Scotch-Irish were gathered for a meeting of the Pan-Presbyterian Alliance. Princeton University President James McCosh, a transplanted Scot, encouraged New York Presbyterian minister John Hall and Princeton biology professor George Macloskie to seek to bring together America's Scotch-Irish into greater community.[53] Hall's close friend Robert Bonner, owner and publisher of the *New York Ledger*, was to be the society's first president. Taylor put Wright in contact with Bonner and they corresponded extensively, planning the first mass meeting. With the aim of celebrating the history and achievements of the Scotch-Irish in America, the planning for the first Scotch-Irish congress began in 1888. Taylor supported the congress by issuing hundreds of invitations to prominent Scotch-Irish individuals and publishing a general call in a thousand leading newspapers.[54] The SISA was formed at the congress, held from 8 to 11 May 1889 in Columbia, Tennessee. At the first congress itself, newspapers reported anywhere from 6,000 to 10,000 attendees.

Bonner emphasized that the society was non-political and non-sectarian, with membership open to anyone with Ulster Scots ancestry regardless

---

50   Schlesinger, 'Biography of a Nation', 19; *Philadelphia Inquirer* 27 May 1890.
51   SISA First Congress, 3; John J. Appel, *Immigrant Historical Societies in the United States, 1880–1950* (New York: Arno, 1980), 64–68. Appel notes that Wright's troubled relationship with Robert Bonner meant his role in running the society was very limited.
52   *Galveston Daily News* 10 May 1891.
53   For the background of this meeting, see Macloskie's eulogy of Hall in SISA Ninth Congress, 246.
54   SISA First Congress, 6–7. See also account of the first congress in *Chicago Daily Inter-Ocean* 10 May 1889.

of religion. Nevertheless, the society was dominated by Presbyterians. Society leaders were determined that the organization would be thoroughly American, not involving itself with any other nation. Throughout each of the ten congresses held between 1889 and 1901, society members were mainly concerned with underscoring their differences with New England Puritans and Irish Catholic immigrants. They were adamant about the unique status of the Scotch-Irish in the history of the American republic, emphasizing their role as pioneers of civilization and guardians of American freedom. Society members hoped to promote social networking amongst the Scotch-Irish, particularly encouraging 'a better acquaintance between northern and southern members of the race'.[55] Twenty-four years after the end of the Civil War and twelve years after the end of Reconstruction, sectional divides were still strongly felt in the United States. Many members of the SISA had proudly participated on one side or the other during the Civil War, but hoped the society would help to erase persisting sectional divides. Tennessee itself was chosen as the location of the first congress because of its historic role as a place of settlement for the Scotch-Irish and home of perhaps the most famous Scotch-Irishman, Andrew Jackson, as well as its central location between north and south.

The society worked to advance the study of Scotch-Irish history, believing that their 'race', while greatly contributing to the formation of America, was behind other ethnicities in the celebration of 'race pride'.[56] Speakers recounted the history of the Scotch-Irish during ancient times, the plantation of Ulster, the emigration across the Atlantic, and the foundation of the American republic. Colonel E.C. McDowell claimed ancient Irish roots for the Scotch-Irish ethnicity. 'In the sixth century, a colony of these Irish-Scots migrated to Northern Britain', from Ireland, he stated in the first congress's opening address, 'and settling in what is now the county of Argyle, established a kingdom, subjugating the Pictish tribes that were before them, and ancient Caledonia was thenceforward the land of the Scots, and Scotland it remains today'.[57] Far from rejecting the Irish part of their identity, the Scotch-Irish claimed to be twice Irish, because the settlers of Scotland had originally migrated from Ireland. Characteristics attributed to the Scotch-Irish 'race' were described as combining the best elements of both the Scottish and the Irish. Dr. D.C. Kelley explained, 'We have thus the indomitable, prudent, calculating, metaphysical, God-fearing, tyrant-hating Scotch, brought by marriage into blood relationship with the brave, reckless, emotional, intuitive, God-loving, liberty-adoring Irish'. This

---

55 SISA First Congress, 4; Appel, *Immigrant Historical Societies*, 53.
56 SISA First Congress, 4.
57 SISA First Congress, 25.

was an ideal combination, he continued, because 'we find these people the cautious builders of free constitutional government, and, at the same time, the pioneers of American civilization'.[58]

Though the society was able to attract thousands of attendees in its early years, in many ways it was driven by Bonner, Hall, and Philadelphia Reverend John S. MacIntosh as individuals. Bonner grew up in Ramelton, County Donegal, and immigrated to the United States in 1839 where he eventually became the owner and publisher of the *New York Ledger*. He was re-elected president of the society every year until his death in 1899.[59] Bonner was a member of the Fifth Avenue Presbyterian Church in New York City, where Hall served as minister. Hall was born in rural County Armagh. He worked as a Presbyterian missionary in County Roscommon during the latter years of the Famine, then became the pastor of the Presbyterian church in the city of Armagh. He came to America as part of an Irish Presbyterian deputation in 1867, and soon after was called to the pastorate of the Fifth Avenue Church. He had been in the United States for twenty-two years at the time of the first congress.[60] MacIntosh was born in Philadelphia in 1839 to Scotch-Irish parents. He moved to Ireland with his family when he was very young, and was educated in Belfast, Edinburgh, and Germany. He worked as a minister at Belfast's May Street Presbyterian Church. MacIntosh went to the United States as a delegate for the Pan-Presbyterian Alliance in 1880, where he received the call to the Second Presbyterian Church of Philadelphia.[61]

Though these three and many other members of the society had relatively recent direct connections to Ireland, the society itself hardly ever examined the Scotch-Irish as an immigrant group after the time of Andrew Jackson. They reinforced the idea of the Scotch-Irish as an old, mainly pre-Revolutionary immigrant group. This implied a distinct split between the Scotch-Irish and the Famine emigration of the Catholic Irish, as well as placing themselves on an equal footing with the Puritans. The Scotch-Irish underscored their differences with Puritans while emphasizing their own roles as pioneers of civilization and guardians of American freedom. The Puritans dominated the writing of American history, whereas the Scotch-Irish saw themselves as 'doers' rather than writers and had neglected to record their own contributions. They were adamant about their

58 SISA First Congress, 140.
59 *NYT* 7 Jul 1899. See Appel, *Immigrant Historical Societies*, 58–60; Thomas C. Hall, *John Hall, Pastor and Preacher: A Biography* (New York: Fleming H. Revell, 1901), 221–222.
60 *NYT*, 18 Sep 1898, 5 Oct 1898. See Appel, *Immigrant Historical Societies*, 60–62; Hall, *John Hall*, 296–297.
61 Appel, *Immigrant Historical Societies*, 62–63.

unique role in the formation of the American republic, and anxious to set themselves apart from the Puritans. MacIntosh explained, 'The world has in the Scotch-Irish a man as distinct from the Puritan as the Puritan is from all other men'.[62] McDowell portrayed the Puritans and Scotch-Irish as having essentially different philosophies on the relationship between the individual and the state. The Puritan ideal was to get the greatest aggregate good for the community, meaning that the individual and family were subordinate to the state. In contrast, for the Scotch-Irish, 'the state is made by and for the people'.[63] This emphasis on the role of the individual led to the important contributions of the Scotch-Irish within American society, distinct from Puritan involvement.

In their rhetoric, the Scotch-Irish were much more interested in contrasting their historic role in the United States against that of older migrant groups such as the Puritans rather than creating a separate identity from the newer Catholic emigrants from Ireland.[64] They were never overtly anti-Catholic. It is difficult to say how much they were actually motivated by the need to form a distinct identity from the Catholic Irish, especially considering that by claiming a Scotch-Irish identity they were asserting an overarching Irish character. Because many Scotch-Irish families had been in America for generations, it was unlikely that any such individuals would be mistaken for more recent Catholic Irish immigrants. Despite frequent assertions that they were a non-sectarian body, the society dealt with a persistent public perception of sectarianism. At one congress business meeting, a resolution was proposed stating, 'That there may be no apprehension as to the purpose of this society, we hereby declare that we are not organized in antagonism to any class of the Irish or Scotch races, from whatever source they may derive their origin'. Hall argued that such a resolution would put the society on the defensive, and he believed they should try to appear as if they never considered the idea of anti-Catholicism.[65] Bonner emphasized, 'Whatever our respective opinions may be as to either religion or politics, or however zealous we may be in advocating them elsewhere, we neither introduce nor discuss them here'.[66]

A church service conducted by a team of Presbyterian ministers became an annual feature of the congresses. The role of the Scotch-Irish in building the American Presbyterian Church was frequently celebrated, and at times the Scotch-Irish were contrasted with Catholic Irish immigrants.[67] John

---

62 SISA First Congress, 195.
63 SISA First Congress, 195.
64 McKee, 'Peculiar and Royal Race', 68–69.
65 SISA Second Congress, 59–60.
66 SISA Third Congress, 26.
67 SISA Third Congress, 214–215.

Appel believes that some of the members did have anti-Catholic intentions in their participation in the society. There were connections between some SISA members and the fiercely anti-Catholic American Protective Association.[68] Even if creating a separate identity from the Catholic Irish was not an overt purpose of the society, there is no doubt that the Scotch-Irish were conscious throughout their congresses of tenuous links with the Catholic Irish and perceptions of sectarianism.

Some Irish-Americans objected to the formation of a Scotch-Irish society on the grounds that it propagated a myth. Largely in reaction to the SISA and the growth of Scotch-Irish ethnic celebrations, the American Irish Historical Society (AIHS) was established in Boston in January 1897. Appel asserts that Boston newspaper debates over the existence of Scotch-Irish ethnicity and the 1895 Little Red Schoolhouse Riot also spurred the formation of the AIHS.[69] The journal of the AIHS and publications of its members accused the Scotch-Irish of falsifying history, attacking them as 'defamers' of the Irish. The AIHS denounced the term 'Scotch-Irish' as a 'delusion'. John C. Linehan wrote that the prejudices of Scotch-Irish writers 'blind their love of truth' as they created 'a new race'.[70] Michael J. O'Brien challenged the idea that there were two traditions in Irish-American history. He contended that early Ulster Protestant immigrants to America were fully 'Irish' in identity. O'Brien emphasized the importance of colonial Catholic migrations from Ireland. The *Irish World* was also critical of the promotion of 'Scotch-Irish' ethnicity, asserting the Irish identity of the early migrants in the American colonies, denying that Ulster was a Protestant province, and declaring the Scotch-Irish neither Irish nor Scottish but instead mongrels. 'Every other man has a country and loves his country', stated one article, 'but here is a creature who hates the land of his birth and loves only her enemies!'[71] The positions of the AIHS and *Irish World* show the controversy

---

68 Appel, *Immigrant Historical Societies*, 74; Donald L. Kinzer, *An Episode in Anti-Catholicism: The American Protective Association* (Seattle: University of Washington Press, 1964), 219.

69 Lee, 'Introduction', 3; Leyburn, *Scotch-Irish*, 327–334; Akenson, *Irish Diaspora*, 254–255; John J. Appel, 'The New England Origins of the American Irish Historical Society', *New England Quarterly* 33, no. 4 (Dec 1960); Samuel Swett Green, 'Scotch-Irish in America' (Worcester, Mass.: Charles Hamilton, 1895), appendix. For more on the Little Red Schoolhouse Riot, see O'Connor, *Boston Irish*, 153–156.

70 John C. Linehan, *The Irish Scots and the 'Scotch-Irish': An Historical and Ethnological Monograph* (Concord: AIHS, 1902), 7. See also J.D. O'Connell, The 'Scotch-Irish' Delusion in America: Historical Reply to President Eliot of Harvard College (Washington, DC: AIHS, 1897); Joseph Smith, *The 'Scotch-Irish' Shibboleth Analyzed and Rejected, with Some Reference to the Present 'Anglo-Saxon' Comedy* (Washington, DC: AIHS, 1898).

71 *Irish World* 7 Jun 1890, 16 Jul 1892, 12 Jan 1895, 13 Jun 1896, 24 Oct 1896, 2 Jul 1898.

of the Scotch-Irish ethnicity. No matter how often the society claimed
to be non-sectarian, it was seen as inherently divisive by members of the
Irish-American community.

From 1889 to 1896, the SISA met annually at congresses in Pittsburgh,
Pennsylvania; Louisville, Kentucky; Atlanta, Georgia; Springfield, Ohio;
Des Moines, Iowa; Lexington, Virginia; and Harrisburg, Pennsylvania. The
Pittsburgh congress in 1890 was probably the most successful year, with
President Benjamin Harrison in attendance. Society secretary A.C. Floyd
wrote,

> In attendance was the president of the United States and members of
> his cabinet, governors of great states, judges of the highest tribunals,
> divines, editors, and congressmen, celebrated lawyers and physicians,
> noted bankers, merchants and manufacturers, substantial farmers,
> mechanics – every trade and profession represented by its best
> elements.[72]

Floyd estimated that 12,000 people 'eagerly sought attendance' to the
congress.[73] The society's leaders believed that with this congress they
achieved worldwide prestige and the notice of the world's press. The Belfast
Chamber of Commerce even delegated one of its ex-presidents, Francis
D. Ward, as a representative to the congress, though he failed to attend,
pleading exhaustion from his travels around the United States.[74]

The society was determined to gain further attention and create a global
Scotch-Irish network through increased communications. They received
congratulatory cablegrams from the mayor and citizens of Belfast, the US
consul in Edinburgh, Wallace Bruce, the mayor of Londonderry, and even
Scotch-Irish citizens of Mexico and the Mexican president, Porfirio Díaz.[75]
MacIntosh, as the society's vice-president general, reported that one of the
duties he took up was wide-ranging correspondence with representatives of
the Scotch-Irish ethnicity throughout the world. He focused particularly on
Ulster and the Scottish lowlands, he explained, 'but it has reached farther
than that, because there are leading men of our blood and kin in Britain,
India, China, and Australia, who in various ways I have been striving
to interest in our work'.[76] MacIntosh was chiefly interested in collecting
personal and inherited recollections, and genealogies written into family

---

72 SISA Second Congress, 7–8; *Washington Post* 1 Jun 1890. On Floyd, see Appel,
     Immigrant Historical Societies, 68.
73 SISA Second Congress, 8.
74 SISA Third Congress, 31; *Rocky Mountain News* 6 Apr 1891.
75 SISA Second Congress, 15, 74; SISA Third Congress, 14–15.
76 SISA Fifth Congress, 45–46.

Bibles. The society sent out its annual volumes of congress proceedings to its members, as well as various libraries around the country. Through the proliferation of these volumes, they believed they were making an impact on the field of American history.[77] The national Scotch-Irish Society also spawned state affiliates in California, Pennsylvania, Tennessee, Virginia, North Carolina, Alabama, Kentucky, Georgia, and Iowa, as well as a Scotch-Irish Society in Atlanta.

Though a large portion of the congresses was dedicated to recounting the role of the Scotch-Irish in American history, speakers did not ignore the current conditions of Ireland. They revealed that they closely monitored relations between Britain, Ireland, and America. Hall was by far the most outspoken society member on Irish matters. He travelled back to his Ulster homeland every summer. It was his regular duty to report on the state of Ireland at each congress. Hall informed the attendees of life in Ulster, how the Ulster Scots' educational and religious values connected them to their Scotch-Irish brethren, and the role of the Presbyterian Church in Ulster society. He especially hoped to counter the American perception that all of the Irish were Catholic.[78]

Hall also emphasized the progression of Ireland's condition over time. Hall considered himself a pronounced Liberal, and according to his son was fascinated by parliamentary debates.[79] Hall frequently stressed that Ulster's political, economic, and social situation had greatly improved within his lifetime, particularly over the course of the previous decade. This indicated support for Conservative policies of constructive unionism. Despite society restrictions on explicit statements of political views, Hall clearly advocated self-determination for Ulster, which implied maintenance of the Union. 'I have had the opportunity to know Ireland', he explained,

> I was born there and brought up there, and I labored for years in Ulster as a minister. I know the whole land, and I tell you, my brethren, that I am not speaking of American politics, but of something in another land – that what is wanted is not to carry out the policy that has been advanced by one great and distinguished man [Gladstone], but to educate her people, train them, inspire them with the thoughts, purposes, and convictions that have made these United States, in the face of difficulties and discouragements what, through the blessings of God Almighty, these United States are to–day.[80]

77 SISA Sixth Congress, 18–19.
78 SISA First Congress, 108. On Hall, see Appel, *Immigrant Historical Societies*, 78–79.
79 Hall, *John Hall*, 139, 261.
80 SISA Third Congress, 188–190.

In 1892, Hall spoke of the Ulster Protestants' fear of Gladstone coming back into power, with the certain renewal of Home Rule policies. He explained that various denominations of Protestants had leagued together to protest against Gladstone's policies.

> My convictions are founded substantially upon that ground that they [Ulster Protestants] take, and, ladies and gentlemen, if you accept to be true those most eloquent statements that were made to us last night and which you applauded, regarding the prudence, the wisdom, the foresight, the sagacity, the integrity of my countrymen and the people of my race, the Scotch-Irish race – if you accept all those, then you must surely come to the conclusion that it is not without reason that this attitude of antagonism is taken to what is known commonly as the Home Rule policy. (Applause.)[81]

The following year, Hall again called on his fellow Scotch-Irish to think of their Ulster brethren. He hoped that Gladstone and the Liberal party would have their eyes opened to see clearly the situation in Ireland, 'and when this is the case, the Protestants of Ireland, that are a unit upon this broad matter, will no longer be filled with apprehension as to perils that may come upon them if the policy of Mr. Gladstone's government should be carried into execution'.[82]

Not only did Hall state his support for unionism, his speeches also reflected the expectation that other members of the society closely followed British and Irish events. Hall hoped that the identification of the Ulstermen with the qualities celebrated by the Scotch-Irish would legitimize the cause of unionism for members of the SISA. If the Ulstermen, like the Scotch-Irish, possessed all of these positive qualities, then they must be justified in their demands for the maintenance of the Union. Others in the society also commented on Irish politics. MacIntosh connected the Home Rule question with the Ulstermen's traditional claim as fighters for liberty, saying,

> The world is hearing a vast deal of the 'Irish Question'. That political porcupine, in its later form, came forth to light in Ulster; and it was selfish English statesmen and most despotic churchmen started it. Though, at this hour, the Ulstermen, as a body, refuse to join with the Nationalists of to-day, Ulster and its wrongs and fierce revolt are the beginning of the later land and folk fights. The Ulsterman was the brewer of the storm. He became the 'Volunteer' for freedom.[83]

81 SISA Fourth Congress, 155–156.
82 SISA Sixth Congress, 70.
83 SISA Second Congress, 100.

The mayor of Springfield, Ohio, James Johnson, urged the society to take a stand on the Home Rule issue, stating,

It if shall be the wisdom of this congress to give expression to its sentiments on the momentous question now pending in which the fate of the mother country is involved, that expression shall display to the world that the Scotch-Irish of America have full confidence in the independence and ability of their race to maintain itself, whatever may be the issue of that question, and that fear, despair, and discouragement have no place in the breast of a genuine Scotch-Irishman. (Applause.)[84]

Dr. William C. Gray, at the sixth congress in 1894, made probably the most extreme recorded statement of support for the Ulster unionists. Gray went so far as praising the efforts of unionist militants: 'It is only a year or so ago that they turned out and organized military companies, and began to drill for the purpose of fighting the queen's government for the privilege of remaining subjects of her government. The like of that was never seen or heard of in the world before'. Gray hoped if Home Rule was passed England would not interfere as the rest of Ireland tried to handle Ulster. He was sure of the outcome: 'The croppies would lie down again. The Scotch-Irish would be found, as soon as the smoke cleared away, where they are everywhere and always: on top'. Gray believed the Scotch-Irish were created in such a way that they would not bend their knees to anyone but God.[85] In contrast, the Atlanta Scotch-Irish Society did not view Ireland as divided along denominational lines. One speech in 1891 even called for the Scotch-Irish to 'make peace between their brethren' and to follow the self-government initiatives of 'the great peacemaker Gladstone'. This was an explicit endorsement of Home Rule that indicated inclusivity and flexibility of Irishness in the southern states.[86]

Two of the society's most illustrious speakers over the years also could not resist giving their opinions on Irish politics. The future Democratic vice president under Grover Cleveland, Adlai E. Stevenson I, gave a speech in 1891 entitled, 'The Scotch-Irish of the Bench and Bar'. Stevenson, whose grandfather was born in Scotland and migrated to Ulster and later the United States, stated that Ireland was in contrast with the United States, where the Scotch-Irish were enjoying liberty in the highest degree.

---

84 SISA Fifth Congress, 25.
85 SISA Sixth Congress, 118.
86 Quoted in Gleeson, 'Smaller Differences', 88–91.

Our thoughts on such an occasion turn to unfortunate Ireland, the ancestral home of our race. Oppressed by merciless exactions, with cruel landlordism, the heritage of each succeeding generation yet struggling against odds for a larger measure of freedom, Ireland challenges at once our sympathy and our admiration. May we not believe that the morning of a brighter day is soon to dawn upon that gallant people, and that the fruits of centuries of suffering, of oppression, and of toil will be to them as to us the principle in action of our race, 'individual freedom and home rule'.[87]

While Stevenson supported the Irish nationalist sentiments of his Democratic Party, William McKinley was only slightly less forthright in his opinions.

McKinley was, at the time of his appearance at the Scotch-Irish congress in 1893, the Republican governor of Ohio. His speech focused mainly on the Scotch-Irish role in America. He stated, 'The Scotch-Irish would not change either ancestry or birthplace if they could. They are proud of both; but they are prouder yet of their new home they have helped to create under the stars and stripes, the best and freest under the sun'. He then briefly touched on the situation in Ireland, saying,

To the Ulsterman across the ocean, to the Celt south of him, each with his virtues, and his faults, I cannot but say in the tender, pleasing language of the venerable Gladstone, the greatest living Englishman: 'Let me entreat you – and if it were with my last breath I would entreat you – to let the dead bury its dead, to cast behind you every recollection of bygone evils, and cherish, to love, to sustain one another through all vicissitudes of human affairs in the times that are to come'.[88]

Gladstone had said these words at the end of his speech introducing the second Home Rule Bill on 13 February 1893, entreating his fellow MPs to support his Irish policy.[89]

Macloskie explained Ulster unionist attitudes to Irish Home Rule at the eighth congress in 1896. He compared contemporary Ulster with 'the good old times', explaining that conditions had greatly improved and the attitude of the British government toward Ireland had changed for the better. According to Macloskie, Ulster unionists believed that,

87 SISA Third Congress, 94.
88 SISA Fifth Congress, 19. Along with McKinley, Theodore Roosevelt also exhibited interest in the revival of Scotch-Irish ethnicity. In his *Winning of the West*, he described Irish Presbyterians as leaders in the push westward, with emphasis on their values of democracy, education, and religion. See Leyburn, *Scotch-Irish*, 318.
89 PD 4th Ser., Vol. 8, 1275.

any independent government which the majority of Irish voters would be able to establish would be a change greatly for the worse. They have observed the methods of the Parnellites and anti-Parnellites under circumstances which should have elicited self-denial, caution, and true patriotism; they have observed the sort of statesmanship exhibited by some of our Irishmen in the great cities of America; after they have, by long and peaceful struggles, shaken off the tyranny of landlordism over their votes as well as their property, and the more galling tyranny of ecclesiasticism over their consciences, they are determined not to permit the reestablishment of a worse ascendancy by a majority who have shown no sympathy with the spirit or prosperity of the northern province. Their intense loyalty to England's crown and constitution, as now represented, is the strongest argument for this determined stand.[90]

Macloskie's sympathetic portrayal of the unionist cause was appended with a disclaimer that he personally did not take a side in the Home Rule argument, as he believed that it was his 'duty as an American citizen not to intermeddle in the politics of other countries'.[91] Even with these forays into Irish politics, America was still foremost in the minds of the Scotch-Irish. Benton McMillan, a United States Congressman from Tennessee, reflected on the society, stating, 'The reason I rejoice that there is Scotch-Irish in my veins, is not simply because it is Scotch-Irish, but because it gives a little more grit and a little more resolution to see the right and to have the courage to do it, and be a better American citizen; for, after all, my greatest ambition is to be one of the best American citizens'.[92] Members of the SISA were primarily driven by American circumstances, which influenced them to play down concerns over contemporary Ireland because they wanted to prove their loyalty to the United States.

The decline of the SISA was caused by several factors. The society had faced diminished attendance after the wildly successful second congress, and since 1894 had dealt with decreasing membership and financial instability.[93] After the eighth congress in Harrisburg, Detroit was chosen as the next host city. Arrangements were in place for a ninth congress when the Detroit Local Committee reported that they believed a successful meeting could not be held in that city. By that time it was too late to make other arrangements for 1897. The following year, the SISA planned a congress in Chicago.

90 SISA Eighth Congress, 103.
91 SISA Eighth Congress, 103.
92 SISA First Congress, 187–190.
93 Appel, *Immigrant Historical Societies*, 48–49.

That fell through when members of the Chicago Local Committee were called away due to the outbreak of the Spanish–American War.[94] Attempts to organize congresses in the following years failed due to the Executive Committee's disarray after the deaths of several key members. Bonner, Hall, and vice president Reverend John H. Bryson all died within the space of a year. Secretary A.C. Floyd had already resigned his position after eight years of service, meaning that there were few experienced leaders left in the Executive Committee.[95] By the time the ninth congress was finally held in 1900 in Knoxville, Tennessee, the society was irreparably damaged. After the Knoxville congress, the SISA managed one final congress in 1901 in Chambersburg, Pennsylvania, before the organization disintegrated.

The only state society to survive the demise of the national organization was the Pennsylvania Scotch-Irish Society (PSIS), founded in October 1889.[96] The PSIS flourished well into the twentieth century, eventually changing its name to the Scotch-Irish Society of the United States. They formed the Scotch-Irish Foundation, which was charged with preserving the history of Ulster, Scotland, and the Scotch-Irish in America. The PSIS's main event each year was an annual dinner, which attracted such speakers as future Presidents Woodrow Wilson and Herbert Hoover, Secretary of the Navy Hilary Herbert, and British Ambassador James Bryce, a Liberal Home Ruler.[97] The PSIS, much like its parent society, intended to promote the historical and literary side of Scotch-Irish identity. In 1911, on the recommendation of Woodrow Wilson, the PSIS commissioned Professor Henry Jones Ford of Princeton University to write the history of the Scotch-Irish.[98] Ford's *Scotch-Irish in America* was published in 1915. His book was one of a wave of new publications celebrating the role of the Scotch-Irish in America, including past president of the SISA, Oliver Perry Temple's *The Covenanter, the Cavalier, and the Puritan*; Charles Hanna's *The Scotch-Irish*; John Walker Dinsmore's *The Scotch-Irish in America*; and Charles Knowles Bolton's *Scotch Irish Pioneers in Ulster and America*.[99]

94 *Chicago Tribune* 12 Apr 1898, 17 Apr 1898.
95 Letter of explanation can be found in SISA Ninth Congress, 6–7.
96 *Philadelphia Inquirer* 29 Oct 1889.
97 *Philadelphia Inquirer* 16 Feb 1895; *NYT* 19 Feb 1909. See Official Programmes from PSIS Annual Dinners, Folder 5, Scotch-Irish Foundation Library and Archives Collection (SIF), HSP 3093; James Bryce, 'The Scoto-Irish Race in Ulster and in America: Address Delivered to the Scotch-Irish Society of Pennsylvania, February, 1909', in *University and Historical Addresses: Delivered During a Residence in the United States as Ambassador of Great Britain* (London: Macmillan, 1913).
98 Meeting of Council 21 Apr 1911, Meeting of Council 28 May 1915, *Council Minutes of Proceedings 12 Jan 1904–20 Dec 1922*, Vol. 9, SIF, HSP; Appel, *Immigrant Historical Societies*, 114–115.
99 Henry Jones Ford, *The Scotch-Irish in America* (Princeton, NJ: Princeton University

At the 19 February 1914 meeting of the council, the minutes reported that PSIS secretary Charles L. McKeehan presented a letter from a member 'suggesting that a telegram of sympathy be sent from the Pennsylvania Scotch-Irish Society to the Scotch-Irishmen of Ulster. After discussion it was moved, seconded and carried that it was unwise for the Society to take part in the present controversy regarding Home Rule in Ireland'.[100] The PSIS carried on the national organization's tradition of official silence on Irish political questions. There are indications that society members, particularly McKeehan, were deeply interested in the events unfolding in Ireland. The society elected a number of Ulstermen and their supporters as honorary members, ostensibly for their help in promoting Ford's book in Ireland, as well as for manifesting 'a very cordial and friendly interest in this Society'. These included Edward Carson; Reverend William Park, Presbyterian minister of Belfast's Rosemary Street church; Reverend James Barkley Woodburn, author of *The Ulster Scot: His History and Religion*; Professor James Heron of the Assembly's College, Belfast; Sir John Byers, Professor of Obstetric Medicine at Queen's University who was known for his interest in Ulster dialect and folklore; J.W. Kernohan, secretary of the Presbyterian Historical Society of Ireland; and Samuel Cunningham, the editor of the *Northern Whig*.[101]

McKeehan carried on extensive correspondence with Cunningham, including the exchanging of books and other ephemera. Cunningham sent McKeehan a copy of F.S. Oliver's *Alexander Hamilton*, to which McKeehan replied, 'I had read a couple of lives of Hamilton, and have also been quite familiar with his own writing. Oliver's treatment of the subject is most interesting and from a somewhat different point of view from the other lives I have read. I thank you very much for sending it to me'.[102] In a letter dated 5 April 1916, McKeehan wrote that he was enjoying Oliver's *Ordeal by Battle*, also sent by Cunningham. 'His chapters on "The Spirit of German Policy" are very able, though I am looking forward with still more interest to his

Press, 1915); Oliver Perry Temple, *The Covenanter, the Cavalier, and the Puritan* (Cincinnati: Robert Clarke Company, 1897); Charles A. Hanna, *The Scotch-Irish; or, the Scot in North Britain, North Ireland, and North America* (New York: G.P. Putnam, 1902); John Walker Dinsmore, *The Scotch-Irish in America: Their History, Traits, Institutions, and Influences, Especially as Illustrated in the Early Settlers of Western Pennsylvania and Their Descendants* (Chicago: Winona Publishing Company, 1906); Charles Knowles Bolton, *Scotch Irish Pioneers in Ulster and America* (Boston: Bacon and Brown, 1910).

100 Meeting of Council 19 Feb 1914, *Council Minutes of Proceedings*, SIF, HSP.

101 Meeting of Council 28 May 1915, *Council Minutes of Proceedings*, SIF, HSP.

102 McKeehan to Cunningham 18 Mar 1916, *Miscellaneous Correspondence 1916–1925*, Vol. 11, SIF, HSP; F.S. Oliver, *Alexander Hamilton: An Essay on American Union* (London: Archibald Constable, 1906).

chapters on "The Spirit of British Policy". I have noticed several references to the book in newspapers and periodicals commenting on Mr. Oliver's criticism of some aspects of British leadership during the war'.[103]

McKeehan credited Cunningham with initiating the 'pleasant and interesting connections that our Society has made in Ulster'.[104] McKeehan also corresponded with Kernohan at the Presbyterian Historical Society in Belfast, noting in 1916 that he sent Kernohan a copy of the PSIS annual report. He also had connections with Park, the pastor of the Rosemary Street congregation in Belfast. McKeehan wrote to Park in March 1916 that he was very glad to have him as a member of the PSIS, and heard that the meeting of the Pan-Presbyterian Alliance had been postponed due to the war. He then commented,

> The progress of the war is watched in this country with an interest second only to the interest felt in Europe. There is nothing neutral about the feelings of this country, in spite of those who would have you believe otherwise. I suppose there is no telling at all when the war will end, but it seems to be growing more and more clear, especially since the drive against Verdun, that Germany has passed the zenith of her strength, and from now on will grow weaker, while the Allies grow stronger.[105]

In addition to McKeehan's correspondence, other members of the PSIS such as Agnew T. Dice, the president of the Philadelphia & Reading Railway Company, also corresponded with Cunningham, Park, and Carson.[106]

After the Battle of the Somme, McKeehan encouraged PSIS members to raise funds to send to Ulster to help relieve distress. McKeehan himself had already donated money to the Ulster Volunteer Force (UVF) Hospital, which had been set up by the UVF Headquarters Council in connection with the War Office at the start of war.[107] At the 23 December 1916 meeting of council, McKeehan reminded the PSIS,

> That the Society had not done anything in a practical way to alleviate the distress in Ulster caused by the war, and after discussion, it was moved, seconded and carried, that Mr. Bayard Henry and the

---

103 McKeehan to Cunningham 5 Apr 1916, *Miscellaneous Correspondence*, SIF, HSP; F.S. Oliver, *Ordeal by Battle* (London: Macmillan, 1915).
104 McKeehan to Cunningham 18 Mar 1916, *Miscellaneous Correspondence*, SIF, HSP.
105 McKeehan to Kernohan 5 Apr 1916, McKeehan to Park 18 Mar 1916, *Miscellaneous Correspondence*, SIF, HSP.
106 H.V. Noble to Dice 3 Mar 1919, *Miscellaneous Correspondence*, SIF, HSP.
107 McKeehan to R. Dawson Bates 17 Feb 1916, *Miscellaneous Correspondence*, SIF, HSP.

Secretary be appointed a committee to raise a fund of not less than $500 among the members of the Society, and present it to the Ulster Volunteer Force Hospital for Wounded Soldiers and Sailors, as a memorial of the Society to the late John McIlhenny.[108]

The PSIS wished to memorialize John McIlhenny, an active member of the PSIS and former treasurer of the SISA born in Milford, County Armagh. McIlhenny, a gas meter magnate, had died on 23 February 1916.[109] At the February meeting of the PSIS council, McKeehan reported that the PSIS had raised a total of $1,000 to donate to the UVF Hospital. The money was sent to Belfast through Cunningham, 'from our Society for Ulster Volunteer Force Hospital in memory of John McIlhenny and in admiration of the splendid spirit of Ulster'.[110] McKeehan also arranged for the PSIS to donate $100 to the Scotch-Irish section of the British-Irish Relief Society bazaar in 1917, which was organized in part by Philadelphia Orange lodges.[111]

In addition to concerns over the relief of Ulster during the First World War, members of the PSIS took note of the influence of Irish-American nationalists and the United States government on Irish policy. On 8 June 1917, McKeehan wrote to Cunningham, 'I entirely agree with you as to America's interfering on the Irish question. On my return, I will send you something on this line for such use as you deem proper'.[112] The appeal to counter American involvement in the Irish question was repeated throughout the years following the First World War. In February 1921, for example, McKeehan wrote to the prospective speakers for the annual dinner that they should feel free to select whatever subject they wished, but if they cared 'to include in what I am sure will be a delightfully witty speech a word of advice to the effect that Americans should stop interfering in the Irish question, it will be entirely in order, and will, I think, strike a responsive chord'.[113] Though they did not directly take a stance on the Irish issue, the urging of the American government to stop interfering in the Irish question was a way to appear fully American while still expressing sympathy for the unionists in Ireland.

108 Meeting of Council 23 Dec 1916, *Council Minutes of Proceedings*, SIF, HSP.
109 See Appel, *Immigrant Historical Societies*, 64.
110 McKeehan to Cunningham (undated; late Dec 1916), McKeehan to Cunningham 1 Oct 1917, *Miscellaneous Correspondence*, SIF, HSP.
111 McKeehan to Bayard Henry 31 Mar 1917, *Miscellaneous Correspondence*, SIF, HSP.
112 McKeehan to Cunningham 8 Jun 1917, *Miscellaneous Correspondence*, SIF, HSP.
113 McKeehan to Judge Harold B. Wells, McKeehan to Rev. Charles Wadsworth, McKeehan to Gerald Campbell, all 10 Feb 1921, *Miscellaneous Correspondence*, SIF, HSP.

Loyal Orange Institution of the United States of America

Irish immigrants founded the first American Orange lodges in New York in the 1820s, affiliated with the Grand Lodge in Ireland. Lodges sprouted in east coast states such as New York, Pennsylvania, Delaware, Massachusetts, and Connecticut, with the first Orange parade held in Boston in 1824.[114] Throughout the nineteenth century, Orangeism gradually grew into a worldwide movement with especially strong presence in Canada where it transformed beyond an immigrant association to attract Protestants of all ethnicities.[115] In the United States, the organization remained limited particularly because of the challenges of adapting to republicanism. Support for the British Empire and monarchy was a major tenet of Orangeism in Ireland and British Commonwealth countries.[116] An 1880 newspaper announcement protested at the impression that members were allied with Great Britain, describing the Order as 'formed by persons desirous to the utmost of their power to support and defend the liberties (civil and religious) of the United States from the designs and intrigues of Popish mercenaries, as well as for the maintenance of the public peace and tranquility'.[117] Orangemen carefully constructed the rules of their organization so as to emphasize loyalties to the

---

114 David N. Doyle, 'Orange Order', in *Ireland and the Americas: Culture, Politics and History*, ed. James P. Byrne, Philip Coleman, and Jason King (Santa Barbara, Calif.: ABC-CLIO, 2008), 739–740; S.E. Long, 'The Orange Family Worldwide: The United States of America', in *A Celebration, 1690–1990: The Orange Institution*, ed. Billy Kennedy (Belfast: Grand Orange Lodge of Ireland, 1990), 86.

115 On Canadian Orangeism, which has a much larger literature than that of America, see Cecil J. Houston and William J. Smyth, 'Transferred Loyalties: Orangeism in the United States and Ontario', *American Review of Canadian Studies* 14, no. 2 (Summer 1984); Houston and Smyth, *Irish Emigration and Canadian Settlement: Patterns, Links, and Letters* (Toronto: University of Toronto Press, 1990), 180–187; Houston and Smyth, *The Sash Canada Wore: A Historical Geography of the Orange Order in Canada* (Toronto: University of Toronto Press, 1980); William Jenkins, 'Ulster Transplanted: Irish Protestants, Everyday Life and Constructions of Identity in Late Victorian Toronto', in *Irish Protestant Identities*, ed. Mervyn Busteed, Frank Neal, and Jonathan Tonge (Manchester: Manchester University Press, 2008); Billy Kennedy, 'The Orange Family Worldwide: Canada', in *A Celebration, 1690–1990: The Orange Institution*, ed. Billy Kennedy (Belfast: Grand Orange Lodge of Ireland, 1990); David A. Wilson, 'The Irish in Canada' (Ottawa: Canadian Historical Association, 1989); *The Orange Order in Canada*, ed. David A. Wilson (Dublin: Four Courts Press, 2007); Donald M. MacRaild, 'The Orange Atlantic', in *The Irish in the Atlantic World*, ed. David T. Gleeson (Columbia: University of South Carolina Press, 2010); William J. Smyth, *Toronto, the Belfast of Canada: The Orange Order and the Shaping of Municipal Culture* (Toronto: University of Toronto Press, 2015); Robert McLaughlin, 'Irish Nationalism and Orange Unionism in Canada: A Reappraisal', *Éire-Ireland* 41, no. 3/4 (Fall/Winter 2006).

116 Long, 'Orange Family Worldwide', 86; Houston and Smyth, 'Transferred Loyalties', 200–203.

117 *Chicago Daily Inter-Ocean* 29 May 1880.

United States: only naturalized American citizens and immigrants who were already Orangemen were allowed to become members of American lodges, which limited organizational growth.[118]

After the Irish Orange Order was dissolved in 1836, Orange members in the United States turned to other organizations such as the American Protestant Association and the Know Nothing party as alternatives to Orange lodges. Later, the Orange Order was closely associated with the American Protective Association and the second generation of the Ku Klux Klan in the 1920s.[119] The abundance of these nativist organizations in part explains the relative weakness of the Orange Order in the United States especially compared to the prolific Canadian Orange Order.[120] By the 1850s, five states had Orange charters. Application was made to the Grand Lodge of Ireland for National Grand Lodge status in the United States, approved in 1870, in the midst of a wider anti-Catholic resurgence in the United States.[121] In the United States as in the wider Orange world, members navigated a path between violence and respectability, as riots marked participation in the organization in Ulster, Canada, Britain, Australasia, and America. Orangeism provided its members with a network throughout the English-speaking world as well as a prescribed world view. While the numbers of Orangemen in the United States were never close to those achieved by their Canadian counterpart, Orange lodge members received similar benefits. Donald MacRaild describes Orange lodges as encompassing a 'social club, pseudo-religious sect, benefit society, and militant political movement' for the Ulster immigrants.[122] As described in a newspaper announcement, part of the purpose of the Orange Order was to 'afford assistance to distressed members of the order and otherwise promote such laudable and benevolent purposes as may tend to the due ordering of religious and Christian charity'.[123] Through such mutual benefits, membership in the Orange Order helped new immigrants find a place within American society.

---

118 Houston and Smyth, 'Transferred Loyalties', 200–203.
119 The Supreme Grand Master of the Orange Order, W.J.H. Traynor, also became president of the APA in 1893. The *NYT* ran a series of articles on the connections between the APA and the Orange Order from June to July 1894. See also Berthoff, *British Immigrants in Industrial America*, 201; Kinzer, *Episode in Anti-Catholicism*, 59, 73, 92, 100.
120 Donald M. MacRaild, *Faith, Fraternity, and Fighting: The Orange Order and Irish Migrants in Northern England, c.1850–1920* (Liverpool: Liverpool University Press, 2005), 299–300.
121 Long, 'Orange Family Worldwide', 86; Higham, *Strangers in the Land*, 61.
122 Donald M. MacRaild, 'The Associationalism of the Orange Diaspora', *The Orange Order in Canada*, ed. David A. Wilson (Dublin: Four Courts Press, 2007), 26; MacRaild, 'Orange Atlantic', 308–309.
123 *Chicago Daily Inter-Ocean* 29 May 1880.

The core beliefs of Orangeism were preserved no matter where the lodge was located. The Orange Order's assertion of a Protestant libertarian vision was transferred from Ireland to the United States, nurtured by transatlantic visits from such figures as William Johnston of Ballykilbeg.[124] Ties to Ulster were emphasized through the names of lodges such as the American Sons of William, Apprentice Boys, Enniskillen True Blues, and Derry Walls. Other lodges had wholly American names such as Abraham Lincoln, George Washington, and Daughters of John Adams, a Ladies' Lodge. At 12 July parades, Orangemen in the United States sang songs which would have been familiar to Ulster Orangemen, such as 'Boyne Water', 'Croppies Lie Down', and 'Protestant Boys'.[125] Irish politics and influence of Irish nationalists in the United States remained important to American Orangemen. They combined their promotion of Irish unionism and traditional Orange values with advocacy of anti-Catholic policies in the United States that were shared with the wider nativist movement. Despite these attempts at nativist appeals, both the Orange Order and Irish Catholic groups at times faced criticism for bringing the conflicts of Ireland to American soil.[126]

With an increased presence in America, Orangemen came into frequent conflict with Irish Catholic immigrants, such as during the 1824 riots in Greenwich Village and the 1831 riots in Philadelphia.[127] The most significant clashes were the 1870 and 1871 Orange Riots in New York City. Violence erupted on 12 July in both years, when Irish Catholic workers attempted to stop Orange parades. In 1870, 2,500 members of the Orange lodges, the American Protestant Association, and their families gathered in Elm Park to listen to a speech by Grand Master John J. Bond. The eruption of violence was sudden, as the Orangemen traded gunfire with Irish Catholic workers. Eight people died and at least fifteen were injured.[128] In 1871, New York Governor John T. Hoffman called out the National Guard to protect the Orangemen during their parade. Plans for an Orange parade were announced weeks prior to 12 July. Rumours that Irish Catholics planned to attack the Orangemen circulated in city newspapers. In the event, as Orangemen again clashed with Irish Catholic workers, the National Guardsmen panicked and opened fire on the crowd. Over sixty people were killed and more than 100 injured.[129]

124 MacRaild, 'Associationalism of the Orange Diaspora', 27.
125 *St. Louis Daily Globe Democrat* 13 Jul 1880; Jones, 'Scotch-Irish', 906.
126 MacRaild, 'Orange Atlantic', 314.
127 Doyle, 'Orange Order', 740.
128 Gordon, *Orange Riots*, 36.
129 Michael A. Gordon, 'The Orange Riots of 1870 and 1871', in *The Encyclopedia of the Irish in America*, ed. Michael Glazier (Notre Dame, Ind.: University of Notre Dame Press, 1999), 748.

Collective memories of historical clashes between Protestant and Catholic groups in Ireland helped shape the riots. The immigrant experience in America was also reflected, as the riots were underlined by religious animosity, tensions caused by ethnic and class divisions within the city, and frustration with the corrupt Tweed Ring that controlled city government.[130] MacRaild also asserts that the Orange Riots were partially caused by the immigrants wanting to emerge from 'sectarian enclaves' to take greater part in American society.[131] The riots spurred wealthy New Yorkers and nativists to launch a crusade to topple the Tweed Ring, which was said to pander to the Irish Catholic masses in exchange for Democratic Party votes. Ultimately, the Tweed Ring was forced from power by reformers who, according to Michael Gordon, sought to return respectability to city government by lessening Irish Catholic influence.[132]

After the riots, the Orange Order found itself increasingly popular, especially in New York. Membership reportedly more than doubled in 1872.[133] By 1875, the Orange Order claimed 120 lodges with 10,000 members nationwide.[134] The records of the Pennsylvania Orange lodges show that they were deeply ingrained within civic society. Philadelphia Orangemen participated in the city's Labor Day parades and Orange delegates attended meetings of various other like-minded organizations within the city, such as the Patriotic League and the Protestant Federation Independent League.[135] In December 1885, the Prince of Orange District Lodge formed the Orange Hall and Literary Association of the City of Philadelphia, with the ultimate goal of erecting a hall to accommodate Philadelphia's Orange lodges.[136] The new Orange Hall on 16th Street held its first meeting on 21 April 1894, a testament to the presence of the Orange Order in Philadelphia.[137] In addition, 12 July parades, picnics, and celebrations were annual features of the Orange programme in cities throughout the country.

In the final decades of the nineteenth century, Orangemen in the United States responded to the developing political situation in Ireland. After the Phoenix Park murders of 6 May 1882, the Grand Master of Massachusetts, D.H.M. McIntire, spoke for all Orangemen in the United States at an all-Ireland meeting in Boston's Faneuil Hall. He announced

130 Gordon, *Orange Riots*, 2.
131 MacRaild, 'Crossing Migrant Frontiers', 58–61.
132 Gordon, *Orange Riots*, 188.
133 Long, 'Orange Family Worldwide', 88.
134 Doyle, 'Orange Order', 740; Kenny, *American Irish*, 158.
135 See examples in *Minutes 4/23/1908–9/5/35*, Royal Black Preceptory (RBP) Star of Liberty Lodge No. 34, Box #2, HSP MSS 89.
136 4 Dec 1885, *Minutes*, Orange Hall Association of Philadelphia, Box #1, HSP MSS 102.
137 4 Dec 1885, *Minutes*, Orange Hall Association of Philadelphia, Box #1, HSP MSS 102.

that 'the Orangemen are ready and most willing to bury the hatchet which has for so many years divided their ranks, and make common cause for the welfare of Ireland. He denounced in strongest terms that the deed had been perpetrated by Irishmen or friends of Irishmen, and promised the utmost co-operation on the part of his order with the Land League to bring the murderers to justice'.[138]

This offer of conciliation with Irish-American nationalists proved short-lived. With the threat of Home Rule looming in 1886, the Grand Orange Lodge of the State of New York passed resolutions censuring Gladstone, denouncing Parnell, and offering assistance to unionists. State Grand Master William B. Kennedy sent a cable dispatch to William Johnston in Belfast, asking what the American Orangemen could do to give effective assistance to the Irish unionists.[139] On 5 March 1886, the Washington Lodge of Philadelphia reported that an Orange brother asked the Lodge for money toward 'helping the committee appointed by the three Districts to hold a publick demonstration to protest against home rule for Ireland and the saying of masses in the house of Correction. It was moved and seconded that the report be received and an order drawn on the treasurer for that amount'.[140] Combining protests against Home Rule with protests against the saying of masses in the Philadelphia jail kept the Orangemen connected to Ireland while at the same time allowing them to be involved with American social and political issues.

The Home Rule crises also aided the growth of Orangeism in the United States. The *Chicago Tribune*, in describing the unusually popular 12 July parades of 1886, stated, 'The anti-home-rule agitation in the north of Ireland and alleged arming and drilling of the Orangemen there have raised a spirit of emulation among the Orangemen of this city, and strong efforts have been made to spread and strengthen the organization and put it on a firm financial footing'.[141] However, at the same time, the Supreme Grand Lodge of the United States voted against a resolution condemning Irish Home Rule because they did not want to be associated with foreign sentiments. The Supreme Grand Master, George Herron, stated that he believed it was important for the American Orangemen to remain officially neutral when it came to Irish politics. However, he declared, 'The Unionists are just getting aroused to the fight and that they are able to defeat the present or any other home-rule movement'.[142] The American Orangemen were therefore

138 *Chicago Daily Inter-Ocean* 10 May 1882.
139 *Kansas City Star* 24 May 1886; *The Times* 17 May 1886.
140 5 Mar 1886, *Minutes 1885–1907*, Washington LOL No. 43, Box #1, HSP MSS 60.
141 *Chicago Tribune* 12 Jul 1886.
142 *Chicago Tribune* 12 Jul 1886.

conflicted in showing their anti-Home Rule sentiments while displaying patriotism for the United States.

The Orangemen's response to the second Home Rule crisis in 1892–1893 showed less concern with the dangers of involvement in a foreign issue. At the 1892 meeting of the Supreme Grand Lodge, held in Alleghany, Pennsylvania, the Orangemen passed a pro-Union resolution. They tendered their support for

> their brethren in Ireland to their resistance of the projected scheme of home rule. This they state is a bold attempt to inaugurate an Irish Roman Catholic parliament. The order deems it a solemn obligation not to support a Roman Catholic who seeks political preferment. If the American republic is to be maintained loyal American citizens should be on guard.[143]

The Orangemen portrayed the Home Rule threat in Ireland as linked to the perceived threat of Catholic influence in the United States. They believed that every American citizen should guard against Catholics seeking preferential political treatment, both at home and abroad. The Supreme Grand Lodge and Massachusetts State Grand Lodge were two of several hundred organizations to send messages of sympathy to be read at the Great Unionist Convention on 17 June 1892.[144]

In 1893, the Pennsylvania State Grand Lodge, having heard the news of a Home Rule Bill 'being imposed upon a Loyal industrious God fearing class of people whose principles are pure and whose allegiance to the government of their Queen never faltered', proclaimed, 'We pray every loyal Protestant of whatever denomination he belongs to not to sell his brothers into Slavery and Papist Bondage by the whims of an old Political Trickster'.[145] Pennsylvania Orangemen urged British Protestants not to betray loyal Irish Protestants by supporting Gladstone's Home Rule policies. The Massachusetts State Grand Lodge also passed a resolution of sympathy for Irish brethren and raised a small sum to send to Ireland.[146] In Illinois, State Grand Master B.P. Reynolds declared his state's support of unionism, but denied rumours of Ulster militancy. He stated, 'These reports and rumors circulated for the past month are absurd. There is no arming, no collecting of money, at least on our side. If there were, the Orangemen here would know of it. I believe that these reports

---

143 *Duluth Daily News* 16 Jun 1892.
144 *BNL* 18 Jun 1892, 5 Sep 1892; *Charlotte Observer* 18 Jun 1892.
145 1893 Meeting, *Minutes*, Pennsylvania State Grand Lodge of the LOI, HSP MSS 93.
146 Mount Horeb Loyal Orange Lodge 19, Somerville, MA, *Meeting Minutes 1892–1895*, HSP, M93–102.

are circulated by the other side. The men of Ulster are quiet and peaceable'.[147] Though the American Orangemen supported the unionist cause, they had not been called upon by Ulster unionists for their tacit support of more militant actions in resisting the implementation of Home Rule.

By 1900, there were Orange lodges in twenty-one states; by 1920, the organization was present in about forty states. They were strongest in the urban and working-class areas of Pennsylvania, Michigan, and New York, but were as far-flung as Georgia, Louisiana, Colorado, Arizona, Idaho, and even had one lodge in Cordova, Alaska.[148] Lodge members met regularly to celebrate Orange history and Protestant values, attempt to counter Irish Catholic political influence and run campaigns to inform Americans about the dangers of Papal power in public institutions, and to provide support for fellow Orange members within their communities.[149] They also spawned several related organizations, including the Ladies' Loyal Orange Association, the Royal Black Institution of the Camp of Israel, Apprentice Boys of Derry Club, Loyal Orange Girls' Lodge, and the Orange Home, an orphanage and retirement centre in Pennsylvania founded in 1902.[150]

Connections to Ireland and other Orange lodges throughout the world were nurtured through triennial meetings of the Imperial Grand Orange Council of the World, founded in 1870. The Triennial Council met in New York City in 1900, where David Graham of New York presided as Imperial Grand President.[151] Lodge members regularly received communications from Orange institutions around the world, including Ireland and Canada. Orangemen in the United States also corresponded with the Irish Grand Secretary, Colonel R.H. Wallace. Irish, British, and Canadian Orangemen visiting the United States attended Orange meetings.[152] Transfer certificates

---

147 *Rocky Mountain News* 24 Mar 1893.
148 Orange Ledger, HSP; Houston and Smyth, 'Transferred Loyalties', 204–206.
149 Long, 'Orange Family Worldwide', 88; Michael A. Gordon, 'Orange Order', in *The Encyclopedia of the Irish in America*, ed. Michael Glazier (Notre Dame, Ind.: University of Notre Dame Press, 1999), 748.
150 Michael F. Funchion, *Irish American Voluntary Organizations* (Westport, Conn.: Greenwood Press, 1983), 223–224; *NYT* 29 Nov 1901. See also the history of the Supreme Grand Lodge of the United States and State Grand Lodges in *Report of the Proceedings of the Thirteenth Triennial Session of the Imperial Grand Orange Council of the Loyal Orange Association of the World. Held in the City of Dublin, Ireland, July 15th and 17th, 1903*, PRONI D1889/6/5A; Patrick Coleman, '"In Harmony": A Comparative View of Female Orangeism, 1887–2000', in *Ireland in the World: Comparative, Transnational, and Personal Perspectives*, ed. Angela McCarthy (New York: Routledge, 2015), 117–119.
151 Long, 'Orange Family Worldwide', 88.
152 4 Jun 1908, 20 Jan 1910, *Minutes*, RBP Star of Liberty Lodge No. 34, HSP MSS 89; 20 Mar 1886, 29 Oct 1886, *Minutes 1885–1907*, Washington LOL No. 43, HSP MSS 60. See Wallace correspondence, PRONI D1889/1/2/3.

show that a significant number of new Orange emigrants from counties Tyrone, Londonderry, Cavan, Down, Antrim, and Fermanagh relocated and joined American lodges throughout this era. However, throughout this time the American Orange Order was beset with factionalism and disaffection which, along with the difficulties associated with transferring a pro-British and monarchist order to the American republic, limited the organization's ability to grow beyond a minority ethnic association.[153] The *Boston Pilot* criticized the Orange Order in 1900, stating, 'Orangemen everywhere put their order ahead of their government, and are terribly desperate fellows when they outnumber their opponents by only ten to one'.[154] Likewise, Catholic Irish-Americans in Minneapolis complained, 'The Orange order is un-American. It is founded on prejudice of the meanest sort. It lives for the sole purpose of antagonizing the Catholics. It has no other object ... Its king, its god, is King William of England'.[155]

American Orangemen remained connected to Ireland throughout the third Home Rule crisis despite facing crippling factionalism. At the meeting of the Supreme Grand Lodge in 1912, William Kirkland, Supreme Grand Secretary, called upon American Orangemen to support the unionists of Ireland, stating:

> We who are the descendants of the men of Derry, Enniskillen, Aughrim and the Boyne, and in whose hearts the old sod will always find a warm spot, and who have many ties that bind us to the dear old Isle; where those whose near and dear to many of us rest beneath its silent clay, and loved ones still roam over its green fields, picturesque hills and enchanted valleys; where nature, with all true grandeur, rules sublime, we can never forget the scenes of our boyhood and early manhood and we can well realize what Home Rule means to the land of our birth, and what would happen to those near and dear if the old Union Jack, mother of our own beloved stars and stripes, was pulled down and the flag of the Vatican took its place on Irish soil. Brethren this must never be and never will be.[156]

Kirkland portrayed Ireland as enchanting, picturesque, and dear to the Orangemen of the United States, while emphasizing the dangers and fears

---

153 Houston and Smyth, 'Transferred Loyalties', 200, 206–208.
154 Reprinted in the *Springfield Daily Republican* 21 Aug 1900.
155 *St. Paul Daily Globe* 13 Jul 1892.
156 Loyal Orange Institution, United States of America, Report of the Thirty-Fourth Session of the Supreme Grand Orange Lodge in the United States of America, held in Odd Fellow's Hall, Atlantic City, NJ, August 13, 14, and 15, 1912 (Wilmington, NC: William H. Kramer, 1912), 47–48.

inherent in Irish self-government, which he equated with the rule of the Vatican. He continued,

> Our brethren in the old land are making a noble fight for free and religious liberty, and it is our duty to render them all the assistance possible. I know they have our sympathy, and while sympathy is all right at times and in its place, yet on this occasion it requires dollars and cents to win the battle. The enemy has had much of this American ammunition, and it is the source of their strongest fighting power. Let us therefore see that some of it is sent to the assistance of our boys.[157]

Kirkland urged his Orange brethren to prove that Irish unionists too had a substantial international backing, to equal the high levels of support for Irish nationalists. Kirkland's words helped lead to resolutions by the Supreme Grand Lodge assuring Ulster unionists of the sympathy and support of the Orangemen in opposition to any form of Home Rule. State lodges such as those in Pennsylvania and New York sent money to Ulster to aid unionist actions.[158] The State Grand Lodge of California also sent letters of support, wishing 'Carson and his brave followers complete success in their efforts to prevent the passage of the Home Rule Bill'.[159]

In 1913, a rift led to the separation of the American Orange Order into two competing branches, and they were not reunited until after 1930. The split was rooted in two brethren, Kirkland and George T. Lemmon, both claiming to be the Supreme Grand Secretary for the United States. This led to the establishment of two separate Supreme Grand Orange Lodges. There was confusion over who held the original charter establishing the Supreme Grand Orange Lodge, which the Triennial Council members agreed would indicate the authentic lodge. The Triennial Council also agreed that this was a dispute to be settled by American Orangemen alone.[160]

Although funds from both factions were funnelled into litigation against each other, the cause of Irish unionism was still present. At the 1914 meeting of Kirkland's faction of the Supreme Grand Lodge, Kirkland reminded the Orangemen,

---

157 Loyal Orange Institution, Thirty-Fourth Session, 1912, 48.
158 1913 Meeting, *Minutes*, Pennsylvania State Grand Lodge, HSP MSS 93; see also Wallace correspondence, PRONI D1889/1/2/3; R.P. Dodds to Edward Carson, 2 Feb 1913; Henry E. Maxwell to Richard Dawson Bates, 10 Apr 1913, PRONI D1327/18/1A/12.
159 *Witness* 22 Mar 1912.
160 Report of the Seventeenth Annual Triennial Meeting of the Imperial Grand Orange Council of the World, held at Belfast, Ireland, on the 15th and 16th of July, 1920, PRONI D1889/6/5C; Long, 'Orange Family Worldwide', 88. See also the newspaper of the Kirkland faction, *The Orange and Purple Courier*.

Our brethren in the Old Land still continues their fight against Home Rule and have made heroic efforts so far in their able resistment of its encroachment. I am afraid, in our confused condition, we have not given them the support during their struggle that we should ... If our hearts are with them, as I know they are, our pockets will be ready to assist financially, and if the worst has to come our hands should be ready to grasp the musket, cross over the pond and under the battle cry of No Surrender, stand shoulder to shoulder with them in the defence of freedom and religious liberty.[161]

Kirkland's words reflected the heightened tensions of the Ulster Crisis, as Ireland came to the brink of civil war in 1914, while urging his fellow brethren to consider their duty to offer military aid to unionists.

When Home Rule was put on hold for the duration of the First World War, American Orangemen joined with other organizations in their local areas to respond to the heavy losses sustained by the troops, especially at the Battle of the Somme. British-American societies in the Philadelphia region came together for 'the purpose of raising funds for the relief of distressed & disabled British soldiers', in which Orange lodges throughout the area took part. Orange delegates were sent to the resultant Scotch-Irish Relief Association, which organized a concert, dance, and bazaar to benefit British soldiers. In the end, the association raised over $5,000 to be donated to the British Red Cross.[162]

Orange members continued to protest against both Home Rule and the role of Irish nationalists in the United States. After the Easter Rising in 1916, they urged the American government to refrain from interfering in the Irish question, fearing that a home rule settlement would be pushed through while wartime hostilities were still taking place. At the 1916 meeting of the Lemmon faction of the Supreme Grand Lodge, Grand Master William A. Dunlap reported,

Ulster in this awful war has marched to the front and many of her loyal men have been killed and wounded, leaving her today a pitiable sight, and John Redmond and Premier Asquith have taken advantage of them in this hour of sorrow and peril, but I believe the time is not far distant when the men of Ulster will trot out as the men from behind the walls

---

161 Loyal Orange Institution, 35th Biennial Report, 1914, 29.
162 16 Nov 1916, 21 Dec 1916, *Minutes*, RBP Star of Liberty Lodge No. 34, HSP MSS 89; 27 Oct 1916, 24 Nov 1916, 12 Jan 1917, May 1917, *Minute Book*, Lily of the Valley LOL No. 167, Box #1, HSP MSS 87; 7 Nov 1916, 6 Mar 1917, 20 Mar 1917, *Records 1885–1986*, Washington LOL No. 43, Box #5, HSP MSS 60.

of Derry did and at the battle of the Boyne, and settle this question once and for all.[163]

He urged the American Orangemen to remember their duty to their 'brothers across the sea', directed pledges of support to be sent to the Irish Orangemen, Carson, the Ulster Volunteers, and others, and endeavoured to publicize the fight against Home Rule in the American press. In 1917, the Pennsylvania State Grand Lodge passed a resolution stating,

> As to the Irish Home Rule ... [we believe] that no state or national government have a right to interfere with the domestic affairs of a foreign nation, we believe the same to be un-American and unpatriotic and that our executive officers be and are hereby empowered to use all means within their power to prevent such action by our public officials of government.[164]

Specifically targeting the Irish-American nationalist efforts, the Pennsylvania Grand Secretary condemned the propaganda of the United Irish League and other similar organizations as 'un-American and unpatriotic'. He warned, 'American Protestants are against being misled by these Roman Catholic societies. Should Ireland desire a different form of government, let the Irish of Ireland decide for themselves'. He welcomed the news of the 1917 Convention as evidence that Irishmen would be able to decide their own affairs without interference by Irish-Americans or the United States government.[165] However, the convention caused dissension in the ranks of American Orangemen as others did not support the British government's tactics for settling the Irish problem.[166]

The Massachusetts State Grand Lodge sent letters of support to Edward Carson, and messages to Woodrow Wilson and David Lloyd George propagating the unionist stance. They protested to Lloyd George that 'real' Americans wished he would 'face the fact that any British Government which yields to the clamor of [Irish-American] critique will merit and receive the detestations of Americans and of all others continuing to exalt truth and self-sacrifice above falsehood and treason'.[167] The New York State Grand Lodge also circulated letters of protest to Wilson, Lloyd George, Arthur

---

163 Loyal Orange Institution, 36th Biennial Report, 1916, 23.
164 1917 Meeting, *Minutes*, Pennsylvania State Grand Lodge, HSP MSS 93.
165 1917 Meeting, *Minutes*, Pennsylvania State Grand Lodge, HSP MSS 93.
166 *NYT* 12 Jul 1917.
167 Grand Lodge of Massachusetts to Edward Carson, 21 May 1918, PRONI D1507/A/27/12–14.

Balfour, Edward Carson, and United States Senators and Representatives. The letters argued against

> the exploitation of alleged American sentiment in favor of Home Rule, and the effort to commit the American Government to any policy or expression of opinion that could counsel or countenance any action by which the British Government would deprive the Protestant population of Ireland of the rights of small peoples, and reward Ulster's glorious contribution to the victorious armies of our Allies by committing that part of Ireland that has rendered the last full measure of devotion to our common cause to the murderous passions of those who have openly defied all the claims of honor and humanity, and illustrated their Germanic Frightfulness in the perfidious assassinations of the Easter Rebellion.[168]

They condemned Irish-American newspapers for supporting German war efforts, and declared that 'sane, self-respecting, liberty-fostering Protestant America' would not stand for the separation of Ireland from the British Empire. They urged Americans and Britons to understand that 'Casements and Germanic co-operators abroad' do not 'speak for America, that they do not serve the Common Cause by the Common Foe'.[169]

After the end of the First World War, Orangemen continued to condemn interference by Americans in the Irish situation. At the 12 July 1919 parade in New York City, Orangemen extended their 'sympathy and support to the Ulstermen and all who are in sympathy with their cause throughout the world'.[170] A few weeks later, the Supreme Grand Lodge drew up resolutions to be sent to Henry Cabot Lodge, Chairman of the Senate Committee on Foreign Relations, as well as all members of the House and Senate, and to the press. The Orangemen protested against the committee receiving representatives of Irish republicanism during their hearings on the Treaty of Versailles. Their letter stated, 'The American Senate has no business meddling with the unquestioned problems of the British Parliament'. They accused Sinn Féiners of conspiring with Germany during the war, and denied that there were any grounds for separation from the United Kingdom. Orangemen also protested that a minority of the United Kingdom's citizens in Ireland could place 'the loyal population of that island in a false light

---

168 Letter of Protest by Albert E. Kelly, Moses A. Allerton, Robert Smith, and George T. Lemmon, c.mid-May 1917, PRONI D1507/A/23/25; *NYT* 2 May 1917.
169 *NYT* 2 May 1917.
170 *NYT* 13 Jul 1919.

before the world'.[171] They believed the Irish–American republicans who addressed the committee did not 'represent American sentiment, nor the will of that Irish people who sent their sons with ours to win the war'. The Orangemen asked that the friends of Ulster's self-determination be granted a hearing.[172] At the Pennsylvania State Grand Lodge meeting of August 1919, two pro-unionist resolutions were passed. They stated,

> that in view of the fact that the Irish Home Rule propaganda has been misleading and that the action of the Senate of the United States has caused the general public throughout the United States to form an opinion that all the Irish race desire home rule, whereas the truth of the matter is that the above is the desire only of the Irish race known as Sinn Feiners and be thus opposed to the Protestant religion as believed by the Ulsterites and their friends in Ireland; be it further Resolved, that we protest against any action by the United States House of Representatives and Senate in support of Home Rule and that we endorse the actions of Sir Edward Carson and his associates who agree with him in his attitude on the home rule question.[173]

The State Grand Lodge sent copies of these resolutions affirming their support of the unionists to Carson and members of the United States House of Representatives and Senate.

Along with these attempts to persuade the United States government to refrain from interfering in the Irish situation, Orangemen also protested against the American visit of Éamon de Valera in 1919. Delegates of the Washington lodge in Philadelphia reported attending a meeting of the Independent Patriotic League of Philadelphia. Attendees of the meeting protested 'against Mayor [Thomas B.] Smith extending a welcome to de Valera' in his visit to the city. On 2 December, the Washington lodge resolved to give the Independent League 'all the help they can to give the view coming from the other side in protest against what de Valera was spreading'.[174] At the next meeting, on 16 December, the delegates reported 'that arrangements had been made to hold a mass meeting on Thurs. Jan. 8, 1920 in the Metropolitan Opera House, where the meeting will be addressed by Ulstermen who were here to speak & tell of conditions in Ireland'. The Orangemen agreed to give that meeting as much publicity

---

171 *NYT* 30 Aug 1919, 2 Sep 1919; Jones, 'Scotch-Irish', 907; Kenny, *American Irish*, 197.
172 *NYT* 2 Sep 1919.
173 1919 Meeting, *Minutes*, Pennsylvania State Grand Lodge, HSP MSS 93.
174 7 Oct 1919, 2 Dec 1919, *Minutes*, Washington LOL No. 43, Box #2, HSP MSS 60.

as possible.[175] The Ulstermen who came to Philadelphia to speak at the Metropolitan Opera House were a seven-member Protestant deputation led by William Coote. They arrived in the United States in December to conduct a speaking tour to tell the Irish unionist point of view. In February, the Philadelphia Orange delegates were able to report a positive conclusion to the Ulster deputation's visit. They stated that the Patriotic League had a fine follow-up meeting, with principal business of setting up collecting cards for the Ulster mission. The total amount collected for the Ulster Protestants by the Philadelphia Orangemen and Independent League was about $4,300.[176] On Coote's second tour of the United States and Canada in 1922, the Philadelphia Orangemen raised over $10,000 for the 'aid of the Protestant Orphans and Refugees of the Irish Free State'.[177]

The Orange Order in the United States was united in its support of Irish unionism and condemnation of the influence of Irish-Americans and the American government in the Irish situation. At the 1920 meeting of the Supreme Grand Lodge, Kirkland declared, 'We as Orangemen should assist Sir Edward Carson in reorganizing and equipping the Ulster Volunteers, that noble, fearless, courageous and undaunted body which won the British Empire laurels by their gallantry and bravery on Flanders' Field, and thus place them in position to protect and defend themselves on home soil which they are well able to do'.[178] While pledged to 'one hundred percent Americanism',[179] they had clear and continuous support for Irish unionists, which grew stronger as they linked Irish nationalists with the enemy in the First World War. However, like Orangemen in Great Britain, Canada, Australia, New Zealand, and South Africa, Americans were never likely to cross the Atlantic to take up arms against the British government and Irish nationalists in the event of civil war.[180]

175 16 Dec 1919, *Minutes*, Washington LOL No. 43, HSP MSS 60.
176 2 Feb 1920, *Minutes*, Washington LOL No. 43, HSP MSS 60.
177 *Orange and Purple Courier* I, no. 83 (Mar–Apr 1923).
178 *Orange and Purple Courier* I, no. 68 (Sep–Oct 1920).
179 *Orange and Purple Courier* I, no. 71 (Mar–Apr 1921).
180 William Jenkins, 'Views from the "Hub of Empire": Loyal Orange Lodges in Early Twentieth-Century Toronto', in *The Orange Order in Canada*, ed. David A. Wilson (Dublin: Four Courts Press, 2007), 140–145; MacRaild, *Faith, Fraternity and Fighting*, 283, 317–318.

Ulstermen and the Celebration of Scotch-Irish Heritage

Around the close of the nineteenth century, Irish unionists began to cultivate an 'Ulsterman' identity. This identity developed through the publication of several books on the history of Ulster and the Ulster Scots character. Irish unionists attempted to assert claims of self-determination and validate arguments for remaining in the Union. The Ulsterman 'type' drew upon the concurrent revival of Scotch-Irish identity in America, and particularly flourished after the development of a separate Ulster Unionist Council in 1904 and during the third Home Rule crisis.[181]

The growth of the Ulsterman 'type' was informed by an Irish Protestant siege mentality in the north. It developed in reaction to the increasing worldwide prominence of Irish nationalism and the changing roles of Catholics within Ulster society. As Frank Wright describes, Protestants faced a decaying colonial structure and frontier conditions in which British and Irish identities went head-to-head. Greater democratization and increased economic opportunities led to greater political and economic equality between Catholics and Protestants in the north. Protestants became increasingly defensive, resulting in mistrust and suspicion by both groups. An Ulsterman identity was a way to minimize the importance of Catholics in the north of Ireland, while ideologically unifying Protestants.[182]

Under these evolving conditions and in the face of the Home Rule threat, Ulstermen worked to develop a united Protestant identity by emphasizing shared historical experiences, such as the 1641 rebellion, the United Irishmen uprising in 1798, and later the Battle of the Somme.[183] The unionist sense of siege and desire to defend themselves against Catholic encroachment also acted as a unifying force. Ulster identity was strengthened by a tradition of loyalty to the crown since 1689 and celebration of a shared British Protestant identity.[184] The Orange Order, traditionally

---

181 Jackson, *Ulster Party*, 14–15. The Ulsterman type developed over time, and there are indications that it was already 'alive' by 1886: James Anderson, 'Ideological Variations in Ulster in Ulster During Ireland's First Home Rule Crisis: An Analysis of Local Newspapers', in *Community Conflict, Partition and Nationalism*, ed. Colin H. Williams and Eleonore Kofman (London: Routledge, 1989), 162.

182 Frank Wright, *Two Lands on One Soil: Ulster Politics before Home Rule* (New York: St. Martin's, 1996), 510–515; Lee, 'Introduction', 4.

183 McIntosh, *Force of Culture*, 7–9; see also Jackson, 'Unionist Myths'; Cathal McCall, 'Political Transformation and the Reinvention of the Ulster-Scots Identity and Culture', *Identities: Global Studies in Culture and Power* 9, no. 2 (2002).

184 Thomas Hennessey, 'Ulster Unionism and Loyalty to the Crown of the United Kingdom, 1912–74', in *Unionism in Modern Ireland: New Perspectives on Politics and Culture*, ed. Richard English and Graham Walker (Basingstoke: Macmillan Press, 1996), 123–126; James Loughlin, 'Joseph Chamberlain, English Nationalism, and the

associated with Anglicanism, also helped to unify Ulster Protestants as it became increasingly associated with symbols of Presbyterianism such as the Ulster Covenant in 1912.

Informed by the popular racial theories and social Darwinism of the time, the Ulstermen laid out the characteristics of their 'type': dour, shrewd, industrious, practical, independent, and naturally gifted with governing abilities.[185] As Graham Walker emphasizes, the Ulsterman 'type' was frequently linked to a Scottish heritage, in part as an attempt to draw support from Scotland for the unionist movement.[186] Presbyterianism was also central to the Ulsterman identity.[187] These Scottish ties, along with Ulster-American connections, were underscored through the celebration of Scotch-Irish achievements in the United States.

Scotch-Irish identity in America broadened over time to include all Irish Protestant immigrants regardless of denomination or region of origin. In contrast, Ulstermen increasingly drew on Scottish and Presbyterian elements, to an extent excluding the Anglo-Irish from their newly formed sense of identity. However, as Anglicans, Methodists, and Presbyterians alike were mobilized in huge numbers through the Ulster Covenant, the Ulsterman identity was able to create cultural hegemony amongst Protestant denominations.[188] This artificially minimized differences to forge a seemingly united Ulster Protestant opposition to Home Rule.

The ties between Scotland, Ulster, and the Scotch-Irish were celebrated in a speech on 1 November 1911 by the American Ambassador to the United

Ulster Question', *History* 77, no. 250 (Jun 1992), 213–214; Alvin Jackson, 'Irish Unionist Imagery, 1850–1920', in *Returning to Ourselves: Second Volume of Papers from the John Hewitt International Summer School*, ed. Eve Patten (Belfast: Lagan Press, 1995).

185 James Barkley Woodburn, *The Ulster Scot: His History and Religion* (London: H.R. Allenson, 1914), 396; McBride, 'Ulster and the British Problem', 7. On social Darwinism, eugenics, and racial theories, see Archdeacon, *Becoming American*, 159–160.

186 See Graham Walker, *Intimate Strangers: Political and Cultural Interaction between Scotland and Ulster in Modern Times* (Edinburgh: John Donald Publishers, 1995), especially chapters 1–2; Walker, 'Empire, Religion, and Nationality in Scotland and Ulster before the First World War', in *Scotland and Ulster*, ed. Ian S. Wood (Edinburgh: Mercat Press, 1994); Walker, 'Ulster Unionism and the Scottish Dimension'. See also Peter Dunn, 'Forsaking Their "Own Flesh and Blood"? Ulster Unionism, Scotland and Home Rule, 1886–1914', *IHS* 37, no. 146 (Nov 2010).

187 Andrew R. Holmes, 'Presbyterian Religion, Historiography, and Ulster Scots Identity, c.1800 to 1914', *Historical Journal* 52, no. 3 (2009), 630–639.

188 Donald H. Akenson, *God's Peoples: Covenant and Land in South Africa, Israel, and Ulster* (Ithaca, NY: Cornell University Press, 1992), 149; Graham Walker, 'Scotland and Ulster: Political Interactions since the Late Nineteenth Century and Possibilities of Contemporary Dialogue', in *Cultural Traditions in Northern Ireland*, ed. John Erskine and Gordon Lucy (Belfast: Queen's University Press, 1997), 93–97; Anderson, 'Ideological Variations', 139.

Kingdom, Whitelaw Reid. Speaking in Edinburgh on 'The Scot in America and the Ulster Scot', he enthused over the contributions of the Scotch-Irish to American history. 'During the whole period, from the Revolution to the Civil War', Reid stated,

> the indomitable Ulster Scots, chiefly from Pennsylvania and the south, were pouring over the Alleghenies, carrying ever westward the frontiers of the country, forming the advance guard of civilization from the Lakes to the Gulf, fighting the Indians and the wild beasts, subduing and planting the wilderness, westward to the Mississippi.[189]

Ulstermen in newspaper articles responded favourably to this well-publicized lecture as well as other by-products of the Scotch-Irish revival such as the annual reports of the Scotch-Irish congresses and books by Hanna, Bolton, Ford, and others.

The roles of the Scotch-Irish in winning the American Revolution and taming the frontier were memorialized by Ulstermen. Gillian McIntosh writes, 'These "historical" events were the beacon buoys for unionists, marking the rocks on which Ulster Protestants had almost foundered in the past but which they had overcome through their own tenacity'.[190] The Scotch-Irish, through their tenacity, had overcome their immigrant status and frontier conditions to become leading members of American society. A *Witness* editorial in 1912 mused, 'The United States owe much of their being, and not a little of their well-being, to the Ulster Scot, and the spirit of rugged and determined resistance of the obstacles of tyrannical government on the one hand or of nature on the other'.[191] James Barkley Woodburn wrote in his *The Ulster Scot*, 'They went hundreds of miles into the unoccupied interior, and made settlements on the slopes and in the valleys of the mountains that run parallel to the coast about two hundred miles inland. Therefore they were sometimes called "the mountainy men", or more commonly, the backwoodsmen'.[192]

The Scotch-Irish backwoodsmen in America were determined to seek liberty to worship and to go beyond the reach of tyrannical civil authority, building new lives for their families. According to Scotch-Irish mythology, they were first to call for independence from the British with the Mecklenburg Declaration of 20 May 1775. As John Harrison wrote in

---

189 Whitelaw Reid, 'The Scot in America, and the Ulster Scot. Edinburgh Philosophical Association Opening Address, 1911–12, Synod Hall, November 1' (London: Harrison and Sons, 1911), 46.
190 McIntosh, *Force of Culture*, 19.
191 *Witness* 29 Mar 1912.
192 Woodburn, *Ulster Scot*, 218.

The Scot in Ulster, they were also foremost in the fighting of the American Revolution: 'The Presbyterian emigrants were among the stoutest soldiers who fought in the War of Independence, and many of the best citizens of the United States spring from the same stock'.[193] Hugh Morrison, in *Modern Ulster*, also credited the Scotch-Irish backwoodsmen, who had gained experience acting as 'the frontier line against Indian aggression', with turning the war in the colonists' favour.[194] Of all their contributions, Woodburn believed that the most important was 'the leading part they took in the winning of the West – the lands between the Alleghenies and the Mississippi'.[195] The Scotch-Irish had acted as a civilizing force for the American frontier.

Ulstermen also celebrated the practical achievements of the Scotch-Irish in American government, religion, and industry. Long lists of American presidents of 'Ulster stock' were enumerated. James Logan, in *Ulster in the X-Rays*, wrote,

When he emigrates, the Ulsterman, like most Irishmen, 'makes good', and he frequently rises to the highest positions. Almost one half of the great line of Presidents of the United States came of Ulster stock, and McKinley's old ancestral home may still be seen in the neighbourhood of Dervock, North Antrim. This is a debt America owes to Ulster which is sometimes forgotten.[196]

The Scotch-Irish achievements in the United States were also victories for Protestantism, with Ulstermen praising the contributions of Francis Makemie and Gilbert Tennent to the American religious establishment.[197]

The industrial achievements of the Scotch-Irish were lauded as well. Harrison wrote, 'It is, indeed, in the practical work of the world that those men of Ulster excel at home and abroad. They have made but little mark in art or literature; but in commerce and manufactures and science, in war and diplomacy, they have done their own share of hard and successful labour'.[198] Robert Fulton, inventor of steam technology, Samuel Morse, inventor of the

193 John Harrison, *The Scot in Ulster: A Sketch of the Scottish Population of Ulster* (Edinburgh: William Blackwood and Sons, 1888), 112.
194 H.S. Morrison, Modern Ulster: Its Character, Customs, Politics, and Industries (London: H.R. Allenson, 1920), 118.
195 Woodburn, *Ulster Scot*, 227.
196 James Logan, *Ulster in the X-Rays: A Short Review of the Real Ulster, Its People, Pursuits, Principles, Poetry, Dialect and Humour* (London: Arthur H. Stockwell, 1922), 35.
197 Woodburn, *Ulster Scot*, 380.
198 Harrison, *Scot in Ulster*, 112–113.

telegraph, and Cyrus McCormick, inventor of the mechanical reaper, were upheld as examples, as well as A.T. Stewart, the entrepreneur who owned the most successful dry-goods business in the world at that time.[199]

These practical contributions to American society, through government, religion, and business, were mirrored with the achievements of the Ulster Scots in the north of Ireland. Through the use of Scotch-Irish examples, the Ulstermen were illustrating their value to Ireland. They asserted their unique place in Irish society as the builders of industry. Their success in industries such as shipbuilding and linen had benefited Protestant and Catholic alike. Ulstermen emphasized dual identities which celebrated devotion to both Ulster and Ireland as a whole. The Ulstermen feared the impact of Home Rule on the industrial north. These American examples were used to illustrate the significance of the Ulstermen's role in Ireland and the need to remain in the Union for continued industrial success.

Emphasis on the American emigration was also used to foster unity amongst Ulstermen. Morrison and W.F. Monypenny both wrote of the oppression of Ulster Presbyterians under the Test Act and the domination of landlords. They fled Ulster for America to avoid oppression and cruel bondage, shun persecution and designed ruin, withdraw from the community of idolaters, and have the opportunity to worship God according to conscience.[200] Woodburn wrote that through the Test Act and restrictions on woollen trade,

> Ulster was drained of the best of her sons. They were driven out of the land which they had saved for England by their swords at Londonderry and Enniskillen, and they carried their enterprise and energy to another land beyond the seas, and played a great part – perhaps the greatest – in building up the largest Republic in the world.[201]

Even those who had not emigrated from Ulster would be familiar with the perceived betrayal and oppression by England. Ulstermen had shared experiences of the conditions that had driven so many to emigrate. The significant impact of emigration itself on families and communities throughout Ulster was also a uniting factor.

Even though those who remained in Ulster had not directly contributed to the Scotch-Irish achievements in the United States still felt pride in the success of their 'race'. In 1912, the editors of the *Witness* wrote:

---

199 Harrison, *Scot in Ulster*, 112–113; Woodburn, *Ulster Scot*, 392.
200 Morrison, *Modern Ulster*, 18–20; W.F. Monypenny, *The Two Irish Nations: An Essay on Home Rule* (London: John Murray, 1913), 37.
201 Woodburn, *Ulster Scot*, 213–214, 228.

The Ulster Scots are as proud as are the people of the United States of the part that the men of their race played of planting, pruning, and preserving the tree of liberty in the Western Continent. They are proud of the part the men of their kith and kin have played in the upbuilding and upkeeping of the great Republic of the West. They are proud of the manliness and independence that characterized them. Theirs was not to reason why, theirs but to do and die for the land of their adoption and for the maintenance of the liberties of that land that were threatened by a fatuous British king and a fatuous government. They fought for what they believed to be the right; they suffered and sacrificed for it. And it is just because the Ulster Scots now represent the same race and same spirit that we regard their attitude on the Home Rule question not as bluff, as their enemies would represent, but as sober, considered, well-regulated, and well-adviced determination.[202]

It was this determination to uphold liberties and fight for what they believed to be right that united Ulstermen on both sides of the Atlantic. The cultivation of the Ulsterman 'type' justified shared claims over Scotch-Irish achievements. As long as they all identified with the 'type', it did not matter if they had actually committed the acts themselves. Furthermore, as Morrison wrote, because of Anglo-American rapprochement and the shared experience of the Great War, Ulstermen on both sides of the Atlantic had been reunited and would continue to fight together for the advancement of human liberty.[203]

The Ulstermen approached the era of colonial and Revolutionary Scotch-Irish achievement as a 'golden age' in their ethnic history.[204] Celebration of this 'golden age' helped to unify the Ulstermen in a time of threat and give them a sense of belonging when they were somewhat isolated from both British and Irish identities. The Scotch-Irish 'golden age' helped to explain Ulster ethnic identity and symbolized its collective achievements, even for those who remained in Ireland. Both the Scotch-Irish in America and Ulstermen emphasized a vision of their ethnic history at a 'flowering' stage, when the Scotch-Irish were at the peak of their pioneering and political powers. Moreover, because of the high levels of emigration in the mid- to late-eighteenth century, this was a time when theoretically the Scotch-Irish were much more closely tied back to Ulster.

---

202 *Witness* 29 Mar 1912.
203 Morrison, *Modern Ulster*, 137.
204 For discussions of an ethnic or national 'golden age', see Anthony D. Smith, *The Ethnic Origins of Nations* (Oxford: Basil Blackwell, 1986), 191–208; Loughlin, *Ulster Unionism and British National Identity*, 2.

Ulstermen's celebration of the contributions of the Scotch-Irish to American society persisted to include contemporary events. As the *Witness* editors wrote on the election of Woodrow Wilson as president, 'An Ulster Scot, or the descendant of an Ulster Scot, is once again in the proud position of President of the great Republic of the West, with which Ulster interests are so bound up, and in the history and in the development of which Ulster Scots have played such a part'.[205] Even though a century had passed since the peak of the Ulster Protestant emigration to America, the Ulstermen continued to assert close ties to the United States and believed that their futures would be determined in part by the continuing relationship with America.

Conclusion

The Scotch-Irish were influenced by American political, social, and economic circumstances as well as the desire to remain connected to Ireland. In late nineteenth-century America, pluralistic ethnic, class, occupational, and sectarian loyalties clashed against the promotion of nativism, social Darwinism, and Anglo-Saxonism. The Scotch-Irish were in a unique position in that they were able to be on both sides of the ethnic-nativist divide simultaneously, reflecting the diverse backgrounds and changing circumstances of immigrants who had come from Ireland over a period of two and a half centuries. This diversity of identities among the Scotch-Irish helps to explain why Ulster unionism did not have greater appeal in the United States.

Those who chose to celebrate a specifically Scotch-Irish identity were embracing their connections to Ireland while separating themselves from Catholic Irish immigrants. The Scotch-Irish ethnic revival emphasized the eighteenth-century roots of immigration and life in America before the time of Andrew Jackson. The rise of Jackson to the presidency represented the time when their ethnic group no longer had to fight their way in the wilderness but had risen to the pinnacle of American politics and society. It was a success story that emphasized full assimilation into American culture, but was not in actuality an accurate portrait of the Scotch-Irish as a whole. Such emphasis on the distant past may have limited connections with contemporary Irish issues, but nevertheless some individuals and organizations supported transatlantic networks maintaining ties to Ulster. These networks have persisted to the modern day despite declining immigration.[206]

205 *Witness* 8 Nov 1912.
206 Blethen and Wood, Introduction, 4.

While the audience for Ulster unionist discourse in America was limited, members of the Scotch-Irish community were open to its dissemination, participated in political movements, and had an impact on cultural developments in Ulster itself. The enduring appeal of the Scotch-Irish heritage in America was underlined by the existence of Ulster Scots heritage groups in Massachusetts, New York, California, Illinois, Michigan, and Pennsylvania into the mid-twentieth century, and the endurance, in smaller form, of the Orange Order and the Scotch-Irish Society of the United States.[207] Recently, James Webb's prominent book *Born Fighting* emphasized the lasting legacy of the Scotch-Irish in the southern United States.[208]

In Ulster, the shared experience of emigration helped to foster unity within unionism. Ulster Scots claimed ownership of the actions of their 'racial' brethren across the Atlantic. The identity of Ulster was closely linked to an image of Revolutionary and frontier America in which the Scotch-Irish fought to uphold liberties and were determined to stand up for what they believed was right. Ulstermen during the Home Rule crises claimed the same determination and pioneering qualities for themselves.

Over the course of the twentieth century and to the modern day, Ulster unionists and loyalists have emphasized ties with the Scotch-Irish. From the publication of historical narratives, poetry, political and tourist pamphlets, promotion of educational exchanges, and preservation of the ancestral homesteads of American presidents, Northern Ireland has been portrayed as 'the cradle of the Scotch-Irish, the pioneers and frontiersmen of early American life', as one pamphleteer asserted.[209] The Ulster-Scots Agency, which was created as a cross-border endeavour of Northern Ireland and the Republic of Ireland, emphasized the United States in its pamphlets, newspaper, and murals. Murals in Northern Ireland have celebrated the Scotch-Irish role in the American Revolution, fighting spirit, and success on the frontier. The Ulster-American Folk Park in County Tyrone, established in 1976, similarly has emphasized the success of the Scotch-Irish and their pioneering character.[210] Likewise, Ulster loyalists attempting to build a

---

207 List of Scotch-Irish organizations as of 1942, Folder 1, Series 4 Miscellaneous, Box #36, SIF, HSP; Jones, 'Scotch-Irish', 907.

208 James Webb, *Born Fighting: How the Scots-Irish Shaped America* (New York: Broadway Books, 2004).

209 Eric Montgomery, 'The Scotch-Irish and Ulster' (Belfast: Ulster-Scot Historical Foundation, 1965), 3. William F. Marshall's *Ulster Sails West: The Story of the Great Emigration from Ulster to North America in the 18th Century* (Baltimore: Genealogical Publishing Company, 1984), first published in 1943, contains the remarkable poem 'Hi! Uncle Sam!' See also the works of Billy Kennedy, such as *The Making of America: How the Scots-Irish Shaped a Nation* (Greenville, SC: Ambassador, 2001).

210 Wendy Ann Wiedenhoft Murphy and Mindy Peden, 'Ulster-Scots Diaspora: Articulating a Politics of Identification after "the Peace" in Northern Ireland', in

support base in the United States have drawn upon images of conflict on the frontier and loyalty to principles of freedom as shared inheritances.[211] Above all, these common themes and continued ties in the modern day reflect the influence of views propagated by the Scotch-Irish in the late nineteenth century as Irish Protestant immigrants and their descendants attempted to find a place within American society while maintaining connections back to Ireland.

Lessons from the Northern Ireland Peace Process, ed. Timothy J. White (Madison: University of Wisconsin Press, 2013), 97–108; Billy Kennedy, 'The Ulster-Scots in the USA Today: How the Bonds Remain' (Belfast: Ulster-Scots Agency, 2009).

211 Niall Ó Dochartaigh, 'Reframing Online: Ulster Loyalists Imagine an American Audience', *Identities* 16, no. 1 (2009), 117.

5

Unionist Visits to America

Over the course of the Home Rule era, Irish unionists continuously engaged with the United States. They hoped to foster the development of a transatlantic unionist community, with resultant moral and financial support, as well as the diminishment of Irish-American nationalist credibility. Transatlantic unionist visits are one particularly revealing aspect of the relationship with the United States, reflecting the approaches and inconsistencies of unionists in direct contact with American audiences. This chapter will examine three unionist trips to America between 1886 and 1920. The visits emphasized the unionists' concern for the cultivation of Anglo-American friendship and Protestant unity, as well as their focus on countering Irish-American nationalist influence.

Irish nationalists frequently travelled to the United States to rally both moral and monetary support from the 'greater Ireland' across the Atlantic. A tradition of sending money from the United States to Ireland had been established through emigrant remittances. Remittances were substantial enough to make an impact on the Irish agricultural economy, social patterns, and family emigration patterns.[1] By the 1840s, Irish-Americans commonly sent money in support of political movements in Ireland. Daniel O'Connell and the Repeal Association collected donations sent by sympathizers in America. O'Connell's insistence on constitutional methods meant that over time he gradually lost American support to the Young Irelanders. Irish-American backing and funds played significant roles in the Young Ireland uprising of 1848, though leaders such as William Smith O'Brien were uncertain about the place of such support in the movement for Irish independence. The 1848 rising shifted the balance of external backing for Irish nationalism from Europe to America, drawn by the high numbers of Irish immigrants and political exiles in the United States.[2]

---

1 Foster, *Modern Ireland*, 371; Adams, *Ireland and the Irish Emigration*, 180–183, 226–227, 355–356, 392.
2 Christine Kinealy, *Repeal and Revolution: 1848 in Ireland* (Manchester: Manchester

As the century wore on, the nationalistic fervour of Irish–America became an important consideration of Fenian proponents. Fenian leader James Stephens arrived in the United States in May 1866, seeking armed aid and funding for a violent insurrection. He promised to lead an Irish revolutionary army against the British. Stephens raised about $60,000 on his trip, which culminated in a final rally in New York on 28 October.[3] Over the next decade, expectations of military support from Irish-American soldiers faded, but monetary and moral support became even more important. The successful tour of Charles Stewart Parnell through the United States in 1880 was so significant as to establish his place 'as the greatest political leader of nationalist Ireland since O'Connell', according to R.F. Foster.[4] Parnell raised money for political purposes and joined together the causes of land reform, relief for the impoverished, and self-government. He appealed to radicals through his platform rhetoric, including his reported 'Last Link' speech in Cincinnati, while officially maintaining constitutional stances. The United States was a significant source of funds for the Parnellite IPP, particularly as it became standard practice to pay IPP Members of Parliament.[5] The importance of American funding was reflected in the regularity of visits by a wide array of Irish nationalists including Parnell, Michael Davitt, T.M. Healy, John Dillon, T.P. O'Connor, John Redmond, William O'Brien, and others.[6]

Like the Irish nationalists, the eyes of Ulster unionists turned westward for moral and monetary support, though to a lesser extent. One of the earliest transatlantic visits by an Irish politician was, in fact, made by Orangeman and MP William Johnston. In 1872, years before the high-tide of Parnellite political tours, he travelled to the United States and Canada speaking on the Protestant ideals of civil and religious liberty.[7] Following the early visit by Johnston, subsequent political trips by Irish unionists were much rarer than those of Irish nationalists. The cases examined in this chapter were in many ways exceptional.

University Press, 2009), 45–48, 77–78, 168–177, 194–195; R.V. Comerford, *The Fenians in Context: Irish Politics and Society, 1848–82* (Dublin: Wolfhound Press, 1985), 15; Mansergh, *Irish Question*, 81–83.

3 Comerford, *Fenians in Context*, 133; Kinealy, *Repeal and Revolution*, 284–286.
4 Foster, *Modern Ireland*, 393, 405.
5 David Sim, *A Union Forever: The Irish Question and U.S. Foreign Relations in the Victorian Era* (Ithaca, NY: Cornell University Press, 2013), 138–142; Foster, *Modern Ireland*, 417; Jackson, *Home Rule*, 41.
6 Ward, *Ireland and Anglo-American Relations*, 12–14; Brundage, *Irish Nationalists in America*, 112–114, 125.
7 Parnell himself came over to the United States in 1871, but this was for personal rather than political reasons. His first political visit was in autumn 1876 with the Fenian John O'Connor Power. See Lyons, *Parnell*, 38–39, 55–57.

This chapter will first look at the 1886 trip by Reverend Dr. Richard Rutledge Kane and barrister George Hill Smith, two representatives of the Ulster Loyalist Anti-Repeal Union (ULAU). They travelled to the United States and Canada following the defeat of the first Home Rule Bill. They aimed to present the unionist case to a North American public that they perceived to be blinded by a pro-nationalist press. Second, it will focus on the aged William Johnston's visit to the Imperial Grand Council of the World, held in New York City in 1900. His visit to the United States exemplified attempts to create transatlantic connections through Orange and Protestant links. Third, the chapter will examine the 1919–1920 Ulster Protestant delegation to America, led by the MP for South Tyrone, William Coote. In an attempt to counter Éamon de Valera and Sinn Féin's American influence, Coote and six Belfast clergymen travelled to the United States to speak at mass meetings and Protestant churches throughout the country.

These three cases, spread across a wide time period, reveal how the unionists marketed themselves while overseas, their approaches to the opposition of the nationalist influence in America, and their views of the United States. The visits also show pitfalls in the unionists' American tactics. Each visit emphasized links between the United States and Ulster through their historic ties and Protestant values. The delegates credited those links with helping to foster greater friendship between Britain and America. Ultimately, these three visits reveal numerous facets of the unionists' attempts to create their own transatlantic community in answer to that of the Irish nationalists.

R.R. Kane and G.H. Smith, September–October 1886

'Our object', declared the Reverend Dr. Richard Rutledge Kane before setting off from Londonderry on a two-month tour of North America,

> is first of all to assure the people of Canada and the United States of our continued friendship, though divided by thousands of miles of ocean, and to receive whatever tokens of their interest in us they may be disposed to make us bearers of, and especially to refute slanders so diligently circulated respecting this country by that bureau of slander, the National League.[8]

Kane and his fellow delegate George Hill Smith, barrister-at-law, were sent to North America by the ULAU. They hoped to enlighten 'the people of

8 *BNL* 28 Aug 1886.

the United States and Canada on the real state of the Irish question'.[9] Their trip, coming soon after the defeat of the first Home Rule Bill, reflected the perceived importance of Irish-American influence in Irish and American politics. It was a response to both the increasingly frequent Parnellite visits across the Atlantic and the anti-unionist propaganda in the United States.

The ULAU, founded in January 1886 as the Ulster Loyalist Campaign Committee, with both Tory and Liberal membership, was one of the longest-standing unionist organizations by the time it disbanded in 1911.[10] The focus of the ULAU was anti-Home Rule propaganda. It acted as a central body for arranging speeches and demonstrations in Ireland, England, and Scotland.[11] The trip of Kane and Smith marked the ULAU's first foray into North America, though members were earlier assigned to engage in letter writing campaigns to the United States and the Empire. The trip was planned after a ULAU meeting on 23 July 1886 to determine whether the organization should remain in existence after the defeat of the Home Rule Bill. The *Belfast News-Letter* reported that not only did members affirm the necessity of the organization's work, but also resolved that a deputation be dispatched to North America to promote the cause of Irish loyalism. A *News-Letter* editorial praised the plan as 'an admirable idea, and we are sure that Canada especially – where there are many of our most loyal colonists – and in the United States also, the members of the deputation will meet with a cordial reception. The people of Ulster wish them every success'.[12]

The two delegates dispatched to North America were prominent within the ULAU and Ulster society. Smith was a barrister from Armagh educated at Queen's College Belfast. He had worked on the North-East Circuit since 1878. In addition to writing several books on law and his own reminiscences, he was a well-travelled speaker for the ULAU throughout England and Scotland. Smith would continue this task for years to come with the Irish Loyal and Patriotic Union and Irish Unionist Alliance.[13]

Kane was a more notorious figure within Belfast society. Born in Omagh in 1841, he was the rector at Belfast's Christ Church from 1882 until his death in 1898, the Grand Master of the Belfast Orangemen, and heavily

---

9 *BNL* 28 Aug 1886.
10 See Savage, 'Origins of the Ulster Unionist Party', 195, which calls the ULAU 'the central core of the unionist party in Ulster'. Alvin Jackson, while acknowledging the group as an 'important source of non-partisan opposition to the Home Rule Bill', believes that Savage exaggerates its importance – see his *Ulster Party*, 41.
11 Jackson, *Ulster Party*, 39–41; *BNL* 15 May 1886.
12 *BNL* 24 Jul 1886.
13 *Who Was Who, 1916–1928* (London: Adam & Charles Black, 1967), 971; George Hill Smith, *The North-East Bar: A Sketch, Historical and Reminiscent* (Belfast: Belfast News-Letter, 1910), 114. See also Smith's *Rambling Reminiscences: Being Leaves from My Note Book as a Public (Political) Speaker* (Newry: Newry Telegraph, 1896).

involved in the unionist politics of the city. As a member of the ULAU, he was on the platform during Lord Randolph Churchill's infamous meeting at Ulster Hall on 22 February 1886. Along with Reverend Dr. Hugh Hanna, Kane was publicly accused of inciting Protestants to riot against the Home Rule Bill in June 1886.[14]

Throughout the time of the North American trip, Kane was a focus of the Belfast Riots Commission. Hanna defended Kane and himself in a letter to the editor of *The Times*, writing, 'One thing, however, can be easily established, that for the last forty years no disturbance was originated in Belfast by the Protestant party'.[15] In the House of Commons, Nationalist MP Tom Sexton accused Kane of fleeing from the Commission by travelling overseas.[16] The editors of the *Belfast News-Letter* championed Kane in response to Sexton's speech, writing, 'Dr. Kane will return to Belfast in October, and is ready to come sooner if the Commissioners require him. Perhaps when he does reach home, Mr. Sexton may have reason to think he has arrived too soon'.[17]

Within the context of defeat of the Home Rule Bill and accusations of inciting the Belfast riots, Kane and Smith departed for North America. Their travels were closely tracked by the *Belfast News-Letter*, although there was a significant time delay on reports of their North American speeches. Interviewed at Londonderry just before setting out, Kane took issue with the nationalist portrayal of Irish loyalists as 'a bigoted set' who 'don't allow Roman Catholics to have the same liberty as themselves'. He termed this portrayal,

> a gross slander and contrary to the whole history of Irish Protestants. And we want to set everyone right as to the real object of these conspirators, to show that it is first to indulge themselves in luxuries which they could not otherwise enjoy; and secondly, to indulge their irrational hatred of empire, Crown, dominion, and influence of Protestant England.[18]

Kane considered extreme nationalists unrepresentative of the Irish as a whole. He stated, 'I believe the moral sense of the vast multitudes of Irish

---

14 Tom Hartley, *Written in Stone: The History of the Belfast City Cemetery* (Belfast: Brehon, 2006), 58–59; John Frederick MacNeice, *The Church of Ireland in Belfast: Its Growth, Condition, Needs* (Belfast: William Mullan & Sons, 1931), 17. See also Kane's obituary and account of his funeral in *BNL* 24 Nov 1898.

15 *The Times* 6 Sep 1886.

16 PD 3rd Ser., Vol. 308, 1609–1610. On the Belfast Riots, see Curtis, *Coercion and Conciliation*, 105–107; Caroline Hirst, *Religion, Politics and Violence in Nineteenth-Century Belfast: The Pound and Sandy Row* (Dublin: Four Courts Press, 2002), 174, 186.

17 *BNL* 9 Sep 1886.

18 *BNL* 28 Aug 1886.

Roman Catholics revolts at the domination of this immoral and atheistic conspiracy, and will hail with delight the dawn of Ireland's emancipation, which I believe to be at hand'.[19] Kane thought the vast majority of Irish Catholics wished not for the corrupt control of nationalists, but for substantive gains that could be achieved by working through the current British political system. He perceptively portrayed Fenians as anti-Catholic and atheistic, as many Fenians had abandoned Christianity. Kane hoped to fight against nationalist propaganda in North America and to secure for the Irish loyalists 'the sympathy and help of all who are interested in the greatness of the United Kingdom and the continued blessings of civil and religious liberty in this country'.[20]

Kane, Smith, and Smith's wife arrived in Quebec City on 6 September 1886. Kane later explained, 'In one sense we wanted to pay our respects to Canada first and last. I have a strong opinion that no one has anything to say to the main question at issue in Ireland but a citizen of the British Empire'.[21] Kane believed that strong imperial ties drew them to Canada, with greater assurances of a positive reception than in the United States. Kane was considerably apprehensive about the potential negative response from nationalist-indoctrinated Americans.

Montreal was the site of the delegates' first meeting, followed by Toronto. Some 2,500 people gathered there to hear them speak on 'Home Rule from an Irish Loyalist Point of View' on 8 September. Over the next month, they toured the eastern half of Canada, speaking at Hamilton, St. Catharines, London, Ottawa, Peterborough, Kingston, and Belleville, as well as smaller agricultural communities. Attendance was generally over a thousand and sometimes much higher.[22]

While speaking at an Orange meeting in Hamilton, Kane compared the 'diabolical deeds' of Irish nationalists to those of 'savage Indians'. A First Nations man responded to his comments by stating, 'It seemed as if their Irish visitors had but a very poor notion of what Indians really were'. He challenged them both 'to go with him to an Indian Reserve Settlement and address a meeting there', which would certainly test Kane and Smith's views of First Nations peoples as 'wild, savage, or uncivilized'.[23] A week later, the delegates found themselves on a First Nations reserve about 25 miles outside of London, Ontario. First Nations representatives, through a translator, expressed their devotion to the Queen and Empire.

19 *BNL* 28 Aug 1886.
20 *BNL* 28 Aug 1886.
21 *BNL* 18 Dec 1886.
22 *BNL* 10 Nov 1886; *The Times* 23 Sep 1886. For Orangeism in Toronto and the Kane/ Smith visit, see Jenkins, 'Ulster Transplanted', 215–216.
23 Smith, *Rambling Reminiscences*, 27.

Both Kane and Smith were taken with the events of the meeting. Smith considered it one of the most extraordinary gatherings in his long speaking career. He enthused, 'Certainly we had travelled a long distance, and broken in on one of our off nights to hold this meeting, but we would not have missed it for all the tour'.[24] Kane remarked,

Even the loyal and educated Indians seemed anxious to surpass all others in extending to us assurances of their devotion to the glorious empire of which they were proud to call themselves citizens. We had an opportunity of addressing a large meeting at an Indian reservation, at which a resolution was passed in their own language similar in terms to those passed at our other meetings; and I cannot soon forget the courtesy and hospitality with which our red brethren received and entertained us.[25]

The expression of loyalty from the First Nations people was used as a symbol of the international appeal of the unionist cause. Kane focused on the visit as symbolizing the strengths of the Empire in uniting a diverse range of people – an Empire to which the Irish unionists themselves were deeply committed.

Smith and Kane held a second meeting in Toronto on 2 October before turning their attention to the United States. Invitations for further speaking engagements were already coming in. Kane believed they could have spent their whole time in Canada. However, he felt obligated to go on to the United States, knowing that 'friends at home will be disappointed and *United Ireland* will say that we knew better than to venture into the great and free Republic with our preaching against justice to Ireland; so we turned our faces to Niagara'.[26] As they travelled through the Niagara Falls area to the United States, the delegates faced their coming task with considerable trepidation because of the large nationalist influence. Kane later remarked, 'We had made up our minds that with Canada our smooth sailing as Loyalist delegates would be at an end, and we trimmed our sails for some stiff breezes. We had yet to learn the true state of things in the United States'.[27] Kane and Smith arrived in Philadelphia, the site of their first meeting in America, on 12 October.

The delegates spoke at the Philadelphia Academy of Music two days later. Philadelphia was one of the key cities of Scotch-Irish settlement and had significant Orange presence. Kane expressed amazement at the level of

24 Smith, *Rambling Reminiscences*, 28.
25 *BNL* 10 Nov 1886, 18 Dec 1886.
26 *BNL* 18 Dec 1886.
27 *BNL* 18 Dec 1886.

support they received starting with a procession to the meeting. He wondered if the crowd was actually made up of Irish nationalist supporters of Parnell and Jeremiah O'Donovan Rossa in disguise, stating, 'A band and brilliant procession appeared outside the hotel to escort us to the place of meeting. Was this band and all this ovation intended by Rossaites and Parnellites and their American sympathizers as a trap to inspire us with false confidence?'[28] Though Rossa's influence was waning by 1886, Kane's reference to him recalled the extremism and violence of the dynamite campaign, which had greatly informed the unionist view of the United States.

In Philadelphia, Kane and Smith were accompanied by 300 Orangemen and members of the American Protestant Association as they processed from the Continental Hotel to the Academy of Music. At least 7,000 people crowded into the amphitheatre, with hundreds turned away for lack of space. Smith noted that this was the largest crowd he addressed over the span of his entire career.[29] Kane described the Philadelphia gathering as 'the most magnificent meeting of our tour', though it was held in what he believed was 'hostile territory'. Newspaper reports of the meeting from the *Philadelphia Times* were so popular that 10,000 additional copies of the issue were printed, and the report was later published in pamphlet form.[30]

The delegates next spoke on 18 October in Boston, which Kane considered to be 'the headquarters of Fenianism'. This was an interesting claim on the part of Kane, because Boston was generally considered to be more of a stronghold of Parnell and constitutional nationalism. For the first time, hostile elements formed a significant part of the audience – about 800 'avowed' Fenians within a total crowd of 3,500. Kane reported that the Fenians 'hissed at the name of the Queen and any reference to the British Empire'. Police removed a few noisy pro-nationalists. Overall, however, Kane believed that the delegates had stood their ground against the Fenians: 'We didn't for a moment lower our flag of loyalty to the Queen and loyalty to the Union, but we held aloft, as in my opinion Irish Loyalists ought ever to hold aloft, our flag of loyalty to Ireland'.[31] The final meetings of the trip, held in New York City and Brooklyn, were less hostile than the Boston gathering, and left Kane encouraged by the delegation's reception in the United States.

Kane and Smith addressed several themes in their speeches to North American audiences. One of their main goals was to refute rampant nationalist propaganda, which they believed was spread because of nationalist control of the press. The majority of Canadians and Americans had never been exposed to pro-Union arguments. Kane recognized, 'Our Nationalist opponents were not slow to appeal to people not only outside Ireland, but outside of the empire of the Queen for sympathy and support in their determined and deliberate efforts to dismember the United Kingdom'.[32] He believed that unionists were hesitant to appeal to the United States because the bounds of the Empire would be broken, which contrasted with nationalist views of America as part of 'greater Ireland'. This hesitancy explains why Kane, Smith, and other unionists were much more confident in their appeals to Canada. It also points to why actively soliciting funds was not made an explicit part of their agenda. They had accused nationalists of being foreign-run and unrepresentative of the Irish because so much of their monetary support came from America. As the first unionist delegation to North America, Kane and Smith had expected hostile reactions and would not have wanted to embarrass themselves by failing to collect significant sums when nationalists had been so successful. They did, however, accept donations from local organizations to fund the trip itself, which otherwise would have been paid for out-of-pocket by Kane, Smith, and the ULAU.[33]

Kane and Smith portrayed the unionists as loyal and proud Irishmen. 'I am an Irishman all over', Kane told the Philadelphia audience, 'and since the Flood none of my family have been born out of Ireland. But it would take a Harvey and a microscope to discover a drop of Irish blood in Charles Parnell's body. The Union secures to my county its central state and her honour'. Irish unionists were as concerned for Ireland's honour and independence as any other part of the Irish population, especially when compared to Parnell's perceived American loyalties. Parnell had well known American heritage and many family members living in the United States.[34] The idea of Irish Protestants as proud Irish patriots, sharing a feeling of Irish nationality, was something Gladstone hoped to pick up on with the Home Rule project. Irish Protestants were deeply invested in Ireland, but most, like Kane, determined that the best chance to secure a prosperous future lay with the Union.[35] These ideas were underscored by the hundreds of thousands of loyal Irishmen who, as Kane described, 'were prepared, if

32 *BNL* 28 Oct 1886, 18 Dec 1886.
33 *BNL* 25 Oct 1886, 2 Nov 1886.
34 R.F. Foster, *Charles Stewart Parnell: The Man and His Family* (Hassocks: Harvester Press, 1976), 54–56, 225–233.
35 D. George Boyce, 'In the Front Rank of the Nation: Gladstone and the Unionists of Ireland, 1868–1893', in *Gladstone Centenary Essays*, ed. David W. Bebbington and Roger Swift (Liverpool: Liverpool University Press, 2000), 187–192.

necessary, once more to draw their swords and prevent the dismemberment of the empire'.[36]

According to Kane, the unionists were prepared to oppose separation from the British Empire 'to the bitter end'. Any Home Rule policy leading to separation from the Empire would degrade the position of Ireland in the world.[37] Kane and Smith especially emphasized imperial unity and power in their Canadian meetings. Under the Union, the Irish like the Canadians were equal members of an Empire which they had helped to build. Home Rule and separation would render Ireland 'a poor nation cut adrift from the British Empire'.[38] Home Rule would also lead to a degraded economic and political position for Ireland as compared to England and Scotland. Ireland would have to pay taxes and contribute to the British armed forces without any representation at Westminster, destroying Irish equality with England and Scotland.[39]

In the United States, the delegates no longer appealed to imperial unity as they had in Canada. Kane explained that they approached their American speeches as 'advocates of Protestant truth and liberty', ideals which would also be in 'deadly peril' under Home Rule.[40] Fear of Catholic domination of Protestants was an element in Kane's speeches throughout North America. Kane asserted that Protestants dreaded the rule of Catholic Archbishops Thomas Croke and William Walsh. He declared that 'Irish Protestants would never be slaves to political adventurers and religious domination'.[41] However, Kane believed the problem lay in the Catholic hierarchy rather than the majority of Irish Catholic people. He felt that the Irish on the whole were satisfied with the full equality, freedom, and prosperity they had gained through the Union.[42]

The main focus of Kane's and Smith's speeches was attacking Parnellism. Kane accused Parnellites of inconsistency in their preaching of Home Rule or separation depending on their location. In Canada, Kane emphasized that Parnellism meant separation, 'that the last link that bound her to England would be broken' and control of Ireland would be in the hands of criminals who had orchestrated such outrages as the Phoenix Park murders.[43] These Canadian speeches accused Parnell of advocating total separation from Britain and the Empire.

---

36 *BNL* 22 Oct 1886, 28 Oct 1886, 18 Dec 1886; *Philadelphia Inquirer* 15 Oct 1886; *NYT* 22 Sep 1886.
37 *The Times* 9 Sep 1886; *BNL* 18 Dec 1886.
38 *BNL* 26 Oct 1886.
39 *BNL* 25 Oct 1886.
40 *BNL* 18 Dec 1886.
41 *BNL* 22 Oct 1886.
42 *BNL* 25 Oct 1886.
43 *BNL* 25 Oct 1886, 26 Oct 1886.

In contrast, when faced with hostile Fenian elements in the United States, Kane emphasized that Parnell was lying to America's Fenians to gain monetary support. Parnell would never follow through with demands for full separation. Kane played on the suspicions that purist American Fenians felt toward Parnellite constitutionalism.[44] Indeed, according to Kane, Fenians and Orangemen had much more in common than either of them with the Parnellites. Kane explained,

Both the Fenians and the Orangemen desire that Ireland should be a nation, not a province paying tribute to a foreign country, but a nation. The Fenians wanted Ireland to be a separate nation from England and a republic. The Orangemen were content that Ireland should be as much a nation as England and the same nation.[45]

Separation in itself was not the problem, although Orangemen would rather remain within the Union. The problem was with a Home Rule policy that would degrade Ireland to the status of a colony paying tribute to the mother country. This idea of unionists preferring full separation to Home Rule was not unique: at times a unionist strand of thought emerged which argued that the unionist minority would be better able to defend its interests in an independent Ireland rather than under a Home Rule system.[46] In this argument, unionist loyalties were not to the Empire in itself, but rather to the protections the Empire was able to offer them as a minority group within Ireland.

Kane and Smith also attacked Parnell's role as the leader of the IPP. Smith accused Parnell of being a megalomaniac with absolute control over IPP members to the extent that they were only able to represent Parnell rather than their constituents.[47] Parnellites, as described by Kane, were 'the most contemptible set of hirelings that have ever appeared in Irish history'. None was worse than Parnell himself.[48] To gain monetary support, Parnellites portrayed Ireland as a 'down-trodden country' when, in reality, according to Smith, 'there was no class of tenantry in the world that enjoyed greater privileges either under the land purchase or eviction bills'. Irishmen were in every way equal to the other citizens of the British Empire, meaning the land agitation was based on a sham.[49] Parnell himself was a landlord

---

44 Foster, *Modern Ireland*, 398–399.
45 *BNL* 18 Dec 1886. See similar remarks by Kane at the New York Cooper Institute, *San Francisco Evening Bulletin* 22 Oct 1886.
46 See Jackson, *Ulster Party*, 122.
47 *BNL* 22 Oct 1886.
48 *BNL* 18 Dec 1886.
49 *BNL* 26 Oct 1886; *Philadelphia Inquirer* 15 Oct 1886.

who enforced payment of rents by the same process of writs he condemned when leading the land agitation movement. He was no better than any other landlord. The only Irishmen benefiting from money donated by Americans and Canadians to the nationalist cause were the Parnellites themselves. They would say anything about the state of the Irish people or their own separatist intentions to gain funds 'from dupes in America and Canada'.[50] According to Smith, this money had been spent lifting Parnell out of poverty and supporting others 'in luxury'. Smith concluded, 'The American people had better keep their money in their pockets, as of the last $40,000 which they sent to Parnell $25,000 of it went into his pockets'.[51]

The reception of Kane and Smith was mostly positive over the course of their tour. They faced hostility from nationalists in Boston. At their meeting in Kingston a nationalist proposed a pro-home rule resolution which garnered controversy but gained little support.[52] Otherwise, following Kane and Smith's speeches, a leading member of each community proposed pro-unionist resolutions assuring the delegates of their sympathy. Reflecting the Orange character of the meeting, the audience at Philadelphia also resolved to 'support those struggling to resist the usurpation of Popery and conspiracy of the Church of Rome against Ireland's rights and liberties'.[53]

In the wake of such support, Kane was left wishing the delegates had more time to spread the unionist message in the United States. He reported to a Belfast audience that their short stay was enough to convince him 'the Irish Loyalist and Protestant loses nothing of his attachment to his principles and to his religion by being transplanted to American soil'. Kane hoped future unionist delegations would continue the work they had begun, which would eventually cause the dominance of Irish-American nationalism to melt away. Without this element, the United States and United Kingdom would naturally gravitate toward each other because of their similar political, social, and moral values. Kane believed in the future the two countries would 'be found shoulder to shoulder, joint and unconquerable guardians of constitutional liberty, political reform, and Scriptural truth'.[54]

Kane and Smith arrived back in Queenstown on 30 October, where they were interviewed by the *Belfast News-Letter* before travelling on to Belfast. Kane reported there had been marked change on the Irish question in North America over the two months of their tour. 'We shall disappoint our friends on the other side of the Atlantic immensely', he stated, 'if we do not continue

50 *BNL* 29 Sep 1886, 25 Oct 1886; *NYT* 22 Sep 1886.
51 *Philadelphia North American* 15 Oct 1886; *NYT* 8 Sep 1886; *Philadelphia Inquirer* 15 Oct 1886.
52 *BNL* 25 Oct 1886; *The Times* 29 Sep 1886.
53 *Philadelphia Inquirer* 15 Oct 1886.
54 *BNL* 18 Dec 1886.

that interchange of sympathy and sentiment and principle, which was begun – so far as organized change is concerned – so auspiciously in the mission'.[55] The *Belfast News-Letter* responded to the support shown for the unionist delegation in North America by observing in an editorial, 'Those who are perpetually boasting about the greater Ireland beyond the sea ought to bear in mind that there are two Irelands beyond the sea'.[56]

William Johnston, July–August 1900

By the time of William Johnston's visit to the United States in 1900, he was a seasoned traveller across the Atlantic. On each of his four trips to North America, he was treated like Orange royalty. Prior to his first visit in 1872, Johnston gained notoriety for defying the Party Processions Act, for which he spent time in jail, and he became well known internationally as an Orange leader. During his North American visits, he promoted stronger ties between Britain and the United States by drawing on Orange principles and international connections.

Johnston was born in Downpatrick in 1829, gaining low-church values from his Episcopalian parents. He became a member of the Ballydonnell Orange Lodge in May 1848. Early on, he had a tumultuous relationship with the Orange Order, centred on his promotion of the Grand Black Chapter and controversy surrounding old higher degrees.[57] Johnston also disagreed with the official Orange policy of cooperating with the provisions of the Party Processions Act of 1850 and Party Emblems Act of 1860. He was determined to influence both the Orange leadership and ordinary brethren who accepted the ban on processions. He toured local Orange halls making speeches attacking the government. He staged an illegal Orange parade on 12 July 1867 in Newtownards, for which he was arrested. His subsequent stint in prison made Johnston an Orange martyr. He was quickly returned as an Independent MP for South Belfast. In Parliament, he acted to repeal the anti-parading acts in 1870.[58]

Johnston was heavily involved in the formation of the Imperial Grand Council of the World. This Triennial Council originated from the desire

---

55 *BNL* 2 Nov 1886, 18 Dec 1886.
56 *BNL* 29 Sep 1886.
57 M.W. Dewar, John Brown, and S.E. Long, *Orangeism: A New Historical Appreciation* (Belfast: Grand Orange Lodge of Ireland, 1967), 141; Aikan McClelland, *William Johnston of Ballykilbeg* (Lurgan: Ulster Society Publications, 1990), 4–20. On the original Grand Black Chapter of Ireland, founded in 1797, see R.M. Sibbett, *Orangeism in Ireland and throughout the Empire* (Belfast: Henderson and Company, 1915), Vol. 2, 161–162.
58 McClelland, *William Johnston*, 26, 41; Dewar, Brown, and Long, *Orangeism*, 142.

of Irish Orangemen to spark closer cooperation between lodges in the United Kingdom and the Empire. Supporting the idea, Johnston proposed a resolution at the December 1865 meeting of the Grand Lodge of Ireland. The resolution provided for regular gatherings of Orange representatives to 'take into consideration the state of Orangeism and Protestantism, with a view of devising means for the furtherance of the cause of Truth, and the extension of the Orange Society'.[59] The subsequent Grand Conference was held in Belfast in 1866, with representatives present from Ireland, England, Scotland, and Canada. This conference organized the Imperial Grand Council of the World, which met for the first time in 1867 at Radley's Hotel in London. American Orangemen first attended the Triennial Council three years later at the 1870 meeting in Toronto.[60]

Before his 1900 trip to the United States, Johnston made three visits to North America, two of which were to attend meetings of the Triennial Council in Canada.[61] Newspaper reports from Canadian cities stated Johnston was treated like royalty on his visits. Processions with thousands of people greeted him on his arrival.[62] In 1872, after spending most of his trip in Canada, he visited New York and addressed an Orange audience at the Cooper Institute. With the visit coming only a year after the deadly New York City Orange Riot of 12 July 1871, police presence at Johnston's meeting was considerable. Superintendent James J. Kelso detailed 275 patrolmen to occupy the hall, with 450 patrolmen held in reserve.[63]

The meeting passed with no instances of conflict. Representatives of the New York Lodges occupied the platform, celebrating Johnston as a 'champion of civil and religious liberty'.[64] The *New York Herald* reported, 'Mr. Johnston has acquired considerable notoriety in Ireland, in consequence of his determined adherence to Orangeism, and also because he had taken high rank in the Order, notwithstanding opposition of some aristocratic persons who are identified with the Orange association'.[65] Johnston was

---

59 McClelland, *William Johnston*, 39.

60 McClelland, *William Johnston*, 38–39; 'Brief History of the Imperial Grand Orange Council', Report of the Proceedings of the Thirteenth Triennial Session of the Imperial Grand Orange Council of the Loyal Orange Association of the World. Held in the City of Dublin, Ireland, July 15th and 17th, 1903, PRONI D1889/6/5A.

61 These were the 1879 Council at Ottawa and the 1891 Council at Toronto.

62 See Johnston's newspaper file at PRONI D880/7/5B, which contains his clippings from the Belleville *Daily Intelligencer*, Kingston *British Whig*, Victoria *Warder and Commercial Advertiser*, *Toronto Sentinel and Orange and Protestant Advocate*, Vancouver *Daily Telegram*, *Manitoba Daily Free Press*, and Toronto *Evening Telegram*, amongst others.

63 *New York Tribune* 13 Aug 1872.

64 *New York Sun* 13 Aug 1872.

65 *New York Herald* 13 Aug 1872.

renowned for his principled stances and as an 'everyman', opposed to the higher ranking brethren who he fought against to repeal the Party Processions Act.

When it came time for him to address the meeting, Johnston spoke on some of the problems which were inherent with the transfer of Orangeism to the United States. Though American Orangemen lived in a republic rather than a monarchy, he said, they still held the same principles celebrated by the Orange Order worldwide:

They felt that they were one with those in the British Isles, and their firm and resolute determination to uphold the cause which was victorious at the Reformation and triumphant at the Boyne gave civil and religious liberty not only to England, Scotland, and Ireland, but also to this great Republic – as much to New York and Boston as to Belfast and Londonderry.[66]

American Orangemen had been seen as a British faction in the United States, where Anglophobia was common since the days of the American Revolution. Johnston stated if American Orangemen were actually supporting Britain, he would not have visited them. He could never support a group which went against its home country's constitution. Johnston concluded his speech by thanking

the audience for the superb welcome they had given him, which he accepted, not as an individual, but as the member of a society bound to spread civil liberty and evangelical truth throughout the world. And above all he begged them never to be separated, in word nor in thought from their Protestant brethren on the other side of the water, and to remember that both had common heroes and common lodges.[67]

The relationship between the United States and the United Kingdom had changed drastically by the time of Johnston's visit to America in 1900. The British response to the Spanish–American War in 1898 was seen as a welcome sign of friendship to the United States. With the settlement of the Venezuela boundary dispute by arbitration in 1899, a rapprochement began between the two countries. This was further solidified by the Hay-Pauncefote Treaty of 1901 on control of the Panama Canal, and the settlement of the Alaska–Canada boundary dispute in 1903. The rapprochement was marked by the rise of Anglo-Saxonist sentiment, heralding the English-speaking nations as

---

66 *New York Herald* 13 Aug 1872.
67 *NYT* 13 Aug 1872.

superior to every other civilization on earth due to their exceptional racial characteristics.[68] The Anglo-American alliance in politics and sentiment was celebrated by Johnston during his visit.

By the time of his trip to New York in 1900, Johnston was an elder statesman within the Orange Order, the only surviving member of the original Triennial Council in 1867. Though his wife was ill at the time, Johnston took the opportunity to attend the twelfth meeting of the Triennial Council, held in New York. He also planned to speak at gatherings in Philadelphia and Boston.[69] He left home on 12 July 1900 to attend the Orange procession in Belfast, at which he presided. Johnston noted in his diary, 'A magnificent demonstration, and a cordial greeting for me'.[70] In his speech to the Orange crowd, Johnston reported his plans for his transatlantic journey, stating that 'it was a pleasing thing for him (the chairman) to be able to stand there on the last day that he expected to spend in Ireland for at least a couple of months, for on the morrow he sailed, please God, from the Maiden City to attend the triennial council of Orangemen in New York'.[71] He planned to tell Americans of 'the loyal Ulstermen – (hear, hear) – and how they rejoiced to know that the Orangemen of the United States were one with the Orangemen of Her Majesty's dominions in upholding the Protestant and Orange cause of Derry's watchword, "No Surrender". (Cheers)'.[72]

The *Belfast News-Letter* reported on Johnston's speech and the rest of the Twelfth celebrations. The reporter mused on the international reach of the Orange organization, writing, 'It is gratifying to remember that the Orange Institution is a world-wide organization'. Though the Orange Order was centred in Belfast, its reach went throughout the world with North America in particular playing an important role. 'It is a power in the United States and in Canada – a power which does much to make firmer ties uniting the different branches of the Anglo-Saxon race. Wherever Orangemen are found they are animated by the same spirit and true to the same principles; their aims are identical and their methods alike'.[73]

Johnston left the next morning for Londonderry, where he boarded the *Furnessia* to New York, arriving on 22 July. He was greeted on the pier by David Graham, the Grand Master of the Supreme Grand Lodge of

68   Ward, *Ireland and Anglo-American Relations*, 30; Charles S. Campbell, *Anglo-American Understanding, 1898–1903* (Baltimore: Johns Hopkins University Press, 1957), 346; Stuart Anderson, *Race and Rapprochement: Anglo-Saxonism and Anglo-American Relations, 1895–1904* (Rutherford, NJ: Farleigh Dickson University Press, 1981), 11–13.
69   McClelland, *William Johnston*, 105; *BNL* 4 Aug 1900.
70   12 Jul 1900, Johnston diary, PRONI D880/2/52.
71   *BNL* 13 Jul 1900.
72   *BNL* 13 Jul 1900.
73   *BNL* 13 Jul 1900.

the United States, and other representatives. Graham was a leader during the New York City Orange Riot in 1871.[74] The next day, Johnston visited meetings of the State Grand Lodge of New York and the Grand Black Chapter of the United States. He was later able to attend a session of the Supreme Grand Lodge of the United States, also held in New York City. A mass meeting was held in Lyric Hall to welcome Johnston along with the other Council delegates.[75] At the meeting, Johnston enthusiastically spoke of his reception to the United States and celebrated the ties between Britain and America through the Orange institution and the wider world. 'Thank God for the existence to-day of the United States and for the existence of the British empire', he said. He read a note from Joseph Chamberlain wishing him well on his visit, and emphasized that the Orange Order 'was not exclusively British, and there was no reason why American Protestants and lovers of liberty should not join it'.[76]

Nevertheless, the Orange Order faced criticism upon Johnston's visit, with the *Boston Pilot* editorializing,

William Johnston, the Irish M.P. for Belfast, is being lionized by his brethren in this country, where he is visiting on a mission to unite the two branches of the 'Anglo-Saxon' race. He is indorsed by Joseph Chamberlain, and recommended to British-Americans who have become naturalized without forswearing their allegiance to the Orange institution, which they hold higher than the British throne.

By implication, Orangemen held their own order higher than their American citizenship as well, and took refuge in the majority to attack the minority Irish Catholics. 'Orangemen', the *Boston Pilot* accused, 'everywhere put their order ahead of their government, and are terrible desperate fellows when they outnumber their opponents by only ten to one'.[77]

The Triennial Council began on 26 July in the auditorium of the Grand Opera House. While there were many Orange members from the United States and Canada, Johnston was the only delegate from Ireland or Great Britain, indicating that the Triennial Council was perhaps more important to Johnston personally than it was to the Grand Lodge of Ireland as a whole.

---

74 22 Jul 1900, Johnston diary, PRONI D880/2/52; Report of the Proceedings of the Thirteenth Triennial Session of the Imperial Orange Council of the Loyal Orange Association of the World. Held in the City of Dublin, Ireland, July 15th and 17th, 1903, PRONI D1889/6/5A.

75 23 Jul, 24 Jul 1900, Johnston diary, PRONI D880/2/52; *BNL* 14 Aug 1900; *NYT* 24 Jul 1900.

76 *NYT* 25 Jul 1900; *Evening Star* 25 Jul 1900.

77 Reprinted in the *Springfield Daily Republican* 21 Aug 1900.

He wrote in his diary, 'We had a grand attendance from Canada and the states. I was the only representative from HOME'. Along with Johnston, the Grand Lodge of Ireland had contacted four Canadian brethren to represent their views at the Triennial Council.[78]

The Triennial Council in 1900 dealt with practical issues, such as the implementation of a universal ritual of induction. The council secretary reported, 'The New York brethren gave the members and delegates a right royal reception, spending thousands of dollars on the same. There were many and successful public meetings, receptions, and an enjoyable excursion to New York harbour, and a parade which included 3000 Orangemen with colours on'.[79] The Orange celebration at New York Harbor took place on 27 July, ending the Triennial Council with Johnston giving a speech.[80]

The next day, 3,000 to 4,000 Orangemen paraded through New York City, their first Orange parade since 1871. Extra police were detailed to line the parade route because of fears that trouble could break out. An Irish-American group, the Sons of Limerick, had applied for a parade permit over the same route and was refused because of memories of the riot years. They threatened to march without a permit. A newspaper report described, 'For two hours this afternoon Fifth Avenue, save for the tall buildings and splendid mansions, might have been taken for one of the principal streets of Belfast'. Orange flags were waved and airs played. The parade passed with only a few incidents of shouting and waving of green flags from the small number of onlookers.[81]

A letter appeared in the *Belfast News-Letter* from James Magowan of New York, reporting the events of the day. He stated that the New York Orangemen refrained from parading on the twelfth in preparation for the Triennial Council parade. Magowan wrote,

Of course, you have no idea how hard it is in New York to be loyal, as many people imagine we are against the U.S., but that is a silly idea of the opposite party. We do not molest them, and they dare not lay a finger on us as a body, because we have the same freedom and privileges as they have on the 17th of March. We have a noble cause to fight for; they have none, although, I am sorry to say, they are away in the majority by a long lead.[82]

78 *Toronto Sentinel* 28 Jun 1900.
79 Imperial Orange Council, Dublin, 1903, PRONI D1889/6/5A.
80 Imperial Orange Council, Dublin, 1903, PRONI D1889/6/5A; 22 Jul 1900, Johnston diary, PRONI D880/2/52.
81 *NYT* 28 Jul 1900, 29 Jul 1900; *Chicago Tribune* 27 Jul 1900; 29 Jul 1900; *Washington Post* 29 Jul 1900.
82 *BNL* 14 Aug 1900.

Magowan said city officials protected their right to process and to wave orange flags and ribbons.

Johnston noted in his diary, 'A brilliant day. At 2, carriages with delegates left the Ashland House for the Parade of Orangemen. Black Knights, in full regalia, headed it. David Graham acted efficiently as Grand Marshall. "Three Cheers for Johnston of Ballykilbeg" was constantly repeated. All went off well'.[83] These New York proceedings so impressed Johnston that he reported back to the Belfast Orangemen that he believed, 'Orangeism has done infinite service in promoting friendly sentiments between the United States and Britain'.[84]

For the rest of his time in New York, Johnston visited old friends, toured the Museum of Art, and saw Central Park. He left for Philadelphia in the company of Orange brethren on 2 August. The American Orangemen escorted Johnston from place to place, and showed him the sights of each city. Johnston wrote in his diary entry for the next day, 'Very fine. Brother Abernethy took me to see the old house where Betsy Ross made the first American flag for Washington. I laid my hands on Franklin's tomb; and stood beside the place where Penn, in 1682, signed treaty with Indians'. He also saw Independence Hall and other Philadelphia sights, and spoke at a picnic of the Kensington Association.

On the afternoon of 4 August, he attended an 'enthusiastic Orange demonstration' at Washington Park, where, he noted, 'hundreds of old friends shook hands. The welcome was touching'.[85] The *Philadelphia Inquirer* reported between 2,000 and 3,000 Orangemen present at the demonstration. The article described Johnston as 'the hero of the crowd, which pressed upon him and almost fought for a chance to grasp his hand. Many of those in the audience had voted for him when he first went to Parliament in 1868, after having been imprisoned for parading on Orangemen's Day, July 12'.[86] Johnston believed the American Orangemen were united by the principles fought for at the Battle of the Boyne, just as America and Great Britain were now united by Anglo-Saxon principles. 'I came here profoundly impressed that God had given the control of the destinies of the world to the Anglo-Saxon race', he told the crowd.

In Great Britain, under God, we think we can take care of ourselves and guess you Americans think the same of yourselves. But I am earnestly

83 28 Jul 1900, Johnston diary, PRONI D880/2/52.
84 S.E. Long, 'Belfast County Grand Orange Lodge Centenary: Official History 1863–1963' (n.p.: Universal Publishing, 1963), 22.
85 4 Aug 1900, Johnston diary, PRONI D880/2/52.
86 *Philadelphia Inquirer* 5 Aug 1900.

glad to see the good understanding between these two nations and I hope it may continue to the judgment day. You know when European potentates wanted to intervene between your government and Spain during the war our statesmen told them Great Britain would not permit any such interference. And we watched your armies in Cuba and in the Philippines and have felt you were fighting for the emancipation of mankind. I believe upon the American armies has rested the blessing of Almighty God.[87]

For Johnston, the Anglo-Saxon race had united together against the European Catholic powers to bring Protestant freedom to the world through imperialism. This Anglo-American alliance, exemplified by the unity of the Orange Order across the Atlantic, stood in sharp contrast to the other transatlantic Irish connection between nationalists.

A banquet was given in Johnston's honour on 6 August. He was excited to note that almost 130 were in attendance.[88] However, the triumphant tone of his visit took a radical shift when he received a letter on 8 August announcing the death of his wife, Georgiana. He wrote in his diary, 'I deeply regret not being at home. Arranged with W. Abernethy to leave at 11 am tomorrow for New York'.[89] All of his other plans, including a trip to Boston, were cancelled and with the help of Orange brothers Abernethy and Graham, Johnston made arrangements to travel to Belfast as quickly as possible. He left New York on 14 August, and arrived back in Belfast eleven days later.[90]

Johnston's message of Anglo-American unity and the spread of Protestant freedom through imperialism chimed well with the mood of the nation. Following the Spanish–American War, jingoistic nationalism swept the United States. At the turn of the century, Americans embraced a 'positive' Anglo-Saxonism, believing the superior Anglo-Saxon race could uplift inferior races in conquered territories. Though racism did not decline, there was a decline in fears that immigration would threaten the nation. The energetic anti-Catholicism which characterized the early 1890s had faded away. The American Protective Association, an organization with strong Orange connections which had briefly flourished from 1893 to 1894, now denied its Orange associations.[91] This left the American Orange Order in a state of transition. Johnston's message helped point the way to a path upon which they

---

87 *Philadelphia Inquirer* 5 Aug 1900.
88 6 Aug 1900, Johnston diary, PRONI D880/2/52.
89 8 Aug 1900, Johnston diary, PRONI D880/2/52.
90 *Boston Globe* 8 Aug 1900; Entries for 9 to 14 Aug 1900, Johnston diary, PRONI D880/2/52.
91 Higham, *Strangers in the Land*, 79–85, 108–111; Kinzer, *Episode in Anti-Catholicism*, 232.

might find greater success in the United States, at least temporarily. However, the American Orange Order also continued to promote anti-Catholicism and ties to Ireland as they struggled to find a place in American society.

Ulster Protestant Deputation, December 1919–February 1920

On 24 November 1919, a seven-member deputation sponsored by the UUC left from Liverpool for a three-month tour of the United States.[92] As representatives of Irish Protestant churches, the delegates aimed to defend their pro-Union stances. They intended to refute 'the gross charges' made against the British government as part of the long-running propaganda efforts of Irish-American nationalists and, more recently, Éamon de Valera and his fellow Sinn Féiners. In a pamphlet written after their return, the delegates outlined the objectives of their trip. They hoped to counter the 'misrepresentation and falsehood' of nationalist reports on the Irish situation; lay before the American people the privileges and liberties that Ireland had gained from the Union; emphasize the historic ties between the north of Ireland and America along with Anglo-Saxon characteristics that helped 'bind the American and British races in mutual hope'; and entreat Americans to refrain from interfering in the Irish question.[93]

William Coote, MP for South Tyrone, led the deputation. An Orangeman and Presbyterian, Coote worked as a businessman in the provisions trade in Tyrone. He held his parliamentary seat from 1916 to 1922.[94] Accompanying him were six ministers from different Protestant churches. Alexander Wylie Blue was a Scottish Presbyterian, born in Argyll and educated at Glasgow University and United Presbyterian Theological College in Edinburgh. After years preaching in Glasgow and Sunderland, he was invited to be the new minister at Belfast's May Street Presbyterian Church. He quickly integrated himself into the Belfast Protestant community, genuinely believing in the strength of 'Ulster's cause'.[95] Like Blue, fellow Presbyterian delegate William Corkey was known as a great platform speaker on the subject of Ulster

---

92 I would like to thank Reverend Robin Roddie at the Methodist Historical Society of Ireland and Dr. Susan Hood at the Church of Ireland RCB Library for help with biographical information on these delegates. See *NYT* and *Chicago Tribune* 23 Nov 1919 for announcements of the delegation's departure.
93 'America and the Irish Question. A Short Account of the Visit of the Delegation from Protestant Ireland to the Churches in the United States of America. December 1919–February 1920. By the Delegates' (Belfast: Belfast News-Letter, 1920).
94 *Who Was Who, 1916–1928*, 226.
95 D. Frazer-Hurst, *'Wylie Blue': The Life of the Rev. A. Wylie Blue, D.D.* (London: James Clarke, 1957), 1–16, 44.

unionism. As the minister at Belfast's Townsend Street Presbyterian Church, Corkey had already written pamphlets on education and the influence of the Catholic Church. He later gained prominence by lobbying for greater Protestant influence on the Northern Irish constitution and educational system. In subsequent writings he used his participation in the deputation to prove the strength of his loyalty to Ulster.[96]

Three Methodists were selected as part of the delegation due to the strength of Methodism in the United States. Frederick E. Harte grew up as the son of a Methodist itinerant minister in the south of Ireland. In 1892, he was accepted as a candidate for the ministry at Belfast's Methodist College. Working at Donegall Square Methodist Church in Belfast since June 1917, he had long wished to visit America. He wrote that he never would have imagined the way in which this dream was fulfilled, going to the United States 'to tell the truth about Ireland'.[97] Edward Hazelton, also the son of a Methodist minister, was born in Arklow in 1852. At the time of the deputation he was a supernumerary minister at Belfast's Falls Road Methodist Church. C. Wesley Maguire, the secretary of the delegation, was born in Lurgan in 1890, educated at Belfast's Methodist College, and served as minister at the Donegall Square Church. In 1921, he resigned from the Methodist Church to join the Church of Ireland ministry. The final member of the deputation was Louis Crooks. He was educated at Belfast's Methodist College, Queen's College Cork, and Trinity College Dublin, and was rector at Knockbreda Episcopal Church. He was also Grand Chaplain of the Grand Orange Lodge of Ireland and Imperial Grand Chaplain.[98]

At the time of the deputation's visit to the United States, David Lloyd George's government had set up a committee on Ireland. Led by former Ulster unionist leader Walter Long, the committee recommended the creation of two separate Home Rule governments, one each in northern and southern Ireland. The committee's recommendations were incorporated into the Government of Ireland Bill, introduced on 22 December 1919. Discussions on the bill in Parliament were ongoing throughout the time of the deputation's visit.[99] Unlike the two previous cases discussed in this chapter, the delegates in 1919 had to deal with the fact that Home Rule had

---

96 William Corkey, *Episode in the History of Protestant Ulster, 1923–1947* (Belfast: Dorman & Sons, 1959), 152. See also Corkey's *The Church of Rome and Irish Unrest: How Hatred of Britain is Taught in Irish Schools* (Edinburgh: William Bishop, 1918).

97 Frederick E. Harte, *The Road I Have Travelled: The Experiences of an Irish Methodist Minister* (Belfast: Wm. Mullan & Son, 1947), 32.

98 *Clergy of Down and Dromore* (Belfast: Ulster Historical Foundation, 1996), Part I, 285; Part II, 155.

99 PD Commons 5th Ser., Vol. 123, 1168–1223; Jackson, *Home Rule*, 197–199; Foster, *Modern Ireland*, 503.

already been conceded. The primary target of the unionist delegates in this case was not the Home Rule party, but more extreme Irish republicans. The early stages of the Anglo-Irish War had already commenced, and Ireland was on the cusp of independence. This context contributed to feelings of frustration and desperation amongst the delegates.

In the United States, the deputation came up against the presence of de Valera, who had travelled in secret to America in June 1919. He intended to conduct a brief tour of the country in pursuance of two goals: the establishment of an American loan for the new Irish republican government through a 'bond-certificate' programme, and official recognition of the Irish republic which would be vital in the international political arena. He made his first public appearance with a press conference at New York's Waldorf-Astoria Hotel on 23 June. Through publicity and propaganda, he continued to garner attention for the cause of the Irish republic for the entire eighteen months of his trip.[100] De Valera faced divisions within Irish-American nationalism and engaged in a power struggle over who would ultimately direct the nationalist movement in the United States. At the same time, he was confronted with the presence of the Ulster Protestant deputation, which arrived in America in early December.

Upon landing in New York, the delegates issued a press statement asserting that they were not on a financial or political campaign, and that their purpose was non-sectarian, raising 'no religious issue'. Rather, they were there to counter the 'radical and destructive' Sinn Féin agenda, which used Bolshevik methods: 'We resent their untruthful propaganda; we are here to help your citizens, who know the falsity of the Sinn Féin appeal, to inform the American public on the real situation'.[101] The deputation had arrived at the height of the post-war red scare in the United States. They highlighted fears of Bolshevik propaganda, radicals, and anarchists in their speeches against Irish nationalism.[102]

Now that they were in the United States, however, the deputation floundered because of organizational failures. Harte later lamented, 'Looking back on this mission, after many years, I see what a mistake it was to send us out to this vast country without having our itinerary previously arranged'.[103] They were stuck in New York for weeks because no meetings were scheduled in advance. Meanwhile, they remained in the public eye because of clashes with de Valera through the press.

---

100 Longford and O'Neill, *Eamon de Valera*, 95, 98, 114; Edwards, *Éamon de Valera*, 81–94; Cronin, *Washington's Irish Policy*, 25–26.
101 *NYT* 5 Dec 1919.
102 Higham, *Strangers in the Land*, 222–233.
103 Harte, *Road I Have Travelled*, 129.

When he heard of their arrival, de Valera challenged the delegates to a debate on Irish freedom. *The Times* reported de Valera's delight at the delegates' arrival, 'for it is hardly possible in the present state of the Irish problem that this mission to "protest against a pernicious propaganda" can have much effect. The Ulstermen have come "in the interests of law and order, truth, honesty, and fair play". Mr. de Valera replies that he stands for the same principles'.[104] Coote refused to debate with de Valera, stating that he 'could see no benefit to the case by indulging in an argument with him'.[105] The delegates also rejected de Valera's invitation to join him in setting up an American commission of investigation to examine the two sides of Irish opinion. He advocated a five-person panel with two members selected by each side and a chairman agreed by all.[106]

Though they refused to engage directly with de Valera, the delegates believed that their very presence in America was creating positive headway against Sinn Féin influence. Harte was amazed by the reception he received at his first speaking engagement on 7 December at St. Paul's Church: 'To my astonishment it was followed by a round of clapping led by the minister. We had a great reception when the service ended. Irish folk came up in the dozens to shake hands and wish us well'.[107] Other delegates found the American public eager to hear the Ulster side of the Irish situation. They began to learn how to shape their message to appeal to an American audience. Blue wrote that the most important thing in relating to an American audience was to satisfy their somewhat naive desire for 'the facts'.[108]

Despite their efforts, the delegates' reception was not entirely positive. They received threatening letters and a bomb threat in New York. They also dealt with hostile elements in audiences at their meetings. The delegates often refused to engage with dissenters. Harte recalled that at the end of one of his speeches the chairman spurned an Irish Catholic audience member by stating, 'This is not a debating society. You have stated your side for years, and this is the first time we have ever heard the other side'.[109] The delegates believed they deserved the chance to tell their side of the story after years of nationalist domination in America. They could not prevent Sinn Féiners from attending their meetings, however, which led to conflict.

Harte was scheduled to preach on 29 December at Grace Methodist Episcopal Church. Due to a confrontation with Catholics at an earlier

104 *The Times* 8 Dec 1919.
105 *NYT* 11 Dec 1919.
106 *The Times* 8 Dec 1919; Hannigan, *De Valera in America*, 133.
107 Harte, *Road I Have Travelled*, 129.
108 A. Wylie Blue, *Fossicker's Fare: Rakings and Recollections* (Belfast: Quota, 1946), 79–81.
109 Harte, *Road I Have Travelled*, 132, 138.

service, he asked Coote to attend with him. At the church they found a large crowd and about a dozen policemen. Harte reported that he was determined to preach 'the plain gospel on the last Sunday of the old year', and he was able to speak without any disturbances. Then Coote started his speech on 'the truth about Ireland'. Harte recalled, 'The M.P. had scarcely opened his lips when ... shouting and free fights with the [police] seemed to break out everywhere. At one time there was a scene of indescribable confusion and disorder'.[110] The Sinn Féiners in the audience shouted, 'Down with England', 'Hurrah for de Valera', and 'To Hell with lying ministers!' After a struggle with the police, they were ejected and Coote was able to continue. 'This is the very thing we have tried to stop in Ireland', he said. 'That is the beast that is trying to ruin our civilization and yours, that is trying to drive a wedge in between two great nations'. As the congregation exited the church, they were 'hooted' by about 50 Sinn Féiners standing outside, which led to further disturbances that took the police half an hour to quell.[111] De Valera responded the next day by condemning the disrupters as unrepresentative of Sinn Féin while simultaneously minimizing the impact of the Ulster delegates. He stated, 'We stand for freedom of speech and freedom of the press everywhere. We welcome the advent of these men from the north-east corner of Ulster'.[112]

By the end of 1919, the Ulster Protestant deputation still had not left the New York City region. Harte reported that he and his companions were anxious to spread their message to a wider audience. He wrote, 'This settling down in one place for so long a time jarred upon us'.[113] On 3 January, the deputation finally left New York for Philadelphia. They were welcomed, as Harte described, by 'thousands of people at the railway depot who raised cheers when they saw us'.[114] The deputation spoke at a wide variety of meetings in Philadelphia, including the annual meeting of the Pennsylvania Scotch-Irish Society. Their time in Philadelphia was capped by a meeting at the Opera House, organized by the Patriotic League and local Orange lodges.[115] Harte reported, 'When we all marched in the band struck up "The Protestant Boys", and there was a scene of indescribable enthusiasm'. The delegates' speeches were designed to appeal to an American audience and counter Sinn Féin propaganda. Hazelton spoke on 'Why I cannot be a Republican', Crooks on 'Is Ireland a Nation?'

110 Harte, *Road I Have Travelled*, 133.
111 *The Times* 30 Dec 1919; *NYT* 29 Dec 1919.
112 *NYT* 30 Dec 1919; Hannigan, *De Valera in America*, 134.
113 Harte, *Road I Have Travelled*, 130–131.
114 Harte, *Road I Have Travelled*, 134.
115 See Washington Loyal Orange Lodge *Minutes* describing arrangements, Washington Loyal Orange Lodge No. 43, Box #2, HSP MSS 60.

and Harte discussed, 'Is Ireland an Oppressed Country?'[116] Though they were not specifically there to raise funds, almost $4,300 was collected for the Ulster mission.[117]

Next the deputation made a day-long visit to Washington, DC where they met with Vice President Thomas Marshall. The delegates reported that he responded to them privately by saying, 'So far as I am concerned there is no Irish Republic!'[118] His remarks had added weight because Marshall was one of the few voices of authority from the Executive branch after President Wilson suffered a stroke the previous October. Some members of the deputation later returned to Washington for a mass meeting at New York Avenue Presbyterian Church. The meeting was so popular that an overflow session was held in the hall below. A resolution was adopted by the crowd stating, 'We assure them that we heartily appreciate their truth and loyalty and invoke for them welcome and sympathy and protection in their arduous and devoted service. We remember keenly the dishonorable past enacted by their opponents amid the blood and battle of the World War, and protest against any action by the United States Congress which would interfere in the internal affairs of a friendly nation or recognize in any way the existence of a so-called Irish Republic'.[119] The deputation also went to Pittsburgh, where they addressed a meeting at Syria Mosque with a similar programme to their Philadelphia meeting, collecting $2,300.[120]

After Pittsburgh, the delegation divided so as to cover as much of the country as possible, as well as make stops in Canada. Harte, Hazelton, and Blue went on to Columbus and Dayton, Ohio. The full deputation met again in Chicago on 17 January as guests of Moody Bible Institute. They held a mass meeting at Medinah Temple on 19 January with two overflow meetings.[121] After Chicago, the deputation once again divided, with Harte and Coote initially visiting Kansas City, where Harte was taken ill. Coote went on to Colorado, California, and Vancouver, while Harte eventually travelled to St. Paul, Minnesota.[122] Delegates also addressed meetings in Boston, where they had the support of the Loyal Coalition, a group formed in response to the Ulster mission. The Loyal Coalition's aim was to preserve the links between the United States and the United Kingdom which were under threat because of the prominence of the Irish question.[123]

116 Harte, *Road I Have Travelled*, 135.
117 *Minutes of the Washington Loyal Orange Lodge*, Box #2, HSP MSS 60.
118 'America and the Irish Question'.
119 *Orange and Purple Courier* I, no. 64 (Jan–Feb 1920).
120 Harte, *Road I Have Travelled*, 135–136.
121 *Chicago Tribune* 17, 18, 20 Jan 1920.
122 Harte, *Road I Have Travelled*, 139.
123 'America and the Irish Question'.

At the beginning of February, the whole deputation met in St. Paul and travelled to Toronto. Harte reported that arriving in Toronto was almost like coming home, as within the Empire they no longer felt like foreigners. They were given a civic reception and held a mass meeting at Massey Hall, 'where there was very great enthusiasm, especially since there were so many Ulster people in Toronto'.[124] The mass meetings held in Toronto were marked by intense displays of sympathy for the Ulster unionists.[125] Afterward, they addressed meetings in Ottawa and Montreal before going back to New York. Their final mass meeting was at Fifth Avenue Presbyterian Church. The next day they had an Orange reception, where Blue, Corkey, and Harte 'paid a grand tribute to American Protestantism and declared that every place they went they met with success and believed their mission accomplished that which Ulster entrusted them with', followed by a farewell dinner at the Society for British and American Friendship.[126]

Though the delegates claimed to espouse non-sectarian views, religion played a large role in their speeches and the pamphlet which they published for their American audience, entitled 'Facts about Ireland'.[127] A focus on the Protestant community was perhaps inevitable given the composition of the delegation. As well as addressing mass meetings for the public, the ministers preached in Protestant churches every Sunday, sometimes several services each.[128] The delegates believed that the thing Ireland needed most, in the words of Harte, was 'the gospel of the Lord'.[129] With Christian teaching, dissension and strife in Ireland could be remedied. These calls for increased gospel teaching contrasted with newspaper reports of appeals made from Catholic pulpits to give support to de Valera's Irish bond drive.[130] The Ulster delegates targeted the Irish Catholic hierarchy as a cause of Ireland's problems. They described in the 'Facts about Ireland' pamphlet: 'Acting sometimes in accordance with the will of the state and at other times opposing that will, the Hierarchy evidences its consistent claim to be the dominating factor in civil as well as religious affairs in Ireland'.[131] They accused the Irish priesthood of impeding trade and industry in the south through advocating boycotts and of promoting religious control of education.

124 Harte, *Road I Have Travelled*, 141.
125 *The Times* 16 Feb 1920.
126 *Orange and Purple Courier* I, no. 65 (Mar–Apr 1920).
127 'Facts about Ireland for the Consideration of American Citizens by the Delegates of the Protestant Churches of Ireland' (Philadelphia: Protestant Federation, 1920).
128 See, for example, advertisement in *Chicago Tribune* 17 Jan 1920, which shows the delegates scheduled to speak at fifteen meetings the following day.
129 *NYT* 15 Dec 1919.
130 *Chicago Tribune* 19 Jan 1920.
131 'Facts about Ireland'.

Archbishop of Dublin William Walsh and other members of the Catholic hierarchy were also charged with killing Irish conscription in 1918.[132]

At the same time, the delegates asserted that most Catholic Irish did not want a republic. Sinn Féin misrepresented the wishes and conditions of the Irish public by claiming that Ireland was oppressed by the British. The delegates maintained in their speeches and through 'Facts about Ireland' that the nation was in actuality overrepresented in Parliament, was not overtaxed as de Valera had claimed, and had a generous land arrangement.[133] Ireland had its own local self-government, and received substantial grants from the British Parliament for education and agricultural development.[134] Sinn Féin did not need American money to help Ireland, only to help themselves. De Valera himself, who claimed to be the president of the Irish republic, preferred to be 'put up at the Waldorf-Astoria on American money now' than go to Ireland to aid his countrymen.[135] In the eyes of the delegates, Sinn Féin was content to fill their coffers with American dollars rather than fight for freedom in Ireland.

Sinn Féin's greed and deception were contrasted with the Ulstermen, who did not ask for American money though they were willing to accept funds donated at their meetings. The delegates called upon Ulster's history of defending liberty throughout the world, not only in the Great War but also as part of Washington's army in the American Revolution. Coote reminded a Chicago audience that the Catholic Irish did not start arriving in large numbers until they were driven to America by the Famine: 'Ulster has sent more men to ... defend the liberties of the world than all the rest of Ireland together'.[136]

Anglo-American friendship, which had been aided by the historic connections between Ulster and the United States, was under attack by Sinn Féin. The delegates asserted that de Valera was attempting 'to sow discord between Great Britain and the United States'. Harte worried, 'Ireland may yet be the great obstacle between English-speaking peoples'.[137] The delegates hoped that their efforts to present the truth about Ireland to the American people would allow the Anglo-American alliance to prosper. They urged the United States government to refrain from interfering in the domestic affairs of a friendly power. They also appealed to the American public, now presented with the facts about Sinn Féin, to halt their monetary support of Irish republicanism.[138]

132 'Facts about Ireland'; *Chicago Tribune* 20 Jan 1920.
133 *NYT* 15 Dec 1919; *Chicago Tribune* 18, 20 Jan 1920; 'Facts about Ireland'.
134 *NYT* 29 Dec 1919.
135 *Chicago Tribune* 18 Jan 1920.
136 *Chicago Tribune* 20 Jan 1920.
137 *NYT* 15 Dec 1919; *Washington Post* 13 Jan 1920.
138 *Chicago Tribune* 20 Jan 1920; *NYT* 20 Jan 1920.

After travelling back to Liverpool on the *Lapland*, the deputation was welcomed in Belfast with a celebration in Donegall Square Methodist Church. They were also given a 'splendid reception' by the UUC on 9 March in Wellington Hall, attended by Edward Carson and James Craig.[139] The delegates claimed to have reached a wide swath of the American public, presenting 'a story much of which America did not know, and which it was good that she should hear. She, too, knows what national integrity means, and she can understand why the oneness of these our British lands should be and must be forever maintained.' Drawing on their own Civil War experiences, Americans were able to appreciate the unionist cause at the same time as they were growing tired of the Irish nationalists' 'perpetual disloyal and disruptive scheme'.[140] However, the effectiveness of the deputation was under debate. *The Times* condemned the deputation for prolonging the settlement process for Ireland.[141] Hugh de Fellenberg Montgomery, a prominent Liberal Unionist landlord, after consulting with his correspondents, revealed a mixed view of the deputation's work.

Montgomery's correspondent, John E. Gunn, Catholic Archbishop of Natchez and Montgomery's former tenant, reported the deputation was doing more harm than good by emphasizing the sectarian nature of the Irish question. Gunn accused them of avoiding 'public debate, [speaking] only behind closed doors and ... [flooding] the country with propaganda matter, mostly published in Belfast. You can imagine how this irritated the American public'.[142] Gunn sent Montgomery a clipping from a Chicago newspaper, *Brann's Iconoclast*, blasting the Ulster delegates as 'Irish traitors' after their meeting at Medinah Temple. 'They came to this country on a mission of hatred for the British government', the newspaper stated, 'and mean to invade all the principal cities of America'.[143]

Montgomery wrote to another correspondent that he worried about 'the growing strength of the Sinn Féin view of matters there'.[144] Nevertheless, he took heart from Gunn's reports because he believed they showed Sinn Féin saw the Ulster delegates as a serious threat. Montgomery hoped further delegations might be arranged. UUC secretary Richard Dawson Bates wrote to Montgomery that he believed 'undoubtedly our last Deputation did an enormous amount of good'. However, he also outlined some of the pitfalls of sending delegates to America. Many people in Belfast would rather have their money spent on 'home purposes'. Many believed the question of

---

139 Harte, *Road I Have Travelled*, 143; UUC Scrapbook, PRONI D1327/18/664.
140 'America and the Irish Question'.
141 *The Times* 8 Dec 1919.
142 Gunn to Montgomery, 26 Mar 1920, PRONI D627/438/12.
143 *Brann's Iconoclast* 30, no. 2, PRONI D627/438/10.
144 Montgomery to Ricardo, 23 Apr 1920, PRONI D627/435/51.

promoting harmony between America and Great Britain should be a focus of the British government rather than the responsibility of Ulster unionists.[145] Montgomery, still optimistic about making a favourable impression on the American public, replied, 'If Coote's deputation did much good, it appears to show that a further deputation of the same sort should go, consisting, if possible, of more important people. I quite agree that the British Government should take the matter up'.[146]

Coote reported to the Orange Triennial Council that their delegation had discovered that the British government had nothing to fear from the American people. He alleged that 'they were sick of the Irish question'. The opinion of the United States therefore should not be used to influence an Irish settlement. Coote hoped 'that the United States and Great Britain would be bound together as one, and that both would hand down to future generations the same principles of civil and religious liberty for which they stood in the Orange Institution'.[147] Coote's claims revealed inconsistencies in the Ulster unionist approach to America. If the United States was indeed sick of the Irish question, the delegates would not feel the need to continue to appeal for American support.

Instead, the delegates aimed to maintain relationships with contacts they made on their trip. They sent out an annual letter to friends in the United States and Canada. Their letter of 1922 called upon North Americans to remember their historic ties to Ulster. The letter urged them to speak out on Ulster's behalf 'so that British politicians shall hear' as they formulated further Irish policy and determined a settlement with the new Irish Free State.[148] Additionally, September 1922 found Coote back in the United States, speaking against Sinn Féin atrocities in Ireland. Coote accused Sinn Féin of murdering and plundering thousands of Protestants in the south of Ireland. He implored audiences to donate funds for the relief of Protestant refugees.[149]

Coote's second visit to the United States showed the depth of his anti-Catholic animosity. In a meeting at Chicago's Western Avenue Methodist Episcopal Church, Coote stated, 'The whole question of this strife in Ireland is religious. I'm an Orangeman and proud of it. And the only trouble is that Catholics are fighting against Protestant England'.[150] A near-riot was sparked in response to his speech, with Sinn Féiners thrown out by ushers and bricks

145 Bates to Montgomery, 5 May 1920, PRONI D627/435/73.
146 Montgomery to Bates, 7 May 1920, PRONI D627/435/77.
147 Report of the Seventeenth Triennial Meeting, PRONI D1889/6/5C.
148 UUC Scrapbook, PRONI D1327/18/664.
149 *Chicago Tribune* 14, 16 Sep 1922.
150 *Chicago Tribune* 16 Sep 1922.

hurtling through the windows of the church.[151] A *Chicago Tribune* editorial defended Coote's right to free speech but criticized his methods. 'He does what Americans generally believe is useless and mischievous. He attacks a religion'.[152] Coote's blatant framing of the Irish question in religious terms during his second visit reflected some of the problems of the original deputation's visit to the United States. Despite their non-sectarian claims, the composition of the delegation and their methods showed that their approach to the Irish question was transparently anti-Catholic in a way which many found unappealing despite the heightened nativism of the 1920s.

On the other hand, Coote was able to raise significant funds from the American Orange Order, including $10,000 from the Philadelphia Orangemen for the 'aid of the Protestant Orphans and Refugees of the Irish Free State'.[153] American Orangemen later accused Coote of soliciting funds that went to his own benefit rather than to the Protestant cause. The Kirkland faction asserted that Coote's methods and actions made it more difficult to raise funds for Ulster.[154] Coote's obituary, however, recorded no such tarnish on his reputation, stating, 'He had travelled widely in the interests of the Ulster and Orange causes ... By Orangemen in Ulster he was held in great esteem and was entrusted with high office'.[155]

Conclusion

The trips to the United States made by Kane, Smith, Johnston, and the Coote deputation are a central element to consider in the Ulster unionist relationship with America. These visits acted as an important counterpart to the frequent Irish nationalist tours overseas. They were part of the unionists' efforts to foster the development of their own transatlantic community. Indeed, all three case studies reveal that Anglo-American friendship and Protestant unity were cultivated by the unionists. Kane and Smith recognized the ties of political, social, and moral values which drew Great Britain and the United States together as 'guardians of constitutional liberty, political reform, and Scriptural truth'.[156] They appealed to the American public to protect 'Protestant truth and liberty' in Ireland, which would be under attack with the passage of Home Rule. As the Anglo-American relationship evolved at the turn of the century, Johnston also drew upon Anglo-Saxonist

151 *Chicago Tribune* 16 Sep 1922; *NYT* 16 Sep 1922.
152 *Chicago Tribune* 18 Sep 1922.
153 *Orange and Purple Courier* I, no. 83 (Mar–Apr 1923).
154 *Orange and Purple Courier* I, no. 88 (Mar–Apr 1924); I, no. 89 (May–June 1924).
155 *The Times* 16 Dec 1924.
156 *BNL* 18 Dec 1886.

ideals in his appeal to American Orangemen. He urged the English-speaking powers to unite against European potentates to spread Protestant freedom throughout the world in the age of imperialism. Finally, the Coote deputation, emphasizing the need for the spread of gospel truth in Ireland against the harmful authority of the Catholic hierarchy, urged Americans to preserve Anglo-American friendship by opposing the influence of Sinn Féin.

Kane, Smith, and the Coote delegation all went to the United States with the express purpose of countering the long-running propaganda of Irish and Irish-American nationalists. Kane's determination to 'refute slanders' of the Parnellites was mirrored by the Coote delegation's desire to spread 'the truth about Ireland' against Sinn Féin falsifications. The context of the two trips, however, was different. Travelling just after the defeat of the first Home Rule Bill, Kane and Smith focused their attention on appealing to Orangemen and Fenians alike through anti-Parnellism. They accused Parnellites of inconsistencies in their message, at times espousing extremist separatism while at others adhering to constitutional Home Rule. Kane and Smith also charged Parnellites with advocating crime and outrage, an accusation that later would be echoed during the Parnell Commission trial. As Home Rule had already been defeated, Kane and Smith had a more distant dialogue with their nationalist opponents than the Coote delegation.

Coote and the six clergymen who accompanied him came into direct confrontation with Sinn Féin in general and de Valera in particular, as he was in America at the time. The Ulster delegation floundered through lack of organization which left them stuck in New York City for over a month. Their greatest blunder, however, may have been not taking advantage of de Valera's offers to open up debate between the two sides. Engaging in debate with de Valera would have gained them greater publicity throughout the country. Instead, they gave the impression they were intimidated by the Sinn Féiners. Like the Coote delegation, Kane and Smith approached their trip to the United States with marked hesitation to confront the nationalist presence. They relied on emphasizing imperial connections while in Canada, and viewed the United States with trepidation because it was out of the bounds of Empire. They appealed to ancestral connections with Ulstermen in Canada, but did not take full advantage of similar connections in the United States.

In contrast, Johnston was very much concerned with the international ties of Ulstermen through the worldwide Orange organization. He was particularly anxious about the challenges that Orangeism faced as it was transplanted to the United States, because so much of Orangeism revolved around the British monarchy and Empire. Not only did Orangemen have to adapt the movement to America's republican system, but they also faced criticism within the United States because they were perceived as being loyal to Britain. This may have been one of the problems inherent with American support of Ulster unionism overall – reconciling its implied links with Britain as a world power with life in the United States, as opposed to support for Ireland in its small-nation quest for self-determination. The strength of Johnston's personal popularity in the United States nevertheless showed that transplanted Ulstermen did retain connections and celebrate the values of their homeland.

In all three of the case studies in this chapter, unionists were able to claim success by attracting sizable crowds and publicity for an Ulster Protestant message. Each, however, was constrained in various ways: Kane and Smith by their hesitation to leave the familiarity of the British Empire and face Fenian opposition in the United States, Johnston because of his limitation to the Orange organization, and the Coote delegation through organizational blunders and unwillingness to rise to challenges from their opponents. If these unionists were aware that there were, as the *Belfast News-Letter* described, 'two Irelands beyond the sea', the question remains as to why the Irish unionists on these visits and on the whole failed to take full advantage of a Scotch-Irish version of 'greater Ireland'.

6

Transatlantic Religious Connections

In 1857, Ulster Protestants received reports of significant religious revival in the United States. Eager to spark their own revival, the Irish Presbyterian General Assembly sent two representatives to America to report on the proceedings. Their reports contributed to the beginnings of Ulster's great revival of 1859, which brought American and British influences together with Ulster Scots evangelical religious culture. American revivalists came to Ulster to lead services and prayer meetings, renewing the traditional religious links that had been maintained throughout the eighteenth and nineteenth centuries.

In their *Evangelical Protestantism*, David Hempton and Myrtle Hill stress the impact of American connections on the Ulster Protestant community. They write, 'With close links established by successive waves of emigrants, the Ulster Scots community was particularly susceptible to the transmission of religious excitement generated by the American frontier experience'.[1] At the same time the American religious establishment was influenced by Ulster religion. From the colonial period onward, American religion received considerable contributions from Scotch-Irish immigrants as well as other Irish Protestants.

Ulster and America forged connections through centuries of shared religious experiences. A transatlantic Presbyterian tradition was formed by reciprocal flows of clergymen from Ulster to America on the one hand, and, on the other, of revivalists and Princeton-educated ministers from America to Ulster. Religious connections between Ulster and the United States increased throughout the nineteenth century with improvements in communications technology, greater ease of travel for revivalists and missionaries, and the formation of international religious organizations such as the Evangelical and Pan-Presbyterian Alliances.

By the Home Rule period, religion and politics were intertwined as

---

1 David Hempton and Myrtle Hill, *Evangelical Protestantism in Ulster Society, 1740–1890* (London: Routledge, 1992), 149.

essential components of Ulster's relationship with the United States. This chapter aims to illustrate the ways in which evangelical religion was utilized to help build a transatlantic unionist community. Scotch-Irish and Ulster Scots connections were born out of religious associations. Ulster Protestants were inspired by the American Protestant example and critical of the roles of Catholics in American society. Irish Protestant churches called upon their American counterparts to support anti-Home Rule stances. Shared religious heritage was a defining feature of the Ulster unionist view of America throughout the Home Rule era.

Transatlantic Evangelicalism and the 1859 Ulster Revival

By the mid-nineteenth century, Ulster and America had developed transatlantic religious connections sustained by visits from missionaries, continuing emigration, and common impact of evangelicalism on religion, politics, and society. In both places, evangelicalism drew upon societal changes and helped to shape political and social outcomes. Evangelical groups played leading roles in the democratization of politics and culture, promoting ideas of volunteerism and individual freedom to act independently from traditional social hierarchical patterns.[2] In Ireland, evangelicalism effectively narrowed the gaps between Presbyterians, Methodists, and the Church of Ireland, and widened those between Protestants and Catholics. For Presbyterians in particular, evangelical ideas of individualism helped certain factions to pursue progressive politics in the eighteenth century. However, the Irish Presbyterian Church gradually became associated with conservative forces in Irish politics.[3]

---

2 Michael Gauvreau, 'The Empire of Evangelicalism: Varieties of Common Sense in Scotland, Canada, and the United States', in *Evangelicalism: Comparative Studies of Popular Protestantism in North America, the British Isles, and Beyond, 1700–1990*, ed. Mark A. Noll, David W. Bebbington, and George A. Rawlyk (New York: Oxford University Press, 1994), 219–220; Dudley Levistone Cooney, *The Methodists in Ireland: A Short History* (Blackrock: Columba, 2001), 14, 26; Griffin, *People with No Name*, 60–64. For evangelicalism's impact on divisions within the Church of Scotland and Irish Presbyterianism, see Marcel Pradervand, *A Century of Service: A History of the World Alliance of Reformed Churches, 1875–1975* (Edinburgh: Saint Andrew Press, 1975), 6–7; Griffin, *People with No Name*, 55; R.F.G. Holmes, *Our Irish Presbyterian Heritage* (Belfast: W&G Baird, 1985), 99. For the impact on the establishment of Irish Methodism, see David Hempton, 'Methodism in Irish Society, 1770–1830', *Transactions of the Royal Historical Society* 5th Ser., 36 (1986), 137; Cooney, *Methodists in Ireland*, 69. For the influence of evangelicalism on the Church of Ireland, see Beckett, *The Anglo-Irish Tradition*, 104–105.
3 Hempton and Hill, *Evangelical Protestantism*, 44; Holmes, *Our Irish Presbyterian Heritage*, 95, Andrew Holmes, 'The Ulster Revival of 1859: Causes, Controversies, and Consequences', *Journal of Ecclesiastical History* 63, no. 3 (Jul 2012), 490, 500–501.

Evangelical links between Ulster and America grew with the emergence of a revival movement in New York in 1857, which soon spread to New England, Texas, New Orleans, the Ohio River Valley, and Canada.[4] Upon hearing news of the revival, the Presbyterian General Assembly decided to dispatch representatives to report on its development and conditions. William Gibson, professor of Christian Ethics at the Assembly's College, visited the United States with Reverend William McClure in 1858.[5] Gibson was elected moderator of the General Assembly in 1859. In the following year, he wrote *The Year of Grace: A History of the Ulster Revival of 1859*. His book related the deputation's experiences in the United States and the impact of the American 'awakening' on Ulster. Gibson reported that news of the American revival 'helped to rekindle in the hearts of God's children a desire for a similar awakening'.[6] He directly linked the revival in Ulster with events in America. After his return, Gibson toured the north of Ireland to report on his experiences. Emigrant letters and pulpit readings of accounts of the American revival also had an impact.[7]

Signs of revival emerged in Connor under the direction of Reverend J.H. Moore. Prayer services and camp meetings were held throughout the north of Ireland. James McConnell reported,

> Soon the whole district was resounding 'with prayers and suppli-cations, with strong crying and tears unto Him that was able to save.' The movement spread gradually over the whole of Ulster, and even extended to Dublin and parts of the South. The universal eagerness with regard to religion was intense, and the most extraordinary agitations of mind and body together were witnessed.[8]

As McConnell noted, the 1859 revival was known for the pathological phenomena displayed at services such as fainting, falling into trances, and seeing apparitions, which were generally associated with American frontier religion.

4   Holmes, *Our Irish Presbyterian Heritage*, 122; William G. McLoughlin, *Revivals, Awakenings, and Reform: An Essay on Religion and Social Change in America, 1607–1977* (Chicago: University of Chicago Press, 1978), 141–143.

5   Hempton and Hill, *Evangelical Protestantism*, 149; David N. Livingstone and Ronald A. Wells, *Ulster-American Religion: Episodes in the History of a Cultural Connection* (Notre Dame, Ind.: University of Notre Dame Press, 1999), 21, 54; Gibbon, *Origins of Ulster Unionism*, 45–46.

6   William Gibson, *The Year of Grace: A History of the Ulster Revival of 1859* (Edinburgh: Andrew Elliot, 1860), 14.

7   Richard Carwardine, *Transatlantic Revivalism: Popular Evangelicalism in Britain and America, 1790–1865* (Westport, Conn.: Greenwood Press, 1978), 172.

8   James McConnell, *Presbyterianism in Belfast* (Belfast: Davidson & M'Cormack, 1912), 37.

Gibson remarked when he visited America that he was surprised by the revival's 'noiseless character and its entire freedom from those tumultuous agitations which have sometimes signalized the progress of kindred movements in that land'.[9] He cited two Princeton professors, Dr. Archibald Alexander and Dr. Charles Hodge, as supporting the view that physical manifestations were not necessary for a revival to be effective.[10] He also quoted a letter sent from Episcopal Bishop of Ohio Charles McIlvaine to the Bishop of Down, Connor and Dromore, Robert Knox. In the letter, McIlvaine recognized the physical phenomena of the Ulster revival as similar to those experienced by Scotch-Irish settlers in Kentucky at the turn of the century. McIlvaine described the Scotch-Irish as 'an intelligent, hardy, industrious, brave, and quiet set of people'. He explained,

the character of the people was precisely that from which you would least expect mere excitement. They were the very ones to suspect and resist all attempts to produce excitement. But among those Scotch-Irish strangely appeared precisely such cases of striking as the same sort of people, in the very region whence their fathers came, have now been exhibiting.[11]

These traditional American frontier behaviours were looked down upon by 'respectable' Belfast classes.[12] Gibson went to some lengths to show these manifestations were not necessary to experience religious revitalization. However, he also attempted to legitimize such experiences through his references to McIlvaine's letter and links to the Scotch-Irish tradition in America.

Some clergy were critical of the revival because of its associations with these physical manifestations, and because of concerns with its doctrinal, ecclesiastical, and moral implications. Anti-revivalists considered the more 'spectacular' or 'miraculous' phenomena to be inauthentic and unnecessary. The American roots of the revival were also criticized. Clergymen such as the Presbyterian Reverend Isaac Nelson and Anglican Reverend William McIlwaine disapproved of American economic speculation, tendency for physical manifestations in revival culture, and, above all, toleration of slavery within the antebellum evangelical community. Ultimately, however,

---

9 Gibson, *Year of Grace*, 336–337.
10 Gibson, *Year of Grace*, 337, 351.
11 Gibson, *Year of Grace*, 338–339.
12 David Miller, 'Religious Commotions in the Scottish Diaspora: A Transatlantic Perspective on "Evangelicalism" in Mainline Denomination', in *Ulster Presbyterians in the Atlantic World: Religion, Politics, and Identity*, ed. David A. Wilson and Mark G. Spencer (Dublin: Four Courts Press, 2006), 35–36.

the revival was supported by a majority of Ulster ministers from multiple Protestant denominations.[13]

The excitement of revival in Ulster triggered visits from the international evangelical community. These visits were a continuation of an American revivalist tradition of touring the United Kingdom, which included Charles Grandison Finney, William Taylor, Absalom B. Earle, and Maggie Van Colt.[14] At the height of the Ulster revival in 1859, American Methodists Walter and Phoebe Palmer visited Belfast to conduct services out of the Donegall Square Methodist Church. Phoebe Palmer was known for drawing converts to the front of the crowd to express commitment and as evidence of conversion. The Palmers held services throughout Ireland, England, and Scotland through 1860. Other preachers from North America, such as Michael Bosner, John Cooke, Theodore Cuyler, John Graves, and Edward Payson Hammond, also visited Ulster during the revival.[15]

The revival took place during a time of industrial and agricultural transition. Ulster Protestants responded to these changes as well as religious influences from America and Britain.[16] In response to the revival, Wesleyan Methodists in Ireland had a one-year membership increase of over 15 per cent, and Primitive Methodist membership rose almost 54 per cent.[17] These increases were short-lived as membership quickly dropped in the years after 1859. The revival also significantly impacted Presbyterians. In addition, Gibson noted the revival had made great inroads among Orangemen.[18]

---

13 Daniel Ritchie, 'William McIlwaine and the 1859 Revival in Ulster: A Study of Anglican and Evangelical Identities', *Journal of Ecclesiastical History* 65, no. 4 (Oct 2014), 811–814, 818–819; Daniel Ritchie, 'Transatlantic Delusions and Pro-slavery Religion: Isaac Nelson's Evangelical Abolitionist Critique of Revivalism in America and Ulster', *Journal of American Studies* 48, no. 3 (2014), 761–774; Holmes, 'Ulster Revival', 502–503; Andrew Holmes, 'Religion, Anti-Slavery, and Identity: Irish Presbyterians, the United States, and Transatlantic Evangelicalism, *c.*1820–1914', *IHS* 39, no. 155 (2015), 386–388.

14 Christopher Adamson, 'God's Continent Divided: Politics and Religion in Upper Canada and the Northern and Western United States, 1775–1841', *Comparative Studies in Society and History* 36, no. 3 (Jul 1994), 425; William G. McLoughlin, *Modern Revivalism: Charles Grandison Finney to Billy Graham* (New York: Ronald Press, 1959), 41, 127, 152–153; Carwardine, *Transatlantic Revivalism*, 16–17; David W. Bebbington, *Evangelicalism in Modern Britain: A History from the 1730s to the 1980s* (London: Routledge, 1989), 116. In addition to Finney's work, Bebbington also discusses American religious writings that had a significant impact on British and Irish religion at this time, such as Asa Mahan's *Scripture Doctrine of Christian Perfection* in 1844 and W.E. Boardman's *The Higher Christian Life* in 1858 (*Evangelicalism in Modern Britain*, 164).

15 Cooney, *Methodists in Ireland*, 74; Carwardine, *Transatlantic Revivalism*, 172, 182.

16 Hempton and Hill, *Evangelical Protestantism*, 150. England saw little revival activity, but the west of Scotland and Wales both responded to evangelical influence.

17 Hempton and Hill, *Evangelical Protestantism*, 148; Cooney, *Methodists in Ireland*, 74.

18 Gibson, *Year of Grace*, 160–165.

The revival influenced the changing composition of the Orange Order, which transitioned from a mainly rural, Anglican organization, to including increasingly urban, Presbyterian membership. After the revival, church leaders such as Reverend Dr. Hugh Hanna gained prominence in Ulster, pairing Conservative politics with conservative religion. This led to the development of fundamentalism similar to that emerging in the southern United States.[19]

The revival increased the religious connections between Ulster and America that had already been facilitated by shared evangelicalism. Ministers from Ireland, including John Edgar, made trips to America to report on Ulster's religious happenings. Edgar was a member of the Secessionist church, professor of Theology at the Assembly's College, and the founder of the Ulster Temperance Society. His visit to America was covered in Belfast newspapers, which reported a warm reception as he relayed news of the great revival.[20] After the mid-nineteenth century, visits by evangelicals to America, Britain, and Ireland became increasingly scheduled and routine, helping to eliminate the spontaneous physical phenomena that previously marked the American frontier experience and the Ulster revival. The visits of Dwight L. Moody and Ira D. Sankey in the 1870s, carefully programmed for weeks in advance, were a reflection of this new control over revival impulses.[21]

Revivalism, Princeton, and Pan-Presbyterianism

In the 1860s, attention turned to the Liberal campaign to disestablish the Church of Ireland, which was achieved in 1869. Many in the Anglo-Irish community believed the Irish Church Act was a breach of the Act of Union which had nominally brought together the Churches of Ireland and England. They saw disestablishment as endangering the constitution and threatening the integrity of the empire. While antidisestablishmentarianism was prevalent amongst church members, the Church of Ireland did see some benefits from disestablishment such as greater lay participation in church governance. The church was now governed by a bicameral General Synod, which was used to air political as well as religious grievances, particularly during the Home Rule crises.[22]

Primitive Methodists were also significantly affected by disestablishment. They had maintained their distinction from Wesleyan Methodists

---

19 Gibbon, *Origins of Ulster Unionism*, 63.
20 McConnell, *Presbyterianism in Belfast*, 27; Livingstone and Wells, *Ulster-American Religion*, 22–23.
21 Miller, 'Religious Commotions', 36.
22 Hempton and Hill, *Evangelical Protestantism*, 165; Beckett, *Anglo-Irish Tradition*, 108.

through their continued connection to the Church of Ireland, working as an evangelical group within the established church. After disestablishment, they received an invitation from the Wesleyan Conference to reunite. The two groups came together as the Methodist Church in Ireland in 1878.[23] The Irish Church Act also withdrew the *regium donum* from the Presbyterian Church, and the Maynooth Grant. In the Presbyterian General Assembly of 1868, an intense, three-day debate resulted in a series of resolutions adopted against the withdrawal of the *regium donum*, though many Presbyterians were supportive of disestablishment itself.[24]

Disestablishment brought new life into the unionist cause through pan-Protestantism. A significant source of division between Presbyterians and Anglicans was taken away, enabling the creation of a more united Irish Protestant identity. Evangelicalism helped to diminish boundaries between different Protestant denominations in Ireland, and also drew Irish Protestants closer to those in Britain, including through attempts to convert Irish Catholics.[25] Historians such as Linda Colley have highlighted the central place of Protestant religion in the formation of national identity in Britain. The importance of Protestantism in identity formation certainly extended to Protestants in Ireland as well as helping to form national identities in America and Europe.[26] Protestantism provided one of the most important bonds between Ulster unionists and Britain;[27] it was also a vital component of the relationship between Ulster unionists and America.

Protestants on both sides of the Atlantic continued to be affected by evangelical visits, especially the tours of Dwight L. Moody, one of the nineteenth century's greatest evangelical leaders. Born in Massachusetts, Moody started his evangelical career in antebellum Chicago where he met his partner, gospel singer Ira D. Sankey. Moody and Sankey left Chicago for Britain in the spring of 1873, landing at Liverpool. As demand for their services increased, they travelled throughout the north of England and Scotland. Moody and Sankey's services were considered some of the greatest public events of the Victorian age, appealing to populist impulses and transcending gender, age, and class in their appeal.[28]

23 Cooney, *Methodists in Ireland*, 77.
24 McConnell, *Presbyterianism in Belfast*, 38. Some 211 members of the Assembly supported the resolutions, with 180 against. On *regium donum*, see R.F.G. Holmes, 'Ulster Presbyterians and Irish Nationalism', in *Studies in Church History*, 18: *Religion and National Identity*, ed. Stuart Mews (Oxford: Blackwell, 1982), 537.
25 Jackson, 'Irish Unionism, 1870–1922', 118; Holmes, 'Ulster Presbyterians', 541.
26 Loughlin, 'Joseph Chamberlain', 213; Linda Colley, *Britons: Forging the Nation, 1707–1837* (New Haven, Conn.: Yale University Press, 1992).
27 Loughlin, *Ulster Unionism*, 30.
28 Edgar J. Goodspeed, *A Full History of the Wonderful Career of Moody and Sankey, in Great Britain and America* (New York: Henry S. Goodspeed, 1876), 60–62; Bebbington,

Moody and Sankey's first Belfast meetings were held on 6 September 1874. Reverend Edgar J. Goodspeed, a Baptist minister from Chicago who accompanied the pair, reported crowded meetings in churches and Ulster Hall, with people travelling long distances to experience the revival. Their final Belfast meeting was held in the Botanic Gardens on 8 October, and they made a stop in Londonderry before going on to Dublin. Goodspeed quoted a Dublin Protestant as reporting,

It was not found necessary to preach those sermons which are generally used as a preparation for revival. The revival commenced immediately. Dublin had been waiting to hear the Gospel preached; and its people, by crowds, when they heard it, eagerly pressed into the kingdom of Christ ... We have never before seen such sights in Dublin as we have seen this last week, night after night, in the Exhibition Palace. It is estimated to hold 10,000 persons. Every night it is filled, and the attention and silence is wonderful.[29]

Goodspeed also noted that Moody was careful to stay away from any divisive reference to Catholicism, thus gaining favourable attention from Dublin's Catholic community.[30] At the meeting of the Pan-Presbyterian Alliance in 1884, Reverend Hamilton Magee of Dublin hoped that the Catholic response toward Moody and Sankey indicated the possibility of conversion among Irish Catholics. He stated,

The Irish are a religious people. They hold some of the foundation truths of our common Christianity with a firm grasp. Agnosticism and Infidelity have, so far, made comparatively little progress among them. Their recent demeanor towards the mission of Mr. Moody and Mr. Sankey in the south of Ireland, and their attitude of mind generally, towards Gospel truth lovingly made known to them, is in a high degree worthy of recognition.[31]

Magee believed Protestants must reach out to Catholics, not merely to pad conversion statistics, but to project Gospel truth into Roman Catholicism.

Evangelicalism in Modern Britain, 162–163; McLoughlin, *Revivals*, 141–145; John Coffey, 'Democracy and Popular Religion: Moody and Sankey's Mission to Britain 1873–1875', in *Citizenship and Community: Liberals, Radicals and Collective Identities in the British Isles 1865–1931*, ed. Eugenio F. Biagini (Cambridge: Cambridge University Press, 1996), 94–105.
29 Goodspeed, *Full History*, 132.
30 Goodspeed, *Full History*, 134.
31 Report of the Pan-Presbyterian Alliance, 1884, 337.

After travelling back to England to tour for another nine months, Moody and Sankey returned to the United States in the second half of 1875. Goodspeed wrote, 'Great expectations had been raised by their success abroad, and eager multitudes awaited their coming'.[32] Back in the United States, Moody and Sankey held services in Philadelphia, Princeton, and New York in 1875 and 1876 before travelling to south and west. Moody made several return trips to the United Kingdom, his last visit in 1892, maintaining the tradition of a transatlantic network of evangelical preachers. Frederick Harte, newly arrived to begin as a student at Belfast's Methodist College, attended the last night of Moody's mission in 1892. He described the gathering, held at the pavilion built for the Great Unionist Convention in the Botanic Gardens:

> There was an enormous gathering, and there came upon me a feeling of intense loneliness, since I did not know a single face in that vast multitude. Moody was just like the photographs of him, which appeared in the papers. He did not strike me as being a great preacher, but somehow he gripped the crowd and one felt that the power of God was with him. The meeting I attended was the last of the series conducted by Moody. So if I had not gone that night I should never have heard him at all. I remember having a feeling of consternation when it was announced that the mission would be continued by a man called the Rev. John McNeill. How could anyone hold the crowd after Moody? But the new preacher did hold the crowd, and held forth night after night with tremendous eloquence and power.[33]

Harte's account illustrated how preachers from both sides of the Atlantic worked together to conduct revival missions. The preacher who had continued Moody's mission, McNeill, was an Ulster Presbyterian minister just beginning his career as a travelling evangelical preacher. He later preached all over the world, including at the Fifth Avenue Presbyterian Church in New York City at the invitation of prominent Ulster emigrant Reverend John Hall.[34]

Ulster Protestants throughout the Home Rule period were interested in and affected by the work of American evangelical preachers. The *Witness* reported the activities of Moody and Sankey in the United States and abroad.[35] The paper also monitored the emergence of new evangelical revivalists coming to

32 Goodspeed, *Full History*, 227.
33 Harte, *Road I Have Travelled*, 32–34.
34 Alexander Gammie, *Rev. John McNeill: His Life and Work* (London: Pickering & Inglis, 1933), 110–137.
35 See, for example, *Witness* 6 Feb 1885, 23 Apr 1886, 21 May 1886, 6 Jan 1893.

prominence in America, such as Reverend Samuel Porter Jones who gained notoriety at the end of the nineteenth century.[36] American Congregationalist Reuben Torrey came to preach in Belfast in 1904. Torrey's work as the Dean of the Bible Institute in Los Angeles linked him to another Ulster evangelical, W.P. Nicholson. Nicholson held successful revivals in Ulster, the United States, and elsewhere after his appointment to the Bible Institute in 1918. Newspaper reports and minutes of church assemblies and synods record numerous visits between Ulster and America by a wide variety of ministers and delegates throughout this period.

This transatlantic network was exemplified in the person of James McCosh, the president of Princeton. McCosh participated in both Ulster's great revival of 1859 and in the American revival services of Moody and Sankey in 1876. He spent much of his life attempting to forge greater connections between transatlantic Protestant groups. McCosh was born in southern Ayrshire and educated at Glasgow and Edinburgh's New College, where he was a student of Thomas Chalmers. As a minister in Scotland, he was caught up in the anti-patronage campaign and ended up separating from the Church of Scotland to join the Free Church in 1843, a disruption which he regarded 'as the greatest event in my life'.[37]

In 1850, McCosh was called to the Chair of Logic and Metaphysics at Queen's College Belfast. An article in the *Princeton Theological Review* of 1903 described McCosh's contributions to Irish society while he was at Queen's:

We find him in the midst of this activity taking an active part in organizing the ministerial support fund for the Irish Presbyterian Church, advocating with cogent arguments for the disestablishment of the Irish Church, and taking a leading part in the organization of the Evangelical Alliance, which held its first meeting in London ... He lived a threefold life of philosophical thinker, educator, and man of affairs.[38]

McCosh was also dedicated to Irish education reform. A strong supporter of the Union during the American Civil War, he travelled to the United States for the first time in 1866 to visit major universities and theological

36 *Witness* 14 Aug 1885, 21 Aug 1885.
37 William M. Sloane, ed. *The Life of James McCosh: A Record Chiefly Autobiographical* (Edinburgh: T. and T. Clark, 1896), 75–76.
38 Alexander T. Ormond, 'James McCosh as Thinker and Educator', *Princeton Theological Review* 3 (Jul 1903), 344–345; David N. Livingstone, 'James McCosh and the Scottish Intellectual Tradition', in *Queen's Thinkers: Essays on the Intellectual Heritage of a University*, ed. Alvin Jackson and David N. Livingstone (Belfast: Blackstaff Press, 2008), 23–24.

seminaries. William Sloane, his biographer, wrote that it was during this trip that McCosh had the idea for the Pan-Presbyterian Alliance.

> During the extended tour he made through America in 1866, he had been much feted, and had made many influential acquaintances in all parts of the United States. Although it was ostensibly a holiday journey, yet he was ever revolving many important schemes in his mind, and among these was a plan for the alliance of Presbyterian churches throughout the world, concerning which he spoke and conversed much with the leading men of all the various Presbyterian denominations.[39]

McCosh became friends with Dr. Samuel Irenaeus Prime, the long-time editor of the *New York Observer*, who suggested him to Princeton's trustees as a potential president. McCosh accepted the appointment as president in 1868.[40]

Princeton had long been a major point of connection between Ulster and America. The university had Presbyterian founders in 1746. It was closely linked to the Princeton Theological Seminary, founded in 1816. For generations, Irish ministerial students crossed the Atlantic, making Irish the most prominent nationality of international students studying at the Theological Seminary.[41] Both Princeton University and Princeton Theological Seminary also maintained close intellectual ties to the Assembly's College in Belfast, particularly through faculty members at each institution. Robert Watts, for example, held the Chair of Theology at the Assembly's College starting in 1866. He was born in County Down, studied at the Princeton Theological Seminary, worked at Philadelphia's Westminster Church, and then became the minister at Gloucester Street Church in Dublin.[42] He was moderator of the Irish Presbyterian General Assembly from 1879 to 1880, and also served as a delegate to the Pan-Presbyterian Alliance. Watts was a staunch unionist, reflected in letters he wrote during the Home Rule crises. Watts hoped to shape the Assembly's College after the model of Princeton. He encouraged the Assembly's College to forge greater links with the American university rather than focus on Edinburgh's New College.[43]

---

39 Sloane, *Life of James McCosh*, 181.
40 Sloane, *Life of James McCosh*, 182–183; Peter Brooke, *Ulster Presbyterianism: The Historical Perspective, 1610–1970* (Dublin: Gill and Macmillan, 1987), 193.
41 Livingstone and Wells, *Ulster-American Religion*, 7–8.
42 McConnell, *Presbyterianism in Belfast*, 153.
43 McConnell, *Presbyterianism in Belfast*, 153; Livingstone and Wells, *Ulster-American Religion*, 36–37; Holmes, 'Religion, Anti-Slavery, and Identity', 391–393; David N. Livingstone, 'Darwinism and Calvinism: The Belfast-Princeton Connection', *Isis* 83, No. 3 (Sep 1992), 412.

McCosh had urged Moody and Sankey to visit Princeton in 1875 after students showed signs of revival impulses. Goodspeed reported that students themselves 'initiated a movement which has had its fruit in an almost unprecedented interest in spiritual things, heightened and spreading day by day, and yet on the increase'.[44] McCosh described the revival by stating, 'Every student, indeed every member of the college, felt awed and subdued. It was estimated that upwards of one hundred were converted'.[45] Around the same time, McCosh was labouring to create a Pan-Presbyterian Alliance, which would unite Presbyterians on a federal basis inspired by the United States government model.[46]

The formation of the Young Men's Christian Association in 1844, Evangelical Alliance in 1846, and Lambeth Conference of Anglican Bishops in 1867 all influenced the creation of the Pan-Presbyterian Alliance. The alliance was organized by an initial conference held in London in 1875, with McCosh as president. The first general council was held in 1877 in Edinburgh, and met every three or four years thereafter. Reverend Robert S. Duff, a Tasmanian representative, described the main subjects dealt with by the Pan-Presbyterian Alliance as modern theological thought, Christian life and worship, roles of ruling elders, distinctive principles of Presbyterianism, religion in relation to philosophy and science, Sabbath schools, temperance, and most importantly, cooperation on foreign missions.[47] The Pan-Presbyterian Alliance was part of a trend toward transnational religious organization. The last quarter of the nineteenth century also saw the creation of other international church bodies, notably the International Congregational Council and World Methodist Council, both founded in London in 1881.

Several future members of the Scotch-Irish Society of America (SISA) were part of the Pan-Presbyterian Alliance, including George Macloskie, John S. MacIntosh, and John Hall. Indeed, it was probably during the 1884 third general council in Belfast that the initial meeting in which McCosh suggested the formation of a Scotch-Irish society took place, as reported by Macloskie.[48] Macloskie had studied in Belfast under McCosh, and arrived in Princeton at McCosh's invitation in 1875 to take the Chair of Natural History. He was ordained in the Irish Presbyterian Church and served in Ballygoney from 1861 to 1873. Macloskie maintained connections with Watts in Belfast, especially as they took part in the transatlantic debate over the

---

44 Goodspeed, *Full History*, 408.
45 Sloane, *Life of James McCosh*, 229; Livingstone and Wells, *Ulster-American Religion*, 12.
46 Sloane, *Life of James McCosh*, 250.
47 Robert S. Duff, *Notes of a Visit to America During the Pan-Presbyterian Council, 1880* (Kilmarnock: Dunlop & Drennan, 1882), 15–17.
48 See Macloskie's description of this meeting in John Hall's obituary, *Ninth Congress of the Scotch-Irish in America*, 231.

role of evolution in the religious sphere.[49] McCosh himself became known for reconciling evolution with Protestantism.[50]

John S. MacIntosh, who represented Ireland at the Philadelphia meeting of the Pan-Presbyterian Alliance in 1880, was another future member of the SISA. MacIntosh, who was born in America and raised in Europe, was the minister at May Street Presbyterian Church in Belfast. In 1881, the Second Presbyterian Church in Philadelphia invited him to take over their ministry.[51] MacIntosh later became one of the most prominent members of the Pennsylvania Scotch-Irish Society, the only Scotch-Irish state society to survive the demise of the national society in 1901.

The Ulster that MacIntosh left in 1881 was a society in which Presbyterians and Catholics were still able to unite in their support of Liberal political issues such as that year's Land Act. Presbyterians were traditional supporters of such Liberal issues as tenant rights, franchise reform, and disestablishment.[52] However, as the movement for Home Rule drew together Irish nationalism and Catholicism, religious cooperation became increasingly unlikely in the political sphere.[53] James J. Shaw, a unionist pamphleteer, urged Irish Presbyterians not to be blindly attached to their traditional liberalism.

> You are not, nor am I, ashamed of the fact that our ancestors were United Irishmen. We do not fear to speak of '98 … But, at the same time, we were taught that every object which our forefathers fought for had been attained. Our forefathers took up arms against an Irish Parliament which represented only a small, and interested faction; against an Irish executive which was dominated by the narrow, prejudiced, and obstinate spirit of George III, the same spirit which drove the Ulster colonists to rebellion in America.[54]

Though Presbyterians fought for civil and religious liberty with the United Irishmen, the Union granted them sufficient space to achieve their goals

49 Livingstone and Wells, *Ulster-American Religion*, 40–45, 48; Livingstone, 'Darwinism and Calvinism', 422.
50 Livingstone has written most extensively on this topic. See 'James McCosh', 24.
51 McConnell, *Presbyterianism in Belfast*, 76.
52 Holmes, *Our Irish Presbyterian Heritage*, 190; Andrew Holmes, 'Covenanter Politics: Evangelicalism, Political Liberalism and Ulster Presbyterians, 1798–1914', *English Historical Review* 75, no. 513 (Apr 2010), 343–344, 367–368.
53 Sean Farrell, *Rituals and Riots: Sectarian Violence and Political Culture in Ulster, 1784–1886* (Lexington: University Press of Kentucky, 2000), 175; Hempton and Hill, *Evangelical Protestantism*, 166.
54 James J. Shaw, 'Mr. Gladstone's Two Irish Policies: 1868 and 1886. A Letter to an Ulster Liberal Elector' (London: Marcus Ward, 1888).

within Irish society. Now during this new battle over Union, marked by the introduction of the first Home Rule Bill in 1886, Irish society and politics were becoming more and more sectarian.

Identity, Anti-Catholicism, and Indebtedness

Celebrations of civil and religious liberty were at the heart of British and Irish Presbyterian use of the American religious example, which helped solidify a Presbyterian identity. Nineteenth-century Presbyterians saw the seventeenth century as a model of religious purity and political principle, which linked with the foundations of American Presbyterianism.[55] At the Pan-Presbyterian Alliance meeting of 1884, Reverend Professor William Garden Blaikie of Edinburgh's New College emphasized that the resistance of Scottish Presbyterians to attempts of the government to control the religious establishment led to the advancement of liberty in the British Empire and the United States. He stated,

> I venture to say that but for their resistance to the Royal claims on Church and State, the civil liberties of the country, as well as the liberty of the Church would not have been established on the firm basis where they now stand. I venture to say that Britain would not have been the country she is; I am sure that Ulster would not have been the province she is; I do not think the United States would have been so great in their independence and in their freedom; and I do not think that our Colonies would have been rising or advancing by strides so rapidly into Empires that bid far to rival one day the islands from which they sprang.[56]

Blaikie linked Presbyterian identity with liberty, as exemplified by the traditions of the United States and the British Empire.

Reverend R.J. Lynd, of Belfast's May Street Presbyterian Church and Moderator of the Irish General Assembly, drew on the history of American Presbyterianism to illuminate the international importance of Ulster's Presbyterians in an 1888 speech to the Pan-Presbyterian Alliance.

> He [Lynd], as an Ulster Presbyterian, was there to assert that the first American Presbytery owed its very existence to an Ulster Presbyterian; and if Ireland could show nothing else but American Presbyterians as

---

55 Holmes, 'Covenanter Politics', 344.
56 Report of the Pan-Presbyterian Alliance, 1884, 97.

the fruit of its own Presbyterians, he thought the Presbyterianism of Ireland need not be afraid to lift its face in the presence of the other Presbyterian Churches of the world.[57]

As Lynd highlighted, Ulster Scots emigrants in America dramatically impacted early religious organization. Prominent ministers such as Francis Makemie and the Tennent family helped to establish Presbyterianism in the colonies.[58] Presbyterianism was the most fundamental aspect of Scotch-Irish identity, carried with them as they migrated from Ulster.[59]

John Hall, an Irish minister who had immigrated to America to serve at New York City's Fifth Avenue Presbyterian Church and prominent member of the SISA, also linked the Presbyterian tradition back to liberty. He stated,

> Church history is to a great degree ignored in many places. Yet we, as Presbyterians, have the deepest interest in making the history of the Church known, since it constitutes so powerful an argument for the substantial elementary principles of the Presbyterian system. Some of our best American historians say that liberty in Great Britain owes its existence to the teachings of John Calvin.[60]

The history of Scottish, Ulster, and American Presbyterians was linked to help forge a transatlantic Presbyterian identity based around the concepts of civil and religious liberty.

At the same time, transatlantic Protestants were also tied through attitudes toward Catholicism. Anti-Catholicism was part of mid-nineteenth-century evangelical movements on both sides of the Atlantic. According to John Wolfe, anti-Catholicism helped to define evangelical identity.[61]

---

57 Report of the Pan-Presbyterian Alliance, 1888, 37.
58 For the history of early American Presbyterianism and its links to Ulster, see Hempton and Hill, *Evangelical Protestantism*, 16; Kevin Kenny, 'The Irish in the Empire', in *Ireland and the British Empire*, ed. Kevin Kenny (Oxford: Oxford University Press, 2004), 97–98; Sydney E. Ahlstrom, *A Religious History of the American People* (New Haven, Conn.: Yale University Press, 1972), 266–270; Ian Adamson, 'The Ulster-Scottish Connection', in *Scotland and Ulster*, ed. Ian S. Wood (Edinburgh: Mercat, 1994), 17; Jones, 'Scotch-Irish', 901; J.M. Barkley, 'Francis Makemie of Ramelton – Father of American Presbyterianism' (Belfast: Presbyterian Historical Society of Ireland, 1994).
59 Barkley, 'Francis Makemie'; Griffin, *People with No Name*, 114.
60 Report of the Pan-Presbyterian Alliance, 1892, 46.
61 John Wolffe, 'Anti-Catholicism and Evangelical Identity in Britain and the United States, 1830–1860', in *Evangelicalism: Comparative Studies of Popular Protestantism in North America, the British Isles, and Beyond, 1700–1990*, ed. Mark A. Noll, David W. Bebbington, and George A. Rawlyk (New York: Oxford University Press, 1994), 179.

Britain, Ireland, and the United States all saw significant agitation against Catholicism. In Ireland, both Presbyterians and Anglicans evangelized to Catholic communities. Protestant missionaries preached throughout the country, distributed Bibles and tracts, and challenged Catholic clergy to religious debates. Evangelical voluntary societies were particularly active in attempts to convert Irish Catholics.[62] While evangelical campaigns ultimately failed in their goal of the mass conversion of Catholics, they did aid in the creation of greater evangelical identity among Irish Protestants. Attendance at churches and communion increased as religion was progressively popularized.[63]

In contrast to the zealous members of evangelical societies, the hierarchies of Protestant churches were more cautious in their approach to converting Irish Catholics. Church leaders retained an awareness of their responsibility to refrain from religious or political conflict, but as the nineteenth century wore on churches were increasingly drawn into controversy. After Catholic Emancipation, there was particular concern over education policies, specifically seen in the hostility to the increased state grant for Maynooth College in 1845. Greater links were being forged between evangelical religion and political conservatism. Just as Daniel O'Connell and the Catholic Association helped to create a distinctly Catholic Irish nationalism, evangelicalism aided working-class and rural Protestants in asserting their own identity. These simultaneous forces created deeper divisions within Irish society.[64]

In the United States, the Catholic Church grew due to the influx of Irish and German immigrants, causing resentment of nativist Americans and concerns over assimilation. Nativists and evangelicals saw Catholic immigrants as threatening to American national identity. While there was relatively little overlap in the membership of evangelical societies and nativist political associations, they both targeted Catholics in the mid-nineteenth century.[65] Catholicism was said to threaten the republican system of the United

---

62 Holmes, *Our Irish Presbyterian Heritage*, 118–119; Beckett, *Anglo-Irish Tradition*, 106; Hempton and Hill, *Evangelical Protestantism*, 48. This was true of British evangelical societies as well: groups such as the Church Missionary Society, the British and Foreign Bible Society, the London Missionary Society, and the Scottish Missionary Society all targeted Ireland as part of their missions.

63 Hempton and Hill, *Evangelical Protestantism*, 61–62; Beckett, *Anglo-Irish Tradition*, 106.

64 Hempton and Hill, *Evangelical Protestantism*, 69, 81; Holmes, 'Religion, Anti-Slavery, and Identity', 391–393.

65 Wolffe, 'Anti-Catholicism', 184; Ray Allen Billington, *The Protestant Crusade, 1800–1860: A Study in the Origins of American Nativism* (New York: Macmillan, 1938), 42–43, 58, 58; Richard Carwardine, 'The Know-Nothing Party, the Protestant Evangelical Community, and American National Identity', in *Studies in Church History*, 18: *Religion and National Identity*, ed. Stuart Mews (Oxford: Blackwell, 1982), 462.

States, acting as a hostile force to civil liberties, religious toleration, and the separation of church and state.[66]

By the Home Rule period, Ulster Protestants showed concern with American Catholicism. Some unionists portrayed the fight against Home Rule as part of an international battle against the influences of Catholicism.[67] The *Witness* reported on 'Roman Catholic Demands in America'.[68] The Pan-Presbyterian Alliance had accounts of 'Romanism in the United States'.[69] English historian James Anthony Froude, who had wide experience in Ireland, wrote a two-part series of articles on 'Romanism and the Irish Race in the United States', which appeared in the *North American Review* in 1879. He praised America as a 'land of wonders', but feared the influence of Irish Catholics who had failed to assimilate into American society. He portrayed Catholicism as a direct menace to the American republic because it did not support the idea of individual freedom.

> The growth of the Irish element has, for some time, disturbed the minds of the Americans. They have absorbed a substance which they have been unable to assimilate, and it interferes with their digestion. A religion, to which the Irish vote has given power and consequence, can already turn the scale among their political parties.[70]

Froude compared the ability of Irish Catholics to influence politics in the United States to their power in the United Kingdom. He claimed if Home Rule was granted to Ireland, Catholics would take over the Dublin parliament, establish Catholicism as the state church, and destroy individual freedom. Froude warned that on both sides of the Atlantic, 'the principles of constitutional government have permitted the growth of a party at once religious and national, which is the natural enemy of religious and political liberty; which demands toleration, yet will concede no toleration; which aspires to undo the work of the Reformation, and turn back the tide of human things'.[71] Therefore, according to Froude, Irish Catholicism was a threat to both the American and British governments, and citizens in both countries should fight against its influence.

---

66 Carwardine, 'Know-Nothing Party', 449, 453.
67 David Hempton, *Religion and Political Culture in Britain and Ireland: From the Glorious Revolution to the Decline of Empire* (Cambridge: Cambridge University Press, 1996), 108–110.
68 *Witness* 21 Aug 1886.
69 Report of the Pan-Presbyterian Alliance, 1884, 15.
70 James Anthony Froude, 'Romanism and the Irish Race in the United States, Part I', *North American Review* 129 (Dec 1879), 525.
71 James Anthony Froude, 'Romanism and the Irish Race in the United States, Part II', *North American Review* 130 (Jan 1880), 46.

At the second meeting of the Pan-Presbyterian Alliance in 1880, Reverend Robert Knox of Belfast's Linenhall Street Church also linked concerns with American Catholics to Irish Catholicism. He addressed the council on 'The Evangelization of Ireland'. Knox worked as a missionary in the south of Ireland in the 1840s, and received a doctorate of divinity from New York's Union College. He stated,

> If you look at Ireland on a map, it is a mere speck in the great Atlantic; and yet that little island has wielded for ages, and continues to wield, a mighty influence on Britain and all the dependencies of Britain, and on this great continent of America. Hence it becomes a matter of supreme importance to bring the Irish people under the power of the gospel, not only for their own sake, but for the sake of those countries whose character and destinies they influence.[72]

Knox explained that William Gladstone's policy of religious equality brought new life to the Catholic cause, exciting 'the most extravagant hopes. From a condition of sullen inactivity Rome has started up "as a giant refreshed with wine." The watchwords now are, "Ireland for the Irish!" – "Ireland for Rome"; "Protestantism must be conquered or expelled"'.[73] Knox saw the hierarchy of the Catholic Church as intensely ultramontane, so that every line – even in Irish politics – converged on Rome. He was especially concerned over the issue of education and the influence of Rome as Catholics tried to gain political power in Ireland.

Knox asserted that the only option for Presbyterians, as a group that had never quarrelled with Irish Catholics in the past, was to attempt to convert Catholics. Because of the influx of Catholic immigrants, Britain and the United States would also have a deep interest in this work.[74] Knox argued that Protestants in Ireland, Britain, and the United States all should fear the influence of Rome in their political and social lives, and therefore ought to be united in combating Catholicism. He maintained that it was not enough for each country to act individually; Catholicism must be fought at its source in Ireland.

Knox concluded that American Presbyterians had special reason to aid the conversion of Catholics in Ireland:

> It was an Irish Presbyterian, from the centre of Donegal, who laid the foundation of the American church; and from the days of Francis

---

72 Report of the Pan-Presbyterian Alliance, 1880, 419.
73 Report of the Pan-Presbyterian Alliance, 1880, 420.
74 Report of the Pan-Presbyterian Alliance, 1880, 423–424.

McKemie [*sic*] till this hour, America has been thinning our ranks and draining our resources. Thousands of what you call the Scotch-Irish are landed every year on your shores. This process, so exhausting to us, has been going on for a century and a half. Not a few of these have become your statesmen and your warriors, your orators, merchants, and ministers of religion. Others have helped to clear your forests and build your great cities, and yourselves would be the first to acknowledge that, in many cases, they form the bone and sinew of your churches. Thus you have become numerous and rich by making us poor.[75]

The contributions of the Scotch-Irish to American history and development meant that Ulster Presbyterians were now unashamed to put a claim upon them. Knox implored,

For your own sakes, and in memory of all you owe Ulster, 'come to the help of the Lord against the mighty.' If we succeed, as by the help of heaven we expect we shall, the richest benefit will be yours, for then you would be receiving, year by year, an influx of free, enlightened, law-abiding Churchmen and women.[76]

The Scotch-Irish essentially owed Irish Presbyterians their aid in converting Catholics because of the great success they had achieved in America at the expense of the Ulster population. Interestingly, the arguments by Knox were made a full nine years before the SISA was founded with the very purpose of promoting the history of Scotch-Irish excellence within American society.

At the 1884 meeting of the Pan-Presbyterian Alliance, Dr. T.Y. Killen was concerned that efforts to convert Catholics in Ireland would not aid in increasing the Protestant population of the country. He stated,

It may be said that we cannot show much fruit of our Roman Catholic mission, and so far as Ireland was concerned, that was true, but what was the reason? Because those who were converted to Protestantism were very often exposed to persecution on the part of their own countrymen, and were obliged to flee to America, and so the [American] brethren in that way got the benefit of the work done in Ireland.[77]

Presbyterians claimed American churches received the benefits of their Irish Catholic missions. New converts were said to have a high rate of

75 Report of the Pan-Presbyterian Alliance, 1880, 425.
76 Report of the Pan-Presbyterian Alliance, 1880, 425.
77 Report of the Pan-Presbyterian Alliance, 1884, 338–343.

emigration from Ireland, which benefited the United States rather than Irish Protestants.

Similar concerns over Protestant population draining were expressed at the Irish Presbyterian General Assembly in 1885. Reverend William Park of Belfast's Rosemary Street congregation asserted,

> For some years past the number of our families and communicants seemed to be growing less, partly from emigration, partly also, perhaps, from a more accurate scrutiny of communion and stipend rolls. This year, rather strangely, there seems to be an advance ... Perhaps the tide of emigration has begun to ebb a little, for times are not so prosperous in America as they were some years ago. There is no doubt that, if we would find a large number of those who have disappeared from our communion and stipend rolls, we would search for them in America. In 1883 and 1884, the total membership of the Presbyterian Church in the Northern States was 687,000, and it had grown by almost 24,000 in one year. A large proportion of the 24,000 were Irishmen.[78]

Presbyterians in Ireland viewed the large numbers of emigrants as advancing Protestantism in the United States, while in Ireland their numbers suffered. As Reverend Charles L. Morrell explained at the Pan-Presbyterian Alliance, this placed an obligation on United States Presbyterians to come to the aid of their brethren in Ireland.

> To our American cousins we can appeal with equal confidence. You owe us something. We have been sending you for years our sons and brothers. They have filled your virgin soil; they have digged from the bowels of your land the iron and the gold; they have filled your Churches and occupied your pulpits; they have been among your honored Senators and illustrious Presidents. In all your wondrous material prospects and spiritual growth, the Ulster Scot has been an important factor. We want your prayers, fathers and brethren, for the Evangelization of Ireland; the prayers of you that stand on the watch-towers of Zion; the prayers of you that make mention of the Lord.[79]

According to Morrell, the high levels of emigration and the success that the Scotch-Irish achieved in the United States meant they were indebted to Ulster Presbyterians, owing them prayers and support in their efforts to convert Irish Catholics.

---

78 *Witness* 5 Jun 1885.
79 Report of the Pan-Presbyterian Alliance, 1884, 338–343.

The idea that American Protestants were beholden to Ulster Protestants was not an attitude that was prevalent only among Presbyterians. In 1886, Irish Methodists sent a delegation to the United States and Canada to raise money for the newly founded Clarke Memorial Church in Portrush. The reporter for the *Irish Times* commented, 'The Clarke Memorial Church, Portrush, has strong claims on American Methodists'.[80]

Forty years later, in 1925, Reverend Frederick Harte of Belfast's Donegall Square Methodist Church participated in a mission to America to raise funds for building work. He wrote,

> The capital sum required was to be raised in the land flowing with dollars, and the building was to be a memorial to the pioneers of American Methodism who went out from Ireland, notably Philip Embry, Barbara Heck, and Robert Strawbridge, and became the founders of the great Methodist Episcopal Church of America.[81]

Harte justified the reasoning behind their approach to American Methodists, explaining,

> I think I may confidently state that we had a really good case to put before the Methodists of America. It was the Irish Methodists who founded American Methodism, and for years Irish Methodism has sent out its best sons and daughters to America. It would be a gracious act if the great Methodist Episcopal Church would make some tangible and worthy expression of an indebtedness which surely exists.[82]

American Protestants were indebted to Ireland for providing the founders of its religious institutions and for drawing the nation's 'best sons and daughters' as immigrants. These attitudes toward emigration and American obligation provided an important context for the Ulster unionist approach to the United States.

By the 1880s, Ulster Protestants closely followed developments within American religion. The *Witness* printed articles on American churches and religious life, essays by McCosh, and regular articles and sermons by Hall and other American ministers.[83] The Pan-Presbyterian Alliance heard accounts of the progress of Presbyterianism in America.[84] With all of

---

80 *Irish Times* 27 Sep 1886.
81 Harte, *Road I Have Travelled*, 155.
82 Harte, *Road I Have Travelled*, 159.
83 See, for example, *Witness* 19 Jun 1885, 26 Jun 1885, 1 Jan 1886, 22 Jan 1886, 26 Mar 1886, 23 Apr 1886, among others.
84 Report of the Pan-Presbyterian Alliance, 1888, 96.

their historic connections, in many ways it was natural for Irish Protestant churches to turn toward the United States when confronted by the threat of Home Rule.

Religion and Politics in the First Home Rule Crisis

Early Home Rule-era Irish unionism incorporated influences of conservative politics, Orangeism, and the Church of Ireland.[85] These three factors were combined in the work of one man, Reverend Dr. Richard Rutledge Kane, minister at Christ Church in Belfast and Grand Master of Belfast Orangemen. John Frederick MacNeice, a Church of Ireland Bishop and father of poet Louis MacNeice, described Kane as extraordinary in his attention to the church, Orange Order, and Irish politics. MacNeice wrote in 1931,

> Much has happened since 1898, and it may well be that no clergyman could again be a foremost political leader as Dr. Kane was. For more than ten years he was, perhaps, the most dominant personality in the public life of Belfast. There will be general agreement now that the minister of religion should not be too intimately associated with politics of a partizan character. The Church invariably suffers when clergy give up to party what was meant for mankind! But as a public man there was something very attractive about Dr. Kane.[86]

MacNeice's view of Kane reflected the changing position of clergy during the Home Rule era. Clergymen such as Kane took opinionated stances on political issues because of the substantial ramifications of Home Rule for the role of religious organizations in Ireland.

As well as working at Christ Church and with the Belfast Orange Order, Kane was an active member of the Ulster Loyalist Anti-Repeal Union (ULAU). Kane travelled to the United States and Canada in 1886 with barrister George Hill Smith on behalf of the ULAU to promote and defend Ulster unionism. He was also concerned with American Catholicism, which he targeted in his sermons. In a sermon of January 1885, he preached,

> It was impossible that the Roman Catholic should be loyal to the State unless the Church – that was, the priest – be supreme. The State must be satisfied with a divided allegiance or receive no allegiance at all. Here was the reason of the chronic disaffection which they met with

---

85 Jackson, 'Irish Unionism, 1870–1922', 116; Harbinson, *Ulster Unionist Party*, 8.
86 MacNeice, *Church of Ireland*, 17.

amongst Popish populations all over the world. At the present time it was beginning in America, and unless the schools and the elections and the civil government in America be subjected to the control of the Church – that was, the priest – America would soon have in her Popish population as disaffected and troublesome a people to deal with as the United Kingdom had in her Popish population.[87]

According to Kane, unless the Pope and priests were able to dictate political policy, disaffection and rebellion would spread amongst Catholics who could only be partially loyal to the state. Now that the Church of Ireland was disestablished it was easier to claim similarities with the United States, separate in its churches and states.

The role of Kane within Belfast society reflected the solidification of sectarianism with the unionist cause, spurred by the emergence of a combined Orange–Church of Ireland element within unionism. By the late nineteenth century, the Orange Order increasingly attracted Presbyterian membership, though it was traditionally associated with Anglicans. This meant that unionism was able to appeal to Protestants across a spectrum of denominations, while barring Catholics from full participation.[88] By 1886, political and religious events transpired to unite almost all Irish Protestants against Home Rule. They believed Gladstone's Home Rule scheme would isolate them from Protestant Britain, leaving them at the mercy of an oppressive Catholic majority in Ireland who were sure to deprive them of civil and religious liberty.[89]

Protestant churches in Ireland became heavily involved in Irish political affairs as they attempted to maintain the Union. Reverend James McConnell reported that after Gladstone introduced the first Home Rule Bill,

> The members of the General Assembly and nearly all Irish Presbyterians became seriously agitated. They feared that if this Bill were to pass their civil and religious liberties would be seriously imperilled. Many of them who had hitherto been Mr. Gladstone's strongest supporters and greatest admirers, now became his most determined opponents.[90]

The Presbyterian General Assembly called a special meeting to consider the state of the country, unanimously resolving against Home Rule. Presbyterians

87 *BNL* 27 Jan 1885.
88 Jackson, 'Irish Unionism, 1870–1922', 118.
89 Hempton and Hill, *Evangelical Protestantism*, 167; Alan Megahey, '"God Will Defend the Right": The Protestant Churches and Opposition to Home Rule', in *Defenders of the Union: A Survey of British and Irish Unionism since 1801*, ed. D. George Boyce and Alan O'Day (London: Routledge), 161.
90 McConnell, *Presbyterianism in Belfast*, 42.

were anxious to resist the forces of ultramontane Catholicism at home and worldwide. They also wished to proclaim support for civil and religious equality and fair settlement of the land question, ideals which remained consistent with their traditional support of Liberal policies.[91]

The Presbyterian General Assembly also prepared an anti-Home Rule statement for publication in the United States, calling on historical linkages and connections they had made through the Pan-Presbyterian Alliance.

The Presbyterian Churches in America being connected by many ties to their brethren in Ireland holding the same creed and maintaining the same church order, and having two years ago cemented their kinship at the meeting of the Pan-Presbyterian Council in Belfast, are naturally deeply interested in the Constitutional changes proposed to be carried out by Mr. Gladstone's Government of Ireland Bill, and are especially desirous to ascertain the views entertained regarding the Premier's proposals by their co-religionists in Ireland.[92]

The assembly believed the historical and religious ties between the two nations would compel American Presbyterians to look to their co-religionists in Ireland to formulate views on Home Rule.

In their address to the United States, the assembly focused on explaining the actions of Irish Presbyterians regarding Home Rule. They described the dangers inherent in the Home Rule settlement:

And if the Constitution foreshadowed in the present bill be imposed on us, which, instead of conferring upon Ireland anything resembling State rights, reduces her to a position in the empire lower than that of a third-class colony, the birth of the new system will be but synchronous with the inauguration of fresh agitation, whose object will be not merely to shake off the disabilities attached to the Constitution, but to shatter to the utmost, and one by one, the ties that remain to bind Ireland to the Empire.[93]

The General Assembly asserted that far from gaining the status of an American state, Ireland would sink to the level of the lowest colony. This relegation would ensure that Home Rule would lead to further rebellion, extremism, and demands for total separation.

---

91 *Minutes of the Proceedings of the General Assembly of the Presbyterian Church in Ireland, 1886*; Holmes, *Our Irish Presbyterian Heritage*, 134; Hempton and Hill, *Evangelical Protestantism*, 171–172.

92 *Witness* 14 May 1886; *BNL* 13 May 1886.

93 *BNL* 13 May 1886.

An editorial in the *Witness* commented that the assembly's statement would 'very effectually meet the objects for which it was primarily prepared. Our friends across the Atlantic will have their minds disabused by it of any false impressions which may have been left upon them by the utterances of men who spoke about us with some appearance of authority'.[94] The paper referred regretfully to the stance of McCosh, who had come out in favour of Home Rule. McCosh believed the passage of Home Rule was inevitable, so Irish Presbyterians would be better off if they accepted it and worked toward the unification of Ireland.[95] The *Witness* worried McCosh's statements would mislead Americans on Irish Presbyterian views of Home Rule.

All the deep respect which is felt for [McCosh] here has not prevented very many from feeling the deepest sorrow, not unmixed with surprise, at the attitude which he has assumed. Men who were only partially acquainted with all the circumstances of the case might possibly imagine that he spoke with some authority on the subject, and that some American journals which followed in his wake were the true exponents of Irish Presbyterian opinion. We are glad, therefore, that the Assembly's Committee has put the real state of the case before the American public, and we trust that public will take their views of the question not from any individual or journal ... but from this deliberate statement agreed upon by the Assembly's Committee. We ought, it may be supposed, to know our own affairs and our own position best.[96]

The *Witness*'s concern with the views of McCosh reflected the importance of American opinion on the Home Rule question. They hoped the assembly's message would convince the American public that the true interests of Irish Presbyterians were with the maintenance of Union.

Presbyterian preoccupation with American opinion was reflected in the paper's articles monitoring opinions across the United States.[97] One article related the contents of a telegram from New York:

The declaration of the Ulster Presbyterians just published here does not meet with the approval of the leading American clergy. Commenting upon it, they take substantially the same view as Dr. M'Cosh sent recently. Dr. Howard Crosby says – 'I do not agree at all with the

94 *Witness* 14 May 1886.
95 *Witness* 30 Apr 1886.
96 *Witness* 14 May 1886.
97 *Witness* 24 Dec 1885.

Irish Church. It takes a selfish, not a broad and liberal, view of Mr. Gladstone's Bill.' The only eminent Presbyterian clergyman agreeing with the Ulster declaration is Dr. John Hall, an Irishman.[98]

One letter to the editor insisted there was far less backing for Gladstone's bill from America than was apparent from press reports. The writer, Thomas West, sent in a copy of the *Presbyterian Journal* of Philadelphia, which revealed that Presbyterians of that city were in sympathy with Ulster.[99]

The *Presbyterian Journal* had devoted an entire page to analysis of the assembly's American statement. The *Witness* reprinted an article from the *Journal* which stated that the Home Rule cause had little support in Philadelphia.

> However it may be elsewhere, that is strictly true of this neighbourhood. Especially we may say that Presbyterians of Irish descent, or connection, have almost wholly held aloof from it. We think we can say with confidence that the Presbyterians who have had anything to do with the movement, from its inception to its completion ... can be counted on one round of the fingers, and we suspect that not three hundred dollars all told of the money raised came from them. We say this that the Presbyterians in Ireland may know that their kindred here have not been faithless to them.[100]

The *Presbyterian Journal* confirmed Irish Presbyterian hopes that their kinsmen in America were not supportive of the Home Rule movement, at least in the Scotch-Irish hub of Philadelphia. However, there was a wide gap between opposing Irish-American efforts to raise money for Home Rule, and actively supporting the preservation of the Union.

The Anglo-Irish used the Church of Ireland General Synod to express total opposition to the policy of Home Rule in 1886. The Church of Ireland focused on all-Irish unionism, emphasizing common ties with other Irish Protestants.[101] At the Synod's special meeting on 23 March 1886, America frequently appeared in the attendees' speeches. Lord Plunket, the Archbishop of Dublin, asserted that Home Rule was not the final goal of Irish nationalists. 'Is it not plain to everyone who is not blind to what is taking place at the present moment, and who is not deaf to what is being said, that there are ulterior aims on the part of those, in this country and

---

98 *Witness* 14 May 1886.
99 *Witness* 16 Apr 1886.
100 Reprinted in the *Witness* 16 Apr 1886.
101 Hempton and Hill, *Evangelical Protestantism*, 170.

in America, who exercise a chief influence among the advocates of this policy?'[102] Plunket claimed the true demands which lurked behind Home Rule were complete separation and advanced socialism, as illustrated by the land war and dynamite campaign. The Bishop of Down, Robert Knox, expressed similar sentiments through quotation of Charles Stewart Parnell's alleged 'Last Link' speech.[103]

Others also emphasized American extremism which they claimed lurked behind the Irish Parliamentary Party's constitutional exterior. The Bishop of Cork, Robert S. Gregg, stated,

> I will not judge men unfairly: I will judge them by their acts and words. Their acts you know too well; as for their words, they have but one voice – a very gentle voice – in the British Parliament, a voice of villainous import in Ireland, and in America absolutely ferocious. The foremost men in the movement have there spoken of the crime which disgusted Europe, when two blameless and highminded men were butchered in cold blood in Phoenix Park, as a 'victory' in which the Irish race rejoiced.[104]

Reverend James Byrne, the Dean of Clonfert, stated that a deep-seated hatred of England was the key motivator for the Irish, particularly in America. He explained, 'That hatred, indeed, cannot quite be overlooked. It is proclaimed in the Irish Press, it is avowed in the Imperial Parliament, it is manifested in the Irish-American plots for dynamite outrage'.[105]

Reverend George Salmon, Professor of Divinity at Trinity College, asserted that Home Rule went against the worldwide trend toward greater union, as exemplified by the American Civil War.[106] Sir Frederick Heygate, the former MP for County Londonderry, believed the idea of Ireland separating from Great Britain baffled the rest of the world.

> The world looks on from the outside with astonishment; the people of every civilized land rub their eyes with surprise that a small country like Ireland, without much capital, should desire to separate from a country like England. The Americans look on and sneer and laugh at

---

102 'The Church of Ireland and the Present Political Crisis: Report for the Special Meeting of the General Synod, Holden at Dublin, March 23, 1886' (Dublin: Hodges, Figgis, 1886).
103 'Church of Ireland and the Present Political Crisis'.
104 'Church of Ireland and the Present Political Crisis'.
105 'Church of Ireland and the Present Political Crisis'.
106 George Salmon, 'Against Home Rule' (Dublin: Irish Loyal and Patriotic Union, 1886).

the infatuation of the people, and regard the situation as a good safety-valve for the discontent of their own people.[107]

Heygate asserted that Americans, given their own history of movement toward union, were not supportive of the principle of Home Rule. However, the American government had its own motivations for indulging Irish-Americans, in that Home Rule kept Ireland as the focus of Irish-Americans dissent rather than the United States.

Gilbert Mahaffy, the curate of Monkstown, wrote an 1886 pamphlet on 'The Attitude of Irish Churchmen in the Present Political Crisis'. He outlined the main reasons the Church of Ireland was opposed to Home Rule:

One reason is that the Home Rule movement has been, from first to last, a movement hostile to British rule. And fostered as it has been on American soil, and supported by American dollars, it is essentially republican. Such being the case, can it be expected by anyone that a Home Rule Parliament would be friendly to England or loyal to the British Crown? The certain result of setting up such a Parliament would be to make Ireland more than ever a source of weakness to England – a perpetual thorn in her side – a cause of trouble to be reckoned with in every complication with foreign nations.[108]

Like others at the special meeting of the Church of Ireland General Synod, Mahaffy propounded anti-American views which contrasted with the generally pro-American views of Presbyterians during the Home Rule crisis. However, criticism of Irish-American extremism was common across all Protestant denominations in Ireland.

The Methodist Church, though hesitant to enter into the political realm, took a stand against Home Rule based in part on reactions to the influence of Irish-American extremism. The *Methodist Recorder* asserted, 'We care nothing for politics or political party. We care not how radical the scheme that can give weary Ireland peace once more. But we protest in the name of Methodism against a scheme which would hand over our Methodist brethren to the tender mercies of Archbishop Walsh and the dynamiters of New York'.[109] Methodists maintained a record of loyalty to the Union and opposition to Catholic causes such as Catholic Emancipation, the Repeal Campaign, and the Maynooth grant. For the minority of Methodists who supported Home Rule, generally those whose livelihood depended on the goodwill of Catholic neighbours, they

---

107 'Church of Ireland and the Present Political Crisis'.
108 Mahaffy, 'Attitude of Irish Churchmen', 12.
109 Reprinted in *Witness* 23 Apr 1886.

also refused to support any extremism in connection with the cause.[110] The majority of Methodists, however, were firmly against Home Rule.

At the Irish Methodist Annual Conference in 1887, church leaders responded to a message from the General Conference of the Methodist Episcopal Church in the United States. The message expressed sympathy with the unionist cause, stating 'that the future of Ireland, in respect of peace and growth, depends largely upon the security of the Protestant element in her population'.[111] The Irish Methodist address in reply asserted they were in favour of removing every political or religious grievance from all classes of the population, but that they did not believe there was 'a single remaining grievance of which Roman Catholics as such have to complain'. The address concluded, 'As with you during your recent civil war we are heartily with the Union as being, in our judgment, of vital importance in relation to the safety and growth of Protestantism, of which you speak, and earnestly hope that under the wise and firm administration of Government the reign of lawlessness and disorder will speedily come to an end'.[112]

The role of the Catholic Church was a common concern amongst Irish Protestants. An editorial in the *Witness* cautioned that Catholic attitudes as revealed by the American priesthood were an indication of the future for Ireland under Home Rule. American priests indicated that the Catholic Church would not tolerate heretics if Catholics became a majority in the United States. The paper warned, 'Just as the Irish [Parliamentary] party have been obliged to accept the doctrines of the Romish hierarchy in regard to their denominational education, whatever their own private opinions may be, as soon as Romish ascendency is again established in Ireland, they will be constrained to swallow Rome's teaching in regard to toleration'.[113]

Another editorial portrayed the American example as indicative of the future for a self-governing Ireland.

We only have to look across at the state of things in New York to learn what is a very real and probable danger. There the dominant Irish party, by wire-pulling and corruption of various kinds, have allocated public funds from time to time to distinctly Roman Catholic projects. The Protestant Press has complained bitterly, denounced and exposed these knavish tricks, but with as yet little or no result. If in Ireland the command of public funds was in the hands of a political party which in turn was manipulated by the priesthood, who can doubt that a

110 Cooney, *Methodists in Ireland*, 97–98.
111 *Irish Times* 21 Jun 1887.
112 *Irish Times* 21 Jun 1887.
113 *Witness* 24 Dec 1885.

growing endowment of Roman Catholic institutions would take place to the detriment of all other parties and the shame of public justice? It is American-Irish ideas that are ruling at present in Ireland. It is American-Irish institutions that would most likely be imported here.[114]

The *Witness* feared the influence of Catholicism on a potential Dublin parliament, as illustrated by Irish Catholics in America.

Thomas Witherow, prominent Presbyterian minister and Professor of Church History at Magee College in Londonderry, used a hypothetical American example to illustrate the dire situation Irish Protestants faced under Home Rule.

If the State of New York were a Roman Catholic State in the proportion of four to one; and if a proposition were made to withdraw New York from the jurisdiction of Congress, and give it a Congress of its own, practically independent; and if this State Legislature were clothed with legislative and administrative power, so as it have under its control the lives, property, religion and liberty of the Protestant minority; and if the Protestant minority had before them the certainty of being governed in perpetuity by such men as the popular vote now casts to the surface in Ireland – we here wonder how all this would be regarded by the Protestant minority in the State of New York? All who understand this will understand perfectly why it is that the idea of an Irish Parliament is repulsive to the General Assembly and to the Protestants of Ireland.[115]

Published in the *Presbyterian Review*, Witherow's analogy was part of an appeal to an international audience of Presbyterians to understand the Irish unionist cause.

At times, Irish Protestants took a different tactic regarding Catholicism and Home Rule. Like the editors of the *Witness*, Mahaffy believed Home Rule would result in complete ascendancy of the Catholic Church. The only way this would not happen, he asserted, was 'if the revolt against priestly power, of which there are many signs here and there – a revolt stimulated by the frequency of intercourse with America – should reach its culmination, there would be a separation between the clerical party and the communistic party'.[116] Irish-American nationalists were sometimes portrayed

---

114 *Witness* 21 May 1886.
115 Thomas Witherow, 'General Assembly of the Irish Church', *Presbyterian Review* 8, no. 32 (Oct 1887), 727; Holmes, 'Covenanter Politics', 353.
116 Mahaffy, 'Attitude of Irish Churchmen', 15–16.

as extreme anti-Catholic and irreligious socialists or communists. In a pamphlet entitled 'Religion and Unbelief in Ireland', Leopold Agar-Ellis warned that the result of an Irish parliament, dominated by American Fenians, would be an attack on all religion, starting with Protestants and ending with the Catholic Church itself. They would persecute the Catholic priesthood and obliterate the Protestants. He asked, 'Is anyone simple enough to suppose that the teaching of the decalogue would be tolerated by an Irish-American government?'[117] Irish-America was portrayed as an irreligious threat to all religious groups in Ireland, which accorded with their extremist image.

The defeat of the Home Rule Bill at its second reading on 8 June 1886 led to protracted and violent rioting in Belfast, with Kane and Hanna accused of fomenting the disturbance.[118] Hanna was the Presbyterian minister at Belfast's St. Enoch's Church. He was ordained in 1852, and an American university had conferred upon him an honorary doctorate.[119] Known for promoting extremely conservative political views from the pulpit, he was a remarkably popular preacher who, like Kane, combined his role as clergyman with participation in the Orange Order and the ULAU.[120] Hanna and Kane's roles as leading figures in Belfast reflected the pronounced religious presence in the unionist movement.[121]

Opposition to Home Rule and Self-Government, 1890–1920

At the Jubilee Assembly of the Irish Presbyterian Church in 1890, Reverend R.J. Lynd asserted that the great traditions of Ulster Presbyterians were evidenced by their outreach to the world.

We have, through the mysterious workings of Providence, sent out men who have planted their faith in foreign lands, and it has grown so bravely that it has far outstripped the Church's growth at home. Who does not know Francis M'Kemie [sic], who founded American Presbyterianism, was a native of County Donegal? and Dr. [John] Hall will tell you, as he alone can, something of what that Imperial

---

117 Leopold Agar-Ellis, 'Religion and Unbelief in Ireland' (London: Remington, 1888), 6–7. Several Fenian leaders had indeed rejected their boyhood Catholicism.
118 Megahey, 'God Will Defend the Right', 163.
119 Gales College in Wisconsin, which was under the direction of the Presbyterian Church.
120 McConnell, *Presbyterianism in Belfast*, 95–96.
121 D. George Boyce, 'Weary Patriots: Ireland and the Making of Unionism', in *Defenders of the Union: A Survey of British and Irish Unionism since 1801*, ed. D. George Boyce and Alan O'Day (London: Routledge, 2001), 26.

Republic owes to the Ulster Scot. All our colonies have a similar experience.[122]

Irish Presbyterian identity was linked to a history of emigration and planting of faith in foreign frontiers. Scotch-Irish heritage and success in America was called upon to develop a sense of distinctiveness among Ulster's Presbyterians, which helped to contribute to a separate Ulster identity within the unionist movement.

Hall, who frequently visited his native Ulster, was present at the Jubilee Assembly. He reported the influence of Ulster on the United States, stating, 'In point of fact there is no doubt about this, that Ulster has sent into these United States a body of people that have exercised the strongest formative influence upon the institutions and the character of this great nation'.[123] He said that opinion had been confirmed by the recent formation of the SISA, whose president, Robert Bonner, was from the same place as Francis Makemie, Ramelton in County Donegal.

Hall was the subject of an Irish Loyal and Patriotic Union pamphlet in 1888, 'The Testimony of a Presbyterian Devine'. It described Hall as an Irish minister who was now in charge of one of the most influential Presbyterian churches in America, New York's Fifth Avenue Presbyterian Church, raising the largest church offering in the world. In the pamphlet, Hall was quoted explaining the view of Americans toward Ireland as being influenced by Irish-American Catholics. He asserted that the Republican and Democratic parties were swayed by their desire to court the Catholic vote, which explained politicians' utterances in favour of Home Rule. Hall said, 'In other cases, American citizens naturally wish to see approximation in other lands to the ways of their own; and they do not always know enough of the circumstances to discriminate'.[124] Thus the American public only seemed to be supporting Home Rule because they had not been properly presented with the other side of the argument.

The Special Commission on Parnellism and Crime influenced views about the role of America in the Home Rule question. Antrim-born Methodist missionary and principal of Belfast's Methodist College, William Arthur, wrote that the Parnellites had been beneficiaries of

the preachers of the lowest forms of crime which have ever been, in a civilized nation, commended in print, as the beneficiary of men

---

122 *Jubilee of the General Assembly of the Presbyterian Church in Ireland, Belfast, July 1890* (Belfast: The Witness Printing Works, 1890), 117.
123 *Jubilee of the General Assembly*, 154–155.
124 John Hall, 'The Testimony of a Presbyterian Devine' (Dublin: ILPU, 1888), 1–2.

like Patrick Ford, a wretch at whose name every honest man ought to
shudder, whom Mr. [Michael] Davitt regards – and told the judges so
– as an admirable example of the Christian and philanthropist[.] How,
I repeat, could those who, with all this proved, would set up Parnell
in the chief place of power in Ireland be acquitted of partaking of his
sins?[125]

Arthur was astonished anyone could support a party so linked with conspiracy,
crime, intimidation, and murder.

After the second Home Rule Bill was introduced in 1893, the *Witness*
similarly condemned the influence of Irish-America. An editorial stated,
'Only one class would be benefitted by the Home Rule legislation. This is
the class of greedy vultures who in the name of patriotism, have fattened
upon political agitation. Gentlemen of the Healy, O'Brien, and Dillon type
and the cadaverous Fenian Yankee beyond the sea would swoop down upon
Ireland, and prey upon her vitals'.[126] The analogy is with the fate of the
fire-bringer Prometheus, tied by Zeus's command to a rock where a vulture
daily devoured his intestines. The IPP was incriminated by association
with Irish-American extremists and funded by those who would prey upon
Ireland if Home Rule was granted.

A special meeting of the Irish Presbyterian General Assembly was
called on 15 March 1893, which resolved 'strenuously [to] oppose' the
enactment of Home Rule.[127] Nevertheless, Gladstone was able to gain
support from a minority of ministers such as the Reverends J.B. Armour
and J.L.B. Dougherty.[128] Irish Methodists and the Church of Ireland also
expressed strong opposition to the second Home Rule Bill.[129] The Parnell
split had left the IPP divided, but Protestants remained threatened by what
they saw as the Catholic Church openly identifying themselves with the
Home Rulers. The condemnation of Home Rule as Rome Rule became a
prominent refrain.[130] The *Witness* used American examples to illustrate the
corruption of the Catholic Church. The newspaper quoted Froude as saying
what happened in America was bound to happen in Ireland as Catholics
were the same throughout the world. The newspaper implored, 'Let Mr.
Gladstone and his colleagues ponder these words of the far-seeing Froude,

---

125 William Arthur, 'Moral Points in the Home Rule Controversy' (Dublin: IUA, 1893).
126 *Witness* 17 Mar 1893.
127 McConnell, *Presbyterianism in Belfast*, 42.
128 Holmes, *Our Irish Presbyterian Heritage*, 136.
129 Cooney, *Methodists in Ireland*, 99; William Nicholas, 'Why are the Methodists of
     Ireland Opposed to Home Rule?' (Dublin: IUA, 1893).
130 Harbinson, *Ulster Unionist Party*, 15.

and there will be no Home Rule granted; but the prosperity and industry of the loyal Unionists will be fostered instead of ruined'.[131]

After the defeat of the second Home Rule Bill in the House of Lords, the issue of Catholic Church involvement in Irish politics and society continued to form an important part of the arguments against Home Rule. This was particularly the case after the papal *ne temere* decree of 1908. The decree, requiring all children of marriages between Catholics and non-Catholics to be raised as Catholics, was a rallying point for Protestants illustrating how the Pope was attempting to dominate the lives of the Irish. The McCann case of 1910, in which a Catholic man left his non-Catholic wife and disappeared with their two children, especially captured the attention of Irish Protestants. The Ulster Unionist Council resolved that the Church's sanction of such events deserved the reprobation of the entire community. They considered the McCann case to be a confirmation of the threat to civil and religious liberty embodied in a potential Home Rule settlement.[132]

The Presbyterian General Assembly in 1911, with Reverend Dr. John Macmillan as moderator, turned its attention to Anglo-American relations. The assembly passed a resolution expressing its 'intense gratification' for President William Howard Taft's proposal for an arbitration treaty between the two countries, which they called 'the two great sections of the English speaking race'. The assembly stated they 'sincerely hope[d] that nothing may prevent the conclusion of this treaty, and that it will be but the first among many such treaties between the great nations of the world, so that the day may be hastened for which we all earnestly pray when peace shall reign over all the earth and men shall learn war no more'.[133] Macmillan, who was the minister of Belfast's Cooke Centenary Church and an 1878 graduate of Princeton, went to the United States in 1912 to speak at the Princeton Theological Seminary centenary. He also represented Irish Presbyterians at the meeting of the General Assembly of the Presbyterian Church in the United States of America.[134]

At the Princeton Theological Seminary centenary, Macmillan gave an address on 'Irish and American Presbyterianism'. He described the plantation of Ulster and foundations of the Irish Presbyterian Church. According to him, early Ulster Scots regarded the Bible as their statute book and library, emphasized the value of education, and lived a humble life, always retaining

131 *Witness* 24 Feb 1893.
132 Ulster Unionist Council 1912 Year Book, PRONI D972/17.
133 *Minutes of the Proceedings of the General Assembly of the Presbyterian Church in Ireland, 1911*, 52.
134 *Minutes of the General Assembly of the Presbyterian Church in the United States of America, 1912*, 20.

close ties with Scotland.[135] He regarded Ireland as the original homeland of the Ulster Scots, which was the 'Scotia major of the ancient world'. Ulster Scots struggled for toleration, and through those struggles became uncompromisingly Presbyterian. According to Macmillan, Presbyterianism, 'with its franchise and freedom of the Kingdom of God enjoyed by women as well as men – is the strongest and most democratic form of Protestantism; and supply the *raison d'être* of Protestantism'.[136]

Macmillan went on to describe the emigration of Ulster Scots to America, leaving a land of bondage to settle in the Lord's land, maintaining focus on religion, education, and humility. He spoke of the roles of Francis Makemie and William Tennent, and those Ulster-Americans who had a direct impact on his own life. He stated,

> Webster, writing in the middle of the last century, declares that Ulster has continued for one hundred and fifty years to be 'the great nursery' of the American Presbyterian Church. When I think of John Glendy, who was the minister of the church of my boyhood, who fled from Ireland in the tragic days of 1798, who became successively chaplain of the U.S. Congress and of the U.S. Senate, and a minister of great eloquence and power; of the incomparable John Hall, who came to New York in 1867 and exercised a unique influence over the American Continent, of which every great Irish Presbyterian was so justly proud; and of the men who in Princeton greeted me as a fellow-countryman and who are rendering such splendid service in this vast and high field, I am convinced that the ministerial succession is still being well maintained.[137]

Macmillan made clear it was not just religious connections between Ulster and America that were celebrated, but that Ulster Scots had been inspired by the American political example: 'The Declaration of Independence gave hope to those who struggled for justice in Ireland, and the struggle at length was crowned with victory. We now have religious equality'.[138] Macmillan expressed the close connection felt by Ulster Scots to America. He concluded,

---

135 *The Centennial Celebration of the Theological Seminary of the Presbyterian Church in the United States of America at Princeton, New Jersey* (Princeton, NJ: Theological Seminary, 1912), 500–505.
136 *Centennial Celebration*, 506–507.
137 *Centennial Celebration*, 515. His reference was to the historian of American Presbyterianism, Richard Webster. See Webster's *A History of the Presbyterian Church in America: From Its Origin until the Year 1760* (Philadelphia: Joseph M. Wilson, 1857), 59.
138 *Centennial Celebration*, 522.

'Although year by year, we suffer from emigration, by which we are deprived of the enthusiasm and enterprise of our youngest and strongest, we do not grudge our youth to our colonies nor to this Republic, which our people regard as almost a second home'.[139]

Macmillan's visit to the United States was part of a larger web of transatlantic visits which continued to be made by ministers and evangelists. At the meeting of the General Assembly of the Presbyterian Church in the United States of America, the Committee on Christian Life and Work reported that Dr. John Wilbur Chapman, a prominent member of the evangelistic circuit who had worked with Moody, spent several months in Britain as a representative-at-large of the committee. He conducted a number of 'successful evangelistic campaigns in Belfast and other points'.[140] Dr. William H. Roberts also visited Europe on behalf of the committee in 1911, meeting with church leaders in Edinburgh, London, Geneva, and Belfast. The committee recounted,

> Dr. Roberts reports a conference of unusual interest with the Presbyterian Church in Ireland, in which 250 ministers and elders were present to meet him at the call of the Moderator, Rev. Dr. McMillan [sic]. Dr. Roberts also reports a deep interest in the subject of Evangelism as presented by him and the general expression of opinion that a world-wide revival of spiritual religion would be the best monument to the great reformers – Luther and Calvin – in connection with the four hundredth anniversary of the Protestant Reformation.[141]

Presbyterians in the United States and Ireland remained dedicated to an international evangelical effort supporting revivalism and collaboration of churches worldwide.

Meanwhile, by the time of the third Home Rule Bill in 1912, the unionist movement became increasingly narrowed on Ulster rather than all-Ireland unionism.[142] McConnell wrote,

> The veto of the House of Lords had since [1911] been destroyed, and an attempt is again being made to pass a Home Rule Bill for Ireland, which the Irish Presbyterians are preparing to resist with all their might. What the result will be may be inferred from the following

---

139 *Centennial Celebration*, 524.
140 *Minutes of the General Assembly of the Presbyterian Church in the United States of America, 1912*, 34.
141 *Minutes of the General Assembly of the Presbyterian Church in the United States of America, 1912*, 34–35.
142 Burnett, 'Modernisation of Unionism', 50.

pronouncement by Lord Rosebery, when presiding at a lecture by the American Ambassador (Mr. Whitelaw Reid) in Edinburgh a short time ago: – 'I love Highlanders and I love Lowlanders, but when I come to the branch of our race which has been grafted on the Ulster stem, I take off my hat with veneration and awe. They are, I believe, without exception, the toughest, most dominant, the most irresistible race that exists in the universe at this moment'.[143]

In the face of increasing focus on Ulster, Protestant churches continued to lend their support to the unionist cause, including staging anti-Home Rule rallies. The Irish Presbyterian Convention was held on 1 February 1912. They received messages of sympathy from the Church of Ireland, Irish Baptists, and Methodists.[144] Methodists organized their own Belfast demonstrations against the third Home Rule Bill in 1912, with simultaneous meetings held in the Exhibition Hall, People's Hall, and Ulster Hall.[145]

The signing of the Ulster Covenant on Ulster Day, 28 September 1912, was the ultimate expression of the distinctive Ulster blend of religion with politics. The text of the Covenant, reflecting the historic Scottish covenants signed by the Ulster Scots' ancestors, was mainly written by a Presbyterian elder, Thomas Sinclair. The moderator of the Presbyterian General Assembly and the Bishop of Down signed the Covenant immediately after Edward Carson and Lord Londonderry at the ceremony in Belfast City Hall. The Covenant gained the signatures of all the northern Irish bishops in the Church of Ireland.[146] Preachers throughout the country insisted the signing of the Covenant was a religious rather than political occasion.[147]

The menace of Irish-America remained part of the discourse against the Home Rule Bill. The Bishop of Kilmore, Reverend Dr. Alfred George Elliott, warned that 'Ireland a Nation' was the motto of the American supporters of the nationalist party.[148] The threat of Catholicism was also prominent, especially amongst members of the Orange Order. The Imperial Grand President, Colonel Robert H. Wallace, addressed delegates from all parts of the British Empire and the United States at the meeting of the Triennial Council in 1912. Wallace stated they hoped to shut the gates of the Empire against Roman Catholic aggression. He called on the worldwide

---

143 McConnell, *Presbyterianism in Belfast*, 43.
144 R.F.G. Holmes, '"Ulster Will Fight and Ulster Will Be Right": The Protestant Churches and Ulster's Resistance to Home Rule, 1912–14', in *Studies in Church History*, 20: *The Church and War*, ed. W.J. Sheils (Oxford: Basil Blackwell, 1983), 324.
145 Cooney, *Methodists in Ireland*, 99.
146 See Scholes, *Church of Ireland*.
147 Holmes, 'Ulster Will Fight', 329–330.
148 *Witness* 13 Sep 1912.

body of Orangemen to fight against Irish Home Rule, because, he stated, 'in our corner of Ulster we are fighting the battle not only of the other Protestants in Ireland, but of the Protestantism of the world'.[149]

Presbyterians also called upon positive links with America, including the traditional Presbyterian association with fighting for civil and religious liberty. An editorial in the *Witness* about the signing of the Covenant stated,

Presbyterianism has flourished, and flourishes still, by resistance to tyranny, and it would be a red day for Presbyterianism and for civil and religious liberty all over the world when Presbyterians would be content to submit to tyranny in any form, ecclesiastical or political. Presbyterianism has ever been in the van of liberty, and it is to Presbyterianism and the Scottish blood that it represents that the United States of America owe much of their liberty, and that the free Constitutions of two continents are in existence.[150]

The traditional Presbyterian defiance of tyranny and celebration of liberty, as embodied in the Scotch-Irish experience in America, was called upon to legitimize the unionists' stance against Home Rule. This also helped to draw Presbyterians into a more unified 'Ulsterman' identity, aiding the unionist movement to become increasingly concentrated in Ulster.

The *Witness* also called upon the American example as they expressed a feeling of betrayal by the British which led to unionist threats of militancy. The editors wrote,

The Southern States of America demanded in practical effort what the Irish are demanding – separation from Great Britain. The North went to war rather than submit to it. The British Government in regard to Ireland represents the Northern States of that day. But they do not fight; they surrender; and with their surrender sacrifice all the interests, all the traditions of their loyal friends in Ireland. It is asking too much of these men to submit to the rod and lash.[151]

This was likening Catholics to American slave-owners, to whom the British willingly submitted the loyal Ulstermen. Presbyterian traditions in Ulster, Scotland, and America were invoked to portray Ulster Scots as liberty-loving

---

149 Report of the Sixteenth Triennial Meeting of the Imperial Grand Orange Council of the World, held at Glasgow, Scotland, on the 17th and 18th of July 1912, PRONI D1889/6/5B.
150 *Witness* 27 Sep 1912.
151 *Witness* 2 Aug 1912.

and loyal, but prepared to stand up for their ideals against tyranny and coercion. Presbyterians believed their traditions were responsible for inspiring the constitutions of the United Kingdom and United States. This made the sense of betrayal all the greater when, as they saw it, the British government attempted to force Home Rule upon them.

Even after the passage of the Home Rule Bill and the conclusion of the First World War, Ulster Protestants continued to call on Scotch-Irish and evangelical religious connections in the United States. They attempted to gain unionist political support in America and counter the influence of Éamon de Valera as he toured the country. The MP for South Tyrone, William Coote, led a delegation of six clergymen in November 1919 on a tour of the United States. The delegates were composed of members of the Church of Ireland, Methodist Church, and Presbyterian Church, illustrating cross-denominational support for unionists to make appeals to the United States. The delegates spoke out against the dangers of Irish nationalism and the domination of the Catholic Church.[152]

Conclusion

The religious and political links called upon by Coote and the Ulster clergymen had continued from the days of the earliest emigration from Ulster to America, and the foundations of American Presbyterianism. Within the larger context of the worldwide growth of evangelicalism, Ulster and America forged a web of connections between individuals and organizations based on shared religious heritage. From the time of Francis Makemie, there was an unlimited flow of Ulster clergy to America. In return, revivalists and Princeton-educated ministers came to Ulster from the United States. Through the connections of individual ministers, voluntary societies, and transatlantic religious organizations, Ulster and America each developed similar evangelical, and in some cases fundamentalist, religious traditions.

Though the connections between Ulster and American religion did not always directly result in support for the unionist cause, they formed an important context vital to understanding Ulster's view of the United States during the Home Rule period. As Macmillan explained in his speech at the Princeton Theological Seminary centenary, Ulster Presbyterians felt pride in Scotch-Irish contributions to America, and because of the prevalence of emigration and historical connections even viewed America as a second home. Presbyterian unionists emphasized Scotch-Irish heritage and success on the frontier to underscore Ulster Scots' distinctiveness and value to the

152 'America and the Irish Question'.

United Kingdom. They stressed the Presbyterian tradition of fighting for civil and religious liberty in the United States and the British Empire. Such rhetoric helped to create a more united Ulster Presbyterian identity in the face of the Home Rule threat.

These positive uses of the United States were complemented by calls from various denominations on their American counterparts to oppose Home Rule, and the use of American historical examples to legitimize unionist stances. America was also approached in a negative light by all three major Irish Protestant denominations through condemnation of Irish-American extremism, separatism, and funding of the Irish nationalist movement. This was also reflected in Irish Protestant views of Catholicism. The example of Catholics in the United States was used to show the threat of Catholicism to a potential Dublin parliament. Anti-Catholicism was used to unify Irish Protestants, who came from a diverse array of social and political backgrounds, within the unionist movement. Anti-Catholicism was also used to appeal to American Protestants to aid unionists, as Catholicism was depicted as a shared menace to the American and British governments. In contrast, Irish-America was sometimes portrayed as an irreligious force that would work to destroy Catholicism as well as Protestantism in Ireland.

Religion and politics were intertwined in the Ulster unionist approach to America. As politics became increasingly sectarian, Irish Protestants called upon their American counterparts and criticized events in the United States. The United States' religious connections to Ulster were an important part of forming closer relations between Irish Protestants as they were increasingly divided from Catholics in the political sphere. They were also vital to the formation of a more unified Irish Protestant identity and the emphasis on the 'Ulsterman', which aided in the evolution of unionism from an all-Ireland movement to one focused almost solely on Ulster.

7

The Idea of America

Confronted with the first Home Rule Bill in 1886, Irish historian W.E.H. Lecky wrote, 'It would be difficult to conceive a policy more opposed to the best tendencies of the time'. He described the unification of Italy led by the Count of Cavour, unification of Germany under Otto von Bismarck, and praised the United States for overcoming the Civil War. He believed Americans had secured the unity of their republic for centuries to come. Lecky concluded, 'These have been the contributions of other nations to the history of the nineteenth century. Shall it be said of English statesmen that their most prolific and most characteristic work has been to introduce the principle of dissolution into the very heart of their empire?'[1]

Lecky saw national movements toward unity as the best tendency of the nineteenth century. The United States example was used to epitomize unification as the spirit of the age. Unionists claimed the British government was turning its back on the inexorable movement toward unity with its Home Rule policies. Appeals to unity as the spirit of the age echoed in unionist speeches and writings throughout the Home Rule period. Unity was said to be embodied in the coming together of the thirteen colonies as the United States, the fighting of the North to save the Union with the South, and enshrined in the American constitution.

Unionists appealed to the American example of national unity to gain legitimacy in their attempts to preserve the Union with Great Britain. American historical and constitutional examples were used by unionists in a wide variety of ways in their movement against Home Rule. This chapter will first examine unionist rhetoric utilizing the American Revolutionary War. Drawing upon ethnic connections with the Scotch-Irish, Ulster unionists emphasized themes of ethnic identity, legitimacy, militancy, and British coercion and betrayal. Next, the chapter will highlight the American Civil War as a historical parallel to the situation of Ulster unionists. The Civil War

---

1 Lecky, 'Nationalist Parliament', 664. On Lecky, see Jackson, 'Irish Unionism', 123; Boyce, 'In the Front Rank', 187–194.

was used to underscore both obligations of the British government to fight to save the Union and the validity of Ulster militancy. Finally, the chapter will explore the unionists' use of the American constitution. Unionists focused on American constitutional provisions and protections of minority rights to suggest solutions to Irish problems and emphasize flaws in the Home Rule system. The United States played a significant role in unionist political thought and rhetoric throughout the Home Rule era, used to emphasize the need to maintain the Union and provide historical justification for unionist actions.

American Revolution

Ulster unionist attitudes toward the American colonial and Revolutionary periods changed over time as the succession of Home Rule bills were introduced in Parliament. In the final quarter of the nineteenth century, the Scotch-Irish were celebrated for making up the backbone of American colonial society. Groups such as the SISA emphasized the Scotch-Irish as a driving force behind the colonists' victory in the War of Independence. Ulster unionists themselves perpetuated this Scotch-Irish mythology. A *Belfast News-Letter* editorial in 1882 remarked, 'When we look into the history of the great nation now known as the United States, we see enough to convince us that the Insurrection would have been a failure but for the Irishmen who supported it'.[2] As members of the same ethnic group, Ulster Scots considered Scotch-Irish achievements as victories for their 'race' as a whole, even for those who remained in Ireland.

In 1775, American events dominated politics both at Westminster and in Ireland. Eighteenth-century Ireland and America shared common political ideologies and heritage. Ulster Scots also shared a Presbyterian political 'language' which influenced the American colonists.[3] Ulster also had valuable trade connections with North America. After fighting commenced, public sentiment as displayed through newspaper articles, pamphlets, and public meetings revealed widespread sympathy for the colonists. Financial matters and the rallying cry of 'no taxation without representation' formed the framework in which most Irish people saw the American conflict, rather than in ideological terms.[4]

---

2 *BNL* 4 Aug 1882.
3 Foster, *Modern Ireland*, 239–242; Stephen Small, *Political Thought in Ireland, 1776–1798: Republicanism, Patriotism, and Radicalism* (Oxford: Oxford University Press, 2002), 2; Maurice J. Bric, 'Ireland, America and the Reassessment of a Special Relationship, 1760–1783', *Eighteenth-Century Ireland* 11 (1996), 88–89.
4 Maurice R. O'Connell, *Irish Politics and Social Conflict in the Age of the American*

In Dublin, the Irish Parliament led by Henry Grattan used the time of war to demand concessions from the British. Irish leaders felt commercial resentment at British wartime measures constricting the Irish economy. In response to Irish demands and after military demonstrations by armed Volunteers, free trade and legislative independence were granted to Ireland in 1779.[5] The United Irishmen, formed in 1791, demanded further reforms. Inspired by the American and French Revolutions, the United Irishmen gained the support of some Belfast merchants, rural Ulster Presbyterians, Dublin intellectuals, and Catholic peasants. The United Irishmen rose up in 1798 demanding a full break from Great Britain and attempting to establish an Irish republic. The Acts of Union were passed in 1800 largely in response to this rising, solidifying the British connection and abolishing the Irish Parliament.[6]

Over the ensuing decades, Ulster Scots gradually became more associated with support of Union with Britain rather than the republicanism and radicalism of the United Irishmen. Ulster Scots' stances were transformed in part by the hardening of sectarian feeling fuelled by evangelicalism, and increasing identification of religious denominations with political movements, à la Daniel O'Connell's Repeal Association. The Union facilitated evolving economic conditions, leading to economic competition between Catholics and Protestants in Ulster.[7] The benefits of the Union itself created unionists, as George Boyce has remarked. Many Ulster Scots came to celebrate the British connection as their best resource for improvements to their own lives. Through the Union, they were able to champion ideals which they saw themselves as consistently supporting: civil and religious liberty, freedom, and economic progress.[8]

By the Home Rule era, the majority of Ulster Scots fervently supported the Union while continuing to celebrate the role of the Scotch-Irish in the American Revolution and the United Irish rising. Both of these events epitomized attempts to destroy connections with Britain. According to one pamphleteer, the demands that Ulster Scots made as part of the United

Revolution (Philadelphia: University of Pennsylvania Press, 1965), 28, 30; Bric, 'Ireland, America', 103–108; J.C. Beckett, 'Belfast to the End of the Eighteenth Century', in *Belfast: The Making of the City, 1800–1914*, ed. J.C. Beckett (Belfast: Appletree, 1983), 22.

5 Foster, *Modern Ireland*, 243, 248–250.

6 Jackson, *Home Rule*, 12; Foster, *Modern Ireland*, 259–286; English, *Irish Freedom*, 95–102.

7 Stewart, *Ulster Crisis*, 30. For a discussion of Protestant and Catholic identities in Ireland during and after the 1798 rising, see S.J. Connolly, 'Culture, Identity, and Tradition: Changing Definitions of Irishness', in *In Search of Ireland: A Cultural Geography*, ed. Britain Graham (London: Routledge, 1997), 52–57.

8 Boyce, 'Weary Patriots', 22; Holmes, 'Covenanter Politics', 343–344, 367–368.

Irishmen were all answered by the Union, making Ulster Scots loyal supporters of the British connection. Ulster Scots continued to celebrate their roles in the United Irishmen and American Revolution because, throughout these events, they believed they exhibited a spirit of determination to fight for their ideals, which did not conflict with their approach to unionism.[9]

Throughout the Home Rule crises, the American Revolutionary War example was utilized to develop themes of legitimacy, coercion, representation, ethnic identity, and militancy in Ulster unionist discourse. George Bancroft, who wrote a multi-volume series on the *History of the United States from the Discovery of the American Continent* (1834–1874), was frequently cited by unionists as an authority and source on the American Revolutionary period.[10] Ulster Scots ethnic identity was touted through Scotch-Irish achievements and identification of America as a Protestant nation. At a Royal Black Preceptory meeting in 1885, District Master William McCormick remarked:

> Protestantism had no exceptional privileges in its favour when it pushed its way into American wilds, levelling all obstruction, and overcoming the numerous difficulties which presented themselves, changing the face of nature from forests and prairie, and vindicating the people's right to liberty, struck the blow for freedom on the very threshold of their Constitution, which secured the priceless blessings of liberty for all and to all in the great Republic of the West.[11]

McCormack tied these pioneering, Protestant achievements to modern-day Ulster Protestants, who led 'in the van of progress and liberty'. He continued,

> But, said some of its leaders here [in Ireland] Protestantism was not able, could not bear the strain, the tug in this case. What! not able to hold its own because the people were being franchised, were being invested with the rights of subjects and citizens of the realm? If so, he [McCormick] would think very little of Protestantism.[12]

For McCormick, America embodied the glorious example of the strength of Protestantism. Protestantism was strong enough to conquer the prairies and

---

9 Shaw, 'Mr. Gladstone's Two Irish Policies', 9; Ian McBride, *Scripture Politics: Ulster Presbyterians and Irish Radicalism in the Late Eighteenth Century* (Oxford: Clarendon Press, 1998), 207–231; J.G.A. Pocock, 'The Union in British History', *Transactions of the Royal Historical Society* 6th Ser., Vol. 10 (2000), 193–194.

10 PD 4th Ser., Vol. 10, 1731–1732; *BNL* 18 Feb 1892.

11 *BNL* 17 Jan 1885.

12 *BNL* 17 Jan 1885.

secure liberty through the American constitution. Therefore, it would be strong enough to face the democratizing electoral system being introduced in Britain and Ireland, which would give rising numbers of Catholics the vote.

After the first Home Rule Bill was introduced, unionists used American examples to illustrate doubts about the system outlined within the bill.[13] William Arthur, former Principal of Belfast's Methodist College, questioned the tax system, which relied on the honesty of nationalist collectors. Arthur used the American Revolutionary War example to illustrate just how important tax policy was: 'Whether was Bunker's Hill fought about local rates or Imperial taxes? Were Receivers "absolute security" in those parts?'[14] Arthur's use of the American example emphasized the validity and seriousness of his concerns over the tax provisions within the Home Rule Bill. Tax policy was a main area of criticism developed by unionists against the first Home Rule Bill. The bill did not provide for Irish members in the Westminster Parliament, yet Ireland would be expected to contribute taxes. A *Belfast News-Letter* editorial asserted that this was to rid Parliament of Parnellite obstruction, commenting,

> Unfortunately for this view of the case, there is no possibility of the obstructionists being got rid of. The principle of 'No taxation without representation' has for hundreds of years formed the basis of the privileges of the British citizen; and not even Mr. Gladstone can hope to be successful in forcing upon the people of Great Britain the new doctrine of taxation without representation.[15]

The editorial continued, 'Parliament has before now faced the obstructives and overcome them'.[16] Fear of obstruction was no reason to take away the basic rights of British citizens.

Stewart Hunter, in his introduction of Joseph Chamberlain at Coleraine, remarked that according to the first Home Rule Bill Ireland would have no voice in foreign affairs, including declarations of war and peace. He wondered how long Ireland would 'pay and look pleasant' under those circumstances. Stewart explained, 'Taxation without representation cost Britain her American colonies in the latter part of the eighteenth century – (hear, hear) – and a repetition of the same error would undoubtedly have separated Ireland from England in the latter part of the nineteenth'.[17]

13 Ward, *Irish Constitutional Tradition*, 72–78.
14 William Arthur, 'Shall the Loyal be Deserted and the Disloyal Set over Them? An Appeal to Liberals and Nonconformists' (London: Bemrose & Sons, 1886), 29.
15 *BNL* 4 May 1886.
16 *BNL* 4 May 1886.
17 *BNL* 14 Oct 1887.

Issues of taxation and representation could have dire consequences for Britain. Hunter feared if Ireland lost its imperial connections through the Westminster Parliament, complete separation would result.

Nationalists also used examples from the American Revolution to support their own movement. These nationalist statements were published by the Irish Loyal and Patriotic Union to illustrate their extreme and dangerous policies. One pamphlet highlighted William Redmond's use of the American example to threaten separation as he likened nationalists to American colonists. Unionists condemned such speeches for their militant, extremist language, all the while using the American Revolution in similar ways to promote unionism.[18]

Unionists used the American Revolution to show that their position was reasonable, legitimate, and had historical precedent. John Ross, MP for Londonderry City, emphasized Ulster unionists' steadfast loyalty to the British Empire, stating, 'It is not a fortunate thing to drive people faithful to you to despair. It was not a fortunate thing to maltreat and trample upon your North American colonies, and I doubt whether it will be more fortunate for England if she treats the loyal people of Ulster as she now proposes to treat them'.[19] Ross portrayed American colonists as faithful and loyal citizens. When maltreated through taxation and coercion, they responded in such a way as to cause the British government regret. This example illustrated the unionist sense of betrayal by the British, who granted generous measures to disloyal Irish nationalists. This comparison aimed to bring legitimacy to Ulster unionism through emphasis on the failure of Britain to stand by its faithful citizens.

Dunbar Barton, MP for Mid Armagh, used the American colonial example to emphasize the long-established nature of the Ulster settlement compared to the American colonies. He stated, 'There was not one of the States of America whose people had such an old title to their lands or province as had the people of Ulster'.[20] Irish Home Rulers might as well be seeking to evict European settlers from the United States if they sought to expel Britons from Ireland. Barton's statement also stressed that Ireland was the native homeland of Ulster Scots because their families had lived there for so long that they believed they belonged there.

Barton frequently used American examples in his critique of Home Rule. Another comparison was with grievances that Ulster would face

18 'The Crimes Act; Before and After: Some Extracts from Parnellite Speeches and Comments Thereon' (Dublin: ILPU, 1888).
19 PD 4th Ser., Vol. 7, 299; see Bell, *Idea of Greater Britain*, 250–253 for both sides' use of lessons taught by the American Revolution.
20 PD 4th Ser., Vol. 10, 1731.

under Home Rule, compared to those of the American colonists before they rebelled. Barton described British statesmen as brushing away grievances by rationalizing, 'America will complain, but America will submit'.[21] Likewise he insisted that the British were not seriously attempting to address unionist concerns and threats of resistance. Barton believed Ulster's case against Home Rule was much greater than the American colonists' case against British rule. America was accepted as having legitimately rebelled – therefore, the unionists' cause was even more justified. Barton continued,

> What was the grievance of the American Colonists? Nothing but taxation. And what was the grievance of the people of Ulster? Taxation was the least part of it. There had been revolutions in history founded and justified on questions of religion, upon questions of defence of property, and on the sentiment of liberty, and upon the question of taxation. Every one of these was a motive in the case of the people of Ulster.[22]

By reducing the American case to a question of taxation, as was consistent with Irish interpretations of the American Revolution, Barton emphasized the legitimacy of the numerous objections of Ulster unionists against the implementation of Home Rule.

Barton also used the American example to justify Ulster threats of rebelling to keep the Union intact. He described Ulster unionists as resolute and determined that the British government would not force the Home Rule Bill upon them. He opined,

> This Bill if it became law would be as dead a letter as the Acts they tried to force upon the colonists of America, Acts which passed this House and the House of Lords, and which never operated in that country. As certainly as the colonists of America refused to obey them, as certainly would the people of Ulster – and he begged to remind the House that those men who refused to obey the laws in America were the same race as the Ulster men. At Bunker Hill England lost 1,100 men and the colonists 500.[23]

Barton hoped the current situation would not yield similar results, but, he concluded, if it did, responsibility would clearly lie with the British government. As unionists threatened to rebel against the implementation of

21 PD 4th Ser., Vol. 10, 1731–1732.
22 PD 4th Ser., Vol. 10, 1731–1732.
23 PD 4th Ser., Vol. 10, 1705.

Home Rule, Barton and others frequently used the example of the American colonists rebelling against the British to break their union. Strikingly, unionists themselves would resort to rebellion to save the Union.

The link between the two periods in history, as Barton pointed out, were British attempts to use coercion on both the American colonists and Ulster unionists. Barton described the force needed to implement Home Rule in Ulster, stating,

> To impose this proposed constitution upon Ulster they would have to use the Army and Navy of the Crown, and the forces of the Crown would have to be kept in Ulster year after year, therefore it was with considerable confidence that he told them that this law had no more chance of becoming operative than any of the other arbitrary Acts that Parliament had sometimes attempted to impose and enforce upon the colonies. (An hon. Member: Coercion.) Yes; and this was the largest coercive Bill that was ever introduced.[24]

Barton believed the British government would resort to coercion to force Ulster out of the Union. Coercion was regarded as one of the worst things a British government could do against its own citizens: forcing laws upon them without their consent. The Home Rule policy was all the more alarming because this coercion was a betrayal by the British of their loyal citizens. Unionists used American examples to justify planned responses to coercion. Like the colonists they planned to rebel, but the rebellion was to stay within the Union.

At the Great Unionist Convention of 1892, the Earl of Erne stated that he recognized similarities of the Home Rule crisis with the build-up to the American Revolution. His comparison illustrated the heights of Ulster unionist fervour against Home Rule, knowing that their actions could result in armed rebellion against the British government.[25] Thomas Sinclair, chairman of the Ulster Liberal Unionist Association, spoke to the Convention about the possibility of passive resistance against a Home Rule government. He stated, 'Our kinsmen of the American revolution have taught us to leave it to those that will force tyranny and injustice upon us to strike the first blow'.[26] Like Barton, Sinclair saw the potential for future defiance or rebellion against coercive implementation of Home Rule. The *Belfast News-Letter* described Sinclair's words of defiance as 'the spirit of the Convention; and it attracted the applause of thousands of Delegates, who

24 PD 4th Ser., Vol. 10, 1706.
25 *BNL* 18 Jun 1892.
26 *BNL* 18 Jun 1892.

were sent from every part of Loyal Ulster to declare to Great Britain, to declare to Disloyal Ireland and to the world that a Parliament in Dublin shall never be permitted to exercise dominion in the North'.[27]

Themes of legitimacy and coercion developed in Ulster unionist rhetoric against the second Home Rule Bill until the bill ended with defeat in the House of Lords. Twenty years later, during the third Home Rule crisis, similar themes emerged in the rhetoric of Ulster unionists. By the time of the Parliament Act of 1911, unionism had grown increasingly focused in Ulster rather than the rest of Ireland, and rhetoric was increasingly militant. The Ulster Volunteer Force (UVF), formally established in January 1913, was the source of many comparisons with American rebels.

Looking back on this period from 1922, Ronald McNeill, Ulster-born MP for St. Augustine's, wrote in *Ulster's Stand for Union* that many commentators viewed Ulster unionists' militant attitudes as 'mere bluster and bluff', but the only reply to these perceptions was contempt. 'There never was anything further from the truth, as anyone ought to have known who had the smallest acquaintance with Irish history or with the character of the race that had supplied the backbone of Washington's army'.[28] McNeill used the Scotch-Irish role in the American Revolution to underscore the seriousness of the UVF. They were not bluffing when they threatened to rebel against the implementation of Home Rule.

Ulster unionist celebration of connections to Scotch-Irish Revolutionary heritage was apparent in parliamentary rhetoric against the third Home Rule Bill. Andrew Long Horner, MP for South Tyrone, stated,

> The Ulster breed has never known defeat. We are scoffed at as a minority. We admit inferiority in numbers, but nothing else. In a miserable minority in former times we yet changed the dynasty of this country. In a miserable minority our race played the most conspicuous part against the mad legislation of the British government that led to the foundation of the American Republic. Take care where this mad legislation of yours to-day will lead you. We have done more as pioneers and colonists than any part of the United Kingdom. Do you think the men who are of our blood and race, controlling, as they do, the greatest interests in our Colonies, will stand by and see you coerce us, your oldest Colony, by force to leave the shelter of the Imperial Parliament and accept the Government of men whose whole careers have been abuse and hatred of us and you?[29]

27 *BNL* 18 Jun 1892.
28 McNeill, *Ulster's Stand*, 18.
29 PD Commons 5th Ser., Vol. 38, 303.

Horner used American Revolutionary connections to prove the strength of Ulster unionists' threat to the British government if they rebelled. He emphasized the power of the Ulster 'race' through historical example and colonial influence. He also echoed the idea of Home Rule as coercion. Horner attempted to legitimize Ulster's stance against Home Rule through the continued emphasis on the legislation as betrayal by the British. Horner saw Home Rule as the British turning their most loyal subjects over to the domination of men who had abused and hated them.

Complaints arose in Parliament that Ulster unionists were making plans for resisting the implementation of Home Rule before they experienced a new Irish parliament. In a 1914 speech, Andrew Bonar Law replied to such complaints, stating, 'The American colonies had done the same thing – they had revolted on a question of principle while suffering was still distant, and for a cause that in itself was trivial in comparison to that of Ulster'.[30] Bonar Law minimized the grievances of the American colonists while amplifying those of the unionists to justify the anti-Home Rule campaign.

As in previous anti-Home Rule campaigns, criticisms against the Home Rule Bill's form utilized American examples. William Mitchell-Thomson, MP for North Down, reminded Parliament that the end of salutary neglect and enforcement of Parliament's inalienable sovereignty over the American colonies led to the American Revolution. With a new Irish parliament, Mitchell-Thomson believed, nationalists would seize control of the Executive and rebel if the Westminster Parliament ever attempted to assert supremacy. Therefore, the establishment of an Irish parliament would lead to total separation. Thus Protestants in Ulster could not rely on the Westminster Parliament to intervene if their rights were ever threatened by a new, nationalist-controlled Irish parliament.[31]

Another problem lay with the breaking of fiscal union between Great Britain and Ireland. Bonar Law asserted that fiscal unity was what held the country together. Without that, complete separation and war were likely outcomes. He referenced the example of Alexander Hamilton, stating that as Secretary of the Treasury it was the work of Hamilton 'to give one fiscal system for the whole United States, and by doing so he made the United States a nation, and you are upsetting that arrangement'.[32] In his criticism of the breaking of fiscal union, Bonar Law was probably drawing upon

---

30 Quoted in McNeill, *Ulster's Stand*, 166; *The Times* 16 Jan 1914.
31 PD Commons 5th Ser., Vol. 38, 129; Ward, *Irish Constitutional Tradition*, 68, 79–81. Westminster parliamentary supremacy was implied in 1886 but written into the 1893 and 1912 Home Rule bills.
32 PD Commons 5th Ser., Vol. 37, 292.

the influential work of F.S. Oliver, a significant figure in the movement for Union of Empire. Oliver published his *Alexander Hamilton: An Essay on American Union* in 1906 in an attempt to use Hamilton as a source of inspiration for the creation of Imperial unity.[33]

Throughout the Home Rule era, unionists emphasized that both America and Ulster faced coercive measures forced on them by the British government. Unionists portrayed Ulster's grievances against Home Rule as greater than any grievances the American colonists might have had against the British government. According to unionists, both American colonists and Ulster unionists were right to rebel against this tyranny, even if British legislation was technically constitutional. This strain of thought is embodied in remarks made by Mitchell-Thomson during the third Home Rule crisis:

> Our position in Ulster is perfectly clear. It was stated for us in terms nearly a century and a half ago by the people of the State of Virginia in the famous resolutions which are called 'The Botetourt Resolutions'. I should like to read one of them. It expresses our position in 1912, as it expressed in February 1775, and when confirmed in 1860, the view of the State of Virginia. It says – 'It is hereby resolved that we desire no change in our system of government while left to the free enjoyment of our equal privileges secured by the Constitution, but that should a tyrannical sectional majority under the sanction of the forms of the Constitution persist in acts of injustice towards us, they and they only must be answerable for the consequences'.[34]

Like the American colonists, Ulster was perfectly happy to retain the connection with Britain as it stood at the time. Like the Americans, Ulster would rebel if that system was changed through coercive measures. The difference was that America rebelled to break the British connection. Ulster unionists were willing to resort to violence and militancy to maintain the Union.

---

33 Oliver, *Alexander Hamilton*. See his conclusion for specific comparisons between the situation in the early American republic and the early twentieth-century British Empire.
34 PD Commons 5th Ser., Vol. 38, 129.

War between the States

Like the Revolutionary War, the American Civil War was a key point of comparison for Ulster unionists. One important difference in the case of the Civil War was that it was easily within living memory during the Home Rule period. Joseph Hernon's article, 'Use of the American Civil War in the Debate over Irish Home Rule', shows how politicians and intellectuals who supported the Northern States later as Liberal Unionists used the Civil War example to oppose Irish Home Rule.[35] Hernon writes that the principles of states' rights in the Civil War, which helped to validate the Confederate standpoint, were used as examples by Liberal Unionists. They feared if Ireland was granted Home Rule, Irish nationalists would use states' rights principles to demand complete separation. Hernon rightly points out the limits to the logic of this parallel, because slavery as a moral issue played such a large role in America.[36] However, fear of states' rights leading to Irish separation was not the only way the Civil War example was employed in unionist rhetoric. The Civil War, considered the greatest war in living memory at the time, was frequently used to develop themes of legitimacy, the sense of betrayal by Britain, and unity as part of the spirit of the age.

During the Civil War, British sympathy for the Confederacy led to severely heightened tensions with the United States. This was complicated by Britain's historical role in campaigning for emancipation.[37] Abraham Lincoln attempted to reassure southerners that he would not threaten the institution of slavery. Onlookers in Britain and Ireland therefore believed the war was primarily about preserving the Union contrary to principles of self-determination.[38] William Gladstone, then Chancellor of the Exchequer, famously supported the Confederacy on the basis of states' rights principles. The Civil War also impacted Anglo-American trade relations. With the outbreak of war in 1861, Northern ships blockaded parts of the Confederacy, cutting off the supply of cotton to Britain. This resulted in increased business for the Belfast linen industry, sparking Belfast dominance in the industry for the rest of the nineteenth century.[39]

---

35 Joseph M. Hernon, Jr., 'The Use of the American Civil War in the Debate over Irish Home Rule', *American Historical Review* 69, no. 4 (Jul 1964).

36 Hernon, 'Use of the American Civil War', 1022, 1026.

37 Leslie Butler, *Critical Americans: Victorian Intellectuals and Transatlantic Liberal Reform* (Chapel Hill: University of North Carolina Press, 2007), 75–77; Joseph M. Hernon, Jr., *Celts, Catholics & Copperheads: Ireland Views the American Civil War* (Columbus: Ohio State University Press, 1968), 68–71.

38 Carroll, *American Presence*, 64–66; Howard Jones, *Abraham Lincoln and a New Birth of Freedom: The Union and Slavery in the Diplomacy of the Civil War* (Lincoln: University of Nebraska Press, 1999), 1–9.

39 Emily Boyle, '"Linenopolis": The Rise of the Textile Industry', in *Belfast: The Making*

For some future British unionists such as John Bright and William Forster, the North's fight to save the Union and emancipate slaves was more appealing than supporting a Southern government propped up by slavery. For some British Tories, the Civil War was proof a republican system built around notions of democratic representation could not work. Irish Protestants were varied according to political creed. Conservatives felt animosity toward the American republic and sympathy toward the Confederacy. Radicals were pro-American and viewed the American republic as their model.[40] Like the Revolutionary War example, Ulster unionists' use of the American Civil War emphasized Ulster Scots' traditional identification with liberal and radical politics as they tried to maintain the Union.

As the United States came out of the Civil War and became increasingly prosperous, views were more sympathetic. America's growing strength on the world stage helped fuel notions of Anglo-Saxon racial unity between Britain and the United States.[41] At the same time, the American Civil War became a prominent example for Ulster unionists searching for historical parallels to their own situation. Kevin Kenny points out that both unionists and nationalists used the American Civil War and the example of Lincoln to address fundamental questions of national sovereignty, the idea of union, secession, political leadership, and civil war.[42] Beyond these themes, unionists used the Civil War to expound ideas of morality, legitimacy, and betrayal.

During the first Home Rule crisis, unionists used the Civil War to develop several themes in their rhetoric. With Gladstone's conversion to Home Rule, the Liberal Party was faced with schism. T.W. Russell, MP for South Tyrone, defended the stance of Liberal Unionists who allied with the Conservatives. He stated in an 1886 speech:

My alternative is – 'Maintain the Union, be scrupulous to redress every Irish wrong, be even generous in view of the past, but govern the Country'. I am told that Democracy will not consent to do this. Let us not be too sure of that ... The great Democracy of the United States answered to Abraham Lincoln, not to Jefferson Davis. And to

of the City, 1800–1914, ed. J.C. Beckett (Belfast: Appletree, 1983), 47–48; Cormac Ó Gráda, *Ireland: A New Economic History, 1780–1939* (Oxford: Clarendon Press, 1994), 290; Hernon, *Celts, Catholics & Copperheads*, 6–7.

40 Hernon, *Celts, Catholics & Copperheads*, 7–8.
41 H.A. Tulloch, 'Changing British Attitudes Towards the United States in the 1880s', *Historical Journal* 20, no. 4 (Dec 1977), 825; Bell, *Idea of Greater Britain*, 95; Curtis, *Anglo-Saxons and Celts*, 90–101.
42 Kevin Kenny, '"Freedom and Unity": Lincoln in Irish Political Discourse', in *The Global Lincoln*, ed. Richard Carwardine and Jay Sexton (Oxford: Oxford University Press, 2011), 158–166.

maintain the Union there the cannon thundered in the valley of the Shenandoah, the musketry rattled on the heights of Fredericksburg, and Grant fought and conquered at Richmond. And the Union was maintained there, just as I firmly believe it will be maintained here.[43]

Russell committed Liberal Unionists to maintaining Liberal social policies in Ireland while supporting the Union. When faced with the question of Home Rule's inevitability, the Civil War provided an example of willingness to commit everything to maintaining unity rather than separation. Many Liberal Unionists maintained that they were willing to give every consideration to bettering Ireland's condition other than destruction of the Union.

Ulster's Liberal Unionists used the American Civil War example to condemn Gladstone's Home Rule stance. Belfast Reverend R.J. Lynd wrote,

Mr. Gladstone is not infallible. Had he his will, the United States of America would now be cut into two kingdoms, and slavery would still retain its grim hold on the kingdom of the South without any control from the North. To us Irish Liberals, who loved him and followed him with a devotion and personal veneration seldom equalled, but never surpassed, there could not be a more melancholy spectacle under the sun than Mr. Gladstone as a Liberal leader presents now.[44]

Gladstone's former supporters accused him of repeating a pattern in his support of the Confederacy and his promotion of Irish Home Rule: an immoral cause would have a hold over a helpless minority in each case.

Unionists were concerned about the Irish Protestant minority, particularly within Ulster. The United States offered its own example of a loyal minority which would have been given over to the disloyal majority were it not for partition. West Virginia seceded from Virginia following a series of conventions in Wheeling in 1861. Principal William Arthur wrote of the West Virginia example in 1886:

We are told of Home Rule in the United States: was there ever a State *put away* from the control of the National Legislature, to give entire practical control over it to a majority composed of men disloyal to the Union, and that against the protest of a powerful minority? Virginia

---

43 T.W. Russell, 'The Case for Irish Loyalists: Being the Substance of an Address Delivered at Grangemouth, Stirlingshire, on Tuesday Evening, May 18, 1886' (Dublin: ILPU, 1888).
44 R.J. Lynd, 'Some Thoughts on the Present Political Crisis' (Londonderry: 'Standard' Steam Printing Works, 1888), 20.

was divided because the minority in West Virginia, loyal to the union, claimed to be exempt from the *régime* of the disaffected majority in the bulk of the State; just as, if the worst came to the worst, Ulster should have to be freed from the yoke she dreads.[45]

The West Virginia example was echoed by Ronald McNeill, writing, 'Ulster could at all events in the last resort take her stand on Abraham Lincoln's famous proposition which created West Virginia: "A minority of a large community who make certain claims for self-government cannot, in logic or substance, refuse the same claims to a much larger proportionate minority among themselves".[46] The West Virginia example was employed to show there was no precedent for the British to abandon the loyal minority within Ireland to a disloyal majority. Indeed, McNeill insisted it would be contradictory for Irish nationalists to demand self-determination and then refuse the same to a strong minority.

The Civil War example was used to deny Irish nationalists the right to compel the Westminster Parliament to change the Union. Reverend George Salmon, Regius Professor of Divinity in the University of Dublin and Chancellor of St. Patrick's Cathedral, believed Irish nationalists might legally be free to pursue Home Rule. Despite its constitutionality, Parliament should not grant Home Rule if it would lead to greater dangers. At the special meeting of the Church of Ireland General Synod in 1886, Salmon stated,

I will remind you of what you can remember took place in America. As far as I understand the law of their Constitution, the Southern States had a perfect right to separate from the Northern if they were so minded. But the Northern States, when asked to submit to such a separation, decided that civil war was preferable. You know what sacrifices of money, of valuable lives, were necessary to conquer the heroic resistance of the South. But what evil or inconvenience that the North could have suffered from the existence of an independent nation in the South is within many degrees comparable to the danger to England from an independent Ireland.[47]

In the United States, Civil War was preferable to the North than allowing the South legally to secede from the Union.[48] In Salmon's view, Home Rule

---

45   Arthur, 'Shall the Loyal be Deserted', 18–19.
46   McNeill, *Ulster's Stand*, 15.
47   'Church of Ireland and the Present Political Crisis', 42.
48   Kenny points out that other unionists such as Ronald McNeill took the opposite view of the legality of secession, that Lincoln had the law on his side while the Ulster unionists

Ireland would similarly threaten Britain because of the dangers of total separation.

Unionists used the Civil War example to show the futility of attempting to use Home Rule to pacify Irish nationalists. At a March 1886 loyalist demonstration in Lurgan, Reverend Michael Beattie stated, 'The integrity and unity of the United Kingdom was at stake. England had won her empire by the sword; America won back the Federal States by the sword. Were thirty-three millions of British people going to be dictated to by Parnell's brigade? ("Never") They should never accept Home Rule'.[49] The North refused to pacify the South during the Civil War. The British government should refuse to pacify Irish nationalists because the majority of British people had a right to overrule the minority Irish nationalists. Colonel Thomas Waring, MP for North Down, also argued if the British attempted to pacify the Irish it would lead to total separation – and worse, civil war in Ireland. He warned that in intensity and fierceness the war 'would only be equalled by that between the Northern and Southern States of America, and which I venture to predict would have a similar result – namely, that those who contend for disintegration shall succumb to those who contend for union'.[50]

The most prominent use of the Civil War example during the first Home Rule crisis promoted this theme of militancy. Lord Randolph Churchill encouraged Ulster to defend its position within the Union in his famous Belfast speech on 22 February 1886. He stated, 'No portentous change such as the repeal of Union, no change so gigantic, could be accomplished by the mere passing of a law. The history of the United States will teach us a different lesson'.[51] Churchill maintained that such a significant change to the Union could not occur without the outbreak of hostilities, justifying Ulster militancy. A few months later he underlined this theme of militancy and ties to the American Civil War in a letter to William Young, using his notorious phrase, 'Ulster will fight; Ulster will be right; Ulster will emerge from the struggle victorious'.[52] Churchill was accused by opponents of encouraging sectarian hatred. Some historians have accused him of inconsistency in his opposition to Home Rule as he opportunistically played the 'Orange card'. R.E. Quinault, however, has argued that Churchill's words indicated his unfailing support of 'enlightened unionism', in that he was loyal to the Conservative policy of unionism but at times went against the Tories by

were resisting the technically legal authority. This made the unionist cause unique in their rebellion to maintain the status quo. Kenny, 'Freedom and Unity', 161.

49   *BNL* 4 Mar 1886.
50   *BNL* 13 Feb 1886.
51   *The Times* 23 Feb 1886.
52   *The Times* 8 May 1886.

supporting progressive measures to strengthen the Union. His use of the Civil War example, according to Quinault, showed that no matter what measures Ulster took to defend the Union, they would be justified by the results. America's peace and prosperity after the Civil War justified the extensive fighting they had gone through.[53] In addition, Churchill maintained that to preserve the Empire, Britain would have to fight for the preservation of the Union with Ireland.

Within the second Home Rule Bill, one of the powers reserved to Westminster was the control over war and peace. All soldiers and officers would come under the control of one army, just as in the United States at the beginning of the Civil War. As J.A. Rentoul, MP for East Down, described, this was no protection from sectional or nationalist sentiments. He stated,

> When the war began, each man seemed to consider that he was a member of a State first, and a member of the Republic afterwards; for we find that those generals who had been born in the Southern States went with the South, such as Johnston, and Jebb, and Lee; and that those generals who had been born in the Northern States went with the North; for example Sherman, and Grant, and Sheridan. Now, will hon. Gentlemen consider whether or not the same result might not be expected in the case of a difference between the Irish Parliament, and the Imperial Parliament?[54]

According to Rentoul, Home Rule was dangerous because it would give credibility to nationalist sentiments that might lead Irish members of the British Army to turn against Great Britain. Home Rule would set up conflicts causing British-trained soldiers to fight against their own army.

In the same speech, Rentoul emphasized that the Westminster Parliament would be going against the worldwide trend toward unity. He asserted, 'In the entire history of the world, no nation has ever done, ever discussed, or even ever dreamed of doing to itself that which is proposed by this Bill'. He gave examples of Italy and France moving toward closer union, before addressing the United States:

> The Southern were different from the Northern States in sentiment, greatly different in race, and different in both habits and education,

---

53 R.E. Quinault, 'Lord Randolph Churchill and Home Rule', in *Reactions to Irish Nationalism* (London: Hambledon Press, 1987), 340, 344–345. See also the chapter 'To the Northern Counties Station: Lord Randolph Churchill and the Orange Card', in R.F. Foster, *Paddy and Mr. Punch: Connections in Irish and English History* (London: Allen Lane, 1993).

54 PD 4th Ser., Vol. 8, 1788–1789.

yet one of the greatest wars of modern times was waged in order to preserve the Republic one and united. The devastation there was nothing ordinary. Bitter and irretrievable ruin was hurled upon tens of thousands, who wanted nothing except the mere sentimental gratification of a simple desire for Home Rule ... In La Vendée, and in the United States of America, we have two instances in the same century of the desperate lengths to which France and America went in order to prevent Home Rule, and yet we are told to grant Home Rule, and told that we are self-seekers, bigots, and fools if we do not grant it at once and with enthusiasm.[55]

Rentoul attempted to discredit Home Rule through emphasizing the great differences between the two sides in the Civil War, which mirrored the differences between Irish unionists and nationalists. The size and devastation of the Civil War illustrated the lengths to which the North was willing to go to preserve the American Union. Like the United States, Ulster unionists were faced with demands for Home Rule. They felt the British government was not making any effort to combat these demands but accommodated them despite the threat of the Union's destruction. Ulster unionists observed the extreme measures taken by the North to prevent the implementation of Home Rule. They resented being painted as bigots and fools by British Liberals and Irish nationalists because they wanted to do the same thing in their country. Unionists felt a sense of betrayal by the British who were unwilling to stand up to Home Rule demands.

In an article for *The Times*, the Duke of Argyll wrote that the question of Home Rule would directly affect the progress of good and evil in the world, and asserted that the unionists' cause was morally right. He explained,

Such was the great issue fought out in the American Civil War. It was very easy then, from good motives, to take the wrong side. Mr. Gladstone probably now sees that he did take the wrong one when he boasted that Jefferson Davis had 'made a nation'. It would have been a nation founded on slavery as its most cherished institution. I have myself the deepest conviction that he is making a similar mistake now. I feel quite sure that our cause, and not his, is the sacred cause. Ours is the cause of personal liberty, of truth, and good faith between man and man – of the predominance of wide and imperial interests over petty and mean and corrupt ambitions.[56]

55 PD 4th Ser., Vol. 8, 1786–1788.
56 Reprinted in *BNL* 5 Jan 1891.

Argyll believed that just as Gladstone misjudged the American Civil War, where the North proved they were the morally right side, he was misjudging the Irish situation. Argyll attempted to discredit Gladstone based on his past support of the Confederacy. He also emphasized the corrupt nature and immorality of the nationalist cause. To Argyll, who supported the North during the Civil War, unionists represented the cause of liberty, truth, and good faith, and the furtherance of 'good' in the world.

In debates over the third Home Rule Bill, unionists questioned the sustainability of nationalistic sentiment in Ireland. Hugh Barrie, MP for North Londonderry, cited historical works by W.E.H. Lecky stating that the spirit of secession which had been so strong in America had by the twentieth century entirely dissipated. Barrie believed the lesser nationalist sentiment in Ireland would similarly disappear over time. Barrie's argument fit with a theme within unionist rhetoric, asserting that Irish nationalists did not represent the Irish people, who were uninterested in Home Rule.[57]

Another common theme was the threat a completely independent Ireland would pose to Great Britain. Many unionists called upon the statements of American Admiral Alfred Thayer Mahan. Mahan had been a naval officer for the North during the Civil War. He continued to serve in the Navy throughout the 1870s and 1880s, and gained prominence through his writings on naval history, including *The Influence of Sea Power upon History*. He wrote an article on imperial federation that touched on the Irish situation in 1902 which was often quoted by Ulster unionists.[58] As described by Ronald McNeill, Ulstermen

> continually strove to make Englishmen realise that far more was involved than loyal support of England's only friends in Ireland; they quoted such pronouncements as Admiral Mahan's 'it is impossible for a military man, or a statesman with an appreciation of military conditions, to look at a map and not perceive that if the ambition of the Irish Separatists were realised, it would be even more threatening to the national life of Britain than the secession of the South was to that of the American Republic ... An independent Parliament could not safely be trusted even to avowed friends'.[59]

---

57 PD Commons 5th Ser., Vol. 37, 2157.
58 Originally published as 'Motives to Imperial Federation', *National Review* (May 1902); reprinted in Mahan, *Retrospect & Prospect*, 100.
59 McNeill, *Ulster's Stand*, 130. Also quoted in, for example, Cave, 'Constitutional Question', 86 and Percy, 'Military Disadvantages', 202; 'New Home Rule and the Old Objections', 17; 'Home Rule and Imperial Defence'.

Unionists believed demands for separation, endangering all of Britain, would inevitably follow the grant of Home Rule. This would leave the government with the choice between full Union and complete separation.

Ulster unionists wondered if the British government would resort to civil war if Irish nationalists attempted complete separation, as the North had done with the South. A 1912 editorial in the *Witness* observed,

> The Southern States of America demanded in practical effect what the Irish Nationalists are now demanding – separation from the North, as the Irish Nationalists are demanding separation from Great Britain. The North went to war rather than submit to it. The British government in regard to Ireland represents the Northern States of that day. But they do not fight; they surrender; and with their surrender sacrifice all the interests, all the feelings, all the traditions of their loyal friends in Ireland.[60]

While North went to war to save their Union, the British government did not fight to prevent Home Rule and future separation. Unionists asserted that Britain was surrendering their loyal citizens to Irish nationalists without any form of resistance, heightening Ulster unionists' sense of betrayal. As Paul Bew asserts, it was this sense of British treachery which increasingly led unionists to turn their arguments from traditional pro-Union political theory. They began to argue instead for the principle of self-determination, which in turn helped lead to partition and the establishment of a separate Northern Ireland Parliament.[61] With the betrayal by the British, Ulster unionists felt they could rely only on their own resources to prevent the implementation of Home Rule.

In Parliament, McNeill declared that civil war between Ulster, Irish nationalists, and the British government was imminent. He opined,

> It seems strange that the present Government, who, if report speaks truly, such is their enlightenment, avoided the thirteenth day of the month for the summoning of Parliament, should have chosen to introduce this Bill on a very significant anniversary. It was on the 11th April, fifty-one years ago, that the first step was taken in the great American Civil War. I say, in all earnestness and with all reverence, that I pray God that on this 11th April, fifty-one years later, the Prime Minister may not by his action have been setting his hand to business which may lead to a similar tragedy.[62]

60 *Witness* 2 Aug 1912; Bew, *Ideology*, 46–47; Boyce, 'Weary Patriots', 28.
61 Bew, *Ideology*, 46–47.
62 PD Commons 5th Ser., Vol. 36, 1514.

In fact, 11 April 1861 was the day before fighting officially broke out at Fort Sumter, the day that negotiations broke down between the North and South in the Civil War. Throughout the third Home Rule crisis, the atmosphere of militancy was ramped up through unionist rhetoric. Pamphleteer Tom Bruce Jones wrote in 1914 that the great lesson of the American Civil War was that it was impossible to withdraw at will from a union. This meant that unionists believed themselves justified in bringing Britain and Ireland to the brink of their own civil war to save the Union.[63]

The American Civil War was used by unionists for a wide variety of purposes as they fought against Home Rule in the late nineteenth and early twentieth centuries. Unionists in both Britain and Ireland so identified with the side of the North that they even used poetry written during the American Civil War to express their own sentiments about the Irish situation. Joseph Chamberlain quoted Henry Wadsworth Longfellow in an 1887 Belfast speech, stating,

> This United Kingdom of ours has been built up by the sacrifices and the resolution of many generations. It has stood the shock of the storm and the rage of the whirlwind. May we not say of it now, in the words of the American poet who lived to witness the greatest contest of our time, waged in order to defend the integrity of the commonwealth: 'Sail on, O ship of State / Sail on, O Union strong and great / Humanity, with all its fears / With all its hopes of future years / Is hanging breathless on thy fate'.[64]

The American Civil War symbolized the power of the Union to endure threats of separation and disconnection if only there were people willing to fight for it.

Constitution of the United States

Throughout the Home Rule period, the American constitution was frequently employed as an example in the political and intellectual arenas. Ulster unionist views of the United States constitution undoubtedly were shaped by concurrent debates over Teutonism, 'Greater' Britain, imperial federation, and democratic reform of the United Kingdom government. These debates have been explored extensively by John Kendle, Christopher Harvie, Michael

---

63 Jones, 'Imperial Peril', 100–101.
64 Boyd, *Mr. Chamberlain's Speeches*, Vol. 1, 298.

Burgess, Duncan Bell, and others.[65] Unionists would have been made aware of the details of the American constitution through the works of British intellectuals such as James Bryce and A.V. Dicey.[66] The American constitutional example was frequently used by those arguing both for and against Home Rule in the United Kingdom, each side shaping their use according to the needs of the situation.[67] Nationalists frequently identified their cause with democracy, constitutional freedoms, and the good of humanity.[68] For unionists there was no coherent system of thought in their application of the American constitutional example. Rather than an exhaustive survey of the uses of the constitutional example, this section contains a sampling of themes intended to illustrate some of the ways in which unionists called upon the American constitution to support their own movement and discredit Home Rule.

Discussion of democracy was a significant theme emerging within unionist rhetoric. The nineteenth century saw considerable changes to the British political system to make it more representative. In the period 1828 to 1832 alone, the Test and Corporation Acts were repealed, Catholics achieved emancipation, and Parliament was reformed. Increasing numbers of British and Irish citizens were enfranchised through the Reform Acts of 1867 and 1884, with the majority of adult males finally getting the vote with the latter Act. Traditional political leaders in the landed gentry began to feel pressure from below for a more democratic decision-making process.[69] For Irish

65 See, for example, John Kendle's *Federal Britain: A History* (London: Routledge, 1997); *Ireland and the Federal Solution: The Debate over the United Kingdom Constitution, 1870–1921* (Kingston: McGill-Queen's University Press, 1989); and *The Round Table Movement and Imperial Union* (Toronto: University of Toronto Press, 1975); Christopher Harvie's *The Lights of Liberalism: University Liberals and the Challenge of Democracy, 1860–86* (London: Allen Lane, 1976) and *Floating Commonwealth*; Michael Burgess's *The British Tradition of Federalism* (London: Leicester University Press, 1995); Bell's *Idea of Greater Britain*.

66 James Bryce, *The American Commonwealth* (London: Macmillan, 1888); A.V. Dicey, *Introduction to the Study of the Law of the Constitution* (London: Macmillan, 1885); Christopher Harvie, 'Ideology and Home Rule: James Bryce, A.V. Dicey and Ireland, 1880–1887', *English Historical Review* 91, no. 359 (Apr 1976).

67 D. George Boyce, 'Moral Force Unionism: A.V. Dicey and Ireland, 1885–1922', in *From the United Irishmen to Twentieth-Century Unionism: A Festschrift for A.T.Q. Stewart*, edited by Sabine Wichert (Dublin: Four Courts Press, 2004), 99–100; Gerlach, *British Liberalism*, 101–106. It is also worth noting that many other countries were used for constitutional analogies in Home Rule discussions, particularly the British dominions of Australia, Canada, and New Zealand, though these are outside of the scope of this chapter. See Ward, *Irish Constitutional Tradition*, 81–84.

68 Eugenio F. Biagini, *British Democracy and Irish Nationalism 1876–1906* (Cambridge: Cambridge University Press, 2007), 372–377.

69 Burnett, 'Modernisation of Unionism', 42–46; Alan O'Day, 'The Ulster Crisis: A Conundrum', in *The Ulster Crisis, 1885–1921*, ed. D. George Boyce and Alan O'Day (Basingstoke: Palgrave Macmillan, 2006), 4; Miller, *Queen's Rebels*, 87.

unionists, the perceived threat of nationalists increased as greater numbers of Catholic middle and working classes were enfranchised, solidifying the nationalist hold in the south. Throughout the United Kingdom, the importance of the landed gentry in politics declined, leading some unionists to feel threatened by the onslaught of democracy.

An 1883 editorial in the *Belfast News-Letter* condemned the track that democracy had taken in the United States. The editorial was examining attempts to implement new democratic reforms in what would become the Representation of the People Act of 1884. The *News-Letter* accused the United States of developing 'the most debasing and corrupt form of administration on the face of the earth'.[70] The *News-Letter*'s views were coloured by the scandals of Ulysses S. Grant's presidential administration and the machine politics of Tammany Hall. The *News-Letter* portrayed democratic government as a way to use a veil of support from 'the people' to benefit a small minority of corrupt politicians at the top. William Ellison Macartney, Conservative MP for South Antrim, also condemned American democracy in a February 1885 lecture. He believed democracy led to mediocrity within politics and society, blocking the progress of potentially great and talented men. According to Macartney, distinguished men:

> would neither be recognized nor esteemed. In all probability, they would be suspected and ridiculed. As in the United States, public affairs would have no charm for them, and would be left by their abstention to the manipulation of unscrupulous politicians. The fact is admittedly one of the evils which ardent Liberals see impending in the Republic of France. The experience of a century of democratic government in the United States confirms its existence.[71]

Macartney went on to say that because democracy represented the 'controlling tendencies of the multitude', it was intolerant 'of individual opinion and personal independence, and its capacity for what I have taken as the definition of tyranny – the abusive exercise of power'.[72] Macartney believed that democracy led to socialism, communism, and tyranny. Nevertheless, it is safe to say that these criticisms of American democracy grew less frequent as the United States became increasingly prosperous after the end of the Civil War, and as the extension of democratic reforms became ingrained within the British system.

During the first Home Rule crisis, another theme emerging within unionist rhetoric was that of American constitutional provisions, cited

70 *BNL* 24 Sep 1883.
71 *BNL* 4 Feb 1885.
72 *BNL* 4 Feb 1885.

to criticize the system set up by the Home Rule Bill. Such criticisms generally focused on the formula for representing Ireland in the Westminster Parliament, Ireland's financial relationship in the United Kingdom, and the formal constitutional relationship between the two countries.[73] In 1886, Lord Salisbury was described in a unionist pamphlet as speaking

> with admiring regret of the difficulties which stood in the way of change in the Constitution of the United States. In a young community not encumbered with traditions, or cursed with the privileged interests which have arisen to corrupt older states, it may be a great advantage to surround constitutional changes with obstacles and delays.[74]

Salisbury, who twenty years earlier had written that the American Civil War proved that the experiment with democracy had failed,[75] now admired constitutional safeguards which made amendments difficult. Unlike the condemnations by unionists in previous years, Salisbury asserted that these constitutional safeguards protected against corruption.

George Goschen, MP for East Edinburgh, denounced the Home Rule Bill for the lack of central authority within its devolved system. In a speech reprinted in the *Belfast News-Letter*, he stated,

> Mr. Gladstone's bill provided for neither such an authority as the United States Supreme Court to decide on the unity of legislation, nor such an authority as the Federal Executive. I do not believe that the American public would for one moment tolerate such a paralysis of the Central Executive in any American State as would have resulted in Ireland from Mr. Gladstone's plan.[76]

Without such central authority as guaranteed by the American system, Goschen believed the Irish government would be paralyzed with conflict and confusion. The Marquess of Lorne insisted that the American Civil War proved that no faction should be given Home Rule powers. American analogies describing the relations between the federal government and the states were 'of little or no use. On the only occasion in which national aspirations other than those pertaining to the whole Union were indulged, the indulgence cost the minor nationalists their fortunes and their political

---

73 Ward, *Irish Constitutional Tradition*, 72–81.
74 William Jeans, 'England and Ireland: An Examination of the Demand for Home Rule' (London: T. Fisher Unwin, 1886), 40–41.
75 Robert Cecil, 'The Confederate Struggle and Recognition', *Quarterly Review* 112, no. 224 (Oct 1862), 538.
76 *BNL* 27 Jul 1886.

rights, after a frightful war lasting four years'.[77] The American federal system could not be copied with a Home Rule government in Ireland because the regionalized nationalist sentiments in the two countries were so distinct. According to Lorne, the Irish situation meant the United Kingdom needed an even stronger central government than the United States.

Others maintained that the establishment of an Irish parliament would inevitably lead to great dangers, no matter what protections were inserted into the system. A *Belfast News-Letter* editorial of 1886 stated,

> Federalism in the United States had to endure a severe test, and now the power of the Central Government is greater than before. As the Marquis of Lorne observes, a century's history has shown the tendency to division in spite of carefully-worded and improved Constitutions, and a great civil war was necessary to put an end to the absolute sovereignty of the various States. The States, however, maintain a degree of sovereignty, notwithstanding the efforts to centralise authority in Washington. Experience teaches that Local Governments are more liable to passion and injustice than a Central Government could possibly be; and a Local Government in Ireland, unable to resist peculiar influences, would be oppressive and intolerable, no matter what guarantees were given for the protection of personal rights.[78]

With Irish nationalists already perceived as formidable foes, unionists could only predict the situation would worsen when the Westminster Parliament was no longer able to provide protection.

National unity was another major theme to emerge in Ulster unionist discourse. As discussed earlier in the chapter, unionists used the example of the United States to prove that unity was 'the spirit of the age'. Unionists insisted there was no example in the history of the nations of the world of deliberately cutting an existing union into fragments.[79] 'Ask the Italians to destroy the unity of their kingdom, and what would be the reply?' questioned a *Belfast News-Letter* editorial. 'Ask the Americans to tear up the Constitution of the United States, and they will point to the dreadful war between the North and the South to preserve the Union'.[80] These countries were willing to defend their unions at all costs. The *News-Letter* asserted that, with Home Rule, the British government asked the people of the United Kingdom to do something no other country would consider.

77   *BNL* 3 Sep 1887.
78   *BNL* 22 Jul 1886.
79   Jeans, 'England and Ireland', 45–46.
80   *BNL* 4 Aug 1887.

After the second Home Rule Bill was introduced, H.O. Arnold-Forster spoke admiringly of the protection against the implementation of *ex post facto* laws in the American constitution. He quoted the Federalist papers as saying, 'Our own experience has taught us that additional fences against those dangers ought not to be omitted'.[81] Arnold-Forster hoped the bill would contain protections such as these even if it was unlikely the Irish parliament would ever impose *ex post facto* laws. He stated,

> The Attorney General had shown no reason whatever why they should take a different view to that adopted by the framers of the American Constitution, and he had entirely failed to meet the contention of those who said there were a thousand reasons of the strongest kind why they should be anxious to give shape in the Bill to the proposals that were thought adequate by the framers of the Constitution.[82]

The Liberal Attorney General in question was Sir Charles Russell, an Ulster Catholic. According to Arnold-Forster, protections thought vital by the framers of the American constitution ought to be taken into consideration as the Westminster Parliament contemplated changes to the British constitutional system.

W.E.H. Lecky posited that the greatest danger of a Home Rule parliament was unjust legislation, because the legislature would be in the hands of disloyal and dishonest men. He worried about those men making laws concerning the seizure of property, due process of law, and just compensation, because the lawmakers themselves were the 'teachers of spoliation'. He found a solution in the American constitution which had not been considered in the bill: 'The invaluable article in the American Constitution which provides that no State can make a law "impairing the obligation of contracts," has no place in Mr. Gladstone's scheme, and it has been abundantly shown that his Legislative Council will be an absolute farce'.[83] Without such protections over contracts and property as the United States constitution provided, Lecky feared that the Legislative Council, the upper house provided for in Gladstone's bill, would be rendered useless by the lower house, the Legislative Assembly.

Dunbar Barton asserted that the weak upper house meant minority rights would not be protected under Home Rule. He believed the American system offered much stronger protections of minority rights. Barton stated,

---

81 Federalist #44, written by James Madison. Arnold-Forster wrongly attributed this article to Alexander Hamilton, another Federalist writer.
82 PD 4th Ser., Vol. 13, 1534–1535.
83 W.E.H. Lecky, 'Some Aspects of Home Rule', *Contemporary Review* 63 (May 1893), 630.

There was no comparison between the American Senate and this miserable House, which it was proposed to set up. There were no limits of age or citizenship provided in the Bill as qualifications for seats in the Upper House, as there were in the case of the American Senate; there was nothing to prevent an alien from becoming a member, and he believed and dreaded that, like the Lower House and Irish society generally, it might be overrun and overwhelmed by American adventurers and returned Fenians, who, having paid their money, would exact this in return.[84]

Barton's views encapsulated the complex nature of the Ulster unionist relationship with America. He admired the constitutional provisions in the United States and minority protections provided for by the American Senate. On the other hand, he feared Irish-American extremists and returned Fenians. He worried that without such protections as the American system provided, Irish-American extremists would flood Ireland and overrun the Irish government.

Macartney also referred to minority rights within the American system. He argued that even with their admirable protections in place, it was still possible to encroach on the rights of American minorities. He cited:

the defiance of President Jackson in the well-known case in which the Supreme Court of the United States came into contact with the local legislature of Georgia. In that case the Cherokee Indians appealed to the Supreme Court of the United States against the proposals of the local legislature of Georgia in their regard, and the Supreme Court held that the proposals of the legislature of Georgia were invalid. But what was the effect of that decision? President Jackson declared – 'John Marshall has pronounced his verdict; let him execute it if he can'. The Chancellor of the Duchy [James Bryce] in his book on the American Constitution, said that the case showed the powerlessness of the Supreme Court to help the unhappy Cherokees; and that the success of the resistance of the State of Georgia gave a blow to the authority of the Court.[85]

To Macartney, this case proved that minority protections were ultimately illusory, and therefore, like the Cherokees, the Irish Protestants would always be at risk under Home Rule.

Related to constitutional provisions, another theme to emerge in unionist rhetoric was federalism. Federalist ideas as applied to the Irish situation

84 PD 4th Ser., Vol. 12, 535.
85 PD 4th Ser., Vol. 10, 1693–1694.

were not new: Daniel O'Connell had been tempted by the federalist plans of William Sharman Crawford in the 1840s, and Isaac Butt had originally started the Home Rule movement in the 1870s with ideas of a federal system in the United Kingdom that would help to address Irish grievances. While not a part of the constitutional system of the United Kingdom, federalism was frequently an undercurrent in British political thought. The United Kingdom became a major 'exporter' of federal systems to other places in the world, as described by Michael Burgess. Federal systems were set up in Australia, Canada, India, Nigeria, and Malaysia, and played an influential role in the unification of South Africa.[86]

Throughout the Home Rule era, federalist ideas were used to illustrate parallels between federalist systems and Home Rule, or as alternatives to Home Rule. Another important element within federalist thought was imperial federation, which operated both within and outside of the Irish Home Rule context. At one time or another, Joseph Chamberlain, W.T. Stead, Lord Acton, J.R. Seeley, J.L. Garvin of the *Observer*, David Lloyd George, Walter Long, L.S. Amery, and Edward Carson all espoused federalist ideas. On the Irish nationalist side, federalism found champions in Moreton Frewen, William O'Brien, and T.M. Healy.[87]

Some unionists viewed Home Rule as introducing a federal-state dynamic into the relationship between Britain and Ireland. Carson questioned why the bills did not adhere more closely to the American system. He reasoned, 'As in America, where they had a distinction between Federal matters and State matters, so under the Bill, where they had a distinction between Imperial matters and local matters, they would necessarily have disputes between the Irish Government and the Imperial Government'.[88] Given the inevitability of conflict, Carson wondered why the Home Rule Bill failed to set up a court system similar to that of the United States. He hoped for a Supreme Court to settle potential disputes between the two governments. In a later speech, Carson again emphasized the parallels with the American system.

86 B.A. Kennedy, 'Sharman Crawford's Federal Scheme for Ireland', in *Essays in British and Irish History in Honour of James Eadie Todd*, ed. H.A. Cronne, T.W. Moody, and D.B. Quinn (London: Muller, 1949); Jackson, *Home Rule*, 25–37; Lawrence J. McCaffrey, 'Irish Federalism in the 1870s: A Study in Conservative Nationalism', *Transactions of the American Philosophical Society* n.s., 52, no. 6 (1962); Michael Burgess, 'Federalism: A Dirty Word? Federalist Ideas and Practice in the British Political Tradition' (London: Federal Trust Working Papers, 1988), 1–3.

87 John Pinder, 'The Federal Idea and the British Liberal Tradition', in *The Federal Idea*, Vol. 1: *The History of Federalism from the Enlightenment to 1945*, ed. Andrea Bosco (London: Lothian Foundation Press, 1991), 110; Boyce, 'Federalism and the Irish Question', 128–130; Bell, *Idea of Greater Britain*, 135–136; Alan J. Ward, 'Frewen's Anglo-American Campaign for Federalism, 1910–1921', *IHS* 15, no. 59 (Mar 1967).

88 PD 4th Ser., Vol. 14, 733.

He questioned, 'The only parallel they had for the Constitution they were now setting up in Ireland was the Constitution of America. It had been taken from the American Constitution, but why did not the Government follow the provision of the American Constitution, which set up a Federal Executive in each State?'[89] Carson wished for greater adherence to the American federal system, including a federated state-style government, to ensure protections of unionist interests and preservation of the Union.

On the other hand, Lecky argued that the federal system did not matter in the slightest if the same Irish nationalist opponents were in charge of the Home Rule parliament. He wrote, 'It is this profound division of classes in Ireland that makes all arguments derived from the example of federal governments in Europe or America so utterly fallacious. The first question to be asked before setting up a local legislature is "Who are the men who are likely to control it?"'[90] Lecky believed the American federalist system would not make a difference given Ireland's problems and divisions. Rentoul pointed out another inherent problem in the comparisons of federalism in the two countries: ultimately, the United States example was the opposite of Home Rule. Rentoul argued,

> There was no one of the United States of America that claimed to be a nation or that asked for national privileges. Each State of the United States gave up certain powers of its own, in order that it might be met by other States giving up those same powers to what I may term a supreme legislature which governed them all … In the United States, then, it was not the case of a number of nations being restrained from exercising their proper rights and privileges, but of States voluntarily giving up to a Constitution, which they themselves had founded, certain of their rights, in order that they might assist in exercising similar rights over other States.[91]

As Rentoul asserted, the federal system of government in the United States was not regulating a number of separate nations devolving power from a central government, as would be the case with Ireland under the Home Rule Bill. The United States represented the exact opposite: a number of states coming together into a voluntary union with each other when they would have otherwise been separate. It was apparent, therefore, that unity was enshrined in the American constitution.

89 PD 4th Ser., Vol. 16, 58–59.
90 W.E.H. Lecky, 'Why I am Not a Home Ruler', in *The Truth about Home Rule: Papers on the Irish Question*, ed. George Baden-Powell (Edinburgh: William Blackwood and Sons, 1888), 167.
91 PD 4th Ser., Vol. 11, 664–665.

By the time of the third Home Rule Bill, federal options gained greater consideration. This was especially the case after the passage of the 1911 Parliament Act meant it was increasingly likely that some form of Home Rule would be implemented. By the end of the Home Rule period, the most important federalist thinkers were F.S. Oliver and the Earl of Selborne.[92] With increased support for federalist options, unionists continued to criticize the Liberals for the system set up in the Home Rule Bill. Many of these criticisms were based on the idea that it was the Liberal Party's intention eventually to implement a federal system for the whole United Kingdom. Oliver was active in this criticism. In a series of letters to *The Times*, he questioned the tariff provisions within the Home Rule Bill, arguing that the United States, Canada, Australia, and South Africa had all fought and sacrificed to get rid of customs barriers. Oliver believed that unity could not be maintained with customs barriers cutting through the heart of the United Kingdom.[93] The Ulster Unionist Council saw the existence of customs barriers within the Home Rule Bill as creating a farce of the idea that the Liberal government ever intended to implement a wide-reaching federal system. In 1912, the UUC issued a resolution stating, 'The hypocrisy of the pretence that the present Bill is the forerunner of a Federal Constitution for the United Kingdom is shown by the Customs barriers proposed to be set up between Great Britain and Ireland, an arrangement unknown in any existing Federal system'.[94]

As with previous Home Rule bills, unionists asserted that greater safeguards were needed for the protection of minority rights. Lord Lansdowne, the leader of the Conservative Party in the House of Lords and a Peer of Ireland, warned, 'Remember who are the men upon whom these safeguards are to be imposed. They are the men who have announced that they mean to dethrone once for all the English Government of their country, the very Government whose supremacy is recognised in this Bill by these carefully drawn clauses'.[95] The Senate was to be one of the main safeguards. However, Lansdowne complained that the upper house provided for in the current Home Rule Bill was even weaker than that of the previous bill.[96] Lansdowne also asserted that due process needed a place as a safeguard in the bill. He asked,

Why is it that you have omitted from this Bill the admirable words which you inserted in your own Bill of 1893, and which found a place in the Constitution of the United States of America? The noble

92 See Boyce and Stubbs, 'F.S. Oliver'; Jackson, *Home Rule*, 187–197.
93 *The Times* 30 Apr 1912.
94 Ulster Unionist Council Committee Year Book 1913, PRONI D972/17.
95 PD Lords 5th Ser., Vol. 13, 791.
96 PD Lords 5th Ser., Vol. 13, 794.

Viscount [John Morley] knows the words I mean – the words which prohibit the Irish Parliament from depriving a person of life, liberty, or property without due process of law, or whereby private property may not be taken without just compensation.[97]

The due process provision was so crucial that Carson, MP for South Londonderry, John Gordon, MP for North Down, William Mitchell-Thomson, and southern unionist Lord Ashbourne all spoke in favour of its addition. Bonar Law emphasized that the significance of due process was affirmed by its place of importance in the American constitution.[98] William Moore, the MP for North Armagh, said that he argued for a provision of due process because he was 'one of the unfortunate people whose life, liberty, and property will be wholly at the mercy of the new Parliament that is being set up'.[99] Given the state of the Home Rule Bill, Moore concluded that he was grateful he did not have to rely on government safeguards. He declared, 'I am thankful that we have in Ulster Unionists and Protestants who will be much better safeguards than the right hon. Gentleman is willing to put in the Bill. We are quite willing and ready to safeguard ourselves when a cowardly Government, in subservient obedience to the Irish vote, is going to filch our liberty and property from us'.[100]

Conclusion

The examples of the American Revolution, Civil War, and constitution formed important parts of unionist rhetoric as they defended their own movement and discredited Home Rule. The idea of unity embodied in the history and government of the United States, as discussed throughout this chapter, was one of the most common illustrations unionists made through employing the American example. Unity was seen as the global spirit of the age, exemplified by the United States. American historical and constitutional examples were common currency in Irish unionist political rhetoric, indicating familiarity with American history and political system. Unionists did not have uniform views toward the American constitution; however, the success of the United States by the turn of the century meant any parallels that could be drawn to the American political system would help lend credibility to unionists' stances.

97 PD Lords 5th Ser., Vol. 13, 791.
98 PD Commons 5th Ser., Vol. 42, 2221–2228, 2233, 2236–2239, 2261; PD Lords 5th Ser., Vol. 13, 733.
99 PD Commons 5th Ser., Vol. 42, 2250.
100 PD Commons 5th Ser., Vol. 42, 2254; Miller, *Queen's Rebels*, 99–100.

Unionists' uses of these examples also reflected a much deeper connection to America. Ulster unionists took ownership of the events in colonial and Revolutionary America, consistently drawing upon ethnic connections with the Scotch-Irish. Ulster unionists celebrated the achievements of the Scotch-Irish as pioneers and fighters for their beliefs, characteristics which they also claimed to embody. The unionist image of America became more important over time as they sought to justify militant stances. The American example, with its emphasis on Scotch-Irish connections, both aided and reflected the transition from all-Ireland unionism to unionism focused in Ulster. While Ulster unionists became increasingly localized and separated from the rest of the United Kingdom, they maintained their own vision of America to support their stances.

8

Conclusion

Following the partition of Ireland and establishment of the Irish Free State, Irish-American interest in Irish nationalism significantly decreased. Irish neutrality in the Second World War and increased Irish-American assimilation further diminished levels of participation in nationalist organizations. The United States government itself pursued a policy of non-intervention in Northern Irish affairs for decades. Nevertheless, American interest in Ireland and Irish culture persisted and left the potential for future political mobilization on Irish issues.[1]

The United States government faced a turning point in its Northern Irish policy in the 1970s, as the Troubles and internment sparked Irish-American protests. Irish-American organizations such as the Irish Northern Aid Committee (Noraid), founded in 1970, raised funds for the republican movement and were accused of fostering close ties with the Provisional IRA. By 1977, British security forces claimed that almost 80 per cent of IRA weapons came from the United States.[2] Other Irish-American organizations worked to lobby the American government. The congressional organization, Friends of Ireland (FOI), founded in 1981, included influential senators Ted Kennedy and Daniel Moynihan, Speaker of the House Tip O'Neill, and New York Governor Hugh Carey. FOI combated IRA fundraising and pressured the United States government to end its non-intervention policy. The organization lobbied for a statement on Northern Ireland from Jimmy Carter, who took a special interest in the Troubles because of his human rights agenda. On 30 August 1977, Carter condemned violence and promised American aid and investment if a peaceful settlement was achieved.[3]

---

1   Andrew J. Wilson, *Irish America and the Ulster Conflict, 1968–1995* (Belfast: Blackstaff, 1995), 285; D. George Boyce, *The Irish Question and British Politics, 1868–1996*, 2nd edn (Basingstoke: Macmillan, 1996), 98.

2   Wilson, *Irish America*, 286–289; Andrew J. Wilson, 'Ulster Unionists in America, 1972–1985', *New Hibernia Review* 11, no. 1 (Spring 2007), 50.

3   Adrian Guelke, *Northern Ireland: The International Perspective* (Dublin: Gill and

During Ronald Reagan's administration, FOI maintained pressure on the Irish question, which, when combined with other elements, helped lead to action. Reagan continued American involvement in Northern Ireland, actively encouraging compromise during the negotiations that produced the 1985 Anglo-Irish Agreement.[4] Many Ulster unionists were hostile to the 1985 agreement and suspicious of American involvement in the peace process. They felt isolated by the perceived pro-republican stances of the United States. Unionists attacked American government involvement, and condemned Noraid and other American organizations for supporting the IRA. Focused on opposition to Irish republicans, unionists did little to present their own vision of Northern Irish society to Americans. The attempts made to engage with the United States were generally unsuccessful. Most prominent were the visits of Ian Paisley, leader of the Democratic Unionist Party (DUP). Paisley focused on religious connections as part of a worldwide network of fundamentalist Protestants. He was condemned by Irish-Americans and became the target of negative media attention.[5]

In 1982, the DUP was joined by the Ulster Unionist Party to organize 'Operation USA', an intensive tour of the United States to promote unionist views. Frustratingly for the two parties, the tour generated little interest. Unionists also attempted to call upon surviving Scotch-Irish organizations for support, such as the American Orange Order, Scotch-Irish Society of the United States, and Ulster-Irish Society. A small number of grassroots supporters formed new organizations such as the Northern Ireland Service Council and Ulster American Loyalists. However, with little subsequent encouragement from Northern Ireland, membership quickly declined. Some American supporters were a liability for unionists because of their extremist views.[6]

Macmillan, 1988), 136–137 and 'The American Connection to the Northern Ireland Conflict', *Irish Studies in International Affairs* 1, no. 4 (1984), 33.

4 James Loughlin, *The Ulster Question since 1945*, 2nd edn (Basingstoke: Palgrave, 2004), 122–123; Boyce, *Irish Question*, 128; Adrian Guelke, 'The United States and the Peace Process', in *The Northern Ireland Question: The Peace Process and the Belfast Agreement*, ed. Brian Barton and Patrick J. Roche (Basingstoke: Palgrave Macmillan, 2009), 227; Andrew J. Wilson, 'The Billy Boys Meet Slick Willy: The Ulster Unionist Party and the American Dimension to the Northern Ireland Peace Process, 1994–9', *Irish Studies in International Affairs* 11 (2000), 121.

5 G.K. Peatling, 'Unionist Identity, External Perceptions of Northern Ireland, and the Problem of Unionist Legitimacy', *Éire-Ireland* 39, 1/2 (Spring/Summer 2004), 215–216; Wilson, 'Ulster Unionists in America', 52, 56–57; Steve Bruce, *God Save Ulster: The Religion and Politics of Paisleyism* (Oxford: Clarendon Press, 1986), 168, 180–184; Andrew J. Wilson, 'Maintaining the Cause in the Land of the Free: Ulster Unionists and US Involvement in the Northern Ireland Conflict, 1968–1972', *Éire-Ireland* 40, 3/4 (Fall/Winter 2005), 222–224.

6 Wilson, 'Ulster Unionists in America', 50–51, 61–70; Wilson, 'Maintaining the Cause', 213–217.

The presidency of Bill Clinton was a defining era in the role of the United States in Northern Irish affairs. For the first time, an American government challenged its relationship with Britain over the Northern Ireland question. Influenced by the ending of the Cold War and continued Irish-American lobbying, Clinton initiated dialogue with both nationalists and unionists. He visited Northern Ireland three times throughout his presidency. Senator George Mitchell, Special Envoy for Northern Ireland, was pivotal in chairing the commission which led to the Good Friday Agreement in 1998. This all-party commission brought the UUP fully into the peace process and made considerable advances with loyalist parties.[7] Ulster politicians realized they were failing to defend their political positions or gain allies amongst the British and Americans. The UUP attempted to establish a presence in Washington, and the party's leader, David Trimble, was active in pursuing connections with the Clinton adminis-tration. Worried about perceptions of promoting a nationalist agenda, Clinton invited Trimble to the White House in September 1995. By the time Clinton left office, Trimble could claim to have met with him more than any other world leader. The UUP established a Washington office and engaged in an American strategy to create networks with the White House, Congress, business community, and Irish-American groups. Unionists still faced negative portrayals in the press, especially compared to Irish nationalists. While some success was achieved in drawing attention to the unionist cause, little impact was made on American government policy. In Northern Ireland, unionists were divided or ambivalent about the direction of American strategy and the peace process.[8]

While George W. Bush was less active in Northern Ireland than his predecessor, for the most part he continued the policies set out by Clinton on the peace process. Acting mainly through the Special Envoy for Northern Ireland, the Bush administration helped to influence IRA weapons decommis-sioning and power-sharing in 2006.[9] The relationship with Northern Ireland

---

7 Guelke, 'United States and the Peace Process', 222–223; Lee A. Smithey, *Unionists, Loyalists, and Conflict Transformation in Northern Ireland* (Oxford: Oxford University Press, 2011), 63; John Dumbrell, 'The New American Connection: President George W. Bush and Northern Ireland', in *A Farewell to Arms? Beyond the Good Friday Agreement*, ed. Michael Cox, Adrian Guelke, and Fiona Stephen, 2nd edn (Manchester: Manchester University Press, 2006), 357–358.

8 Smithey, *Unionists, Loyalists*, 62–63; Wilson, 'Billy Boys', 125–129, 132–136; Wilson, 'Maintaining the Cause', 237–238; Guelke, *Northern Ireland*, 145; Mary Alice C. Clancy, 'The United States and Post-Agreement Northern Ireland, 2001–2006', *Irish Studies in International Affairs* 18 (2007), 165–167; Christopher Farrington, *Ulster Unionism and the Peace Process in Northern Ireland* (Basingstoke: Palgrave Macmillan, 2006), 41–42.

9 Dumbrell, 'New American Connection', 361–364; Clancy, 'United States and Post-Agreement Northern Ireland', 173; Roger Mac Ginty, 'Post-Agreement Loyalism

continued under the administration of Barack Obama, particularly on the issue of devolution of justice and policing powers. Both nationalists and unionists in Northern Ireland generally continued to be positively disposed toward the United States, helping to account for the continued prominent role of America on Northern Irish issues.[10] For unionists, power relations shifted in the early 2000s making the DUP, rather than the UUP, play the greater role in interacting with the American government. Despite the United States' regard for appearing impartial and maintaining Anglo-American relations, however, Ulster unionists had significant difficulties in shaping the role of the United States on Northern Irish issues.

After the Good Friday Agreement, the situation in Northern Ireland went through a period of remarkable change, symbolized by the opening of the Northern Ireland Assembly, with its devolved, power-sharing government, on 8 May 2007. Unionists and loyalists demonstrated engagement with the peace process, even as there were problems along the way to creating a non-conflict society. In a time of transition, unionists pursued both new and continuing relationships with the United States. While the contexts changed drastically, and the two eras are by no means analogous, it is worthwhile to contemplate comparisons between the modern Ulster unionist relationship with the United States and that of the Home Rule period. Unionists' inability to deal successfully with the United States had roots in the relationships of the Home Rule era. Ulster unionist responses at the turn of the twenty-first century echoed the problems and precedents of the anti-Home Rule campaign between 1880 and 1920.

Unionism in both eras evolved gradually yet significantly over time. As Richard English describes, 'Unionism has always been open to the process of gradual change, to rolling evolution according to the perceived demands of the day. The shift from the Irish, landlord unionism, epitomised by the late Victorian Edward Saunderson, to an Ulster-centred, more urbanised unionism, more familiar during the twentieth century, provides an important example'.[11] Likewise, twentieth-century changes and contexts had a large impact on unionism: the decline of the British empire and resultant impact on the meaning of British identity; the advent of devolution; changes to the Republic of Ireland over the course of the past one hundred years; changing

and the International Dimension', in *Ulster Loyalism after the Good Friday Agreement: History, Identity, and Change*, ed. James W. McAuley and Graham Spencer (Basingstoke: Palgrave Macmillan, 2011), 44.

10 Adrian Guelke, 'The USA and the Northern Ireland Peace Process', *Ethnopolitics* 11, no. 4 (Nov 2012), 433–437.

11 Richard English, 'The Growth of New Unionism', in *Changing Shades of Orange and Green: Redefining the Union and the Nation in Contemporary Ireland*, ed. John Coakley (Dublin: University College Dublin Press, 2002), 96.

attitudes toward nationalists and the potential of working together to create a peaceful Northern Ireland.

Both eras highlighted the complexities of unionism. It was never a monolithic, homogenous movement. Unionists in the Home Rule era were drawn together under an Ulsterman identity, concealing divisions between Liberals and Conservatives; urban and rural; working class and landlords; diverse religious traditions; differing views on the Land League, Orangeism, militancy, and passive resistance to Home Rule. Modern unionism likewise contained a variety of textures and layers, symbolized by the fracturing of unionist political parties. Unionists were divided in their responses to the peace process and Good Friday Agreement, with some willing to make a degree of accommodation to Irish nationalism. The UUP under Trimble particularly made strides in seeking conciliation in this regard, in an attempt to ensure effective governance in Northern Ireland. On the other hand, loyalists were largely absent from the internationalization of the peace process and faced struggles in societal transitions.[12]

While the diversity of backgrounds, experiences, and viewpoints within unionism was an enduring characteristic, vulnerability and insecurity contributed to a Manichean view of the situations in Ireland and Northern Ireland. Identities of unionists and nationalists were each artificially homogenized. During the Home Rule era, unionists increasingly associated Irish-America with extremism, violence, and separatism, leading to anxiety and fears over potential impact on a Dublin parliament. They emphasized the monetary influence of Irish-America over Irish nationalism, accusing nationalists of concealing their true separatist intentions. The image of an extremist Irish-America provided a representation by which unionists characterized all Irish nationalists. Unionists used Irish-American extremism to legitimize their own moves toward militancy. At the same time, unionists expressed a sense of betrayal by the British for rewarding Ulster loyalty with hated Home Rule, meaning unionists were increasingly isolated and fearful of compromise. In the modern era, divisions and conflict remained in Northern Ireland. Throughout the peace process, unionist and loyalist groups expressed distrust of the British and American governments, and condemned Irish-American participation. Delegates to the United States felt there was a complete lack of understanding of unionism. Many unionists were suspicious of republicans' pledges to decommission weapons and of power-sharing and cross-border institutions. In what was termed a 'discourse of perpetuity', for some unionists all developments in the peace process were assumed to contain a threat to

12 English, 'Growth of New Unionism', 97; Mac Ginty, 'Post-Agreement Loyalism', 37–48.

Protestant interests. Such views led to even greater senses of isolation and embattlement.[13]

Although at times causing frustration for unionists, the United States presented opportunities in both eras. Unionists frequently hoped to take advantage of the long history of transatlantic links between Ulster and America, forged through two and a half centuries of emigration, Protestant networks, and shared cultural values. Religion frequently played a prominent role in connecting Ulster and America, and religious institutions provided opportunities for the transnational promotion of unionism. Religion and politics were closely intertwined during the Home Rule era, as Irish Protestants from a variety of denominations called upon their American counterparts for support. Unionists regularly emphasized transnational ties through evangelicalism, anti-Catholicism, and shared Protestant heritage, which helped to unify Ulster Protestants against the Home Rule threat. Even though Presbyterian symbols were prominent in the 'Ulsterman' identity of this era, as Andrew Holmes describes, the artificial homogenization of Ulster Protestantism to unify unionists undermined the distinctive character of Presbyterian politics. The influence of transnational and transdenominational evangelicalism led to the rise of non-denominational fundamentalism in the modern era. Ian Paisley became the most prominent individual in his efforts to form transatlantic religious relationships, including with American fundamentalists such as Reverend Carl McIntire and Dr. Bob Jones, Jr. These international bonds contributed to Paisley's approach to civil rights and other political issues in Northern Ireland.[14]

In each era, unionists celebrated Scotch-Irish heritage, pioneering spirit, and ties to American presidents. Anxious to show that unionism had international appeal during the Home Rule era, unionists conducted tours of the United States and attempted to cultivate Anglo-American friendship and Protestant unity overseas. The high levels of assimilation, success, and diversity among the Scotch-Irish, however, meant limited support for unionist politics. In Ulster, the Scotch-Irish ethnic revival was influential in the ways unionists defined themselves. The identity of Ulster was linked to an image of Revolutionary and frontier America in which the Scotch-Irish fought to uphold liberties and were determined to stand up for what they believed was right. These qualities and Scotch-Irish ties are celebrated to this day, through loyalist murals, heritage sites, and postcards of presidential

---

13 Smithey, *Unionists, Loyalists*, 62–63; Wilson, 'Ulster Unionists', 50–52, 60, 66, 72–72; James W. McAuley, *Ulster's Last Stand? Reconstructing Unionism after the Peace Process* (Dublin: Irish Academic Press, 2010), xxv–xxvi.

14 Holmes, 'Religion, Anti-Slavery, and Identity', 398; Richard Lawrence Jordan, *The Second Coming of Paisley: Militant Fundamentalism and Ulster Politics* (Syracuse, NY: Syracuse University Press, 2013), 9, 170–198, 246–253.

homesteads. In the modern era, Ulster unionists made significant efforts to reach out to the United States to gain political support and to promote cultural tourism.[15]

In both the Home Rule and modern eras, unionists hoped to awaken and mobilize the American diaspora. Ulster unionists were less insular and more internationally focused than generally portrayed. However, political activity regarding America was inconsistent from the late nineteenth century onward. Ulster unionist approaches to the United States were marked by unevenness and contradictions which limited their effectiveness. Unionists frequently denounced American government involvement in Irish and Northern Irish issues. They also condemned Irish-American participation, but were reluctant to engage with their adversaries when in the United States. They paradoxically both spurned and sought American involvement. Thus the United States was both a boon and a burden for Ulster unionists, as they sought opportunity in their share of the 'two Irelands beyond the sea'.

15 Smithey, *Unionists, Loyalists*, 114, 134–136, 165–166, 217; Farrington, *Ulster Unionism and the Peace Process*, 41–42.

Bibliography

Primary Sources

Archival Sources

Public Record Office of Northern Ireland
Carson Papers
Johnston of Ballykilbeg Papers
Montgomery Papers – Family of Blessingbourne
Papers of the Irish Unionist Alliance
Papers of John Aiken McClelland
Papers of the Wallace Family, Downpatrick
Records of J.M. Barbour
Saunderson Papers
Ulster Unionist Council

Historical Society of Pennsylvania
Lily of the Valley Loyal Orange Lodge No. 167
Orange Hall Association of Philadelphia
Pennsylvania State Grand Lodge of the Loyal Orange Institution
Royal Black Preceptory Star of Liberty Lodge No. 34
Scotch-Irish Foundation Library and Archives Collection
Washington Loyal Orange Lodge No. 43

Government Documents

Parliamentary Debates, 3rd, 4th, and 5th Series
Papers Relating to the Foreign Relations of the United States. *Lansing Papers, 1914–1920*, Vol. 2. Washington, DC: Government Printing Office, 1940.
Treaty of Peace with Germany: Hearings before the Committee on Foreign Relations, United States Senate. 66th Congress, 1st Session. Washington, DC: Government Printing Office, 1919.

Organization Minutes and Reports

Churches and Religious Organizations

The Centennial Celebration of the Theological Seminary of the Presbyterian Church in the United States of America at Princeton, New Jersey. Princeton, NJ: Theological Seminary, 1912.

Jubilee of the General Assembly of the Presbyterian Church in Ireland, Belfast, July 1890. Belfast: The Witness Printing Works, 1890.

Minutes of the General Assembly of the Presbyterian Church in the United States of America.

Minutes of the Proceedings of the General Assembly of the Presbyterian Church in Ireland.

Reports of the Proceedings of the Alliance of Reformed Churches Holding the Presbyterian System (1880–1886).

Scotch-Irish Organizations

Loyal Orange Institution, United States of America. Biennial Reports of the Sessions of the Supreme Grand Orange Lodge in the United States of America.

The Scotch-Irish in America: Proceedings and Addresses of the Scotch-Irish Congresses (1889–1900).

Newspapers

Belfast News-Letter
Bloomington Daily Leader
Boston Globe
Brann's Iconoclast (Chicago)
Charlotte Observer
Chicago Daily Inter-Ocean
Chicago Tribune
Decatur Republican
Detroit Free Press
Duluth Daily News
Evening Star (Washington, DC)
Galveston Daily News
Irish Times (Dublin)
Irish World (New York)
Kansas City Star
Los Angeles Herald
Los Angeles Times
New York Tribune
New York Herald
New York Sun
New York Times
Notes from Ireland (Dublin)
The Orange and Purple Courier (Washington, DC)
Philadelphia Inquirer
Philadelphia North American
Purple Bell (Boston)

Rocky Mountain News (Denver)
Sacramento Union
St. Louis Daily Globe Democrat
San Francisco Evening Bulletin
The Times (London)
Toronto Sentinel and Orange and Protestant Advocate
Washington Post
Witness (Belfast)

Books, Pamphlets, and other Printed Material

Agar-Ellis, Leopold. 'Religion and Unbelief in Ireland'. London: Remington, 1888.
'America and the Irish Question. A Short Account of the Visit of the Delegation from Protestant Ireland to the Churches in the United States of America. December 1919–February 1920. By the Delegates'. Belfast: Belfast News-Letter, 1920.
Amery, L.S. 'The Case against Home Rule'. London: West Strand Publishing, 1912.
—— *Union and Strength: A Series of Papers on Imperial Questions*. London: Edward Arnold, 1912.
Anderson, Robert. *Sidelights on the Home Rule Movement*. London: John Murray, 1906.
Arnold-Forster, H.O. 'The Truth about the Land League, Its Leaders, and Its Teaching'. 2nd edn. London: National Press Agency, 1882.
Arthur, William. 'Shall the Loyal be Deserted and the Disloyal Set over Them? An Appeal to Liberals and Nonconformists'. London: Bemrose & Sons, 1886.
—— 'Moral Points in the Home Rule Controversy'. Dublin: IUA, 1893.
Bagenal, Philip H. 'Parnellism Unveiled; or the Land-and-Labour Agitation of 1879–80'. Dublin: Hodges, Foster, and Figgis, 1880.
—— *The American Irish and their Influence on Irish Politics*. London: Kegan Paul, 1882.
Birmingham, George A. *The Red Hand of Ulster*. London: Smith, Elder, 1912.
Blue, A. Wylie. *Fossicker's Fare: Rakings and Recollections*. Belfast: Quota, 1946.
Bolton, Charles Knowles. *Scotch Irish Pioneers in Ulster and America*. Boston: Bacon and Brown, 1910.
Bonar Law, Andrew. 'Home Rule: The Unionist Point of View. Speech in Bootle, on December 7th, 1911'. Westminster: National Conservative Union, 1912.
Boyd, Charles W., ed. *Mr. Chamberlain's Speeches*. 2 vols. London: Constable, 1914.
Bryce, James. *The American Commonwealth*. London: Macmillan, 1888.
—— 'The Scoto-Irish Race in Ulster and in America: Address Delivered to the Scotch-Irish Society of Pennsylvania, February, 1909'. In *University and Historical Addresses: Delivered During a Residence in the United States as Ambassador of Great Britain*. London: Macmillan, 1913.
Carroll, Francis M., ed. *The American Commission on Irish Independence, 1919: The Diary, Correspondence and Report*. Dublin: Irish Manuscripts Commission, 1985.
Carson, Edward. Introduction to *Against Home Rule: The Case for the Union*, edited by S. Rosenbaum. London: Frederick Warne, 1912.
Cave, George. 'The Constitutional Question'. In *Against Home Rule: The Case for the Union*, edited by S. Rosenbaum. London: Frederick Warne, 1912.
Cecil, Robert. 'The Confederate Struggle and Recognition'. *Quarterly Review* 112, no. 224 (Oct 1862): 535–570.

'The Church of Ireland and the Present Political Crisis: Report of the Special Meeting of the General Synod, Holden at Dublin, March 23, 1886'. Dublin: Hodges, Figgis, 1886.

Corkey, William. *The Church of Rome and Irish Unrest: How Hatred of Britain is Taught in Irish Schools*. Edinburgh: William Bishop, 1918.

—— *Episode in the History of Protestant Ulster, 1923–1947*. Belfast: Dorman & Sons, 1959.

'The Crimes Act; – Before and After: Some Extracts from Parnellite Speeches and Comments Thereon'. Dublin: ILPU, 1888.

Dawson, Richard. *Red Terror and Green*. London: John Murray, 1920.

Dicey, A.V. *Introduction to the Study of the Law of the Constitution*. London: Macmillan, 1885.

Dinsmore, John Walker. *The Scotch-Irish in America: Their History, Traits, Institutions and Influences, Especially as Illustrated in the Early Settlers of Western Pennsylvania, and their Descendants*. Chicago: Winona Publishing, 1906.

Duff, Robert S. *Notes of a Visit to America During the Pan-Presbyterian Council, 1880*. Kilmarnock: Dunlop & Drennan, 1882.

Escouflaire, R.C. *Ireland: An Enemy of the Allies?* London: John Murray, 1919.

'Facts about Ireland for the Consideration of American Citizens by the Delegates of the Protestant Churches of Ireland'. Philadelphia: Protestant Federation, 1920.

Ford, Henry J. *The Scotch-Irish in America*. Princeton, NJ: Princeton University Press, 1915.

Froude, James Anthony. 'Romanism and the Irish Race in the United States, Part I'. *North American Review* 129 (Dec 1879): 519–536.

—— 'Romanism and the Irish Race in the United States, Part II'. *North American Review* 130 (Jan 1880): 31–50.

Gibson, William. *The Year of Grace: A History of the Ulster Revival of 1859*. Edinburgh: Andrew Elliot, 1860.

Goodspeed, Edgar J. *A Full History of the Wonderful Career of Moody and Sankey, in Great Britain and America*. New York: Henry S. Goodspeed, 1876.

Green, Samuel Swett. 'The Scotch-Irish in America'. Worcester, Mass.: Charles Hamilton, 1895.

Hall, John. 'Testimony of a Presbyterian Devine'. Dublin: ILPU, 1888.

Hamilton, Ernest W. *The Soul of Ulster*. London: Hurst and Blackett, 1917.

Hanna, Charles A. *The Scotch-Irish, or, the Scot in North Britain, North Ireland, and North America*. 2 vols. New York: G.P. Putnam, 1902.

Harrison, John. *The Scot in Ulster: A Sketch of the History of the Scottish Population of Ulster*. Edinburgh: William Blackwood and Sons, 1888.

Harte, Frederick E. *The Road I Have Travelled: The Experiences of an Irish Methodist Minister*. Belfast: Wm. Mullan & Son, 1947.

Hendrick, Burton J., ed. *The Life and Letters of Walter H. Page*. 3 vols. London: William Heinemann, 1922.

'Home Rule and Imperial Defence. Admiral Lord Beresford's Views'. Belfast: Ulster Unionist Council, 1919.

'The Home Rule "Nutshell" Examined by an Irish Unionist. (Being a Reply to "Home Rule in a Nutshell" by Mr. Jeremiah MacVeagh, MP)'. Dublin: Unionist Associations of Ireland, 1912.

Hurlbert, William Henry. *Ireland under Coercion: The Diary of an American*. 2 vols. Edinburgh: David Douglas, 1888.

—— *England under Coercion: A Record of Private Rights Outraged and of Public Justice Betrayed by Political Malice for Partizan Ends*. Genoa: R. Istituto Sordo-Muti, 1893.

Imperium Et Unitas. 'Irish Home Rule and British Industry. An Appeal to the British Voter'. Leicester: S. Barker, 1892.

Irish Imperialist. 'The Old Conspiracy: An Attempt to Present in Popular Form the Leading Points in Connection with the Present Home Rule Agitation and to Demonstrate the Impossibility of a Final Settlement of the Irish Question by Means of the Proposed Legislation'. London: Simpkin, Marshall, Hamilton, Kent, 1911.

Irish Liberal. 'Irish Issues: Letters Addressed to the Right Hon. John Morley, M.P.' Dublin: E. Ponsonby, 1888.

Irish Loyal and Patriotic Union, Publications Issued During the Year 1888. Dublin: ILPU, 1888.

James, Henry. *The Work of the Irish Leagues: Replying in the Parnell Commission Inquiry*. London: Liberal Unionist Association, 1890.

Jeans, William. 'England and Ireland: An Examination of the Demand for Home Rule'. London: T. Fisher Unwin, 1886.

Jones, Tom Bruce. 'The Imperial Peril: One Hundred Reasons against Home Rule'. Edinburgh: Oliver & Boyd, 1914.

Kerr-Smiley, Peter. *The Peril of Home Rule*. London: Cassell, 1911.

Le Caron, Henri. *Twenty-Five Years in the Secret Service*. London: William Heinemann, 1892.

Lecky, W.E.H. 'A "Nationalist" Parliament'. *Nineteenth Century* 19, no. 110 (Apr 1886): 636–644.

—— 'Why I am Not a Home Ruler'. In *The Truth About Home Rule: Papers on the Irish Question*, edited by George Baden-Powell. Edinburgh: William Blackwood and Sons, 1888.

—— 'Some Aspects of Home Rule'. *Contemporary Review* 63 (May 1893): 626–638.

—— *Historical and Political Essays*. London: Longmans, Green, 1908.

Linehan, John C. *The Irish Scots and the 'Scotch-Irish': An Historical and Ethnological Monograph*. Concord: American-Irish Historical Society, 1902.

Logan, James. *Ulster in the X-Rays: A Short Review of the Real Ulster, Its People, Pursuits, Principles, Poetry, Dialect, and Humour*. London: Arthur H. Stockwell, 1922.

Londonderry, Marquess of. 'The Ulster Question'. In *Against Home Rule: The Case for the Union*, edited by S. Rosenbaum. London: Frederick Warne, 1912.

Lynd, R.J. 'Some Thoughts on the Present Political Crisis'. Londonderry: 'Standard' Steam Printing Works, 1888.

McConnell, James. *Presbyterianism in Belfast*. Belfast: Davidson & M'Cormack, 1912.

MacNeice, John Frederick. *The Church of Ireland in Belfast: Its Growth, Condition, Needs*. Belfast: William Mullan & Sons, 1931.

McNeill, Ronald. *Ulster's Stand for Union*. London: John Murray, 1922.

Mahaffy, Gilbert. 'The Attitude of Irish Churchmen in the Present Political Crisis'. Dublin: George Herbert, 1886.

Mahan, Alfred Thayer. *Retrospect & Prospect: Studies in International Relations, Naval and Political*. Boston: Little, Brown, 1902.

Monypenny, W.F. *The Two Irish Nations: An Essay on Home Rule*. London: John Murray, 1913.

Moore, F. Frankfort. *The Truth about Ulster*. London: Eveleigh Nash, 1914.

Morrison, H.S. *Modern Ulster: Its Character, Customs, Politics, and Industries*. London: H.R. Allenson, 1920.

'Mr. Chamberlain and the Birmingham Association: Speech Delivered in the Town Hall, Birmingham, April 21, 1886'. London: Liberal Unionist Committee, 1886.

'The New Home Rule and the Old Objections'. Dublin: Unionist Associations of Ireland, 1909.

Nicholas, William. 'Why Are the Methodists of Ireland Opposed to Home Rule?' Dublin: IUA, 1893.

O'Brien, William. *The Irish Revolution and How It Came About*. London: George Allen & Unwin, 1923.

O'Connell, J.D. *The 'Scotch-Irish' Delusion in America: Historical Reply to President Eliot of Harvard College*. Washington, DC: American-Irish Historical Society, 1897.

Oliver, F.S. *Alexander Hamilton: An Essay on American Union*. London: Archibald Constable, 1906.

—— *Ordeal by Battle*. London: Macmillan, 1915.

Ormond, Alexander T. 'James McCosh as Thinker and Educator'. *Princeton Theological Review* 3 (Jul 1903): 337–361.

Palmer, Henry Norton. 'Ireland: Past and Present'. Exeter: Henry S. Eland, 1888.

Percy, Earl. 'The Military Disadvantages of Home Rule'. In *Against Home Rule: The Case for the Union*, edited by S. Rosenbaum. London: Frederick Warne, 1912.

Pim, Joseph T. 'Ireland in 1880, with Suggestions for the Reform of Her Land Laws'. London: W. Ridgway, 1880.

Plunkett, Horace. 'A Better Way. An Appeal to Ulster Not to Desert Ireland'. Dublin: Hodges, Figgis, 1914.

Reid, Whitelaw. 'The Scot in America, and the Ulster Scot. Edinburgh Philosophical Institution, Opening Address, Season of 1911–12, Synod Hall, November 1st'. London: Harrison and Sons, 1911.

Rudyard Kipling's Verse: Definitive Edition. London: Hodder and Stoughton, 1966.

Russell, T.W. 'The Case for Irish Loyalists: Being the Substance of an Address Delivered at Grangemouth, Stirlingshire, on Tuesday Evening, May 18, 1886'. Dublin: ILPU, 1888.

Salmon, George. 'Against Home Rule'. Dublin: Irish Loyal and Patriotic Union, 1886.

Saunderson, Edward. 'Two Irelands; or, Loyalty Versus Treason'. London: P.S. King & Son, 1884.

Shaw, James J. 'Mr. Gladstone's Two Irish Policies: 1868 and 1886. A Letter to an Ulster Liberal Elector'. London: Marcus Ward, 1888.

Sims, William Sowden, and Burton J. Hendrick. *The Victory at Sea*. Garden City, NY: Doubleday, Page, 1921.

Sloane, William M., ed. *The Life of James McCosh: A Record Chiefly Autobiographical*. Edinburgh: T. and T. Clark, 1896.

Smith, George Hill. *Rambling Reminiscences: Being Leaves from My Note Book as a Public (Political) Speaker*. Newry: Newry Telegraph, 1896.

—— *The North-East Bar: A Sketch, Historical and Reminiscent*. Belfast: Belfast News-Letter, 1910.

Smith, Goldwin. 'The Conduct of England to Ireland: An Address Delivered at Brighton, Jan. 30. 1882'. London: Macmillan, 1882.

Smith, Joseph. *The 'Scotch-Irish' Shibboleth Analyzed and Rejected, with Some Reference to the Present 'Anglo-Saxon' Comedy*. Washington, DC: American-Irish Historical Society, 1898.

Temple, Oliver Perry. *The Covenanter, the Cavalier, and the Puritan*. Cincinnati: Robert Clarke, 1897.

Thynne, Robert. 'Plain Words from Ireland'. London: Swan Sonnenschein, 1892.

'Ulster and Home Rule. Unionist Council Meeting. Sir Edward Carson's Advice'. Belfast: Ulster Unionist Council, 1919.

'Unionist Manifesto. Mansion House Claims Refuted'. Belfast: Ulster Unionist Council, 1918.

Urquhart, Diane, ed. *The Minutes of the Ulster Women's Unionist Council and Executive Committee, 1911–40*. Dublin: Irish Manuscripts Commission, 2001.

Webster, Richard. *A History of the Presbyterian Church in America: From Its Origin until the Year 1760*. Philadelphia: Joseph M. Wilson, 1857.

'What Shall Be Done with Ireland?' *Quarterly Review* 153, no. 306 (Apr 1882): 583–604.

Wicks, Pembroke. *The Truth About Home Rule*. With a foreword by Edward Carson. London: Sir Isaac Pitman & Sons, 1913.

Wilson, Philip Whitwell. *The Irish Case before the Court of Public Opinion*. New York: Fleming H. Revell, 1920.

Witherow, Thomas. 'General Assembly of the Irish Church'. *Presbyterian Review* 8, no. 32 (Oct 1887): 724–727.

Woodburn, James Barkley. *The Ulster Scot: His History and Religion*. London: H.R. Allenson, 1914.

Secondary Sources

Articles and Essays

Adamson, Christopher. 'God's Continent Divided: Politics and Religion in Upper Canada and the Northern and Western United States, 1775 to 1841'. *Comparative Studies in Society and History* 36, no. 3 (Jul 1994): 417–446.

Adamson, Ian. 'The Ulster-Scottish Connection'. In *Scotland and Ulster*, edited by Ian S. Wood. Edinburgh: Mercat, 1994.

Akenson, Donald H. 'The Historiography of the Irish in the United States of America'. In *The Irish World Wide*, Vol. 2: *The Irish in the New Communities*, edited by Patrick O'Sullivan. Leicester: Leicester University Press, 1992.

—— 'No Petty People: Pakena History and the Historiography of the Irish Diaspora'. In *A Distant Shore: Irish Migration & New Zealand Settlement*, edited by Lyndon Fraser. Dunedin: University of Otago Press, 2000.

Anderson, James. 'Ideological Variations in Ulster During Ireland's First Home Rule Crisis: An Analysis of Local Newspapers'. In *Community Conflict, Partition and Nationalism*, edited by Colin H. Williams and Eleonore Kofman. London: Routledge, 1989.

Appel, John J. 'The New England Origins of the American Irish Historical Society'. *New England Quarterly* 33, no. 4 (Dec 1960): 462–475.

Barkley, J.M. 'Francis Makemie of Ramelton – Father of American Presbyterianism'. Belfast: Presbyterian Historical Society of Ireland, 1994.

Barry, Colman J. 'Some Roots of American Nativism'. *Catholic Historical Review* 44, no. 2 (Jul 1958): 137–146.

Bayly, C.A., et al. 'On Transnational History'. *American Historical Review* 111, no. 5 (Dec 2006): 1441–1464.

Bayor, Ronald H., and Timothy J. Meagher. Introduction to *The New York Irish*, edited by Ronald H. Bayor and Timothy J. Meagher. Baltimore: Johns Hopkins University Press, 1996.

Beckett, J.C. 'Belfast to the End of the Eighteenth Century'. In *Belfast: The Making of the City, 1800–1914*, edited by J.C. Beckett. Belfast: Appletree, 1983.

Bew, Paul, and Frank Wright. 'The Agrarian Opposition in Ulster Politics, 1848–87.' In *Irish Peasants: Violence and Political Unrest, 1780–1914*, edited by Samuel Clark and James S. Donnelly, Jr. Madison: University of Wisconsin Press, 1983.

Blessing, Patrick J. 'Irish Emigration to the United States, 1800–1920: An Overview'. In *The Irish in America: Emigration, Assimilation, and Impact*. Irish Studies 4, edited by P.J. Drudy. Cambridge: Cambridge University Press, 1985.

Blethen, H. Tyler, and Curtis W. Wood, Jr. Introduction to *Ulster and North America: Transatlantic Perspectives on the Scotch-Irish*, edited by H. Tyler Blethen and Curtis W. Wood, Jr. Tuscaloosa: University of Alabama Press, 1997.

Boyce, D. George. 'Federalism and the Irish Question'. In *The Federal Idea*, Vol. 1: *The History of Federalism from Enlightenment to 1945*, edited by Andrea Bosco. London: Lothian Foundation Press, 1991.

—— 'In the Front Rank of the Nation: Gladstone and the Unionists of Ireland, 1868–1893'. In *Gladstone Centenary Essays*, edited by David W. Bebbington and Roger Swift. Liverpool: Liverpool University Press, 2000.

—— 'Weary Patriots: Ireland and the Making of Unionism'. In *Defenders of the Union: A Survey of British and Irish Unionism since 1801*, edited by D. George Boyce and Alan O'Day. London: Routledge, 2001.

—— 'Moral Force Unionism: A.V. Dicey and Ireland, 1885–1922'. In *From the United Irishmen to Twentieth-Century Unionism: A Festschrift for A.T.Q. Stewart*, edited by Sabine Wichert. Dublin: Four Courts Press, 2004.

Boyce, D. George, and J.O. Stubbs. 'F.S. Oliver, Lord Selborne and Federalism'. *Journal of Imperial and Commonwealth History* 5, no. 1 (Oct 1976): 53–81.

Boyle, Emily. '"Linenopolis": The Rise of the Textile Industry'. In *Belfast: The Making of the City, 1800–1914*, edited by J.C. Beckett. Belfast: Appletree, 1983.

Boyle, J.W. 'The Belfast Protestant Association and the Independent Orange Order, 1901–10'. *Irish Historical Studies* 13, no. 50 (Sep 1962): 117–152.

Bric, Maurice J. 'Ireland, America and the Reassessment of a Special Relationship, 1760–1783'. *Eighteenth-Century Ireland* 11 (1996): 88–119.

Brown, Thomas N. 'Origins and Character of Irish-American Nationalism'. *Review of Politics* 18, no. 3 (Jul 1956): 327–358.

Brownlow, Graham. 'The Political Economy of the Ulster Crisis: Historiography, Social Capability, and Globalisation'. In *The Ulster Crisis, 1885–1921*, edited by D. George Boyce and Alan O'Day. Basingstoke: Palgrave Macmillan, 2006.

Brundage, David. '"In Time of Peace, Prepare for War": Key Themes in the Social Thought of New York's Irish Nationalists, 1890–1916'. In *The New York Irish*, edited by Ronald H. Bayor and Timothy J. Meagher. Baltimore: Johns Hopkins University Press, 1996.

Buckland, Patrick. 'The Southern Unionists, the Irish Question, and British Politics, 1906–14'. *Irish Historical Studies* 16, no. 59 (Mar 1967): 228–255.

Burgess, Michael. 'Federalism: A Dirty Word? Federalist Ideas and Practice in the British Political Tradition'. London: Federal Trust Working Papers, 1988.

Burnett, David. 'The Modernisation of Unionism, 1892–1914?' In *Unionism in Modern Ireland: New Perspectives on Politics and Culture*, edited by Richard English and Graham Walker. Basingstoke: Macmillan Press, 1996.

Campbell, Malcolm. 'The Other Immigrants: Comparing the Irish in Australia and the United States'. *Journal of American Ethnic History* 14, no. 3 (Spring 1995): 3–22.

Carey, Hilary M., and Colin Barr. Introduction to *Religion and Greater Ireland: Christianity and Irish Global Networks, 1750–1950*, edited by Colin Barr and Hilary M. Carey. Montreal: McGill-Queen's University Press, 2015.

Carroll, Francis M. 'The American Committee for Relief in Ireland, 1920–22'. *Irish Historical Studies* 23, no. 89 (May 1982): 30–49.

—— 'Admiral Sims Incident: Irish Americans and Social Tensions in the 1920s'. *Prologue* 25, no. 4 (Winter 1993): 335–346.

—— 'The Collapse of Home Rule and the United Irish League of America, 1910–18: The Centre Did Not Hold'. In *Ireland's Allies: America and the 1916 Easter Rising*, edited by Miriam Nyhan Grey. Dublin: University College Dublin Press, 2016.

Carwardine, Richard. 'The Know-Nothing Party, the Protestant Evangelical Community, and American National Identity'. In *Studies in Church History*, 18: *Religion and National Identity*, edited by Stuart Mews. Oxford: Blackwell, 1982.

Clancy, Mary Alice C. 'The United States and Post-Agreement Northern Ireland, 2001–6'. *Irish Studies in International Affairs* 18 (2007): 155–173.

Coffey, John. 'Democracy and Popular Religion: Moody and Sankey's Mission to Britain 1873–1875'. In *Citizenship and Community: Liberals, Radicals and Collective Identities in the British Isles 1865–1931*, edited by Eugenio F. Biagini. Cambridge: Cambridge University Press, 1996.

Coleman, Patrick. '"In Harmony": A Comparative View of Female Orangeism'. In *Ireland in the World: Comparative, Transnational, and Personal Perspectives*, edited by Angela McCarthy. New York: Routledge, 2015.

Connolly, S.J. 'Culture, Identity, and Tradition: Changing Definitions of Irishness'. In *In Search of Ireland: A Cultural Geography*, edited by Brian Graham. London: Routledge, 1997.

d'Alton, Ian. 'Southern Irish Unionism: A Study of Cork Unionists, 1884–1914'. *Transactions of the Royal Historical Society* 23 (1974): 71–88.

—— '"A Vestigial Population"? Perspectives on Southern Irish Protestants in the Twentieth Century'. *Éire-Ireland* 44: 3/4 (Fall/Winter 2009): 9–42.

Delaney, Enda. 'Our Island Story? Towards a Transnational History of Late Modern Ireland'. *Irish Historical Studies* 37, no. 148 (Nov 2011): 83–105.

Delaney, Enda, and Donald M. MacRaild. Introduction to *Irish Migration, Networks and Ethnic Identities since 1750*. London: Routledge, 2007.

Diner, Hasia R. '"The Most Irish City in the Union": The Era of the Great Migration,

1844–1877'. In *The New York Irish*, edited by Ronald H. Bayor and Timothy J. Meagher. Baltimore: Johns Hopkins University Press, 1996.

Doyle, David N. 'The Irish and Christian Churches in America'. In *America and Ireland, 1776–1976: The American Identity and the Irish Connection*, edited by David N. Doyle and Owen Dudley Edwards. Westport, Conn.: Greenwood Press, 1980.

—— 'Scots Irish or Scotch-Irish'. In *Making the Irish American: History and Heritage of the Irish in the United States*, edited by J.J. Lee and Marion R. Casey. New York: New York University Press, 2006.

—— 'Orange Order'. In *Ireland and the Americas: Culture, Politics and History*, edited by James P. Byrne, Philip Coleman, and Jason King. Santa Barbara, Calif.: ABC-CLIO, 2008.

Dugdale, Blanche E.C. 'The Wyndham-MacDonnell Imbroglio, 1902–1906'. *Quarterly Review* 511 (Jan 1932): 15–39.

Dumbrell, John. 'The New American Connection: President George W. Bush and Northern Ireland'. In *A Farewell to Arms?: Beyond the Good Friday Agreement*, 2nd edn, edited by Michael Cox, Adrian Guelke, and Fiona Stephen. Manchester: Manchester University Press, 2006.

Dunn, Peter. 'Forsaking Their "Own Flesh and Blood"? Ulster Unionism, Scotland and Home Rule, 1886–1914'. *Irish Historical Studies* 37, no. 146 (Nov 2010): 203–220.

Edwards, Owen Dudley. 'American Diplomats and Irish Coercion, 1880–1883'. *Journal of American Studies* 1, no. 2 (1967): 213–232.

—— 'Kipling and the Irish'. *London Review of Books* 10, no. 3 (4 Feb 1988): 22–23.

English, Richard. 'The Growth of New Unionism'. In *Changing Shades of Orange and Green: Redefining the Union and the Nation in Contemporary Ireland*, edited by John Coakley. Dublin: University College Dublin Press, 2002.

Fair, John D. 'The Anglo-Irish Treaty of 1921: Unionist Aspects of the Peace'. *Journal of British Studies* 12, no. 1 (Nov 1972): 132–149.

Fanning, Ronan. 'The Unionist Party and Ireland, 1906–1910'. *Irish Historical Studies* 15, no. 58 (Sep 1966): 147–171.

Foner, Eric. 'Class, Ethnicity, and Radicalism in the Gilded Age: The Land League and Irish America'. In *Politics and Ideology in the Age of the Civil War*. New York: Oxford University Press, 1980.

Fraser, T.G. Foreword to *Ulster and North America: Transatlantic Perspectives on the Scotch-Irish*, edited by H. Tyler Blethen and Curtis W. Wood, Jr. Tuscaloosa: University of Alabama Press, 1997.

Gailey, Andrew. 'Unionist Rhetoric and Irish Local Government Reform, 1895–9'. *Irish Historical Studies* 24, no. 93 (May 1984): 52–68.

Gauvreau, Michael. 'The Empire of Evangelicalism: Varieties of Common Sense in Scotland, Canada, and the United States'. In *Evangelicalism: Comparative Studies of Popular Protestantism in North America, the British Isles, and Beyond, 1700–1990*, edited by Mark A. Noll, David W. Bebbington, and George A. Rawlyk. New York: Oxford University Press, 1994.

Gleeson, David T. 'Smaller Differences: "Scotch Irish" and "Real Irish" in the Nineteenth-Century American South'. *New Hibernia Review* 10, no. 2 (Summer 2002): 68–91.

Gleeson, David T. and Brendan J. Buttimer. '"We are Irish Everywhere": Irish Immigrant Networks in Charleston, South Carolina, and Savannah, Georgia'. In

Irish Migration, Networks and Ethnic Identities since 1750, edited by Enda Delaney and Donald M. MacRaild. London: Routledge, 2007.

Golway, Terry. 'John Devoy and the Easter Rising'. In *Ireland's Allies: America and the 1916 Easter Rising*, edited by Miriam Nyhan Grey. Dublin: University College Dublin Press, 2016.

Gordon, Michael A. 'Orange Order'. In *The Encyclopedia of the Irish in America*, edited by Michael Glazier. Notre Dame, Ind.: University of Notre Dame Press, 1999.

——— 'Orange Riots of 1870 and 1871'. In *The Encyclopedia of the Irish in America*, edited by Michael Glazier. Notre Dame, Ind.: University of Notre Dame Press, 1999.

Griffin, Patrick. 'The People with No Name: Ulster's Migrants and Identity Formation in Eighteenth-Century Pennsylvania'. *William and Mary Quarterly* 3rd Series, 58, no. 3 (Jul 2001): 587–614.

——— 'The Two-Migrations Myth, the Scotch-Irish, and the Irish American Experience'. In *Re-Imagining Ireland*, edited by Andrew Higgins Wyndham. Charlottesville: University of Virginia Press, 2006.

Guelke, Adrian. 'The American Connection to the Northern Ireland Conflict'. *Irish Studies in International Affairs* 1, no. 4 (1984): 27–39.

——— 'The United States and the Peace Process'. In *The Northern Ireland Question: The Peace Process and the Belfast Agreement*, edited by Brian Barton and Patrick J. Roche. Basingstoke: Palgrave Macmillan, 2009.

——— 'The USA and the Northern Ireland Peace Process'. *Ethnopolitics* 11, no. 4 (Nov 2012): 424–438.

Harvie, Christopher. 'Ideology and Home Rule: James Bryce, A.V. Dicey and Ireland, 1880–1887'. *English Historical Review* 91, no. 359 (Apr 1976): 298–314.

Hempton, David. 'Methodism in Irish Society, 1770–1830'. *Transactions of the Royal Historical Society* 5th Ser., 36 (1986): 117–142.

Hennessey, Thomas. 'Ulster Unionism and Loyalty to the Crown of the United Kingdom, 1912–74'. In *Unionism in Modern Ireland: New Perspectives on Politics and Culture*, edited by Richard English and Graham Walker. Basingstoke: Macmillan Press, 1996.

Hernon, Joseph M., Jr. 'The Use of the American Civil War in the Debate over Irish Home Rule'. *American Historical Review* 69, no. 4 (Jul 1964): 1022–1026.

Higham, John. 'Another Look at Nativism'. *Catholic Historical Review* 44, no. 2 (Jul 1958): 147–158.

Holmes, Andrew. 'Presbyterian Religion, Historiography, and Ulster Scots Identity, c.1800 to 1914'. *Historical Journal* 52, no. 3 (2009): 615–640.

——— 'Covenanter Politics: Evangelicalism, Political Liberalism and Ulster Presbyterians, 1798–1914'. *English Historical Review* 75, no. 513 (Apr 2010): 340–369.

——— 'The Ulster Revival of 1859: Causes, Controversies and Consequences'. *Journal of Ecclesiastical History* 63, no. 3 (Jul 2012): 488–515.

——— 'Religion, Anti-Slavery, and Identity: Irish Presbyterians, the United States, and Transatlantic Evangelicalism, c.1820–1914'. *Irish Historical Studies* 39, no. 155 (2015): 378–398.

Holmes, R.F.G. 'Ulster Presbyterians and Irish Nationalism'. In *Studies in Church History*, 18: *Religion and National Identity*, edited by Stuart Mews. Oxford: Blackwell, 1982.

——— '"Ulster Will Fight and Ulster Will Be Right": The Protestant Churches and

Ulster's Resistance to Home Rule, 1912–14'. In *Studies in Church History*, 20: *The Church and War*, edited by W.J. Sheils. Oxford: Basil Blackwell, 1983.

Hopkinson, Michael. 'President Woodrow Wilson and the Irish Question'. *Studia Hibernica* 27 (1993): 89–111.

Houston, Cecil J., and William J. Smyth. 'Transferred Loyalties: Orangeism in the United States and Ontario'. *American Review of Canadian Studies* 14, no. 2 (Summer 1984): 193–211.

Jackson, Alvin. 'Irish Unionism and the Russellite Threat, 1894–1906'. *Irish Historical Studies* 25, no. 100 (Nov 1987): 376–404.

—— 'Unionist Myths, 1912–1985'. *Past & Present* 136 (Aug 1992): 164–185.

—— 'Irish Unionist Imagery, 1850–1920'. In *Returning to Ourselves: Second Volume of Papers from the John Hewitt International Summer School*, edited by Eve Patten. Belfast: Lagan Press, 1995.

—— 'Irish Unionism'. In *The Making of Modern Irish History: Revisionism and the Revisionist Controversy*, edited by D. George Boyce and Alan O'Day. London: Routledge, 1996.

—— 'Irish Unionism, 1870–1922'. In *Defenders of the Union: A Survey of British and Irish Unionism since 1801*, edited by D. George Boyce and Alan O'Day. London: Routledge, 2001.

Jenkins, William. 'Views from the "Hub of Empire": Loyal Orange Lodges in Early-Twentieth-Century Toronto'. In *The Orange Order in Canada*, edited by David A. Wilson. Dublin: Four Courts Press, 2007.

—— 'Ulster Transplanted: Irish Protestants, Everyday Life and Constructions of Identity in Late Victorian Toronto'. In *Irish Protestant Identities*, edited by Mervyn Busteed, Frank Neal, and Jonathan Tonge. Manchester: Manchester University Press, 2008.

Jones, Maldwyn A. 'Ulster Emigration, 1783–1815'. In *Essays in Scotch-Irish History*, edited by E.R.R. Green. Belfast: Ulster Historical Foundation, 1969.

—— 'Scotch-Irish'. In *Harvard Encyclopedia of American Ethnic Groups*, edited by Stephan Thernstrom. Cambridge, Mass.: Harvard University Press, 1980.

Keller, Kenneth W. 'What is Distinctive about the Scotch-Irish?' In *Appalachian Frontiers: Settlement, Society & Development in the Pre-Industrial Era*, edited by Robert D. Mitchell. Lexington: University Press of Kentucky, 1991.

Kelly, Mary C. 'The Hand of Friendship: Protestants, Irish Americans, and 1916-Era Nationalism'. In *Ireland's Allies: America and the 1916 Easter Rising*, edited by Miriam Nyhan Grey. Dublin: University College Dublin Press, 2016.

Kennedy, Billy. 'The Orange Family Worldwide: Canada'. In *A Celebration, 1690–1990: The Orange Institution*, edited by Billy Kennedy. Belfast: Grand Orange Lodge of Ireland, 1990.

—— 'The Ulster-Scots in the USA Today: How the Bonds Remain'. Belfast: Ulster-Scots Agency, 2009.

Kennedy, B.A. 'Sharman Crawford's Federal Scheme for Ireland'. In *Essays in British and Irish History in Honour of James Eadie Todd*, edited by H.A. Cronne, T.W. Moody, and D.B. Quinn. London: Muller, 1949.

Kennedy, Líam. 'The Rural Economy, 1820–1914'. In *An Economic History of Ulster, 1820–1939*, edited by Líam Kennedy and Philip Ollerenshaw. Manchester: Manchester University Press, 1985.

Kennedy, Thomas C. 'War, Patriotism, and the Ulster Unionist Council, 1914–18'. *Éire-Ireland* 40, no. 3/4 (Fall/Winter 2005): 198–211.

Kenny, Kevin. 'Diaspora and Comparison: The Global Irish as a Case Study'. *Journal of American History* 90, no. 1 (Jun 2002): 134–162.

—— 'The Irish in the Empire'. In *Ireland and the British Empire*, edited by Kevin Kenny. Oxford: Oxford University Press, 2004.

—— '"Freedom and Unity": Lincoln in Irish Political Discourse'. In *The Global Lincoln*, edited by Richard Carwardine and Jay Sexton. Oxford: Oxford University Press, 2011.

King, Carla. 'Defenders of the Union: Sir Horace Plunkett'. In *Defenders of the Union: A Survey of British and Irish Unionism since 1801*, edited by D. George Boyce and Alan O'Day. London: Routledge, 2001.

Leary, William M., Jr. 'Woodrow Wilson, Irish Americans, and the Election of 1916'. *Journal of American History* 54, no. 1 (Jun 1967): 57–72.

Lee, J.J. 'Introduction: Interpreting Irish America'. In *Making the Irish American: History and Heritage of the Irish in the United States*, edited by J.J. Lee and Marion R. Casey. New York: New York University Press, 2006.

Light, Dale B., Jr. 'The Role of Irish-American Organisations in Assimilation and Community Formation'. In *The Irish in America: Emigration, Assimilation, and Impact*, Irish Studies 4, edited by P.J. Drudy. Cambridge: Cambridge University Press, 1985.

Livingstone, David N. 'Darwinism and Calvinism: The Belfast-Princeton Connection'. *Isis* 83, no. 3 (Sep 1992): 408–428.

—— 'James McCosh and the Scottish Intellectual Tradition'. In *Queen's Thinkers: Essays on the Intellectual Heritage of a University*, edited by Alvin Jackson and David N. Livingstone. Belfast: Blackstaff Press, 2008.

Long, S.E. 'Belfast County Grand Orange Lodge Centenary: Official History 1863–1963'. n.p.: Universal Publishing, 1963.

—— 'The Orange Family Worldwide: The United States of America'. In *A Celebration, 1690–1990: The Orange Institution*, edited by Billy Kennedy. Belfast: Grand Orange Lodge of Ireland, 1990.

Loughlin, James. 'Joseph Chamberlain, English Nationalism, and the Ulster Question'. *History* 77, no. 250 (Jun 1992): 202–219.

Lowry, Donal. 'Ulster Resistance and Loyalist Rebellion in the Empire.' In *'An Irish Empire'? Aspects of Ireland and the British Empire*, edited by Keith Jeffery. Manchester: Manchester University Press, 1996.

Lyons, F.S.L. 'The Irish Unionist Party and the Devolution Crisis of 1904–5'. *Irish Historical Studies* 6, no. 21 (Mar 1948): 1–22.

—— '"Parnellism and Crime", 1887–90'. *Transactions of the Royal Historical Society* 5th Ser., no. 24 (1974): 123–140.

—— 'The Watershed, 1903–7'. In *A New History of Ireland: Ireland Under the Union II, 1871–1921*, edited by W.E. Vaughan. Oxford: Oxford University Press, 2010.

McAuley, James White. 'Under an Orange Banner: Reflections on the Northern Protestant Experiences of Emigration'. In *The Irish World Wide, Vol. 5: Religion and Identity*, edited by Patrick O'Sullivan. London: Leicester University Press, 1996.

McBride, Ian. 'Ulster and the British Problem'. In *Unionism in Modern Ireland: New Perspectives on Politics and Culture*, edited by Richard English and Graham Walker. Basingstoke: Macmillan, 1996.

McCaffrey, Lawrence J. 'Irish Federalism in the 1870's: A Study in Conservative Nationalism'. *Transactions of the American Philosophical Society* n.s., 52, no. 6 (1962): 1–58.

—— 'Diaspora Comparisons and Irish-American Uniqueness'. In *New Perspectives on the Irish Diaspora*, edited by Charles Fanning. Carbondale: Southern Illinois University Press, 2000.

McCall, Cathal. 'Political Transformation and the Reinvention of the Ulster Scots Identity and Culture'. *Identities: Global Studies in Culture and Power* 9, no. 2 (Jan 2002): 197–218.

McCarthy, Dennis J. 'The British'. In *The Immigrants' Influence on Wilson's Peace Policies*, edited by Joseph P. O'Grady. Lexington: University of Kentucky Press, 1967.

Mac Ginty, Roger. 'Post-Agreement Loyalism and the International Dimension'. In *Ulster Loyalism after the Good Friday Agreement: History, Conflict, and Change*, edited by James W. McAuley and Graham Spencer. Basingstoke: Palgrave Macmillan, 2011.

McKee, Matthew. '"A Peculiar and Royal Race": Creating a Scotch-Irish Identity, 1889–1901'. In *Atlantic Crossroads: Historical Connections between Scotland, Ulster, and North America*, edited by Patrick Fitzgerald and S.J.S. Ickringill. Newtownards: Colourpoint, 2001.

McKivigan, John R., and Thomas J. Robertson. 'The Irish American Worker in Transition, 1877–1914: New York City as a Test Case'. In *The New York Irish*, edited by Ronald H. Bayor and Timothy J. Meagher. Baltimore: Johns Hopkins University Press, 1996.

McLoughlin, Robert. 'Irish Nationalism and Orange Unionism in Canada: A Reappraisal'. *Éire-Ireland* 41, no. 3/4 (Fall/Winter 2006): 80–109.

McNickle, Chris. 'When New York Was Irish, and After'. In *The New York Irish*, edited by Ronald H. Bayor and Timothy J. Meagher. Baltimore: Johns Hopkins University Press, 1996.

MacRaild, Donald M. 'Crossing Migrant Frontiers: Comparative Reflections on Irish Migrants in Britain and the United States During the Nineteenth Century'. *Immigrants and Minorities* 18, no. 2/3 (Jul/Nov 1999): 40–70.

—— 'The Associationalism of the Orange Diaspora'. In *The Orange Order in Canada*, edited by David A. Wilson. Dublin: Four Courts Press, 2007.

—— 'The Orange Atlantic'. In *The Irish in the Atlantic World*, edited by David T. Gleeson. Columbia: University of South Carolina Press, 2010.

MacRaild, Donald M., and Malcolm Smith. 'Migration and Emigration'. In *Ulster since 1600: Politics, Economy, and Society*, edited by Líam Kennedy and Philip Ollerenshaw. Oxford: Oxford University Press, 2013.

Meagher, Timothy J. Introduction to *From Paddy to Studs: Irish-American Communities in the Turn of the Century Era, 1880 to 1920*, edited by Timothy J. Meagher. New York: Greenwood Press, 1986.

Megahey, Alan. '"God Will Defend the Right": The Protestant Churches and Opposition to Home Rule'. In *Defenders of the Union: A Survey of British and Irish Unionism since 1801*, edited by D. George Boyce and Alan O'Day. London: Routledge, 2001.

Miller, David W. 'Religious Commotions in the Scottish Diaspora: A Transatlantic Perspective on "Evangelicalism" in Mainline Denomination'. In *Ulster Presbyterians in the Atlantic World: Religion, Politics, and Identity*, edited by David A. Wilson and Mark G. Spencer. Dublin: Four Courts Press, 2006.

Miller, Kerby A. 'Class, Culture, and Immigrant Group Identity in the United States: The Case of Irish-American Ethnicity'. In *Immigration Reconsidered: History, Sociology, and Politics*, edited by Virginia Yans-McLaughlin. New York: Oxford University Press, 1990.

—— '"Scotch-Irish" Myths and "Irish" Identities in Eighteenth- and Nineteenth-Century America'. In *New Perspectives on the Irish Diaspora*, edited by Charles Fanning. Carbondale: Southern Illinois University Press, 2000.

—— 'Ulster Presbyterians and the "Two Traditions" in Ireland and America'. In *Making the Irish American: History and Heritage of the Irish in the United States*, edited by J.J. Lee and Marion R. Casey. New York: New York University Press, 2006.

Miller, Kerby A., Bruce D. Boiling, and Líam Kennedy. 'The Famine's Scars: William Murphy's Ulster and American Odyssey'. In *New Directions in Irish-American History*, edited by Kevin Kenny. Madison: University of Wisconsin Press, 2003.

Montgomery, Eric. 'The Scotch-Irish and Ulster'. Belfast: Ulster-Scot Historical Foundation, 1971.

Moody, T.W. 'The New Departure in Irish Politics, 1878–9'. In *Essays in British and Irish History in Honour of James Eadie Todd*, edited by H.A. Cronne, T.W. Moody and D.B. Quinn. London: Muller, 1949.

—— 'Irish-American Nationalists'. *Irish Historical Studies* 15, no. 60 (Sep 1967): 438–445.

Murphy, Richard. 'Faction in the Conservative Party and the Home Rule Crisis, 1912–14'. *History* 71 (1986): 222–234.

O'Day, Alan. 'The Ulster Crisis: A Conundrum'. In *The Ulster Crisis, 1885–1921*, edited by D. George Boyce and Alan O'Day. Basingstoke: Palgrave Macmillan, 2006.

Ó Dochartaigh, Niall. 'Reforming Online: Ulster Loyalists Imagine an American Audience'. *Identities* 16, no. 1 (2009): 102–127.

Ó Gráda, Cormac. 'Irish Emigration to the United States in the Nineteenth Century'. In *America and Ireland, 1776–1976: The American Identity and the Irish Connection*, edited by David N. Doyle and Owen Dudley Edwards. Westport, Conn.: Greenwood Press, 1980.

Ollerenshaw, Philip. 'Industry, 1820–1914'. In *An Economic History of Ulster, 1820–1939*, edited by Líam Kennedy and Philip Ollerenshaw. Manchester: Manchester University Press, 1985.

Peatling, G.K. 'Unionist Identity, External Perceptions of Northern Ireland, and the Problem of Unionist Legitimacy'. *Éire-Ireland* 39, no. 1/2 (Spring/Summer 2004): 215–236.

—— 'Thomas Dixon, Scotch-Irish Identity, and the "Southern People"'. *Safundi* 9, no. 3 (Jul 2008): 239–256.

Pinder, John. 'The Federal Idea and the British Liberal Tradition'. In *The Federal Idea, Vol. I: The History of Federalism from Enlightenment to 1945*, edited by Andrea Bosco. London: Lothian Foundation Press, 1991.

Pocock, J.G.A. 'The Union in British History'. *Transactions of the Royal Historical Society* 6th Ser., Vol. 10 (2000): 181–196.

Quinault, R.E. 'Lord Randolph Churchill and Home Rule'. In *Reactions to Irish Nationalism*. London: Hambledon Press, 1987.

Ritchie, Daniel. 'Transatlantic Delusions and Pro-slavery Religion: Isaac Nelson's Evangelical Abolitionist Critique of Revivalism in America and Ulster'. *Journal of American Studies* 48, no. 3 (2014): 757–776.

—— 'William McIlwaine and the 1859 Revival in Ulster: A Study of Anglican and Evangelical Identities'. *Journal of Ecclesiastical History* 65, no. 4 (Oct 2014): 803–826.

Savage, D.C. 'The Origins of the Ulster Unionist Party, 1885–1886'. *Irish Historical Studies* 12, no. 47 (Mar 1961): 185–208.

Schlesinger, Arthur M. 'Biography of a Nation of Joiners'. *American Historical Review* 50, no. 1 (Oct 1944): 1–25.

Schmuhl, Robert. 'Bifocalism of US Press Coverage: The Easter Rising and Irish America'. In *Ireland's Allies: America and the 1916 Easter Rising*, edited by Miriam Nyhan Grey. Dublin: University College Dublin Press, 2016.

Sewell, M.J. 'Rebels or Revolutionaries? Irish-American Nationalism and American Diplomacy, 1865–1885'. *Historical Journal* 29, no. 3 (Sep 1986): 723–733.

Smith, Jeremy. 'Bluff, Bluster and Brinkmanship: Andrew Bonar Law and the Third Home Rule Bill'. *Historical Journal* 36, no. 1 (1993): 161–178.

Thompson, J. Lee. '"To Tell the People of America the Truth": Lord Northcliffe in the USA, Unofficial British Propaganda, June–November 1917'. *Journal of Contemporary History* 34, no. 2 (Apr 1999): 243–262.

Tulloch, H.A. 'Changing British Attitudes Towards the United States in the 1880s'. *Historical Journal* 20, no. 4 (Dec 1977): 825–840.

Urquhart, Diane. '"The Female of the Species Is More Deadlier Than the Male"? The Ulster Women's Unionist Council, 1911–40'. In *Coming into the Light: The Work, Politics, and Religion of Women in Ulster, 1840–1940*, edited by Janice Holmes and Diane Urquhart. Belfast: Institute of Irish Studies, 1994.

Walker, Brian M. 'The Land Question and Elections in Ulster, 1868–86.' In *Irish Peasants: Violence and Political Unrest, 1780–1914*, edited by Samuel Clark and James S. Donnelly, Jr. Madison: University of Wisconsin Press, 1983.

Walker, Graham. 'Empire, Religion and Nationality in Scotland and Ulster before the First World War'. In *Scotland and Ulster*, edited by Ian S. Wood. Edinburgh: Mercat Press, 1994.

—— 'Scotland and Ulster: Political Interactions since the Late Nineteenth Century and Possibilities of Contemporary Dialogue'. In *Cultural Traditions in Northern Ireland*, edited by John Erskine and Gordon Lucy. Belfast: Queens University Press, 1997.

—— 'Ulster Unionism and the Scottish Dimension'. In *Ulster and Scotland, 1600–2000: History, Language, and Identity*, edited by William Kelly and John R. Young. Dublin: Four Courts Press, 2004.

Ward, Alan J. 'Frewen's Anglo-American Campaign for Federalism, 1910–1921'. *Irish Historical Studies* 15, no. 59 (Mar 1967): 256–275.

—— 'America and the Irish Problem, 1899–1921'. *Irish Historical Studies* 16, no. 61 (Mar 1968): 64–90.

Whelan, Bernadette. 'The Wilson Administration and the 1916 Rising'. In *The Impact of the 1916 Rising Among the Nations*, edited by Ruán O'Donnell. Dublin: Irish Academic Press, 2008.

Wiedenhoft Murphy, Wendy Ann, and Mindy Peden. 'Ulster-Scots Diaspora: Articulating a Politics of Identification after "the Peace" in Northern Ireland'. In *Lessons from the Northern Ireland Peace Process*, edited by Timothy J. White. Madison: University of Wisconsin Press, 2013.

Wilson, Andrew J. 'The Billy Boys Meet Slick Willy: The Ulster Unionist Party and the American Dimension to the Northern Ireland Peace Process, 1994–9'. *Irish Studies in International Affairs* 11 (2000): 121–136.

—— 'Maintaining the Cause in the Land of the Free: Ulster Unionists and US Involvement in the Northern Ireland Conflict, 1968–72'. *Éire-Ireland* 40, no. 3/4 (Fall/Winter 2005): 212–39.

—— 'Ulster Unionists in America, 1972–1985'. *New Hibernia Review* 11, no. 1 (Spring 2007): 50–73.

Wilson, David A. 'The Irish in Canada'. Ottawa: Canadian Historical Association, 1989.

—— Introduction to *The Orange Order in Canada*, edited by David A. Wilson. Dublin: Four Courts Press, 2007.

Wolffe, John. 'Anti-Catholicism and Evangelical Identity in Britain and the United States, 1830–1860'. In *Evangelicalism: Comparative Studies of Popular Protestantism in North America, the British Isles, and Beyond, 1700–1990*, edited by Mark A. Noll, David W. Bebbington and George A. Rawlyk. New York: Oxford University Press, 1994.

Books

Adams, William Forbes. *Ireland and Irish Emigration to the New World from 1815 to the Famine*. New York: Russell & Russell, 1932.

Ahlstrom, Sydney E. *A Religious History of the American People*. New Haven, Conn.: Yale University Press, 1972.

Akenson, Donald H. *God's Peoples: Covenant and Land in South Africa, Israel, and Ulster*. Ithaca, NY: Cornell University Press, 1992.

—— *The Irish Diaspora: A Primer*. Toronto: P.D. Meany, 1993.

Allen, H.C. *Great Britain and the United States: A History of Anglo-American Relations, 1783–1952*. Hamden, Conn.: Archon, 1969.

Anbinder, Tyler. *Nativism and Slavery: The Northern Know Nothings and the Politics of the 1850s*. New York: Oxford University Press, 1992.

Anderson, Stuart. *Race and Rapprochement: Anglo-Saxonism and Anglo-American Relations, 1895–1904*. Rutherford, NJ: Farleigh Dickinson University Press, 1981.

Appel, John J. *Immigrant Historical Societies in the United States, 1880–1950*. New York: Arno, 1980.

Archdeacon, Thomas J. *Becoming American: An Ethnic History*. New York: Free Press, 1983.

Bagwell, Philip S., and G.E. Mingay. *Britain and America, 1850–1939: A Study of Economic Change*. London: Routledge & Kegan Paul, 1970.

Bebbington, David W. *Evangelicalism in Modern Britain: A History from the 1730s to the 1980s*. London: Routledge, 1989.

—— *William Ewart Gladstone: Faith and Politics in Victorian Britain*. Grand Rapids: William B. Eerdmans, 1993.

Beckett, J.C. *The Anglo-Irish Tradition*. London: Faber and Faber, 1976.

Bell, Duncan. *The Idea of Greater Britain: Empire and the Future of World Order, 1860–1900*. Princeton, NJ: Princeton University Press, 2007.

Berthoff, Rowland Tappan. *British Immigrants in Industrial America, 1790–1950*. Cambridge, Mass.: Harvard University Press, 1953.

Bew, Paul. *Ideology and the Irish Question*. Oxford: Clarendon Press, 1994.

—— *Ireland: The Politics of Enmity 1789–2006*. Oxford: Oxford University Press, 2007.

Biagini, Eugenio F. *British Democracy and Irish Nationalism 1876–1906*. Cambridge: Cambridge University Press, 2007.

Billington, Ray Allen. *The Protestant Crusade 1800–1860: A Study of the Origins of American Nativism*. New York: Macmillan, 1938.

Boyce, D. George. *The Irish Question and British Politics, 1868–1996*. 2nd edn. Basingstoke: Macmillan, 1996.

Brooke, Peter. *Ulster Presbyterianism: The Historical Perspective, 1610–1970*. Dublin: Gill and Macmillan, 1987.

Brown, Thomas N. *Irish-American Nationalism, 1870–1890*. Philadelphia: Lippincott, 1966.

Bruce, Steve. *God Save Ulster: The Religion and Politics of Paisleyism*. Oxford: Clarendon Press, 1986.

Brundage, David. *Irish Nationalists in America: The Politics of Exile, 1798–1998*. New York: Oxford University Press, 2016.

Buckland, Patrick. *Irish Unionism I: The Anglo-Irish and the New Ireland, 1885–1920*. Dublin: Gill and Macmillan, 1972.

—— *Irish Unionism II: Ulster Unionism and the Origins of Northern Ireland, 1886–1922*. Dublin: Gill and Macmillan, 1973.

—— *Irish Unionism, 1885–1922*. London: Historical Association, 1973.

Burgess, Michael. *The British Tradition of Federalism*. London: Leicester University Press, 1995.

Butler, Leslie. *Critical Americans: Victorian Intellectuals and Transatlantic Liberal Reform*. Chapel Hill: University of North Carolina Press, 2007.

Campbell, Charles S. *Anglo-American Understanding, 1898–1903*. Baltimore: Johns Hopkins University Press, 1957.

Campbell, Malcolm. *Ireland's New Worlds: Immigrants, Politics, and Society in the United States and Australia, 1815–1922*. Madison: University of Wisconsin Press, 2007.

Carroll, Francis M. *American Opinion and the Irish Question, 1910–23: A Study in Opinion and Policy*. Dublin: Gill and Macmillan, 1978.

—— *The American Presence in Ulster: A Diplomatic History, 1796–1996*. Washington, DC: Catholic University of America Press, 2005.

Carwardine, Richard. *Transatlantic Revivalism: Popular Evangelicalism in Britain and America, 1790–1865*. Westport, Conn.: Greenwood Press, 1978.

Clergy of Down and Dromore. 2 vols. Belfast: Ulster Historical Foundation, 1996.

Cole, J.A. *Prince of Spies: Henri Le Caron*. London: Faber and Faber, 1984.

Colley, Linda. *Britons: Forging the Nation, 1707–1837*. New Haven, Conn.: Yale University Press, 1992.

Comerford, R.V. *The Fenians in Context: Irish Politics and Society, 1848–82*. Dublin: Wolfhound, 1985.

Cooney, Dudley Levistone. *The Methodists in Ireland: A Short History*. Blackrock: Columba, 2001.

Cronin, Seán. *Washington's Irish Policy, 1916–1986: Independence, Partition, Neutrality*. Dublin: Anvil, 1987.

Curtis, L.P., Jr. *Coercion and Conciliation in Ireland, 1880–1892: A Study in Conservative Unionism*. Princeton, NJ: Princeton University Press, 1963.

—— *Anglo-Saxons and Celts: A Study of Anti-Irish Prejudice in Victorian England*. Bridgeport, Conn.: University of Bridgeport, 1968.

Daniels, Roger. *Not Like Us: Immigrants and Minorities in America, 1890–1924*. Chicago: Ivan R. Dee, 1997.

Dewar, M.W., John Brown, and S.E. Long. *Orangeism: A New Historical Appreciation*. Belfast: Grand Orange Lodge of Ireland, 1967.

Dinnerstein, Leonard, Roger L. Nichols, and David M. Reimers. *Natives and Strangers: A History of Ethnic Americans*, 5th edn. Oxford: Oxford University Press, 2010.

Edwards, Owen Dudley. *Éamon De Valera*. Cardiff: GPC, 1987.

English, Richard. *Irish Freedom: The History of Nationalism in Ireland*. London: Macmillan, 2006.

Erickson, Charlotte. *Invisible Immigrants: The Adaptation of English and Scottish Immigrants in Nineteenth-Century America*. London: Weidenfeld & Nicolson, 1972.

Farrell, Sean. *Rituals and Riots: Sectarian Violence and Political Culture in Ulster, 1784–1886*. Lexington: University Press of Kentucky, 2000.

Farrington, Christopher. *Ulster Unionism and the Peace Process in Northern Ireland*. Basingstoke: Palgrave Macmillan, 2006.

Foster, R.F. *Charles Stewart Parnell: The Man and His Family*. Hassocks: Harvester, 1976.

—— *Lord Randolph Churchill: A Political Life*. Oxford: Clarendon Press, 1981.

—— *Modern Ireland, 1600–1972*. Harmondsworth: Penguin, 1988.

—— *Paddy and Mr. Punch: Connections in Irish and English History*. London: Allen Lane, 1993.

Frazer-Hurst, D. *'Wylie Blue': The Life of the Rev. A. Wylie Blue, D.D.* London: James Clarke, 1957.

Funchion, Michael F. *Irish American Voluntary Organizations*. Westport, Conn.: Greenwood Press, 1983.

Gammie, Alexander. *Rev. John McNeill: His Life and Work*. London: Pickering & Inglis, 1933.

Gantt, Jonathan. *Irish Terrorism in the Atlantic Community, 1865–1922*. London: Palgrave Macmillan, 2010.

Gerlach, Murney. *British Liberalism and the United States: Political and Social Thought in the Late Victorian Age*. Basingstoke: Palgrave, 2001.

Gibbon, Peter. *The Origins of Ulster Unionism: The Formation of Popular Protestant Politics and Ideology in Nineteenth-Century Ireland*. Manchester: Manchester University Press, 1975.

Gordon, Michael A. *The Orange Riots: Irish Political Violence in New York City, 1870 and 1871*. Ithaca, NY: Cornell University Press, 1993.

Griffin, Patrick. *The People with No Name: Ireland's Ulster Scots, America's Scots Irish, and the Creation of a British Atlantic World, 1689–1764*. Princeton, NJ: Princeton University Press, 2001.

Guelke, Adrian. *Northern Ireland: The International Perspective*. Dublin: Gill and Macmillan, 1988.

Hall, Thomas C. *John Hall, Pastor and Preacher: A Biography*. New York: Fleming H. Revell, 1901.

Hannigan, Dave. *De Valera in America: The Rebel President's 1919 Campaign*. Dublin: O'Brien, 2008.

Harbinson, John. *The Ulster Unionist Party, 1882–1973: Its Development and Organisation*. Belfast: Blackstaff, 1973.

Hartley, Stephen. *The Irish Question as a Problem in British Foreign Policy, 1914–18*. Basingstoke: Macmillan Press, 1987.

Hartley, Tom. *Written in Stone: The History of Belfast City Cemetery*. Belfast: Brehon, 2006.

Harvie, Christopher. *The Lights of Liberalism: University Liberals and the Challenge of Democracy, 1860–86*. London: Allen Lane, 1976.

—— *A Floating Commonwealth: Politics, Culture, and Technology on Britain's Atlantic Coast, 1860–1930*. Oxford: Oxford University Press, 2008.

Hempton, David. *Religion and Political Culture in Britain and Ireland: From the Glorious Revolution to the Decline of Empire*. Cambridge: Cambridge University Press, 1996.

Hempton, David, and Myrtle Hill. *Evangelical Protestantism in Ulster Society, 1740–1890*. London: Routledge, 1992.

Hennessey, Thomas. *Dividing Ireland: World War I and Partition*. London: Routledge, 1998.

Hernon, Joseph M., Jr. *Celts, Catholics & Copperheads: Ireland Views the American Civil War*. Columbus: Ohio State University Press, 1968.

Higham, John. *Strangers in the Land: Patterns of American Nativism, 1860–1925*. New Brunswick, NJ: Rutgers University Press, 1955.

Hirst, Caroline. *Religion, Politics and Violence in Nineteenth-Century Belfast: The Pound and Sandy Row*. Dublin: Four Courts Press, 2002.

Holmes, R.F.G. *Our Irish Presbyterian Heritage*. Belfast: W&G Baird, 1985.

Hook, Andrew. *Scotland and America: A Study of Cultural Relations, 1750–1835*. Glasgow: Blackie, 1975.

Houston, Cecil J., and William J. Smyth. *The Sash Canada Wore: A Historical Geography of the Orange Order in Canada*. Toronto: University of Toronto Press, 1980.

—— *Irish Emigration and Canadian Settlement: Patterns, Links, and Letters*. Toronto: University of Toronto Press, 1990.

Hyde, H. Montgomery. *Carson: The Life of Sir Edward Carson, Lord Carson of Duncairn*. Melbourne: William Heinemann, 1953.

Iriye, Akira, and Pierre-Yves Saunier, eds. *The Palgrave Dictionary of Transnational History: From the Mid-19th Century to the Present Day*. Basingstoke: Palgrave, 2009.

Jackson, Alvin. *The Ulster Party: Irish Unionists in the House of Commons, 1884–1911*. Oxford: Clarendon Press, 1989.

—— *Sir Edward Carson*. Dublin: Historical Association of Ireland, 1993.

—— *Colonel Edward Saunderson: Land and Loyalty in Victorian Ireland*. Oxford: Clarendon Press, 1995.

—— *Ireland, 1798–1998*. Oxford: Blackwell, 1999.

—— *Home Rule: An Irish History, 1800–2000*. Oxford: Oxford University Press, 2003.

Jackson, Daniel M. *Popular Opposition to Irish Home Rule in Edwardian Britain.* Liverpool: Liverpool University Press, 2009.

Janis, Ely M. *A Greater Ireland: The Land League and Transatlantic Nationalism in Gilded Age America.* Madison: University of Wisconsin Press, 2015.

Jones, Howard. *Abraham Lincoln and a New Birth of Freedom: The Union and Slavery in the Diplomacy of the Civil War.* Lincoln: University of Nebraska Press, 1999.

Jordan, Richard Lawrence. *The Second Coming of Paisley: Militant Fundamentalism and Ulster Politics.* Syracuse, NY: Syracuse University Press, 2013.

Kaufman, Jason. *For the Common Good? American Civic Life and the Golden Age of Fraternity.* Oxford: Oxford University Press, 2002.

Kendle, John. *The Round Table Movement and Imperial Union.* Toronto: University of Toronto Press, 1975.

—— *Ireland and the Federal Solution: The Debate over the United Kingdom Constitution, 1870–1921.* Kingston: McGill-Queen's University Press, 1989.

—— *Federal Britain: A History.* London: Routledge, 1997.

Kennedy, Billy. *The Making of America: How the Scots-Irish Shaped a Nation.* Greenville, SC: Ambassador, 2001.

Kenny, Kevin. *Making Sense of the Molly Maguires.* New York: Oxford University Press, 1998.

—— *The American Irish: A History.* Harlow: Longman, 2000.

Keown, Gerard. *First of the Small Nations: The Beginnings of Irish Foreign Policy in the Interwar Years, 1919–1932.* Oxford: Oxford University Press, 2016.

Kinealy, Christine. *Repeal and Revolution: 1848 in Ireland.* Manchester: Manchester University Press, 2009.

King, Carla. *Michael Davitt.* Dundalk: Dundalgan, 1999.

Kinghan, Nancy. *United We Stood: The Story of the Ulster Women's Unionist Council, 1911–1974.* Belfast: Appletree, 1975.

Kinzer, Donald L. *An Episode in Anti-Catholicism: The American Protective Association.* Seattle: University of Washington Press, 1964.

Leyburn, James G. *The Scotch-Irish: A Social History.* Chapel Hill: University of North Carolina Press, 1962.

Livingstone, David N., and Ronald A. Wells. *Ulster-American Religion: Episodes in the History of a Cultural Connection.* Notre Dame, Ind.: University of Notre Dame Press, 1999.

Longford, Frank Pakenham, Earl of, and Thomas P. O'Neill. *Eamon De Valera.* London: Hutchinson, 1970.

Loughlin, James. *Ulster Unionism and British National Identity since 1885.* London: Pinter, 1995.

—— *The Ulster Question since 1945.* 2nd edn. Basingstoke: Palgrave, 2004.

Lucas, Reginald. *Colonel Saunderson, M.P.: A Memoir.* London: John Murray, 1908.

Lyon, Peter. *Success Story: The Life and Times of S.S. McClure.* New York: Charles Scribner's Sons, 1963.

Lyons, F.S.L. *Charles Stewart Parnell.* London: Collins, 1977.

McAuley, James W. *Ulster's Last Stand? Reconstructing Unionism after the Peace Process.* Dublin: Irish Academic Press, 2010.

McBride, Ian. *Scripture Politics: Ulster Presbyterians and Irish Radicalism in the Late Eighteenth Century.* Oxford: Clarendon Press, 1998.

McCaffrey, Lawrence J. *Textures of Irish America.* Syracuse, NY: Syracuse University Press, 1992.

McCarthy, Angela, ed. *Ireland in the World: Comparative, Transnational, and Personal Perspectives.* New York: Routledge, 2015.

McClelland, Aiken. *William Johnston of Ballykilbeg.* Lurgan: Ulster Society Publications, 1990.

McDowell, R.B. *The Irish Convention, 1917–18.* London: Routledge & Kegan Paul, 1970.

McGaughey, Jane G.V. *Ulster's Men: Protestant Unionist Masculinities and Militarization in the North of Ireland, 1912–1923.* Montreal: McGill-Queen's University Press, 2012.

McIntosh, Gillian. *The Force of Culture: Unionist Identities in Twentieth-Century Ireland.* Cork: Cork University Press, 1999.

McLoughlin, William G. *Modern Revivalism: Charles Grandison Finney to Billy Graham.* New York: Ronald Press, 1959.

—— *Revivals, Awakenings, and Reform: An Essay on Religion and Social Change in America, 1607–1977.* Chicago: University of Chicago Press, 1978.

MacRaild, Donald M. *Faith, Fraternity and Fighting: The Orange Order and Irish Migrants in Northern England, c.1850–1920.* Liverpool: Liverpool University Press, 2005.

Mansergh, Nicholas. *The Irish Question, 1840–1921: A Commentary on Anglo-Irish Relations and on Social and Political Forces in Ireland in the Age of Reform and Revolution.* Toronto: University of Toronto Press, 1975.

—— *The Unresolved Question: The Anglo-Irish Settlement and Its Undoing, 1912–72.* New Haven, Conn.: Yale University Press, 1991.

Marshall, William F. *Ulster Sails West: The Story of the Great Emigration from Ulster to North America in the 18th Century.* Baltimore: Genealogical Publishing Company, 1984.

Miller, David W. *Queen's Rebels: Ulster Loyalism in Historical Perspective.* Dublin: University College Dublin Press, 2007.

Miller, Kerby A. *Emigrants and Exiles: Ireland and the Irish Exodus to North America.* New York: Oxford University Press, 1985.

—— *Ireland and Irish America: Culture, Class, and Transatlantic Migration.* Dublin: Field Day, 2008.

O'Brien, Conor Cruise. *Parnell and His Party, 1880–90.* Oxford: Clarendon Press, 1957.

O'Callaghan, Margaret. *British High Politics and a Nationalist Ireland: Criminality, Land and the Law under Forster and Balfour.* New York: St. Martin's, 1994.

O'Connell, Maurice R. *Irish Politics and Social Conflict in the Age of the American Revolution.* Philadelphia: University of Pennsylvania Press, 1965.

O'Connor, Thomas H. *The Boston Irish: A Political History.* Boston: Northeastern University Press, 1995.

O'Day, Alan. *Irish Home Rule, 1867–1921.* Manchester: Manchester University Press, 1998.

Ó Gráda, Cormac. *Ireland: A New Economic History, 1780–1939.* Oxford: Clarendon Press, 1994.

Peatling, G.K. *British Opinion and Irish Self-Government, 1865–1925: From Unionism to Liberal Commonwealth.* Dublin: Irish Academic Press, 2001.

Pletcher, David M. *The Awkward Years: American Foreign Relations under Garfield and Arthur*. Columbia: University of Missouri Press, 1961.

Pradervand, Marcel. *A Century of Service: A History of the World Alliance of Reformed Churches, 1875–1975*. Edinburgh: Saint Andrew Press, 1975.

Ryan, Mary P. *Civic Wars: Democracy and Public Life in the American City During the Nineteenth Century*. Berkeley: University of California Press, 1997.

Sanders, M.L., and Philip M. Taylor. *British Propaganda During the First World War, 1914–18*. London: Macmillan, 1982.

Schmuhl, Robert. *Ireland's Exiled Children: America and the Easter Rising*. Oxford: Oxford University Press, 2016.

Scholes, Andrew. *The Church of Ireland and the Third Home Rule Bill*. Dublin: Irish Academic Press, 2010.

Schrier, Arnold. *Ireland and the American Emigration, 1850–1900*. Minneapolis: University of Minnesota Press, 1958.

Shannon, William V. *The American Irish*. New York: Macmillan, 1963.

Sherling, Rankin. *The Invisible Irish: Finding Protestants in the Nineteenth-Century Migrations to America*. Montreal and Kingston: McGill-Queen's University Press, 2016.

Short, K.R.M. *The Dynamite War: Irish-American Bombers in Victorian Britain*. Dublin: Gill and Macmillan, 1979.

Sibbett, R.M. *Orangeism in Ireland and throughout the Empire*. 2 vols. Belfast: Henderson, 1915.

Sim, David. *A Union Forever: The Irish Question and U.S. Foreign Relations in the Victorian Era*. Ithaca, NY: Cornell University Press, 2013.

Small, Stephen. *Political Thought in Ireland, 1776–1798: Republicanism, Patriotism, and Radicalism*. Oxford: Oxford University Press, 2002.

Smith, Anthony D. *The Ethnic Origins of Nations*. Oxford: Basil Blackwell, 1986.

Smithey, Lee A. *Unionists, Loyalists, and Conflict Transformation in Northern Ireland*. Oxford: Oxford University Press, 2011.

Smyth, William J. *Toronto, The Belfast of Canada: The Orange Order and the Shaping of Municipal Culture*. Toronto: University of Toronto Press, 2015.

Stewart, A.T.Q. *The Ulster Crisis: Resistance to Home Rule, 1912–1914*. London: Faber, 1967.

—— *The Narrow Ground: Aspects of Ulster, 1609–1969*. Belfast: Blackstaff, 1997.

Thompson, Frank. *The End of Liberal Ulster: Land Agitation and Land Reform, 1868–1886*. Belfast: Ulster Historical Foundation, 2001.

Thompson, J. Lee. *Politicians, the Press & Propaganda: Lord Northcliffe & the Great War, 1914–1919*. Kent, Ohio: Kent State University Press, 1999.

Urquhart, Diane. *Women in Ulster Politics, 1890–1940: A History Not Yet Told*. Dublin: Irish Academic Press, 2000.

Walker, Graham. *Intimate Strangers: Political and Cultural Interaction between Scotland and Ulster in Modern Times*. Edinburgh: John Donald Publishers, 1995.

Ward, Alan J. *Ireland and Anglo-American Relations, 1899–1921*. London: Weidenfeld & Nicolson, 1969.

—— *The Irish Constitutional Tradition: Responsible Government and Modern Ireland, 1782–1992*. Washington, DC: Catholic University of America Press, 1994.

Ward, John William. *Andrew Jackson: Symbol for an Age*. New York: Oxford University Press, 1955.

Webb, James. *Born Fighting: How the Scots-Irish Shaped America*. New York: Broadway Books, 2004.

Whelan, Bernadette. *United States Foreign Policy and Ireland: From Empire to Independence, 1913–29*. Dublin: Four Courts Press, 2006.

——— *American Government in Ireland, 1790–1913: A History of the US Consular Service*. Manchester: Manchester University Press, 2010.

Whelehan, Niall. *The Dynamiters: Irish Nationalism and Political Violence in the Wider World, 1867–1900*. Cambridge: Cambridge University Press, 2012.

——— ed. *Transnational Perspectives on Modern Irish History*. New York: Routledge, 2015.

Who Was Who, 1916–1928. London: Adam & Charles Black, 1967.

Willson, Beckles. *America's Ambassadors to England (1785–1928): A Narrative of Anglo-American Diplomatic Relations*. London: John Murray, 1928.

Wilson, Andrew J. *Irish America and the Ulster Conflict, 1968–1995*. Belfast: Blackstaff, 1995.

Wright, Frank. *Two Lands on One Soil: Ulster Politics before Home Rule*. New York: St. Martin's, 1996.

Zebel, Sydney H. *Balfour: A Political Biography*. Cambridge: Cambridge University Press, 1973.

Index